Landmarks Revisited

The *Vekhi* Symposium

100 Years On

**CULTURAL REVOLUTIONS: RUSSIA IN THE 20TH CENTURY**

**SERIES EDITOR**
    Boris WOLFSON—*Amherst College*

**EDITORIAL BOARD:**
    Anthony ANEMONE—*The New School*
    Robert BIRD—*The University Of Chicago*
    Eliot BORENSTEIN—*New York University*
    Angela BRINTLINGER—*The Ohio State University*
    Karen EVANS-ROMAINE—*Ohio University*
    Jochen HELLBECK—*Rutgers University*
    Lilya KAGANOVSKY—*University Of Illinois, Urbana-Champaign*
    Christina KIAER—*Northwestern University*
    Alaina LEMON—*University Of Michigan*
    Simon MORRISON—*Princeton University*
    Eric NAIMAN—*University Of California, Berkeley*
    Joan NEUBERGER—*University Of Texas, Austin*
    Ludmila PARTS—*Mcgill University*
    Ethan POLLOCK—*Brown University*
    Cathy POPKIN—*Columbia University*
    Stephanie SANDLER—*Harvard University*

# Landmarks Revisited
# The *Vekhi* Symposium 100 Years On

EDITED BY
ROBIN AIZLEWOOD AND RUTH COATES

BOSTON / 2013

Library of Congress Cataloging-in-Publication Data:
A bibliographic record for this title is available
from the Library of Congress.

Copyright © 2013 Academic Studies Press
All rights reserved

ISBN 978-1-61811-828-8
ISBN 978-1-61811-287-3 (electronic)

Book design by Ivan Grave

Published by Academic Studies Press in 2013
28 Montfern Avenue
Brighton, MA 02135, USA
press@academicstudiespress.com
www.academicstudiespress.com

*In memory of*
**Oliver Smith**
*(1979-2013)*

# Contents

Preface   8

Introduction   10
   *by Robin Aizlewood, Ruth Coates, and Evert van der Zweerde*

**Part I: *Vekhi* and the Russian Intelligentsia**

1. Word Games? The Russian "Intelligentsia"   49
   as a Question of Semantics
   *by Frances Nethercott*

2. Perversions and Transformations:   69
   A. S. Izgoev and the Intelligentsia Debates, 1904–22
   *by Stuart Finkel*

3. The Intelligentsia Fights Back:   86
   The Left-wing Response to *Vekhi* and its Significance
   *by Christopher Read*

**Part II: *Vekhi* and Political Philosophy**

4. The Rise of the People and the Political Philosophy   104
   of the *Vekhi* Authors
   *by Evert van der Zweerde*

5. Individual Freedom and Social Justice:   128
   Bogdan Kistiakovskii's Defense of the Law
   *by Vanessa Rampton*

6. Russian Political Theology in an Age of Revolution   146
   *by Randall A. Poole*

**Part III: *Vekhi* and the Russian Intellectual Tradition**

7. Chaadaev and *Vekhi* 171
    by Robin Aizlewood
8. Lev Tolstoi, Petr Struve and the "Afterlife" of *Vekhi* 192
    by G. M. Hamburg
9. Aleksei Losev and *Vekhi*: 214
    Strategic Traditions in Social Philosophy
    by Elena Takho-Godi

**Part IV: *Vekhi* and the Russian Religious Renaissance**

10. Inside Out: 243
    Good, Evil, and the Question of Inspiration
    by Oliver Smith
11. D. S. Merezhkovskii Versus the *Vekhi* Authors 263
    by Bernice Glatzer Rosenthal
12. Feuerbach, Kant, Dostoevskii: 287
    The Evolution of "Heroism" and "Asceticism"
    in Bulgakov's Work to 1909
    by Ruth Coates

List of Contributors 308

Index 311

# Preface

The present collection of essays arose out of the *Vekhi* Centenary Conference 1909–2009, held in July 2009 at the University of Bristol, and below we list our grateful acknowledgement to those who supported the conference and made it possible. The conference, of course, could not have taken place without the presence of all who attended it for some or all of the three days. We would also like, therefore, to thank all the participants at the conference for their invaluable contributions to the event in terms of papers presented and discussions engaged in, all of which have fed into and enriched this volume.

We have adopted the Library of Congress transliteration system for the rendering of Russian names and terms, including the names of Russian authors familiar to an English-speaking readership. We have opted to give titles of Russian and other foreign-language works in the original on first mention, and thereafter in English translation, except in the case of the *Vekhi* symposium itself, which we refer to consistently as *Vekhi*, partly to avoid having to make the difficult choice between its translation as *Landmarks* or *Signposts*, but also in acknowledgement of the widespread currency of the term *Vekhi* in the scholarship and teaching on the symposium. All quotations from *Vekhi* are taken from: *Vekhi/Landmarks: A Collection of Articles about the Russian Intelligentsia*, trans. and ed. Marshall S. Shatz and Judith E. Zimmerman (Armonk, NY: M. E. Sharpe, 1994).

We would like to acknowledge the Bristol Institute for Research in the Humanities and Arts (BIRTHA), which underwrote the costs of the conference and provided full administrative support in the person of Samantha Barlow, to whom we are particularly grateful for the successful delivery of the conference. Our thanks go also to the British Association for Slavonic and East European Studies (BASEES), the University of Bristol Alumni Foundation, the University of Bristol Faculty of Arts Research Director's Fund, and University College London (UCL) through the School of Slavonic and East European Studies (SSEES), all of which provided additional financial support. The University of Bristol Conference Office and Wills Hall also made a valuable administrative contribution to the staging of the conference. We offer our sincere gratitude to UCL SSEES for its assistance in the publication of this book.

# Introduction

*Robin Aizlewood, Ruth Coates, Evert van der Zweerde*

The collection of essays entitled *Vekhi*, published in 1909 and usually translated as "Landmarks" but also as "Signposts" or "Milestones," is indeed one of the landmark texts of Russian intellectual history, and more broadly of Russian political, philosophical, and religious culture. It is the central text of what became in effect a trilogy, starting with *Problemy idealizma* (*Problems of Idealism*, 1902) and ending with *Iz glubiny* (*Out of the Depths*, 1918), with a substantially common set of contributors from among the leading figures in Russian intellectual life. Of the seven *Vekhi* authors—Nikolai Berdiaev, Sergei Bulgakov, Semen Frank, Mikhail Gershenzon, Aleksandr Izgoev, Bogdan Kistiakovskii, and Petr Struve—all except Gershenzon and Izgoev appear in *Problems of Idealism*, and all except Gershenzon and Kistiakovskii in *Out of the Depths*.[1] Taken together, the three works chart a trajectory from a relatively benign, constructive intellectual climate at the start of the century to the tumult of the 1917 revolution, with *Vekhi*, written in the aftermath of the 1905 revolution, in between.[2] What unites the three symposia is a critique of the "positivist" (materialist, utilitarian, crudely rationalist) ideology of the Russian radical intelligentsia, from a predominantly (though not exclusively) liberal and neo-idealist perspective that was informed by the neo-Kantian movement in German academic philosophy originating in the last third of the nineteenth century and lasting into the twentieth. While *Problems of Idealism* offers this critique in measured academic terms, *Vekhi* is more polemically directed against the intelligentsia, the bearer of "positivism," and the role that it played in the revolution of 1905. *Out of the Depths*, a book that scarcely saw the light of day in its time, offers a cry of biblical despair in response to the revolutionary apocalypse of 1917, analysing its spiritual, intellectual, social, and cultural roots.

Introduction

The trenchant critique of the Russian revolutionary intelligentsia put forward in *Vekhi* did more than touch a nerve: it generated an extraordinary range of responses, mainly and from all sides critical, and within a year it had been reprinted in its fifth edition (which included a bibliography of some 200 articles and reviews provoked by the collection).[3] The republication of *Vekhi* at the end of the Soviet period, sanctioned at the highest level, can be considered the central symbolic event in relation to intellectual history at the time in the "return of Russian philosophy":[4] if *Vekhi* could be published, any pretence of ideological control was at an end. As far as testaments to the seriousness with which ideas have at times been taken in Russia are concerned, *Vekhi* is right up there in the first rank.

The scholars who have contributed to this volume, which has grown out of a centennial conference in 2009, have found it most interesting to locate *Vekhi* in a very wide range of contexts, in terms of history of ideas, discipline, and theory: to read it not as a "landmark" or "signpost" in an evaluative sense, but as a point of focus, intersection, or liminality, perhaps a "crossroads," to borrow the title proposed by one of the *Vekhi* contributors, Frank.[5] *Vekhi* is not, however, just any point of focus for wider and diverse analyses of Russian intellectual history, whether of its own particular period or in longer perspective, for three reasons. First, and not least, it contains some formidable essays. Second, the strength and urgency of *Vekhi* in its specific and broader contexts—as a reaction to the 1905 revolution and larger social processes, on the one hand, and as evidence of the level of richness and diversity that had been reached in Russian intellectual culture of the early twentieth century, the so-called Silver Age, on the other; and in both respects in relation to the subsequent fate of Russian society and culture—make it one of those documents that come to have, or in this case almost immediately acquire, a significance which goes beyond its contents as otherwise viewed. The third reason relates to what one may call the neo-idealist project, with philosophical, religious, and political dimensions in Russian culture, which had been given its most cogent articulation in *Problems of Idealism*.[6] This project is at a moment of crux in *Vekhi*, where its vital and fruitful contribution is accompanied by a sense, albeit nascent, latent, or even resisted, of its "limitations" in the Russian context. This is a constructive moment. In terms of intellectual history, it is of considerable significance and importance.

Contemporary reception and scholarship alike have elaborated on the common critique of the intelligentsia's worldview, which, it should be noted, is a problematic notion in itself,[7] while also, in some cases, highlighting differences of both emphasis and fundamental principle amongst the *Vekhi* contributors.[8] The common understanding that the *Vekhi* contributions were produced independently of each other, and that their joining together behind the central platform of the collection is a sign of the strength and urgency of the critique, should of course be seen in the context of various interactions over some years between the contributors (which continued to be carried on in conversation and correspondence leading up to the publication).[9] It is perhaps not all that surprising that Gershenzon, the initiator of *Vekhi*, could aspire in his "Preface" to read a "common platform" into the collection,[10] and could do so to a large extent successfully, although it is also clear that the "common platform" was easier to maintain as a shared negative critique than as a set of positive principles.[11] This "common platform" is "the recognition of the theoretical and practical primacy of spiritual life over the external forms of community, in the sense that the inner life of the person is the sole creative force of human existence and it, not the self-sufficient principles of the political order, is the sole firm basis for any building of society" (xxvii). The "Preface" refers to a gathering of "people who have united here in a common task," but at the same time there is an explicit recognition that in some other respects the contributors could "differ greatly among themselves both on basic questions of 'faith' and in their practical preferences" (xxvii). In referring to *Vekhi* as a "common task," Gershenzon appropriates an intelligentsia catchword going back to Chernyshevskii, while the contributors' unity with autonomy provides a model directly opposed to the mass ideological conformity, in the *Vekhi* critique, of the radical intelligentsia.

Gershenzon's presentation of the collection as a unity of different, autonomous voices touches upon larger questions that are variously present in the foreground and/or background of *Vekhi*. One such question concerns unity and difference, all-unity and polyphony, to name just some

Introduction

of the concepts involved in discussing, for example, thinkers as diverse as Leont'ev, Solov'ev and Bakhtin. This is a central subject of inquiry in Russian thought. *Vekhi* also offers an encounter between conceptions of community and the individual person that are activated within complex historical and contemporary frameworks. In keeping with our suggestion that *Vekhi* represents a moment of crux in the neo-idealist project in Russian thought of the Silver Age, we can see here an encounter, whether of conciliation or contestation, between the evolving notion of community in the Russian intellectual and cultural tradition (itself with roots in German thought) and the autonomous person of the Kantian tradition, belatedly entering the arena having hitherto been a relatively minor strand in conceptions of the person in Russian philosophy.[12] Indeed, given the unequivocal advocacy in Gershenzon's essay of each individual's "creative self-consciousness" as the necessary pre-requisite for any positive transformation, alongside his advocacy of the Slavophile legacy with its notions of integral wholeness, community, and *sobornost'*, one may posit an unresolved tension within Gershenzon himself, as well as across *Vekhi*, as to the competing tendencies inherent in the notion of a unity of different, autonomous voices. We return to this question—in a different, broadly political key—in the conclusion to our Introduction.

While the themes of philosophical truth and religious values, which are to the forefront in the essays of Berdiaev, Bulgakov, Frank, and Gershenzon, are readily harnessed in support of the collection's advocacy of the "primacy of spiritual life over the external forms of community," the same is not so self-evident of sociology, law, and politics, which are to the forefront in the essays of Izgoev, Kistiakovskii, and Struve. It may be a valid criticism to say that *Vekhi* does not conceptualize the hierarchy and relation of the inner and the external in an adequate way, although the key concept of "creativity" and creative agency is clearly central to this relation, but it is not the case—contrary to the impression that the "Preface" may produce—that the external is deemed insignificant. In fact, concern for external forms is both prominent and pervasive, alongside advocacy of the "primacy of spiritual life." *Vekhi* presents itself as a "theme with variations," in which philosophical, religious, and socio-political strands combine to make up the collection's content in support of the "common platform." The collection promotes each of its strands as *an* overarching theme of the collection as a whole, but not *the* overarching theme.

In a wide range of ways, the articles in this volume address these same, diverse questions, but from a perspective 100 years on. One of the many things that make *Vekhi* such a productive point of focus for scholarly attention is precisely that it both coheres and points in many directions. These directions include: theoretical questions of Russian religious, political, legal, and speculative philosophy, as well as trends and narratives in this tradition (Poole, van der Zweerde); the same questions approached through the lens of individual thinkers in their evolution and their past and present affinities and interactions (Aizlewood, Coates, Hamburg, Rampton, Rosenthal, Smith, Takho-Godi); topics concerning the object of the critique, the intelligentsia (Finkel, Read); and, last but not least, tropes and rhetoric in Russian culture and the invocation of the Russian literary tradition in the *Vekhi* critique (Nethercott). Indeed, the *Vekhi* authors' rhetorical strategies are commented upon in a number of articles.

In the next three sections of our Introduction we address the question of *Vekhi* and politics, philosophy, and religion. In each case this question is approached somewhat differently, and includes, to a greater or lesser extent, consideration of the question of the intelligentsia (the subject also of individual articles in the volume). In relation to politics, *Vekhi* is placed in the context of—and is used as a lens through which to view—Russian social and political processes of the early twentieth century in the light of theoretical formulations of political form, the *politeia*. In relation to philosophy, the question posed is how Russian philosophy appears from a reading of *Vekhi* in historical, contemporary, and present-day perspectives. In relation to religion, a thorough-going critique is made of *Vekhi*'s conceptualization of the religious sphere, both doctrinally and in respect to Russian religious actualities and practice. This tri-partite view of *Vekhi* and Russian political, philosophical, and religious culture is accompanied by appropriate references to articles from the volume as we proceed.

Introduction

## *VEKHI* AND RUSSIAN POLITICS

It is a commonplace to state that Russia, in the late nineteenth and early twentieth centuries, went through a period of rapid and often tumultuous political, economic, social, demographic, intellectual, and cultural development. It is also a commonplace to state that the autocratic political system failed to respond adequately to these developments: its attempts at reform were half-hearted, and the regime was often paralyzed by internal opposition between reformists and reactionaries. *Vekhi* provides a lens—one among many—through which these political realities can be viewed and put into perspective. But it does more than that: it also reflects these developments in the very position of its authors' collective, viz. in the shifting place of *intelligenty* in a society that was undergoing a process of societal differentiation.

The year of publication of *Vekhi*, 1909, is partway between the revolution of 1905 and those of 1917. At the time, obviously, it could not be known that within five years Russia would be engaged in a war of unprecedented scale that would lead, among other consequences, to the decomposition of all three European empires. From a contemporary perspective, 1909 was a few years after the 1905 revolution, which had brought half-hearted political reforms. The October Manifesto by Nicholas II was, although clearly a concession, not a move toward constitutional monarchy; rather, it served to constrain "the new constitutional liberties into the old legal framework of the autocracy."[13] The battle between monarchist and parliamentary forces that went on between 1905 and 1917 remained undecided, but the parliamentary experiment was "definitely over" after the Second Duma was dismissed in June 1907 (the First Duma had functioned less than three months in 1906; the Second served a little over three months)—the Third Duma lasted its full term (1907–12), but was "custom-made to fit the government's requirements," and none of the *Vekhi* authors served in it.[14]

With all the setbacks of generalization, it seems fair to qualify the first decade of the twentieth century in Russia as a period in which it still proved impossible to find a broadly accepted appropriate political form for a society that had changed very rapidly in terms of economy, industrialization, urbanization, demography, education, and (civil) society.

To be sure, none of the processes under way in Russia was specifically "Russian"—on the contrary, Russia was rapidly picking up processes that should be qualified as generally European and, partly at least, global. The nineteenth century was a period of profound societal transformation, of which industrialization, urbanization, and (social) democratization are key markers.[15] The Russian Empire took part in these developments belatedly and "inconsistently." After a period of reforms initiated by Alexander II, which matched and facilitated these developments (e.g., the abolition of serfdom), subsequent Russian governments embarked on a road of essentially conservative policies that oscillated between reluctant reform and reactionary restoration of the old order. In the early twentieth century, this increasingly generated tensions between the autocrat, who clung to the old regime, and the government (led by Witte and later Stolypin, who was prime minister in 1909), which often was more realistic, but which tended to impose reform without seeking popular support.[16] Oppositional movements differed in their assessment of these social processes, but shared the conviction of their inevitability. Russia, finally, was quickly becoming more strongly connected, socially, economically, and intellectually, with the rest of Europe, as can be seen, for example, in foreign investment in nascent Russian capitalism, but also in the fact that many young Russian intellectuals received parts of their educations in west European countries (this applied to all but one of the *Vekhi* contributors).

All across Europe, and beyond its boundaries, these socio-economic processes were accompanied by calls for political reform that had varying degrees of success and different outcomes: Russia was not the only country in which World War I ended with political revolution. If we depart from a primacy of the social in the sense that there must be *something* that has political form, we can say that political forms are attempts to "match" social reality, i.e., to re-form the political form of society. At the same time, however, the question as to which forms do match better or worse is itself a political, not a "technical" one: direct democracy or popular government, representative or parliamentary government, liberalism and corporatism thus are mutually contesting proposals to deal with a potentially conflictual social reality that is taking shape. The general assumption behind these remarks is that to the extent to which the external conditions and/or the inner dynamics of a given society change, the political form or regime of that society must adapt, re-gauge, and re-invent itself, and at this point different, mutually exclusive alternatives are always present.[17] In Western Europe and North America, the chosen alternative was generally one or another form of representative democracy, which, along with a tendency toward the generalization of suffrage, accounts for the so-called "first wave of democratization" theorized by the late Samuel Huntington.[18] If abstraction is made from post-1917 developments, it is clear that in the early twentieth century Russia was riding this wave, too.

The notion of "regime" deserves some attention here. If we follow Leo Strauss, we can understand it as a rendering of the classical concept of *politeia*, i.e., the overall political life-form of a society: "Regime is the order, the form, which gives society its character … the manner of living of society and in society … that whole, which we today are in the habit of viewing primarily in a fragmentized form…."[19] Regime thus includes such things as parliaments, political parties, governments, and constitutions; it covers the forms of both state (*Staatsform*) and government (*Regierungsform*); it includes various procedures, repertoires, and practices; it includes, finally, a particular *ethos*, i.e., a set of matching values and virtues. It is in this sense that we can see the period under consideration as a period of transition from the *old* to a yet-unknown *new* regime. Both the creation of a book like *Vekhi* and the debate around it, as public events in a relatively free Russia, fall within the horizon of the regime as far as the conditions of their possibility and legitimacy are concerned. The fact that both were legitimately there is indicative of the "actually existing" regime of Russian society at the time: it is hard to imagine *Vekhi*'s publication prior to 1900 or after 1920.

If the regime is the overall political life-form, society is what this life-form is the form of. The crux to understanding the *Vekhi* episode from the perspective of political culture lies, arguably, in the discrepancy between the attempts to devise a new regime on the one hand, and the ongoing development and differentiation of society on the other. Here, it may be helpful to invoke the notion of functional differentiation as developed by Niklas Luhmann: it describes the development of relatively autonomous and (as Luhmann put it) autopoiètic "social systems" like church, market, state bureaucracy, and civil society, unimaginable in antiquity and absent or kept out in pre-modern societies like tsarist Russia.[20] The gradual replacement of a hierarchical society by a functionally differentiated one goes hand-in-hand with societal democratization in the Tocquevillean sense referred to above: given the fact that Russia was, comparatively speaking, a strongly hierarchical society, these changes acted as a shock. This societal differentiation comes to the fore in democratization, in the professionalization of parts of the population—think of the increasing political weight of the so-called *zemstvo* professionals (doctors, lawyers, statisticians, engineers, etc.), or of the military officers,[21] and in individualization—all of which came not only at the expense of the old, tsarist regime, but also at the expense of the Russian intelligentsia as it had come to understand itself. On this point Mikhail Gershenzon proved himself a visionary when he wrote:

> The crisis of the intelligentsia is still just beginning. [...] Instead of society shifting direction along the whole front..., the personality *on its own* will begin to determine the direction of society. [...] Now we are entering a new era fraught with many difficulties. It is an era when ... each one will have to determine the meaning and direction of his life for himself, and each will feel responsible for all he does and all he fails to do. (66–67)

The liberalization of Russian political and cultural life after 1905 had allowed for a plurality of political parties, but also for a large number of professional organizations and trade unions (legalized in 1906 and already numbering several dozen by that time).[22] It had, with new legislation on religion initiated by Witte, put an end to the close connection between the autocratic state and the synodal church, thus depriving the state of its "central ideological pillar," facilitating the economic and political participation of non-Orthodox citizens, and eventually liberating the Russian Orthodox Church from its subordination to the state.[23] It had also, finally, made possible the very publication of *Vekhi* itself, and of the pluriform debates around it. The authors of *Vekhi* were both beneficiaries and supporters of this liberalization: in this respect, they were "natural liberals" and their shift from social-democratic to constitutional-democratic (*kadet*) positions is unsurprising.

Introduction

It is against this backdrop of, on the one hand, differentiation, democratization, and individualization, and, on the other, the failed attempt at a constitutional regime, that we must understand both *Vekhi* and the often vehement reactions to it (see Finkel and Read, in this volume). Whether in acceptance or contestation, *Vekhi* reflects upon the very societal differentiation of which it is an instance, e.g., the differentiation of philosophy and religion from each other, and of both from politics. The religious idealism to which, following Vladimir Solov'ev in this respect, some of the *Vekhi* authors subscribed was already a reaction against the separation of philosophical thought and traditional religion that had taken place in Russian academic circles (though see Poole on an emerging new model of political theology in *Vekhi*). A differentiation of philosophy, religion, and politics, however, also puts an end to the traditional idea that it is from philosophers or thinkers that one would have to expect an answer to society. At this point, in addition to the shift in political position, there is a shift in position vis-à-vis politics. (On *Vekhi* and political philosophy, see van der Zweerde's contribution.)

What *Vekhi* clearly does not do is present its readers with a political program or substantiate a particular political position or ideology, as its precursor *Problems of Idealism* had arguably done. As Lionel Kochan and John Keep put it, "it must be admitted that the *Vyekhi* group were better at raising questions than providing answers."[24] It should be noted, however, that members of this group had been much more explicit and positive at an earlier stage, both intellectually, as seen in *Problems of Idealism*, and in a directly political sense. If *Vekhi*, therefore, contains a sense of doubt and despair, this reflects not only a change in philosophical outlook, but also actual disappointment in reformist politics, something in which several of the authors had been actively engaged.

Indeed, the authors of *Vekhi* were much better at raising questions than in providing answers. In doing so, they undermined the primacy of the "What is to be done [*chto delat'*]?" question, and refused to sacrifice their intellectual seriousness to the urgency of matters political. But there is more at stake: if we see 1905–17 as a period in which Russia rapidly got rid of its "Old Regime," as Richard Pipes has called it,[25] and if we connect this with the notion of a "Crisis of Authority," as Orlando Figes qualified the 1891–1917 period, with crisis referring to political, religious, and intellectual crises,[26] we should invoke at this point Claude Lefort's idea that the transition from *ancien régime* to political modernity—the modern, liberal-democratic regime—is connected to a "dissolution of the markers of certainty [*dissolution des repères de la certitude*]."[27] Politically, the markers of certainty that had characterized the "old regime" and that had received ideological expression in the triplet "Autocracy, Orthodoxy, Nationality" (*Samoderzhavie, Pravoslavie, Narodnost'*) as a would-be expression of national unity, had been replaced by the shallow and partisan "God, Tsar, and Fatherland" of the Union of the Russian People, representing a part rather than the whole of Russian society.[28] Neither of these slogans, nor the triplet of "People, Revolution, and Socialism" of the Left, could convince intellectuals like the *Vekhi* contributors, and certainly not those of the stature of Bulgakov, Frank, or Kistiakovskii. Their key categories—truth, law, virtue, justice, faith, value (these are the core ones, but the list is open to debate)—were *not* alternative "markers of certainty" for a society as a whole, but rather for those "scattered individuals" (Berdiaev: 1) who had to "determine the meaning and direction" of their own lives and could only hope to become part of "a mighty, *unconscious* instrument of God's terrestrial purpose" (Gershenzon: 67, 69). So, indeed, *Vekhi* was "symptomatic of the intelligentsia's new mood of doubt and self-questioning,"[29] but then this mood itself was symptomatic of the advent of a new type of society that radically put an end to the idea of the intelligentsia as a kind of alternative absolute authority. Rather than milestones on an unknown and pluriform path, the *Vekhi* were landmarks in an intellectual, not political, landscape, and if they were signposts, they were of such a kind that the key notions engraved on their surface—truth, law, justice, and more—were of greater importance than the direction in which they pointed (on the special relationship of Kistiakovskii to the questions of law, truth, and justice, see Rampton).

A key aspect of *Vekhi*, pointing at both the eternal question of the relation of intellectuals to political power—to put it platonically, the relation between philosopher and king—and the societal transformation of Russia at the time of its appearance, is thus connected to what is both author and object of the collection of essays, the famous intelligentsia (one of the words that Russia contributed to international parlance, along with *pogrom* and *sobornost'*) as a political factor. Three phenomena deserve to be mentioned here. First of all, during the latter part of the nineteenth century, the meaning of "intelligentsia" had shifted, as Richard Pipes puts it, from "descriptive and objective" to "normative and subjective": "By the 1890s it was no longer enough for a Russian to have an education and play a part in public life in order to qualify; one had to stand in staunch opposition to the entire political and economic system of the old regime, and be willing to participate actively in the struggle for its overthrow."[30] As a normative concept, the intelligentsia had become radical and revolutionary. Secondly, in the first decade of the twentieth century, this self-appointed revolutionary force faced real changes, both economically and politically, which made the self-perception of the intelligentsia problematic. *Vekhi* was written by people who "were certainly themselves members of the intelligentsia in the eyes of the government and its supporters," and yet questioned the very status of the group to which they belonged.[31] Thirdly, as a sociological category, descriptive and objective, the notion underwent change, too, with the increasing importance, as noted above, of a new, professional *zemstvo* intelligentsia made up of lawyers, doctors, engineers, etc., who aspired to political influence and had begun to organize themselves after 1905, for example in the League of Unions led by Pavel Miliukov, yet lacked the overall revolutionary orientation of the radical intelligentsia. (On *Vekhi* and the intelligentsia, see Finkel, Nethercott, and Read.)[32]

Particularly interesting in this respect is the position of the academic intelligentsia which populated the universities under conditions of increased intellectual freedom: all the *Vekhi* authors had a university education, and Berdiaev, Bulgakov, Frank, Kistiakovskii, and Struve taught at university, the latter three even at the time they were working on *Vekhi*.[33] If *Vekhi*, therefore, is a book that reflects confusion, it is not so much academic confusion about the meaning of the notion of "intelligentsia," but rather the confusion of that very group itself.

A major reason for the continued appeal of *Vekhi*, finally, making it interesting not only as the historical document which it is, is that it addresses a number of issues that are of continuing relevance to modern society: the differentiation of society into a plurality of relatively autonomous (sub-) systems, the rise of the masses of the population as a political factor, most clearly manifested in the gradual extension of the franchise, the gradual shift from merely policing society to actually shaping it, and the role of the intellectual vis-à-vis political power. *Vekhi* is, itself, both a "piece of history," and a text that raises issues which, if not of "eternal" relevance, take it well beyond its context. Certainly this has to do with the fact that at least three of its authors—Berdiaev, Bulgakov, and Frank—are important twentieth-century thinkers in their own right, who continue to be widely read and translated, and continue to receive mention in encyclopedias and general histories of philosophy.[34]

## *VEKHI* AND RUSSIAN PHILOSOPHICAL CULTURE

The *Vekhi* collection was published at a very interesting moment in the history of Russian philosophy. Twenty years before, Solov'ev and Fedorov were well established in their philosophical paths, but they were still "works in progress"; twenty years after, nearly all of the *Vekhi* contributors (to consider this partial but significant sample) had been exiled from Soviet Russia,[35] and their philosophical positions had developed and clarified in directions only adumbrated at the time of *Vekhi*. Moreover, the Silver Age in Russian philosophy is quite a different phenomenon from its counterpart in literature: Russian literature at the start of the twentieth century (more broadly, from 1890 to 1930) knew, as it were, what it was—including in European contexts—and knew this to an extremely self-conscious degree that was hugely productive and not atrophying. Russian philosophy, on the other hand, knew (or had reason to know) that it had become something, but was still in the early stages of knowing for sure what that was: this too proved to be hugely productive. The early twentieth century was an unprecedented period of publication and republication of primary philosophical sources from the nineteenth century, of the most diverse new philosophical endeavors, and, last but not least, of the scholarly analysis of Russian philosophy at a level not undertaken before, including on the part of Russian philosophers themselves.[36]

Introduction

Our purpose in this section of the Introduction is to ask the same question posed, explicitly or implicitly, by the *Vekhi* authors: how does Russian philosophy appear from the perspective of *Vekhi*? How does the history of Russian philosophical thought present itself, what is the range of thinkers included and which among them are foregrounded, how would one characterize the state of Russian philosophy toward the end of the first decade of the twentieth century? In this connection it is important to note that, as similarly proposed in the previous section, *Vekhi* both reflects on and embodies the philosophical situation of which it is part, and interesting questions are again raised as to whether and how we might wish to interpret *Vekhi* as "landmarks," "milestones," "signposts," or all or none of these. An immediate answer might be that *Vekhi* offers none of the above, in that it shows a cast of thinkers still orienting themselves philosophically in a dynamic, contested, and evolving field, still seeking to define their own understanding of a philosophical tradition that, in Berdiaev's words, "must be both universal and national—only then will it be culturally fruitful" (13). On the other hand, *Vekhi* populates the past and present philosophical landscape it surveys with a wide range of figures, including "landmarks" (such as, in the concluding paragraph of the "Preface," Chaadaev, Solov'ev and Tolstoi [xxxviii]). It also calls, at a more general level, for the embedding of philosophical culture in Russia, clearly echoing the original such call on the part of Chaadaev some 80 years before (see Aizlewood's article).

Two main things emerge, and both pose for the contemporary and present-day reader alike some key—and to this day open—questions about the scope of Russian philosophy and/or philosophy in Russia. First, somewhat against the grain of the neo-idealism that may be supposed to define, more or less, the philosophical orientation of the collection, *Vekhi*, whether by design or not, locates itself in a more heterogeneous tradition or in a plurality of traditions: classical, European, and Russian. The primary traditions may be, on the one hand, neo-Kantian, reflecting the fact that several of the *Vekhi* contributors had studied in Germany and experienced the Kantian tradition first-hand; and, on the other hand, "concrete idealism"—to adopt the term Berdiaev uses, following Sergei Trubetskoi—which starts from Khomiakov and features the "brilliant phenomenon" that is Solov'ev (12–13). But *Vekhi* also recognizes the presence of other strands in the tradition in which it is located, including a strand or tradition that is "anti-philosophical," and emphasizes the importance of Russian literature in any account of Russian philosophy. So far, therefore, it seems that *Vekhi* would position both itself and Russian philosophy in a relative rather than absolute position vis-à-vis Boris Groys's elegant and fruitful insight that Russian philosophy constructs itself as "other" to western philosophy (or its perceived mainstream), and shows the closest affinity with that tradition's internal "other."[37] Such a conceptual framework may also apply, at least in part, to the strand that Berdiaev identifies as "distinguished by an anti-philosophical spirit" (14), with "anti-philosophical" understood as radical alterity. However, alterity and the "anti-philosophical" need not necessarily indicate lack of philosophical culture. A case in point here would be Shestov (who does not figure within *Vekhi*'s range of vision): he pursues a lifelong project of unmasking the pretensions of rationalist philosophy, from Socrates onward, while being steeped in philosophical culture. Shestov leads us to the second main thing to emerge: the date of *Vekhi* (1909) means that the wealth and diversity of Russian philosophy in the first third of the twentieth century was as yet far from fully apparent, and this indeed applies equally to the *Vekhi* authors Berdiaev, Bulgakov, and Frank themselves, whose main philosophical direction and output were still in the future.

Let us start with one particular aspect of the question as to the state of Russian philosophy: namely, does it tend toward optimism or pessimism. As Randall Poole, one of the contributors to this volume, has pointed out in his "Introduction" to *Vekhi*'s precursor volume *Problems of Idealism*, that collection represents a "more constructive work than its successors: its positive task was to advance neo-idealism as a theory of liberalism," while *Vekhi* and *Out of the Depths* concentrated on critique.[38] Indeed, *Problems of Idealism* is a confident work and one which is impressive in a different way from *Vekhi*, concerned as it is more fully and more strictly with philosophical material. It is not only that *Vekhi*, in contrast, concentrates on the prevalence of a "very low level of philosophical culture" (1) among the intelligentsia, as Berdiaev puts it. In addition, the rhetoric at times posits just a handful of people on the other side. Berdiaev sets the tone early on in the essay with which *Vekhi* opens: "Only scattered individuals possessed a high philosophical culture" (1). However, his critique of the intelligentsia's ignorance of "original Russian philosophy," to go with their superficial borrowing of European ideas, brings with it an account of Russian philosophy and some of its protagonists over a span of 80 years (12-15): this is not, one might judge, such a fragile tradition. But ambivalence of this kind lurks throughout *Vekhi*, most plaintively when the expression of hope or call for reorientation, a rhetorical flourish with which each essay (apart from Izgoev's) concludes, is read against the overwhelmingly damning critique that has preceded it.

It makes a difference to the collection as a whole—and to the way we read the questions about Russian philosophy it poses—that it is Berdiaev who takes up the specific theme of philosophy in the opening essay. One can put forward a number of reasons for this assertion, which may involve a certain retrospectivity of reading in light of his subsequent career. First, he already has a diverse philosophical background and, in line with the highly individual cast that his philosophy will assume, is temperamentally averse to thinking within a school; second, he is remarkably open to engagement with a wide range of Russian thinkers and through his career is a prolific author of studies of both individual thinkers and the Russian tradition as a whole.[39] So what, then, is Berdiaev's account of Russian philosophy in his *Vekhi* essay? Overall what emerges is mainly a religious philosophy, but not exclusively so. This is also true of the collection as a whole. As such, *Vekhi* is in line with a major strand in the historiography, including what for many is still the most accomplished history of Russian philosophy, that of Zen'kovskii.[40] Conversely, it is ironic that the line of logic that links *Vekhi* and its critique to the 1917 revolution is reflected also in the dominant paradigm or framework applied to Russian intellectual history through much of the twentieth century, namely that it leads from the Enlightenment to Marxism and the revolution.

When decrying the way that Russian thinkers of the intelligentsia have not only borrowed superficially but have also distorted as they did so, Berdiaev effectively denies that a whole succession of Russian thinkers of positivist, populist, Marxist, empiriocritical, and Nietzschean inclinations (Chernyshevskii, Pisarev, Lavrov, Mikhailovskii, Bogdanov, Lunacharskii, et al.) can be thought of as philosophers—indeed, Berdiaev places the word in inverted commas when talking of them. Implicitly or explicitly, this view is shared by the other *Vekhi* contributors and is taken over from *Problems of Idealism* (even if that volume goes out of its way to be emollient).[41] This is not the place in which to argue the individual cases, but suffice it to say that this view has its merits in most cases (which does not mean that these thinkers may not be significant from other perspectives). On the other hand, in a nod toward himself and his fellow contributors, Berdiaev's assessment of Russian engagement with Neo-Kantianism, as well as with Kant, Fichte, and German idealism, is positive (10). When he goes on to consider the "original Russian philosophy" that is ignored by the intelligentsia (12–15), his account—as has already been noted—combines plurality with the proposed main, distinctive trend of "concrete idealism," centred on Vladimir Solov'ev (not surprisingly, given Solov'ev's huge presence in Russian philosophy of the late nineteenth century onwards) and associated also with Sergei Trubetskoi (author of a magisterial essay, "What the History of Philosophy Teaches," in *Problems of Idealism*).[42] Berdiaev devotes a page or so to characterizing this trend, which develops in opposition to "Hegel's abstract idealism and rationalism" (12–14).

Before and after this, however, Berdiaev paints a heterogeneous picture, which raises important questions about the scope of philosophy in the Russian case. These questions are familiar now, but were not so then, as is indicated in the opening paragraph of this section. In his opening paragraph on "original Russian philosophy," the first name he mentions is that of Chaadaev, whose *Lettres Philosophiques/Filosoficheskie pis'ma* (*Philosophical Letters*, 1828–30) offer a critique of Russian philosophical culture some 80 years before *Vekhi*. Chaadaev is followed in this pantheon by Solov'ev and Dostoevskii, the latter "of course" being "the greatest Russian metaphysician" (12). Berdiaev then generalizes to refer to the "metaphysical spirit of the great Russian writers," which apparently includes Tolstoi, even though Tolstoi is equated with the intelligentsia in his hostility to "higher philosophy and creation" (12). (On the combination of ambivalence and hostility between Tolstoi and *Vekhi* see Hamburg, in this volume). When seeking to show that Russian philosophy is not just the "brilliant phenomenon" that is Solov'ev, Berdiaev goes on to list a number of philosophers, including the Slavophile Khomiakov, the Hegelian Chicherin, and more recent philosophers of a broadly idealist, intuitivist, and/or religious persuasion (Kozlov, Sergei Trubetskoi, Lopatin, Losskii) as well as Nesmelov, the "most profound" figure from the theological academies (13). Reinforcing his awareness of academic philosophy, earlier in the essay he has also mentioned Iurkevich (3). Apart from the recognition that there is more to Russian philosophy than Solov'ev and his philosophical line (which indeed, however important it may be, does not define Berdiaev's own subsequent development), the key point here concerns the implied common quality of philosophical culture, irrespective of philosophical tendency. This same question recurs, more problematically, at the end of his account, when he turns to "modern Russian mysticism," which shares "the intelligentsia's traditional hostility to philosophical endeavor" and lacks a "clear philosophical consciousness": "Our most outstanding mystics—Rozanov, Merezhkovskii, Viacheslav Ivanov—do furnish rich material for a new statement of philosophical themes, but they themselves are distinguished by an anti-philosophical spirit, and anarchistic denial of philosophical reason" (14; on Merezhkovskii's relationship to *Vekhi* see Rosenthal in this volume). Leaving aside the appropriateness (severally) of the characterization as mystics, this formulation—like the earlier formulation in respect to Tolstoi—is interestingly ambiguous or open, and may not exclude these thinkers from a contribution to philosophy. Thus, while maintaining the *Vekhi* line that due attention to philosophical reason is vital for philosophical culture, Berdiaev's analysis seems to allow for a more inclusive approach too. This tension is one of the intriguing and illuminating features in exploring what one might call the broad borderlands of Russian philosophical thought. Moreover, Berdiaev will become a case in point. While few if any would exclude Berdiaev as a philosopher, he is not known for his adherence to logical exposition.[43]

Although Russian philosophy is less foregrounded by the other *Vekhi* authors than it is by Berdiaev, the picture that nevertheless continues to emerge is one of a heterogeneous phenomenon. To some extent a disciplinary demarcation of subject matter between the articles is observed, as, for example, in Izgoev (sociology) and Kistiakovskii (law, see Rampton), but the rhetorical strategy of the whole tends to erode such boundaries. Heterogeneity is also conveyed through the repeated references to Russian literature and its great writers. On the one hand, these are lined up in opposition to the intelligentsia's worldview, for example, by Struve (121); on the other hand, following Berdiaev, Dostoevskii and Tolstoi are clearly seen to transcend the purely literary realm: Dostoevskii is a recurrent presence in Bulgakov's essay (see Coates), he is of fundamental significance for Frank's critique of the intelligentsia's "ethical nihilism," and Gershenzon identifies him as one of our "best minds," along with Chaadaev and the Slavophiles (59). Gershenzon it is who, amplifying Berdiaev's reference to Khomiakov as the starting point for the Russian critique of the extreme "abstract idealism" reached in Hegel, gives considerable prominence to the Slavophiles in his essay: this may be incompatible with some others, such as Kistiakovskii, but it shows how the contributors to the "common platform" of *Vekhi* can trace quite different ideational genealogies.

Struve is the one author after Berdiaev who lists a good number of intellectual figures, not only writers, in opposition to the intelligentsia: these extend from Radishchev and Chaadaev to Solov'ev (120), with the father of the intelligentsia identified as Bakunin. It is particularly interesting that Struve sees Herzen, despite his atheism, as someone alien to the intelligentsia type, even if he at times wears its "uniform" (121); Bulgakov, on the other hand, locates Herzen in the intelligentsia camp (20). It is true that Struve's criterion for the honor of not being an *intelligent* is not philosophical, and that Herzen is another case in point when it comes to the borderlands of philosophy in the Russian tradition, but it is interesting how *Vekhi* reveals an ambiguity over where he may stand in that tradition on account of his liberal aristocratic conception of the freedom and autonomy of the person. Despite the different fundamental starting points of Herzen and *Vekhi*, the typological similarities that arise are not trivial. This is not a novel observation about Herzen in general, but nevertheless it is one that is worth making in the context of *Vekhi*. Thus, the first half of Berdiaev's closing sentence, which reads "We will be freed from external oppression only when we are freed from internal bondage" (16), could be taken word for word from Herzen. Many of the contemporary reactions to *Vekhi* can be interpreted as protest against the *Vekhi* contributors' refusal to yield to "external bondage," i.e., political demands in the direct sense.

## Introduction

Among the nineteenth-century thinkers that have so far emerged, two important figures have not been mentioned, and indeed they are not mentioned in *Vekhi*. They are, first, Nikolai Fedorov, whose "philosophy of the common task" (an appropriation of this catchphrase in a key quite different from that of Gershenzon in the "Preface") calls for the unity through resurrection of all mankind and represents the second great project of all-unity (alongside that of Solov'ev) in late nineteenth-century Russian culture; and second, Konstantin Leont'ev, a philosopher of culture and values who is one of the most original of all Russian thinkers (and sometimes called the Russian Nietzsche). In different ways, Fedorov for his extravagant utopianism and Leont'ev for his unpalatable reactionary positions, neither fits comfortably into some narratives of Russian thought, and their subtextual presence in *Vekhi* may strike the reader as surprising, even outlandish. In the case of Fedorov, the presence is marginal, but not to be dismissed. It is to be found in Bulgakov, when the larger theme of the intelligentsia's wilful ignorance of historical continuity and the narrower theme of generational discord ("fathers and sons") focuses specifically on the question of progress and attitude to fathers: "Humanistic progress, on the other hand, is scorn for the fathers, aversion to the past and complete condemnation of it, historical and sometimes even personal ingratitude; it legitimizes the spiritual discord between fathers and children" (39). Whether consciously or not, Bulgakov is here articulating the "fathers and sons" motif in a way which echoes Fedorov in his wonderful critique of progress as immoral because of its scornful relegation of the fathers to the historical dustbin.[44] The presence of Leont'ev, far less marginally, is to be found in Frank. Almost certainly, too, Frank is well aware that he is drawing on Leont'ev, since in *Out of the Depths* he identifies Leont'ev as a thinker of "genius" who was "completely unnoticed" by the Russian intelligentsia.[45] Frank pays considerable attention to cultural creativity and wealth, and the most eloquent and profound philosopher of culture in nineteenth-century Russia is precisely Leont'ev. In particular—in the framework of a cyclical understanding of history—it is Leont'ev's conception of the decline of culture in terms of "secondary simplification"[46] that is relevant here, for "simplification" is also an idea that recurs in Frank's critique of the intelligentsia's negative attitude to culture and its creative potential for the betterment of the human condition. This is expressed, for example, in the following: "The Russian *intelligent* feels a positive love for the simplification, impoverishment, constriction of life" (150).

Let us now return to the questions of how to deal with those whom Berdiaev implicitly relates to Russian philosophy, for example Tolstoi and Rozanov, but who are "anti-philosophical" in spirit, and how to deal with Dostoevskii and other figures from the Russian literary tradition. These are important and open—not to mention contested—questions. In both cases, a reading of *Vekhi* would argue against a limiting approach to Russian philosophy that either excluded Dostoevskii, Tolstoi, and Rozanov, or did not address how Russian philosophical thought could be conceptualized in a way which related them, however conditionally, to philosophy. Fluidity in definitions of philosophy and philosopher in the Russian case (thought and thinker are sometimes preferred) is not in itself indicative of anything amiss, but the well-known, and not easily tractable, problem in approaching Russian philosophy is to find a way to maintain an appropriate rigor in defining how Russian thinkers, and in specific cases, such as Dostoevskii's, Russian writers too, may be defined as engaged in a philosophical enterprise, and to recognize the fact that the Russian philosophical tradition is not fruitfully limited to a homogenizing definition of philosophy. A key concept facilitating the traverse of borders in *Vekhi* is creativity, which recurs in a number of essays and is especially prominent in Gershenzon and Frank; needless to say, it has a large conceptual reach. It addresses the border, and its traversing, between literature and philosophy, and also a no less important border and traversal: that between philosophy and religious metaphysics (with Dostoevskii a case in point for both, if we follow Berdiaev's characterization of him as "the greatest Russian metaphysician" [12]).[47] Interpretations of Russian philosophy have addressed these borders variously. For example, as Galin Tihanov points out, the prominent philosopher of the late Soviet period Merab Mamardashvili, while taking care, on the one hand, "to distinguish between Russian philosophy and Russian literature," nevertheless avoided, on the other hand, "drawing an impenetrable line between philosophy and religious thought in Russia," and "essayed to see them as discursive formations that often occupied the same territory and were involved in a dialectic of exchange and competition."[48]

In addressing the flow between literature and philosophy, Edith Clowes has sought to illuminate the literariness of Russian philosophy, while—from the other direction—James Scanlan has undertaken a philosophical approach to Dostoevskii, which is methodologically and conceptually important.[49] Indeed, one might suggest that Russian philosophy presents itself as an excellent testing ground for interdisciplinary approaches.

In conclusion, for all that the picture of Russian philosophy which emerges from *Vekhi* is marked by plurality and heterogeneity, alongside a certain dominant line of "concrete idealism," it is nevertheless striking how much fuller and more diverse, compared to *Vekhi*, is our retrospective view of that philosophy in the first quarter of the twentieth century. Such a view emerges when we take into account, first, the subsequent development of the *Vekhi* philosophers themselves, and of those, such as Rozanov, who feature in *Vekhi* but whose most original and important oeuvre still lay ahead (the "late, great Rozanov," as it is called), and, second, those philosophers who pass unnoticed in *Vekhi* or who have yet to make their entrance onto the philosophical scene. These include Bakhtin, Florenskii, Karsavin, Shestov, and Shpet, to name just a few; to these one would of course add the last of the great Silver Age thinkers, Aleksei Losev, the subject of Takho-Godi's article. The sense of heterogeneity in the Russian philosophical tradition, which emerges somewhat against the grain in *Vekhi*, is a crucial intuition. It is curious and ironic that the hopes of the *Vekhi* contributors for a reorientation of the intelligentsia—to avert a still greater national disaster which remains more or less unnamed, but which provides the tragic occasion for *Out of the Depths* in 1918—are confounded, while, on the other hand the remarkable flowering of Russian philosophical culture still has much to reveal. One could ask why the intelligentsia's ignorance of Solov'ev and other Russian philosophers, lamentable as this may be and however relevant it is to the critique of the intelligentsia as an intellectual phenomenon, has any bearing on the capacity of this philosophy to flourish. Intrinsically, it has little or no direct bearing. We should not forget, however, the subsequent fate of that culture, and of individual philosophers, in the Soviet period. In this respect, the pessimistic undercurrent of *Vekhi* is more than justified.

Robin Aizlewood, Ruth Coates, and Evert van der Zweerde

## *Vekhi* and Religion

It is striking how central a focus Sergei Bulgakov is in the articles in this volume (Coates, Poole, Smith) that concern themselves with the religious dimension of *Vekhi*. Given that the entire collection is commonly taken to represent not least a rejection of the atheist orientation of the revolutionary intelligentsia, one might expect the critical net to be cast rather more widely. That it is not is suggestive of the possibility that Bulgakov's essay treats the religious theme in an atypical and richer way. In this section of the Introduction we aim to review *Vekhi*'s status as a religious text, or at least as a text that promotes religious values. How does the rhetoric of *Vekhi* encourage the reader to construct the volume as religious? What does the use of religious language and imagery reveal about the nature of the *Vekhi* authors' religious values? What is the relationship between the religious dimension of *Vekhi* and the religious culture of Russia, as embodied in the Russian Orthodox Church or expressed in the Slavophile tradition of Russian thought? We will argue that the essays tend overwhelmingly to engage what one might call the positive content of religion, that is, its concrete historical forms of expression, metaphorically as a weapon against the intelligentsia; and that the essays substantially reveal what the religious values of their authors are by making plain through this strategy what they are not. With the exception of Bulgakov's essay, the contributions tend toward an abstract theism that is consistent with the Kantian orientation of the majority of their authors. Though this abstract theism has a certain austere nobility, it not only marks a transient moment in the development of Russian religious thought (Berdiaev, Bulgakov, and Frank would all move on to other methodologies), but is also at odds with the broad thrust of Orthodox culture and thought. It is a great irony that a collection that promotes national cultural wealth should itself be religiously poor.

In his "Preface" to *Vekhi*, Gershenzon famously declares that the common platform of its contributors is "the recognition of the theoretical and practical primacy of spiritual life [*dukhovnoi zhizni*] over the external forms of community" (xxxvii). We might take note of how broad a term "spiritual life" is as Gershenzon employs it, and how typical his use of the adjective "*dukhovnyi*" is of the volume as a whole. Without exception the *Vekhi* authors employ "spiritual" as deriving from the broader Russian meaning of "spirit" (*dukh*), that is, as "consciousness, thought, psychological capacities; the principle that determines behavior, actions,"[50] and only residually, if at all, in its narrower, strictly religious sense. Thus, Berdiaev writes of "the basic spiritual features of the intelligentsia's world" (1), Bulgakov of the intelligentsia's "spiritual arsenal" (18), Izgoev of the "spiritual qualities" of Russian youth (76), and Frank of the "spiritual forces" of the intelligentsia, which he qualifies as "its beliefs, its life experiences, its values and tastes, its intellectual and moral tone" (132). These quotations all apply the term "spiritual" to the intelligentsia, whose materialism and atheism is of course a defining feature. An interesting question to ask might be how much of the intelligentsia's negative reaction to *Vekhi* was stimulated by the mere imputation to it of a "spiritual" life, and how far it sought in its own discourse to avoid such philosophically idealist language. How closely did intelligentsia materialists associate the broad semantic range of "*dukhovnyi*" with religious belief? Perhaps they did so more closely than one might expect, given the hyper-sensitivity of the socialist intelligentsia to any concept sharing a border with the sphere of religion. Be that as it may, as native English-speakers reading *Vekhi* in translation we should be aware of how our own contemporary primary understanding of "spiritual" as "concerned with sacred or religious things" or "concerned with the soul or spirit"[51] colors our reading of a text in which "*dukhovnyi*" is consistently translated as "spiritual." It is possible that part of our perception of *Vekhi* as a religious text can be attributed to this.

A further part of this perception is almost certainly due to the *Vekhi* authors' extraordinarily widespread use of religious metaphor in relation to the intelligentsia. The very broad range of non-literally applied religious terms includes "faith," "worship," "salvation," "repentance," "idolatry," "sin," "martyrdom," "deification," "iconoclasm," "monasticism," and "holiness" (this list is not exhaustive). Only Bulgakov's essay explicitly foregrounds as its central theme "the religious nature of the Russian intelligentsia," and therefore has a formal and thematic rationale for the use of religious metaphor, yet a majority of the *Vekhi* authors (Kistiakovskii and Struve being the exceptions) to a greater or lesser extent choose religious imagery to characterize the intelligentsia. It would be very interesting to attempt a formal linguistic analysis of religious metaphorical language in *Vekhi*. It ranges from conventionalized, "dead" metaphor (for example, the use of "faith" in Kistiakovskii's statement that the intelligentsia "puts unusual faith in the articles and paragraphs of organizational statutes" [105]), to highly self-conscious extended metaphor, as in the following passage from Gershenzon's essay:

> The political faith, like any other, by its nature demanded a heroic deed. But in every faith the same story is repeated: since only a few individuals are capable of heroic deeds, the crowd, which cannot perform them but wishes to be in communion with the faith, devises for itself some platonic confession that involves no practical commitment. And the priests and martyrs themselves tacitly legitimize this deception in order to keep the laymen at least formally within the church. In our political radicalism, the rank-and-file *intelligenty* constituted the laymen. One had only to acknowledge oneself a true son of the church and occasionally participate in its symbolism in order to ease one's conscience and satisfy society. (67)

In part, this use of religious language by the *Vekhi* authors testifies to the fact that it had become conventional, even a cliché, to view revolutionary socialism as an ersatz religion, or even in some way, following Solov'ev, as genuinely religious. Struve's resistance to religious language follows from his principled rejection of this convention as based on a concept of religion that is "formal" and has "no intellectual content" (119). Yet several of the contributors, even as they challenge the convention, buy into it with their imagery. (It is these tensions that Gershenzon has in mind when he half apologizes, in his "Preface," for the apparent contradictions of his contributors on the question of the intelligentsia's religiosity.) For example, Izgoev is happy to refer to the intelligentsia as a "monastic order," as "sanctifying" everything that ends in death (85), but rejects the "frequent attempts to identify the contemporary revolutionaries with the ancient Christian martyrs" on the grounds that these are "two completely different spiritual types" (87). Frank, who after Bulgakov makes the most intensive use of religious imagery (not least in his expansion on the *intelligent* as a "militant monk of the nihilistic religion of earthly well-being" [150–51]), at the same time explores the use of religious metaphor, acknowledging it as "inevitable and often helpful" but castigating it as imprecise and "an inaccurate use of words" (134). He acknowledges the psychological proximity of "authentic" religious faith and the intelligentsia's faith in the future happiness of the people (141–42) while asserting that all genuinely religious worldviews involve "faith in the real existence of the absolutely valuable" (134). Bulgakov is the most self-conscious in employing religious imagery to depict intelligentsia ideology as religion "inside out" (see Smith), but at the same time he too is critical of the tendency, originating with Belinskii, to view the intelligentsia as carrying out the work of Christ (40). Ultimately, all the *Vekhi* authors agree that the religious analogy is imperfect, but this only begs the question as to why most find it so compelling.

An important *effect* of the prolific use of religious imagery is, as mentioned above, that it encourages the reader to construct the text of *Vekhi* as "religious." At the same time, however, it tells us something very interesting about the nature of the *Vekhi* authors' religiosity. We would suggest that two kinds of religiosity are at play in *Vekhi*, one serving as the mirror image of the other (cf. Smith): a pure religiosity and a defective one associated with empirical religion, which is manifested principally as negatively valorized metaphor used polemically against the radical intelligentsia. It is more often than not the case that if the *Vekhi* contributors attribute a religious quality to the intelligentsia through such negatively valorized metaphor, that quality is rejected in terms of their own conception of religion. A striking example of this is the negative assessment of the intelligentsia's worldview as "dogmatic," as betokening an unacceptable rigidity of thought, an assessment prevalent particularly in the very writers who are commonly deemed the most religious. For Berdiaev the intelligentsia's views are "fixed, like dogmas" (4); Bulgakov writes of the intelligentsia's creedal atheism and "abstract dogmatism" (22, 27); and for Frank, intelligentsia revolutionism has "all the force of religious dogma" (144). In institutional Christianity, dogma has the positive role of asserting and protecting the central beliefs of the faith. In their negative interpretation of dogma, the *Vekhi* authors reveal their own, perhaps unconscious, debt to the very Enlightenment of which many are so critical. Uses of the terms "obscurantism" and "fanaticism" also reveal that debt, as do negatively slanted references to "catechism," "credos," and "miracle."

The *Vekhi* authors' disdain for dogma is reflected in the doctrinal sparseness of their promotion of religious values. Apart from Bulgakov's essay, which is the exception that demonstrates the rule, the contributions include little if any theological substance, indeed little that is identifiably Christian. (It should not be forgotten that three of the seven authors were Jewish.) Berdiaev shows a sympathetic awareness of patristic anthropology when he grounds the equality of human beings in their common status as children of God, and when he asserts that love reveals "God's own image in every human being" (6), but this remains undeveloped.[52] Struve's reference to the "mystique of the state" (118), set in its context of a critique of the anarchic and atheistic features of intelligentsia ideology, does no more than connote a body of Orthodox thought on theocracy, from which nevertheless, intuitively, one feels that Struve would surely want to distance himself.[53] Finally, Gershenzon's religious philosophy is (uniquely in *Vekhi*) articulated in pantheistic terms very remote from Christian dogmatics, though he is not averse to coloring it with Christological language, such as when he writes of "a genuine transfiguration of universal flesh in an individual hypostasis" (54).

In general, the question of the value of the institutional church—the Russian Orthodox Church—is completely neglected in *Vekhi*, despite the fact that one of its main concerns is for the impoverished state of culture and civil society in Russia. Berdiaev makes a single quasi-positive comment about the ecclesiastical academies (major educational institutions in pre-revolutionary Russia),[54] to the effect that they represent "a milieu far from the intelligentsia's heart" (13). Struve throws in a reference to Patriarch Hermogen (116). Izgoev appreciates the clergy as "the physically strongest group in the nation" (78)! Even Bulgakov, who was unique among the *Vekhi* contributors in descending from a priestly family and who in 1909 had already begun his slow return to the church, ignores the institutional expression of Christianity (priesthood, liturgy, sacrament) and celebrates instead the figure of the ascetic, whose charismatic authority, as Irina Paert has recently documented, was at odds with the authority of the priestly hierarchy.[55] Bulgakov's essay goes furthest to explain why the *Vekhi* authors refer to the institutional church only in terms of negatively valorized metaphors with which to condemn the intelligentsia with its oblique reference to the "numerous evils of church life" under the Synodal system, "which we have no desire to either minimize or deny" (47). He is no less vague, however, about the positive aspects of "church life" that left their trace on the first intelligentsia generation of ex-seminarians (21). Beyond these references, the authors have nothing to say about the Orthodox Church at all.[56]

It is also worth commenting that while the *Vekhi* authors see intelligentsia ideology as "sectarian" in comparison to mainstream Russian thought (Berdiaev develops this metaphor most fully), which all agree is at the same time more profound and religious-philosophical in character, they are ambivalent about the Slavophile tradition. Bulgakov, whose very Dostoevskian essay on the face of it appears to sit rather comfortably with aspects of Slavophile thinking, expressly wishes to avoid falling into the "clichés" of the Slavophiles' "naive, rather starry-eyed" faith (17). Just as interestingly, Izgoev disavows the Slavophiles while simultaneously promoting conservative family values that he himself admits were best embodied in the prominent Slavophile families (73). Kistiakovskii is highly critical of the Slavophiles' romantic disregard for legal values (95). The *Vekhi* authors' individualism precludes them from an appreciation of Slavophile social thought and from a creative reception of its central philosopheme, *sobornost'*. As van der Zweerde, in this volume, points out, in *Vekhi* the "people" are by and large treated as an undifferentiated mass and as passive beneficiaries, or victims, of the intelligentsia's agency, and not as an organic community of equals. It might be expected that Kireevskii's "integral reason" would lend itself to adaptation by the *Vekhi* authors in their thinking about the "primacy of spiritual life over the external forms of community." However, the importance of Kantian ethics for the majority forestalls this, too: practical reason serves instead of mystical intuition as the vehicle by which the Divine is apprehended. Gershenzon's essay is the only one which is explicitly Slavophile (and by the same token the least Kantian) in spirit, with its specific tracing of the intelligentsia's ills to the Petrine reforms, its analysis of the "disintegration of the personality" (57) as reason becomes separated from the sensual-volitional life, and its insistence on the qualitatively different soul of the people (61), which Gershenzon attributes to their "religious and metaphysical" (he does not say "Christian") ideas and beliefs (62). On this last point Bulgakov agrees, maintaining with the Slavophiles that "[t]he people's world-view and spiritual outlook are determined by the Christian faith" (44).

Absence from *Vekhi* of the Slavophile polemic against the West, including its religious dimension, is one of its most striking features. This is where Dostoevskii and Bulgakov part company, as Bulgakov pleads for "a more profound, historically conscious Westernism" to replace the "superficial" Westernism of the intelligentsia (25). Running through the essays in particular is an appreciation for the Protestant Reformation, which has produced in the West the religious individualism (as opposed to the neo-pagan individualism promoted by the Renaissance) that the *Vekhi* authors are seeking to cultivate in Russia. Following Max Weber, Bulgakov accepts the idea that the Reformation created the conditions for the development of both the legal state with its protection of individual freedoms and the industrial enterprise that is indispensable for the creation of wealth, including cultural wealth (24). Particular appreciation is shown for British government and culture (in five of the seven essays). As examples of the transformative power of sustained introspection, the Slavophile Gershenzon adduces the biographies of the Protestants John Bunyan and Thomas Carlyle (54), and Struve argues that even Calvinism and Jansenism, despite their emphasis on predestination, promoted the idea of personal achievement (119).

All of these observations about the religious attitudes displayed in *Vekhi* are consonant with what we know to be the shared philosophical orientation of all the contributors but Gershenzon: Kantian idealism. A non-dogmatic religious cosmopolitanism, individualism, and rationalism are in evidence that derive from Kant's position as a late Enlightenment thinker of Protestant extraction who promoted "religion within the bounds of reason alone." Of the six Kantians, only Bulgakov has moved decisively into a Christ-centred religion of revelation, though in terms of his philosophical methodology he has not yet abandoned Kant for Schelling, as he would in 1912 (with the publication of *Filosofiia khoziaistva* [*The Philosophy of Economy*]). The remainder are content with an abstract conception of religion as "faith in the real existence of the absolutely valuable," to use Frank's expression (134). It is natural that Kantian ethics should lead the *Vekhi* authors to stress the importance of the individual's inner work on herself or himself that is highlighted by Gershenzon in his "Preface." Nevertheless, precisely because their vision is for a rich and creative national Russian culture founded on the aggregate productive labor of conscientious individuals (see Frank, 139), the contributors are preoccupied with the problem of asceticism (only for Bulgakov is asceticism the solution, see Coates, in this volume). Their disparaging comparison of the revolutionary intelligentsia to monks is informed by a widespread prejudice against Russian Orthodox monasticism as life- and world-denying, undoubtedly informed by Vladimir Solov'ev's anti-monastic views. In contradistinction to this type of asceticism, the *Vekhi* authors promote Weber's *innerweltliche Askese* (ascesis in the world), which is, tellingly, another Protestant phenomenon.

In their religious individualism, just as much as in their political liberalism and philosophical idealism, the *Vekhi* contributors show themselves to be an isolated minority voice in Russian public discourse, as far removed from popular piety and the national institutional church as they are from the collectivism and atheist "faith" of the revolutionary socialists. In contemporary Russia, too, the resurgence of a nationalist and anti-rational Orthodoxy means that, in religion as in political philosophy, the voice of the *Vekhi* authors can surely be expected to have only marginal appeal.

## Conclusion

*Vekhi*, as the central text in the trilogy that starts with *Problems of Idealism* and ends with *Out of the Depths*, can be seen as a sustained intervention by a core group of concerned intellectuals in Russia's public affairs. Despite the fact that, like many interventions by intellectuals, it "failed" in the sense of not achieving its intended and stated goals, its relevance goes well beyond this prolonged episode. First of all, if we see this intervention as, primarily, a warning, we should note that it was followed by seventy years of the kind of regime that it had warned against; the warning, in that sense, was very much to the point. Of course, a "failure" can only be stated with the advantage of hindsight, and we should not too lightly project later developments onto *Vekhi* itself. Was the sense of "sadness" that we read on its pages shared by the authors at the time of writing? Which kind of "success" is presupposed in its qualification as a "failure"? Secondly, the failure of an intervention does not exclude the possibility that valuable arguments are made in the intervention, arguments that go beyond the situation and context themselves. This applies, for example, to the reflections on nihilism, asceticism, and legal consciousness. Finally, *Vekhi* offers an example, arguably a historically unique one, of such an intervention by a core group of established intellectuals. If we compare the *Vekhi* group with, for example, the Charter 77 group around Václav Havel in Czechoslovakia, we find that—at the time of intervening—the *Vekhi* contributors were dissidents within the intelligentsia, not with respect to the regime, as shown by the fact that the attacks on them came from other *intelligenty*, not from the authorities. In all these ways, *Vekhi* can be seen as part of an important case of possible interaction between "thought" and "society."

*Vekhi* is of continued interest in the intellectual history of humankind for another reason, too. We might see it as an attempt to enter a "public sphere" in the Habermasian sense of *Öffentlichkeit*, as part of a functionally differentiating society. Such a public sphere was clearly on the rise in late nineteenth- and early twentieth-century Russia. At the same time, however, the status of that public sphere was still unclear: was it a sphere of public *opinion*, or was this sphere directed to public *affairs*? Several of the contributors to *Vekhi* were intellectuals who also occupied, or had occupied, public positions, such as Duma membership. The fate of *Vekhi* shows it ending up as a contribution to public opinion only, without making much of a political or societal impact, but at the time of its appearance it was unclear which model was at stake: the traditional "Platonic" model of the philosopher-king; in Enlightenment terms, the model of the enlightened absolute monarch to whom intellectuals could send letters, petitions, and projects (think, for example, of Radishchev, Karamzin, Aksakov, Solov'ev, and Fedorov); or again the more plural and diffuse model of a public arena in which intellectuals present their ideas and considerations, and which may have an indirect effect on the policies of the powers-that-be. Part of what makes *Vekhi* so fascinating is that it is projected into a space the nature of which it is not sure about. At this point, interesting parallels can be drawn with the situation in Russia and other countries today, a century later: a thriving public debate in a partly free space (Russians are speaking

Introduction

and publishing far more freely than they did in Soviet times, both on the internet and in printed publications) with an impact on public affairs that is as diffuse as it is uncertain.

Finally, *Vekhi* draws our attention to the boundaries and interactions between religion and philosophy, philosophy and politics, politics and law, etc. It presents an example of an intellectual tradition that has tended toward disciplinary fusion (think of Solov'ev's conception of "integral knowledge" or the diffuse boundary between philosophy and literature)[57] and now finds itself in a situation in which its field of action is apparently not limited to the intellectual domain, but may in actuality move beyond into the social, blurring the dichotomy between the two. At the same time, Russian society was going through a rapid process of professionalization and disciplinary differentiation, of which several of the authors were themselves part in their roles as politicians, university professors, party organizers, etc. From this angle, *Vekhi* offers a highly pertinent example of problems of interdisciplinarity: how are academic disciplines like law and political economy related to the type of reflection that had dominated the Religious-Philosophical societies in Moscow and St. Petersburg, which functioned in roughly the same period (1901–17), and of which three of the four *Vekhi* authors who participated in all three volumes—*Problems of Idealism*, *Vekhi*, and *Out of the Depths*—i.e., Berdiaev, Bulgakov, and Frank, had been active members?[58] How to relate the differentiation of academic disciplines and public discourses to the "holistic" approach that not only is typical of "Russian religious philosophy," but also would be necessary, in the eyes of many of our contemporaries, for any intellectual endeavor with serious social and political import.

The world of the early twenty-first century, obviously, is not the same as that of one century earlier, nor is today's Russia the same as the Russia of 1909. Still, there are several points of principle that need to be addressed in all times, such as the relations between politics and ethics, between politics and philosophy, between philosophy and religion, and between philosophy and literature. Even if the answers given by the *Vekhi* contributors may not immediately appeal to the present-day reader, and may stand in need of contextualization, the questions they raise are fully relevant. The articles in the present volume offer the contextualization that is needed, paradoxically, to decontextualize the original publication and appreciate the extent to which it addresses issues that should interest the present-day reader as well. It then becomes clear that *Vekhi* was not simply a publication about Russia by Russians and for Russians, but is part of something like a "global political memory" (much as the 1905 and 1917 revolutions themselves were), and constitutes a "relevant intellectual event" well beyond the pale of relevance of Russia then or now. The *Vekhi* authors' battle—if that is what it was—was indeed lost, but the event of *Vekhi* opens up the question of the role of intellectuals in a "democratized" public sphere/debate, the question of the quality of that debate, the question of elites, the role of the humanities, the question of possible or real impact on government. Those questions are with us as they were with those original authors.

## Notes

1   For biographical information about each of the *Vekhi* authors, see the Introduction to the English translation of *Vekhi* that we are using in this book: *Vekhi/Landmarks: A Collection of Articles about the Russian Intelligentsia*, trans. and ed. Marshall S. Shatz and Judith E. Zimmerman (Armonk, NY: M. E. Sharpe, 1994), viii–x.

2   Caryl Emerson writes of *Problems of Idealism* as follows: "What strikes one in this book ... is its overall sweet-temperedness, its generosity to individual thinkers and lack of ad hominem attack. These pages abound with appreciations, even to movements that have proved to be far more culprit than friend." See Caryl Emerson, "Foreword," in *Problems of Idealism: Essays in Russian Social Philosophy*, ed. and trans. Randall A. Poole (New Haven, CT: Yale University Press, 2003), vii–xviii (xiv).

3   *Vekhi. Iz glubiny*, ed. A. A. Iakovlev (Moscow: Pravda, 1991) was the most authoritative publication of the two texts at the time, as part of the series "Iz istorii otechestvennoi filosofskoi mysli" of the journal *Voprosy filosofii*. The publication of *Vekhi* is based on the fifth edition in 1910 and includes the bibliography attached to that edition (200–06). Concerning the polemics around *Vekhi*, see Ailin Kelli (Aileen Kelly), "Prilozhenie. Polemika vokrug 'Vekh'," ibid., 548–53. See also V. V. Sapov, "Vokrug 'Vekh.' (Polemika 1909–1910 godov)," in *Vekhi: pro et contra. Antologiia*, ed. V. V. Sapov (St. Petersburg: Izdatel'stvo Russkogo Khristianskogo gumanitarnogo instituta, 1998), 7–22.

4   For an account of this phenomenon and its pre-history, see Stanislav Bemovich Dzhimbinov, "The Return of Russian Philosophy," in *Russian Thought after*

Introduction

*Communism: The Recovery of a Philosophical Heritage*, ed. James Scanlan (Armonk, NY: M. E. Sharpe, 1994), 11–22.

5   Concerning the pre-history and publication history of *Vekhi*, including discussion of the title, see M. A. Kolerov, N. S. Plotnikov, "Primechaniia," in *Vekhi. Iz glubiny*, 500–48 (500–08; on the title, 503). See also the letters from the other contributors to Gershenzon published in V. Proskurina and V. Alloi, "K istorii sozdaniia 'Vekh,'" *Minuvshee. Istoricheskii al'manakh* 11 (1991): 249–91.

6   On *Problems of Idealism*, including its neo-Kantian foundations, see Randall A. Poole, "Editor's Introduction: Philosophy and Politics in the Russian Liberation Movement," in Poole, *Problems of Idealism*, 1–78.

7   While the *Vekhi* contributors and their contemporary readers seem in the main to have accepted the idea of *the* intelligentsia with *its* worldview, scholars now avoid or deconstruct the phenomenon as a singular or homogeneous entity in terminological, socio-historical, and national/global perspectives. See also, for example, G. M. Hamburg, "Russian intelligentsias," in *A History of Russian Thought*, ed. William Leatherbarrow and Derek Offord (Cambridge: Cambridge University Press, 2010), 44–69.

8   Among the wide range of scholarship on *Vekhi*, we would like to mention here the first major book on the subject, by Christopher Read, who is also a contributor to this volume: Christopher Read, *Religion, Revolution and the Russian Intelligentsia 1900–1912: The* Vekhi *Debate and Its Intellectual Background* (London and Basingstoke: Macmillan, 1979). The centenary of *Vekhi* occasioned a large number and variety of publications in Russia, including collections: see, for example, A. A. and E. A. Takho-Godi, eds., *Sbornik "Vekhi" v kontekste russkoi kul'tury* (Moscow: Nauka, 2007); and G. Aliaev and T. Sukhodub, eds., *Fenomen filosofskoi kritiki v kul'ture rossiiskogo serebrianogo veka (k 100-letiiu vykhoda sbornika statei o russkoi intelligentsia "Vekhi"* (Poltava: OOO "ASMI," 2009). Extensive further references to the scholarship on *Vekhi* can be found in the individual articles that make up this volume.

9   See Note 5 above.

10  Mikhail Gershenzon, "Preface to the First Edition," in Shatz and Zimmerman, *Vekhi/Landmarks*, xxxvii–xxxviii (xxxvii). Subsequent references are given in parentheses in the text.

11  In a note to the second edition of *Vekhi*, Izgoev adds a comment as follows: "I feel obliged to make a reservation in regard to the 'platform' formulated in the Preface to this book: I fully accept the *basic thesis* propounded there, but disagree with the other authors on the *principles* used to support it" (90). The next author that one would most likely identify as at some odds with the "common platform" would be Kistiakovskii, who subsequently acknowledged: "Unfortunately, we had very little discussion of the content, plan and rationale of our collection as a whole" (Kolerov and Plotnikov, "Primechaniia," 501). In his correspondence with Gershenzon, Frank identified the convergence around a negative critique and wrote that in respect of a "new ideal" there is "no hope of unanimity among the contributors" (Proskurina and Alloi, "K istorii," 253). Ideas were also floated, this time led by Struve, to produce a second volume which would, according to Frank, "develop in a collective work the *positive*

content of those ideas which had been expressed in *Vekhi* in the negative form of a critique of the intelligentsia worldview" (S. L. Frank, *Biografiia P. B. Struve* [New York: Izdatel'stvo imeni Chekhova, 1956], 87). In many respects, the odd one out among the *Vekhi* contributors was Gershenzon, who was not in fact a contributor to *Problems of Idealism* and *Out of the Depths* (on Gershenzon, see, for example, Vera Proskurina, "Tvorcheskoe samosoznanie Mikhaila Gershenzona," *Literaturnoe obozrenie* 9 [1990]: 93–96).

12  Concerning conceptions of the person in Russian philosophy, see Nikolaj Plotnikov, "Preface," *Studies in East European Thought* 61 (2009), "Special Issue: The Discourse of Personality in the Russian Intellectual Tradition," ed. Nikolaj Plotnikov: 71–75. See also G. M. Hamburg and Randall A. Poole, "Introduction: The humanist tradition in Russian philosophy," in *A History of Russian Philosophy 1830–1930: Faith, Reason, and the Defense of Human Dignity*, ed. G. M. Hamburg and Randall A. Poole (Cambridge: Cambridge University Press, 2010), 1–23.

13  Orlando Figes, *A People's Tragedy: The Russian Revolution, 1891–1924* (New York: Penguin, 1996), 215.

14  John Keep and Lionel Kochan, *The Making of Modern Russia* (London: Penguin, [1962] 1997), 238.

15  By "social democratization" we mean roughly what Alexis de Tocqueville had in mind when he diagnosed the United States of America: a situation in which there does not exist, among citizens, any a priori inequality based, for example, on differences in blood or breeding. For example, any citizen can become head of state upon being elected president, which is crucially different from becoming king—or tsar—on grounds of pedigree. (We omit here the obvious fact that in the course of that same nineteenth century racial divisions—such as those used against colored people in the USA, and Jews in Europe, among others—replaced the old feudal divisions.) See Alexis de Tocqueville, *De la démocratie en Amérique* (Paris: Garnier-Flammarion, [1832–40] 1981).

16  Keep and Kochan, *The Making of Modern Russia*, 240–42.

17  It may very well be that some of these alternatives are more "realistic" or "practical" than others, but that does not make them less political, because "realism" (and "pragmatism" even more) itself is one among several options.

18  Samuel P. Huntington, *The Third Wave: Democratization in the Late Twentieth Century* (Norman, OK: University of Oklahoma Press, 1991), 13–26.

19  Leo Strauss, *What is Political Philosophy? And Other Studies* (Chicago: University of Chicago Press, [1959] 1988), 34.

20  For an illuminating systems-theoretical analysis of this transitional period in Russia, see Dirk Kretzschmar, *Identität Statt Differenz* (Frankfurt am Main: Peter Lang, 2002), 104ff.

21  Figes, *A People's Tragedy*, 56–61 and 162–64, and Kochan and Keep, *The Making of Modern Russia*, 206.

22  Kochan and Keep, *The Making of Modern Russia*, 186, 229.

Introduction

23  Figes, *A People's Tragedy*, 69.
24  Kochan and Keep, *The Making of Modern Russia*, 251.
25  Pipes in the very title of his book: *Russia under the Old Regime* (London: Penguin, [1974] 1995); cf. also Figes in the title of the first part of *A People's Tragedy*.
26  Figes, *A People's Tragedy*, Part 2, 157-303.
27  Claude Lefort, "La question de la démocratie," in *Le retrait du politique*, ed. Philippe Lacoue-Labarthe and Jean-Luc Nancy (Paris: Galilée, 1983), 84; also in Claude Lefort, *Essais sur le politique, XIXe-XXe siècles* (Paris: Éditions du Seuil, 1986), 29.
28  Figes, *A People's Tragedy*, 69 and 241.
29  Ibid., 209.
30  Pipes, *Russia under the Old Regime*, 252.
31  Ibid.
32  See Kochan and Keep, *The Making of Modern Russia*, 233.
33  Information gathered from various editions of *Vekhi* as well as from P. V. Alekseev et al., eds., *Filosofy Rossii XIX-XX stoletii* (Moscow: Kniga i biznes, 1995), and A. D. Sudov, ed., *Sto russkikh filosofov. Biograficheskii slovar'* (Moscow: Mirta, 1995).
34  Berdiaev's heyday internationally may have been mostly in the 1950s and 1960s, but Bulgakov and Frank currently are the subject of PhD and other studies, while recent translations of their works into English and German testify to their perceived relevance beyond the academic contexts of Slavic and Russian studies. The multivolume German edition of Frank's work under the guidance of Peter Ehlen, for example, seeks its audience among philosophers and theologians rather than among Slavists and experts on Orthodoxy (who can read the original anyway).
35  For the story of the expulsion of philosophers from Soviet Russia, see Lesley Chamberlain, *The Philosophy Steamer: Lenin and the Exile of the Intelligentsia* (London: Atlantic Books, 2006).
36  For a critical account of the historiography, which looks at the whole tradition of histories of Russian philosophy as background to the remarkable boom in such histories in the last 20 years, see Alyssa DeBlasio, "Writing the History of Russian Philosophy," *Studies in East European Thought* 63 (2011): 203-26 (on the early twentieth century, 208-10). DeBlasio's overarching question concerns how Russian philosophy might step out of its marginality and assert itself internationally (204, 222-24), while her account of the historiography laments the tendency toward the essentializing of distinctive traits and historiosophy; she also quotes from recent debates about the lack of ideas in contemporary Russian culture (205). The extant writing about Russian philosophy in the early twentieth century is in fact far more extensive than DeBlasio's necessarily summary account conveys, and includes an array of books (on Khomiakov, Leont'ev, Dostoevskii) and articles by Berdiaev alone.
37  Boris Groys, "Russia and the West: The Quest for Russian National Identity," *Studies in Soviet Thought* 43 (1992): 185-98.

38  Poole, "Editor's Introduction," 2.

39  Berdiaev's most famous work as a historian of Russian thought is *Russkaia ideia* (*The Russian Idea*, trans. R. M. French [London: G. Bles, 1947]).

40  V. V. Zen'kovskii, *Istoriia russkoi filosofii*, 2 vols. (Paris: YMCA Press, [1948] 1989), vol. 1, 18; in English: V. V. Zenkovsky, *A History of Russian Philosophy*, trans. George L. Kline (London: Routledge and Kegan Paul, 1953), 6.

41  See Caryl Emerson's comment on *Problems of Idealism* quoted in Note 2 above.

42  S. N. Trubetskoi, "What the History of Philosophy Teaches," in Poole, *Problems of Idealism*, 258–73.

43  See, for example, Berdiaev's own words on the subject in his autobiography: Nikolai Berdiaev, *Sobranie sochinenii*, ed. N. A. Struve, vol. 1, *Samopoznanie (opyt filosofskoi avtobiografii)* (Paris: YMCA Press, 1989), 253–59.

44  See N. F. Fedorov, "Vopros o bratstve, ili rodstve, o prichinakh nebratskogo, nerodstvennogo, t.e. nemirnogo, sostoianiia mira i o sredstvakh k vosstanovleniiu rodstva (Zapiska ot neuchenykh k uchenym, dukhovnym i svetskim, k veruiushchim i neveruiushchim)," in *Sobranie sochinenii v chetyrekh tomakh*, ed. A. G. Gacheva and S. G. Semenova (Moscow: Progress, 1995–99), vol. 1, 51–54.

45  Iakovlev, *Vekhi. Iz glubiny*, 494.

46  This idea is a recurrent one throughout Leont'ev's work and features also in his correspondence with Rozanov before his death (and in Rozanov's commentary on the correspondence). See K. N. Leont'ev, *Vostok, Rossiia i slavianstvo. Filosofskaia i politicheskaia publitsistika. Dukhovnaia proza, 1872–1891*, ed. G. B. Kremnev (Moscow: Respublika, 1996); Konstantin Leont'ev, *Pis'ma k Vasiliiu Rozanovu* (London: Nina Karsov, 1981).

47  It may also be useful to adapt the notion of a "threshold work" or "metaparody"—"designed to resonate between opposing genres and interpretations"—which Gary Saul Morson introduced in his seminal study of Dostoevskii's *Dnevnik pisatelia* (*Diary of a Writer*, 1873–81), as a conceptual and hermeneutic framework for approaching the borderlands of Russian philosophy. See Gary Saul Morson, *The Boundaries of Genre: Dostoevsky's* Diary of a Writer *and the Traditions of Literary Utopia* (Austin, TX: University of Texas Press, 1981), 142–46, 181–82.

48  Galin Tihanov, "Continuities in the Soviet period," in Leatherbarrow and Offord, *A History of Russian Thought*, 311–39 (320).

49  Edith Clowes, *Fiction's Overcoat: Russian Literary Culture and the Question of Philosophy* (Ithaca, NY: Cornell University Press, 2004); James P. Scanlan, *Dostoevsky the Thinker* (Ithaca, NY: Cornell University Press, 2002).

50  S. I. Ozhegov, *Slovar' russkogo iazyka*, 22nd ed., s.v. "dukh."

51  *The Concise Oxford Dictionary*, 9th ed., s.v. "spiritual."

52  For an authoritative statement of the patristic anthropology of image and likeness, see Vladimir Losskii, *The Mystical Theology of the Eastern Church* (Cambridge: James Clarke & Co., 1957), Chapter 6, "Image and Likeness."

Introduction

53   Struve's essay exhibits a fascinating tension between a conservative religious ideal of the state modelled on the early Romanov dynasty, which emerged from a movement of "national and religious" self-defense (115), and a seemingly incompatible emphasis on personal responsibility as the defining feature of "[r]eligion *in any form acceptable to contemporary man*" (120, our emphasis). Struve himself appears either not to notice, or not to find theologically problematic, the question as to how the "Kingdom of God" can be principally "within you" (120) and also principally in the seat of government.

54   See, for example, Patrick Michelson's account of the role of the academies in making patristic theology available to the reading public over the course of the nineteenth century through its large-scale and systematic translation project: Patrick Lally Michelson, "'The First and Most Sacred Right:' Religious Freedom and the Liberation of the Russian Nation, 1825–1905" (PhD diss., UW-Madison, 2007).

55   Irina Paert, *Spiritual Elders: Charisma and Tradition in Russian Orthodoxy* (DeKalb, IL: Northern Illinois University Press, 2010).

56   This is all the more remarkable for the fact that Orthodox culture, and religious culture more generally, was thriving in the late imperial period, as has been documented in a wealth of recent historical research, including: Heather J. Coleman, *Russian Baptists and Spiritual Revolution, 1905–1929* (Bloomington, IN: Indiana University Press, 2007); Jennifer Hedda, *His Kingdom Come: Orthodox Pastorship and Social Activism in Revolutionary Russia* (DeKalb, IL: Northern Illinois University Press, 2008); Scott M. Kenworthy, *The Heart of Russia: Trinity-Sergius, Monasticism, and Society after 1825* (New York: Oxford University Press, 2010); Valerie A. Kivelson and Robert H. Green, eds., *Orthodox Russia: Belief and Practice under the Tsars* (University Park: The Pennsylvania State University Press, 2003); Laurie Manchester, *Holy Fathers, Secular Sons: Clergy, Intelligentsia, and the Modern Self in Revolutionary Russia* (DeKalb, IL: Northern Illinois University Press, 2008); Vera Shevzov, *Russian Orthodoxy on the Eve of Revolution* (New York: Oxford University Press, 2004); and Mark D. Steinberg and Heather J. Coleman, eds., *Sacred Stories: Religion and Spirituality in Modern Russia* (Bloomington, IN: Indiana University Press, 2007).

57   Recently translated into English by Valeria Z. Nollan: Vladimir Solovyov, *The Philosophical Principles of Integral Knowledge* (Grand Rapids, MI: William Eerdmans, 2008).

58   For details, see Jutta Scherrer, *Die Petersburger Religiös-Philosophischen Vereinigungen* (Wiesbaden: Harrassowitz, 1973), and Kristiane Burchard, *Die Moskauer "Religiös-Philosophische Vladimir-Solov'ev-Gesellschaft (1905-1918)"* (Wiesbaden: Harrassowitz, 1998).

Part I
# *VEKHI* and the RUSSIAN INTELLIGENTSIA

# 1

# WORD GAMES?
## The Russian "Intelligentsia" as a Question of Semantics

*Frances Nethercott*

Endeavors to define the intelligentsia, or to chart its origins and development, have generated a vast literature attesting to both its complexity as a peculiarly Russian phenomenon and its importance as a tool for analyzing the interconnecting strands of the nation's political, social, and cultural history. Among the more widely accepted definitions in modern and some contemporary scholarship is one that differentiates between "cultured" and "ideologically committed" elites. In his seminal essay on the mid- to late-nineteenth century intelligentsia, published in the early 1960s, Richard Pipes used this distinction to characterize the former as predominantly a social category, which he equated with educated society or the reading public more broadly. However, in his analysis of the "ideologically committed" elite, Pipes focused on its professed revolutionary esprit de corps, worldview, and beliefs. Drawing upon a history of ideas approach in order to reconstruct the substance of the debate that members of this group engaged in, and the terms of their self-ascribed mission to transform society, he effectively placed his analysis of the intelligentsia, more narrowly defined, at one remove from socio-historical enquiry.[1]

It is this second aspect, namely the articulation or formulation of opinions by members of the intelligentsia about themselves that concerns me here. An analysis of the lexicon used in intelligentsia debates, particularly the terms referencing, across generations, the deeply embedded problem of collective identity and self-definition shows that members of the pre-revolutionary, and specifically, the pre- and non-Marxist intelligentsia rarely drew on sociological criteria; rather, their endeavors to categorize the "*intelligent*"/"intelligentsia" tended to rely on a variety of "rhetorical textual strategies" sourced in Russia's rich literary canon.[2] The *Vekhi* text bears out this observation very well. All the contributors engaged in a complex exercise of semantics as a means to demolish idealized images of the *intelligent* which, beginning in the 1860s and 1870s, had been assiduously fostered by activists in their work as literary critics and authors of *romans à thèse*. In its place, the liberal authors of the *Vekhi* collection projected an alternative image of a "religious humanistic intelligentsia," as Frank expressed it (155).[3] Inspired, in part, by the example of the "spiritual pioneers" of the 1830s and 1840s, and their successors in the latter part of the century, the *Vekhi* authors' "model" *intelligent* had no obvious fictional counterpart, as such; indeed, their obvious preference for historical exemplars of humanistic ideals could be interpreted as an attempt to reinstate the boundaries between fact and fiction that the radical intelligentsia had for so long creatively ignored. But, if the substance of the *Vekhi* authors' quest for collective self-definition challenged the ethos of the radical intelligentsia, the form of that quest nevertheless remained consistent with the practice, perfected by their adversaries, of drawing on the nation's rich literary heritage to advance socio-political and philosophical ideas. Throughout the volume, the reader frequently encounters references to leading novelists and their protagonists, and to literary tropes such as metaphor, irony, and stereotyping, all of which worked together to provide, paradoxically, a composite resource for the construction of an ostensibly socio-political discourse in the run-up to the revolution of October 1917. In order, then, to explore how the *Vekhi* authors conceived the intelligentsia, as well as the humanistic alternative they proposed, study of the rhetorical and polemical devices they employed is arguably just as important as an analysis of the content of the views they espoused.

## Typecasting the Revolutionary Intelligentsia

In probing the mentality of the intelligentsia, the *Vekhi* contributors independently identified a number of salient character traits which, taken together, serve as an identikit of the "typical *intelligent*." The principal features include: student-youth culture (*studenchestvo*), which Aleksandr

Izgoev associated with bad education, and Bogdan Kistiakovskii with unruly behavior ("socially and individually"), nihilism, maximalism, and atheism (91).[4] In sum, these traits targeted the populist tradition, as Semen Frank states: "In his ethical core, the Russian *intelligent* has remained a stubborn, inveterate *populist* from the 1870s, approximately, to the present day. His God is the people, his one aim is the happiness of the majority, and his morality consists of service to this goal combined with ascetic self-restraint and with hatred or disdain for spiritual interests of intrinsic value" (140).[5] Throughout the collection, these traits of the "typical *intelligent*" are twinned with their opposites, thereby providing a simple yet effective device to pass judgement. Time and again, the contributors contrast "youth," both physiological and psychological, with maturity, as, for example, when Izgoev writes that "the highest praise you can give a Russian *intelligent* is to call him an old student" (77).[6] For the *Vekhi* contributors, the *intelligent*'s refusal to grow up and accept responsibility for his actions betrays a slavish mentality endemic to the intelligentsia as a whole. Depicted as a faceless, anonymous social group, the intelligentsia thus stands in stark contrast with the *Vekhi* contributors' own elected pantheon of great thinkers and artists, all of whom are identified by name in tribute to their independence of mind. Mikhail Gershenzon and Izgoev, for example, contrasted the common or garden *intelligent* (rendered as "the intelligentsia mass," "the average *intelligent*," "the average mass *intelligent*") to the elite Russian thinkers, Chaadaev, the Slavophiles, and Dostoevskii.[7] "Only scattered individuals," Nikolai Berdiaev wrote, "possessed a high philosophical culture, and this in itself set them apart from the world of the intelligentsia [*intelligentshchina*]" (1).[8] According to Gershenzon, the incontestable sign of creative genius is one's inner freedom. In view of the intelligentsia's social-utilitarian morality, he could only conclude that, "in Russia, an almost infallible gauge of the strength of the artist's genius is the extent of his hatred for the intelligentsia. We need mention only the greatest of them: Lev Tolstoi and Dostoevskii, Tiutchev and Fet" (60).[9]

As a "moral type," as Frank labelled them (153), the atheism and nihilism professed by the intelligentsia described the sharpest opposition of all to the personalist Christian faith that a number of the *Vekhi* authors shared. Yet, as well as openly reinforcing this contest of opinions, they also drew attention to a common advocacy of social engagement in order to perform a substantive critique of the radical intelligentsia's worldview in the guise of rhetorical undermining. Not only did they strike at the contradictions embedded in the intelligentsia's social credo, they also produced some of the most memorable cameos of the intelligentsia's state of mind. Building on Dostoevskii's original critique of the intelligentsia's conscious appropriation of religious qualities, the *Vekhi* authors introduced the idea of monastic contemplation, effectively subverting the *intelligent*'s vocation of transforming society. Berdiaev and Sergei Bulgakov noted that, despite his declared commitment to social welfare, the *intelligent* had remained cloistered, remote from the world. Like a monk (an image which both Gershenzon and Frank used), he found "worldly vanity or diversions" deeply disturbing. But, inscrutably, if the *intelligent* shunned reality by inhabiting a world of phantoms, dreams, and pious faith, he also fervently sought to transform the world from within the "walls of his monastery and to propagate his faith in it." "In summary," wrote Frank, "we can define the classic Russian *intelligent* as a *militant monk of the nihilistic religion of earthly well-being*" (151; 150).

## Literary Models and Inflections

In their analysis of the symptoms of intelligentsia behavior, the *Vekhi* contributors drew quite extensively on the national literary canon. In doing so, they were in many respects following in the footsteps of the radical intelligentsia. However, whereas their predecessors had made enormous demands on literature so that it became a vehicle for social and political critique, the *Vekhi* authors sought to restore the autonomy of the cultural sphere, and they did so, in part, by appealing to a body of literature that the first-generation intelligentsia had rejected as socially irrelevant, but which had, for their critics, a powerful moral, aesthetic, and metaphysical resonance. Parrying references to *intelligent*-poets and novelists, such as Nekrasov, Uspenskii, or Garshin with the names of Chekhov, Dostoevskii, Fet, and Tolstoi, they mapped out the mutually exclusive worlds that— in Gershenzon's words—these genuine artists, as bearers of "artistic" and "living truth," on the one hand, and the intelligentsia, on the other, respectively inhabited:

> What the intelligentsia lived by quite literally did not even exist [for our best people—FN]; at the peak of the civic movement Tolstoi was glorifying the wise "stupidity" of Karataev and Kutuzov, Dostoevskii was studying the "underground," Tiutchev was singing of primordial chaos, and Fet of love and eternity. [...] The intelligentsia applauded ... but it was not swayed. Moreover, through its spiritual leaders, the critics and journalists, it set up a tribunal to try the free truth of creativity, and it convicted Tiutchev of inattention and Fet of mockery, while Dostoevskii was pronounced reactionary and Chekhov indifferent. Its deeply prejudiced consciousness closed the intelligentsia's soul to artistic as well as living truth. (60–61)

If the intelligentsia could, with some justification, dismiss the works of Chekhov and Dostoevskii as socially irrelevant, it was compelled either to ignore or to deny the hostile and rather troubling portrayals of the intelligentsia types that these writers created. Gershenzon noted that within Chekhov's carefully drawn gallery of character studies, "there are barely five or six normal individuals. Nine-tenths of our *intelligenty* are neurasthenic" (65).[10] Bulgakov sourced a similar observation in Dostoevskii's novels:

> Following Dostoevskii, it has frequently been noted that the Russian intelligentsia's spiritual make-up contains elements of religiosity which sometimes even approximate Christianity. The intelligentsia's historical predicament was primarily responsible for fostering these traits: on the one hand, government persecution gave it a feeling of martyrdom and confessorship, while forcible isolation from life, on the other, produced dreaminess, occasional starry-eyed idealism, utopianism, and, in general, an inadequate sense of reality. (20)[11]

Besides deferring to an alternative set of literary authorities, the *Vekhi* authors also relied on stylistic cadences of their own, both as a means to parody the intelligentsia's self-representation as the progressive elite and to diagnose its sense of mission as a form of neurosis, as the following passage from Gershenzon illustrates: "The average *intelligent* ... felt more unwell with every passing year. He was already living very badly in the mid-eighties. [...] Scarcely any of them are healthy—they are all jaundiced, morose, anxious figures deformed by some secret dissatisfaction" (65).

Izgoev mimicked the intelligentsia's *profession de foi*: "Your convictions will lead you to your crucifixion: they are holy, they are progressive, you are right ..." (84).[12] Similarly, Bulgakov presented the *intelligent* as an aspiring "hero" in his own narrative, his youthfulness and courage fortified by the suffering and martyrdom he willingly endured. The ironic sting in the tale, as Bulgakov tells it, however, is that, having donned the "uniform of the *intelligent*," "those heroic youths ... in later life so easily and imperceptibly turn into 'superfluous men' or into Chekhovian and Gogolian types, ending up with wine or cards, if not worse" (33). In building his portrait, Bulgakov referenced a number of Russian (and German)[13] romantic poets and novelists, but his depiction of the intelligentsia's mental world and beliefs in terms of a man-deifying "all is allowed" motto obviously found its deepest inspiration in the novels of Dostoevskii: "The heroic *intelligent* ... is not content with the role of the modest worker.... His dream is to be the savior of mankind, or at least, of the Russian people. He demands (in his dreams, of course) not the secure minimum but the heroic maximum" (28).[14] Even where the *Vekhi* authors identified leading representatives of the 1860s–1870s generation by name, the focus still privileged a classification of the intelligentsia mentality. Thus Pisarev, the "barbaric iconoclast," as Frank called him, emerges as the quintessential *intelligent*, the embodiment of his age's "spiritual mood"— a utilitarian ethic of rational egoism: "Muffled and uncertain, the voice of aesthetic conscience sounds even more faintly and more timidly in the Russian *intelligent*'s soul. In this respect Pisarev and his puerile dethronement of our greatest national artist (Pushkin), and the entire Pisarev episode, that turbulent revolt against aesthetics, was not merely an isolated incident in our spiritual development. It was, rather, a lens that focused the rays of barbaric iconoclasm that still burns unquenched in the intelligentsia's consciousness onto a single bright point" (134). In other respects, the *Vekhi* portrayal of the intelligentsia was, as the foregoing quotations suggest, closely modelled on the self-image of the early revolutionaries, which they had projected either through their fictional creations or by playing out their own lives "in character" as "new people" in accordance with the rules of the ideologically-engaged aesthetic they espoused.[15] Among the most notorious and often-cited instances of this practice was the radical writer Dmitrii Pisarev and his alter-ego,

## Word Games? The Russian "Intelligentsia" as a Question of Semantics

Evgenii Bazarov, Turgenev's anti-hero in his celebrated novel *Ottsy i deti* (*Fathers and Sons*, 1862). Pisarev singled out Bazarov as the model of "our young generation"; he encapsulated its spiritual physiognomy.[16] Bazarov "acknowledges no rule above or outside him, no moral law or principle,... espouses no elevated purpose, is not prone to self-reflection, yet despite—or because—of that possesses enormous power."[17] Pisarev's indebtedness to Turgenev's fictional creation is again obvious in his own "credo of iconoclasm," which he devised for the "thinking realist": "[S]hatter what can be shattered—the test of what is worthwhile is that which resists the force of the blow. All the rest, broken into a thousand pieces, is nothing but useless, obsolete rubbish. In any case, strike out to the left and to the right: it won't do any harm."[18]

Whether Pisarev's readers approved or condemned his "guide to life," they all seemed prepared to suspend disbelief, ignoring the boundaries, however porous, that exist between fact and fiction. Among his older contemporaries, the literary critic Nikolai Strakhov, for example, contended that Pisarev had made himself the "lyrical hero" of his articles, and thus was not so much a "theorist of *bazarovshchina*," as a distorted reflection (*inobytie*) of Bazarov himself. In the process he rendered the fictional hero, if not more real, then certainly more profound, than his real-life admirer: "It goes without saying that Bazarov does not look at things the way Pisarev does. Even though he denies art its real value, Pisarev does in fact acknowledge it as such, whereas Bazarov rejects it outright because he has a deeper understanding of it."[19] According to Strakhov, Pisarev's Bazarov-style ramblings and homilies, together with an excessive preoccupation with his own "Bazarov image," steered him along a false path resulting in numerous contradictions and empty claims, all of which placed him well below the "real Bazarov."[20] In much the same vein, the *Vekhi* contributors ignored the boundaries between fact and fiction. On the (largely correct) assumption that they required no contextualization for a Russian audience, fictional characters appear in their arguments to illustrate a point. Thus Frank, for example, could with complete ease refer to "our Bazarov" and the consequences of his cold, irrefutable logic for the intelligentsia worldview without referencing the names of either his creator or the novel in which he played out his nihilistic system.[21]

Definitions of the intelligentsia by both first generation radicals and their Silver Age critics, then, were sourced in a single semantic field of paired oppositions (youth versus maturity, sons versus fathers, nihilist versus idealist, atheist versus Christian believer) and a stock of literary types—from the "superfluous man" to the rational egoist and repentant nobleman. By simply inverting the positive and negative qualifiers originally attached to *intelligenty*, men of letters, or the educated classes more broadly, the *Vekhi* contributors succeeding in transforming the heroes of early *intelligenty* narratives into caricatures. But if the force of the *Vekhi* critique depended on a mastery of rhetoric, metaphor, and parody, their engagement with the "intelligentsia question" was also informed by a new accent in literary criticism, which is perhaps best summarized as a preoccupation with questions of a metaphysical order, of religion and personhood that was symptomatic of the more speculative and apocalyptic mood of the Silver Age generation. Against the radical intelligentsia's designs to champion an ideologically-engaged aesthetics, the *Vekhi* authors perceived the novel as an opportunity to explore man's inner spiritual realm.[22] Dostoevskii's masterpieces, in particular, whose protagonists exemplified aspects of the human condition, and probed the deeper moral questions of good and evil, clearly answered the *Vekhi* authors' concern to address the social and material goals of the radical intelligentsia in terms of their frightening moral implications. Thus, if, at one level, Nikolai Shelgunov's assertion that Pisarev was "the prophet of the young generation," and Frank's verdict that his attempt to dethrone "our greatest national artist" (Pushkin) was "puerile," read as straightforward polemical sallies, their respective broader assessments of Pisarev's place in the intelligentsia movement referenced a shift in the literary-critical paradigm. Accordingly, Pisarev passed from the embodiment of a "social type," worthy of emulation, into a very dangerous "psychological type," driven by a fanatical abnegation and unswerving dedication to science. Berdiaev made a similar point in his contribution to *Iz glubiny* (*Out of the Depths*, 1918), the sequel volume to *Vekhi* written in response to the 1917 revolution. If, during the mid-nineteenth century, literary critics treated Gogol' as the founder of the "realist" trend in Russian literature, early twentieth-century readers, caught up by a sense of imminent crisis and apocalypse, recast his work as "an artistic revelation of evil." This was not, Berdiaev stressed, a revelation "of a social and external evil linked with political backwardness and lack of enlightenment," but evil "as a metaphysical and internal principle."[23]

## DEFINING THE *VEKHI* CONTRIBUTORS

Endeavors by the *Vekhi* contributors to distance themselves from the intelligentsia tradition, and to redefine the social role and ideology of a radically different "critically thinking elite," foreground a number of ambiguities with regard to their own identity as a group and their place in the intelligentsia tradition more broadly. If the substance of the *Vekhi* critique established unequivocally their rejection of the radical intelligentsia's anti-statism and utilitarian aesthetics, formal self-designation proved elusive.

Writing at the turn of the century, the historian of philosophy Sergei Trubetskoi noted that to be a "cultured person [*kul'turnyi chelovek*]" was aspirational, but to be called an "*intelligent*," which to his mind carried the same negative connotations as "bureaucrat [*chinovnik*]," was an insult.[24] In view of the *Vekhi* authors' open disavowal of the original intelligentsia model, it is tempting to class them as would-be intellectuals. However, there are several factors militating against this. Although in the *Vekhi* collection the word "intellectual" does occur, it is only as an adjective: for example, "the *intelligent* lacks what Nietzsche called 'intellectual conscience' [*intellektual'naia sovest'*]" (134).[25] As a noun, the term did not, as yet, have much currency; in west European languages it had only recently been coined in an attempt to "recapture and reassert," as Zygmunt Bauman argues, "that societal centrality and those global concerns which had been associated with the production and dissemination of knowledge during the age of Enlightenment."[26] Neither the *Vekhi* contributors nor their immediate contemporaries, who expressed a dislike for the term "intelligentsia," were able to offer a single alternative label to profile their own self-ascribed role as a "critically thinking elite." For want of a better solution, it was common practice to place the term "intelligentsia" in inverted commas or to seek circumlocutions when referring to a cultural elite that eschewed revolutionary extremism while still actively deliberating on questions of social justice. Thus, in their bid to restore the values associated with the "spiritual pioneers" of the 1830s and 1840s and their successors active at the close of the nineteenth century, the *Vekhi* contributors glossed their elected role models variously as "thinkers [*mysliteli*]," "people of profound education [*liudi glubokoi obrazovannosti*]," "of profound intelligence [*glubokogo uma*]," people who are "especially talented [*osobo darovitye*]."[27] Otherwise, the term "intelligentsia" (with or without quotation marks) is annoyingly ubiquitous, and requires close attention to the context in which it appears: "Obviously, by 'intelligentsia,' we do not mean attending balls at the Nobles' Assembly. Nor do we even mean the 'educated class' … with its cultural function of spreading enlightenment. […] The intelligentsia is a totally unique factor in Russian political development, its historical significance stemming from its attitude to both the idea and the actuality of the state" (117–18).[28] Petr Struve's remarks, cited here, suggest that he was conscious of the need to position himself with respect to the original intelligentsia model, and he did so by historicizing it. Berdiaev also recognized the importance of distinguishing between a genuine intelligentsia and its epigones, as his inclusion of the pejorative "*-shchina*" suffix to create the neologism "*intelligentshchina*" suggests.[29] In addition, he transposed this suffix to a partner noun to speak of "*intelligentskaia kruzhkovshchina*"— a rhetorical strategy that gave "intonational weight" to his condemnation of the intelligentsia's failure to recognize the importance of individual responsibility.[30] That said, Berdiaev only used the derogatory term "*intelligentshchina*" a handful of times, and the reader is, again, forced to rely on the context in order to gauge who or what is meant by "intelligentsia." Other contributors were less rigorous; rather than distancing themselves, they muddied the waters with intermittent inclusions of a broad-based "we," in guilty recognition of the part they had played in the failure of the 1905 revolution. Bulgakov began his essay with a mea culpa account of the failure of the revolution, in which he, like all of the contributors, had been directly involved. Gershenzon openly positioned himself as an *intelligent*, and although he did not, of course, align himself with the "rank and file" (*massovaia*) intelligentsia, he persistently blurred the distinction between the two categories to produce in places an (unfortunate) all-inclusive "we." His "we are cripples" is a clear instance of self-castigation; his exclamation of shame—"our best people looked at us with disgust and refused to bless our cause" (51, 60)—was arguably, in view of the polemical intentions of the volume as a whole, not an admission of guilt other contributors would be prepared to make.

It goes without saying that, despite their disavowal of the intelligentsia, the *Vekhi* authors remained no less committed, through the written and spoken word, to encouraging awareness among the public of the need for social change. This explains why they were seemingly reluctant to equate their concept of the genuine *intelligent*, or enlightened man of letters, with the image of an "intellectual-scholar." Again, in fictional depictions, the latter was associated with disinterestedness and uninspiring academia. If both the *intelligent* and the educated elite were portrayed as "westernized" in upbringing and formal education, narrative accounts of their sharply contrasting lifestyles worked to dramatic and comic effect. While the errant (when not exiled) *intelligent*, opponent of tsarist autocracy and participant in the underground, conspiratorial *kruzhki* where he plotted radical social change, made for an exciting storyline, the aloof, sedentary, and usually conformist scholar or man of letters, who enjoyed the refined rituals of salon culture and the country estate, did not. Likened to the German "cabinet professor," the intellectual scholar was either the butt of sarcastic criticism (Pisarev) for his abstract theorizing and lack of social commitment or viewed as an exotic species (Chekhov's "Skuchnaia istoriia" ["A Dreary Story," 1892]) cultivating private interests and producing nothing.[31]

Struve furnished possibly the most comprehensive list of *intelligenty* and their opposites, which is worth quoting in full:

> We need only compare Novikov, Radishchev, and Chaadaev with Bakunin and Chernyshevskii to understand the ideological gulf that separated the luminaries of the educated class from the luminaries of the Russian intelligentsia. [...] The great writers, Pushkin, Lermontov, Gogol', Turgenev, Dostoevskii, and Chekhov, do not have the lineaments [*lik*] of *intelligenty*. Belinskii's greatness is not as an *intelligent*, as Bakunin's pupil, but chiefly as the interpreter of Pushkin and his national significance. Even Herzen, despite his socialism and atheism [i.e., attributes of the *intelligent*—FN], waged a constant inner struggle with his *intelligent*'s image. Or rather, he sometimes wore the uniform, as it were, of the Russian *intelligent*. [...] Mikhailovskii is an example of a ty-

pical *intelligent*.... Vladimir Solov'ev is not an *intelligent* at all. Saltykov, who, as an individual, has little in common with Herzen, is very similar to him in one regard: although he was in no way an *intelligent*, he too wore the intelligentsia uniform, and quite submissively. Dostoevskii and Tolstoi, each in his own way, tore this uniform off and threw it far away. (120–21)[32]

The suggestion here is that once branded *intelligenty*, these men of otherwise outstanding talent sacrificed their individuality and reverted to type. By contrast, the image of the ideal enlightener which the *Vekhi* authors endorsed is not sourced in the literary imagination: it primarily identifies individuals of intellectual and creative greatness who espoused theoretical, aesthetic, and religious values, and who were challenged or victimized for their independence of thought. Moreover, in opposition to the *intelligent*, defined as a product of Russia's long tradition of repressive censorship, the "non-" or "anti"-*intelligent* had a resonance that potentially crossed national borders and time frames. Indeed, there are grounds for suggesting that the intellectual-cum-moral role model which is advanced in *Vekhi* anticipated the emergence of the *"philosophe engagé"* we associate with French leftist intellectuals in the twentieth century, just as, in some ways, it was reminiscent of the enlightened *philosophe* as defined by Voltaire. What distinguished the *Vekhi* role model was, of course, the pre-eminence of a religious dimension in the authors' account of man and society, a component not found in the more secular worldviews of Enlightenment thought and twentieth-century west European existentialism.

## Between History and Sociology

"The word 'intelligentsia,'" Struve remarked, "can of course be used in various senses. The history of this word in colloquial and literary Russian might be the subject of an interesting specialized study" (117). For the purposes of his argument, namely that the intelligentsia was a historically specific phenomenon, Struve identified the term as the expression of an attitude toward the regime ("atheistic dissociation from the state," 121). But his observation also suggests that he was deeply aware of the difficulties presented to anyone endeavoring to offer a definition of the intelligentsia. It is worth noting that, initially, the dominant definitional criteria used in historical surveys of the intelligentsia, which began to appear in this period, were moral and ideological. The authoritative Brokgaus-Efron encyclopaedia, for example, highlighted the intelligentsia's self-ascribed mission to serve the people as a feature exclusive to the most "progressive sector of educated society," thereby making its worldview integral to the definition.[33] The critic and historian of populist persuasion Ivanov-Razumnik, who made explicit the link between the history of the intelligentsia and the history of social thought more generally, specified hostility to the "bourgeois [*meshchanstvo*]" as the hallmark of a genuine intelligentsia across the successive phases in its development. In view of its "classless nature [*vneklassovost'*]," the collective identity of the intelligentsia derived from a bond of consciousness and a shared moral passion.[34] Increasingly, though, as Marxist literature prevailed, definitions of the intelligentsia acquired a more evident social referent building upon the original definition advanced by the popularizer, Boborykin, as "the most educated, cultured and progressive section of society in any given country."[35]

This double set of definitions—one a functionalist definition pitched in terms of a specific social referent (progressive, educated), the other more "culturalist," emphasizing a professed outlook and self-image—has also fed competing views concerning the transferability of the concept to other cultures.[36] If the *Vekhi* authors, subscribing to the second definition, regarded the intelligentsia as a unique, historically defined phenomenon, and continued to do so in their émigré publications, others, such as the historian and Kadet leader Pavel Miliukov, and the literary historian D. N. Ovsianiko-Kulikovskii, in addition to Boborykin, just mentioned, made a case for the existence of comparable sub-cultures across continental Europe.[37] Doing so, however, was possibly at the cost of conflating terms. For example, Miliukov's argument against a nationally specific definition of the intelligentsia derived from his view that the characteristics separating the intelligentsia and the educated class were not stable; depending on the context, differences between them could either dissolve or be exacerbated by the terms of hostile polemics.[38] With no fixed distinction between the two, the task of identifying comparable phenomena elsewhere thus becomes far less problematic. Certainly, as Stefan Collini has argued in his study of British intellectuals, the term "intelligentsia" was an influential foreign import, which in the early twentieth century was assumed to "identify a sociologically distinct group" who, by virtue of an education that set them apart from an almost wholly illiterate society, were committed to being critical of political and religious authority.[39] He cites Karl Mannheim's 1929 study, *Ideologie und Utopie* (published in an English translation in 1936) as an illustration of the facility with which the term was absorbed into sociological discourse: "In every society there are social groups whose special task it is to provide an interpretation of the world for that society. We call these the 'intelligentsia.'" But, as Collini notes, Mannheim was essentially using the term as the plural or categorical form of "intellectuals."[40] Informed by a nascent social science and class analysis inspired by European Marxism, the intelligentsia acquired a collective identity as an epistemic authority. Should their interpretations of society and politics be received as criticism (in authoritarian regimes, for example), they may become marginalized, dissident, or oppositional, but these associations do not, according to Collini, form an intrinsic part of the concept as such.[41] In sociological terms, then, the concept of intelligentsia qua intellectuals has a universal resonance: "Like the knowledge they produce, intellectuals are not bound by localized, communal traditions. They are, together with their knowledge, extra-territorial."[42]

In her study of the attitudes non-Marxist Russians held toward Bolshevism, Jane Burbank noted that "without the Russian Revolution, the category 'intelligentsia' might not have entered the vocabulary of twentieth-century social science and politics."[43] While her observation neatly dovetails with the foregoing comments, in view of the émigré sources she analyzes, her remark also implies that our understanding of the collapse of tsarism and revolution has to a large extent been shaped by the reflections of individuals—including former *Vekhi* contributors—who had witnessed these events firsthand and suffered the consequences in their personal lives thereafter. In memoirs and historical diagnoses of the deeper meaning of events culminating in October, leading émigré voices, such as Berdiaev and Georgii Fedotov, presented the intelligentsia to a western audience as a uniquely Russian phenomenon, the comprehension of which required examination of the specific context in which it emerged, together with a reasoned account of the worldview it professed. Arguably, the majority of western-language studies of Russian intellectual and political culture have taken up Berdiaev's and Fedotov's cue: it has become customary among historians of Russia and the Soviet Union, especially since the latter part of the twentieth century, to argue for the distinctiveness of the intelligentsia as a socio-cultural category. Whether they opt for a socio-historical or a history of ideas approach (or some combination of the two), analyses generally seek to safeguard the historical and cultural distinctiveness of the Russian intelligentsia, even as they confront the evident splits and factions within it that surfaced over time. As I mentioned at the beginning of this essay, Richard Pipes addressed this issue by distinguishing between what he termed "cultured" and "ideological" intelligentsia. Scholars of the final years of Imperial rule have tried to accommodate the fragmentation within the ranks of the intelligentsia by employing a series of labels—radical, revolutionary, liberal, religious, artistic, even "academic"—in order to convey the growing complexity of the phenomenon—without, however, shattering the illusion of a shared identity as an oppositional force to the regime.[44] Despite differences in background, skills, or profession, turn-of-the-century *intelligenty*, which now included poets, philosophers, political thinkers, and university professors, continued to express a concern for the oppressed of Russia. These labels may be workable, short-hand solutions for research into, for example, the history of Russian liberal thought or Soviet dissidence, but they side-step the issue of the intelligentsia's obsession with its own identity. Writing in the early 1970s, Michael Confino pointed out that "none of the definitions given during the past sixty years or so has been found entirely satisfactory, and recent research has clearly shown the vagueness of the term, its many ambiguities and the strains between the outlook and the self-image of those who used it and the social and intellectual reality it is supposed to represent."[45] The point, as Confino's remarks imply, is that since its inception, the word "intelligentsia" operated as a sort of catchword in verbal slanging matches among rival groups, and was actually used to refer to different sets of people. Given an evident lack of formal or definitional consensus, attempts to affirm or demolish the social significance of peers and rivals involved qualifiers that tended to be "persuasive in nature" and actually targeted image/identity as much as, if not more than, deeds.[46] Adjectives such as "true," "real," "young," evocative metaphors—"the beautiful class," "crippled souls," or "dung-hill"—and literary motifs—"repentant noblemen," or "superfluous men"—which originally colored the intelligentsia question, suggest that the *intelligenty* were troubled by a quest to determine who or what they were, as much as by the need to establish their role in society as bearers of ideas and remedies for Russia's socio-political problems. The *Vekhi* episode clearly testifies to this dilemma.

## Notes

1. Richard Pipes, ed., *The Russian Intelligentsia* (New York: Columbia University Press, 1961). See also Vladimir C. Nahirny, *The Russian Intelligentsia: From Torment to Silence* (New Brunswick: Transaction Books, 1983); Philip Pomper, *The Russian Revolutionary Intelligentsia* (New York: Thomas Y. Crowell Co., 1970); Christophe Charle, *Les Intellectuels en Europe au XIXe siècle. Essai d'histoire comparée* (Paris: Seuil, 1996). For a study of the genealogy of the intelligentsia, see Marc Raeff, *The Origins of the Russian Intelligentsia: The Eighteenth-Century Nobility* (New York: Harcourt, Brace and World, 1966).

2. I have taken this expression from Edith Clowes in her *Fiction's Overcoat: Russian Literary Culture and the Question of Philosophy* (Ithaca: Cornell University Press, 2004), Introduction. The nineteenth-century literary origins of the terms "intelligentsia" and *"intelligent"* are well documented. Used by Turgenev in his "Strannaia istoriia" ("A Strange Story," 1869), yet widely (if mistakenly) associated with the work of a relatively minor novelist, P. D. Boborykin, in the 1860s, the terms soon after entered the rival discourses of populists and liberals. See Gary Hamburg, "Russian Intelligentsias," in *A History of Russian Thought*, ed. William Leatherbarrow and Derek Offord (Cambridge: Cambridge University Press, 2010), 44–69.

3. This is Semen Frank's expression in his essay "Etika nigilizma" ("The Ethic of Nihilism.") Citations from *Vekhi* in English are taken from Marshall S. Shatz and Judith E. Zimmerman, eds. and trans., *Vekhi/Landmarks: a Collection of Articles about the Russian Intelligentsia* (Armonk, NY: M. E. Sharpe, 1994). Further references to this volume are given in parentheses in the text.

4. Bogdan Kistiakovskii, "V zashchitu prava. (Intelligentsiia i pravosoznanie)" ("In Defense of Law: The Intelligentsia and Legal Consciousness"), 91-114.

## Word Games? The Russian "Intelligentsia" as a Question of Semantics

5   Berdiaev made very similar observations in his essay "Philosophical Verity and Intelligentsia Truth": "This period of Populist obscurantism is long since over, but the bacillus has remained in our blood." And: "[T]he Marxists' victories over Populism did not lead to a fundamental crisis within the Russian intelligentsia—even in the European garb of Marxism it remained Populist, true to the old belief" (2, 4).

6   Aleksandr Izgoev, "Ob intelligentnoi molodezhi. (Zametki ob eia byt' i nastroeniiakh)" ("On Educated Youth: Notes on its Life and Sentiments"), 71-90. On youth versus maturity, see also the comments by Bulgakov and Struve, cited below.

7   "*Intelligentskaia massa*" is Gershenzon's expression; "*srednii massovyi intelligent*" is Izgoev's. Citations from the Russian are taken from A. A. Iakovlev, ed., *Vekhi. Iz Glubiny* (Moscow: Pravda, 1991), 82, 119.

8   By "scattered individuals," Berdiaev had in mind such figures as Solov'ev, Bukharev, and Sergei Trubetskoi.

9   Mikhail Gershenzon, "Tvorcheskoe samosoznanie" ("Creative Self-consciousness"), 51-70.

10  Chekhov himself made his views known in a letter addressed to I. I. Orlov: "I do not believe in our intelligentsia—hypocritical, false, uncouth, lazy. I do not even believe in it when it suffers and complains, because their oppressors all come from the same nest." Letter to I. I Orlov, dated 22 February 1899, cited in K. B. Sokolov, *Rossiiskaia intelligentsiia XVIII-nachala XX vv.: Kartina mira i povsednevnost'* (St. Petersburg, 2007), 33-34.

11  Sergei Bulgakov, "Geroizm i podvizhnichestvo. (Razmyshlenii o religioznoi prirode russkoi intelligentsii)" ("Heroism and Asceticism. [Reflections on the Religious Nature of the Russian Intelligentsia]"), 17-50.

12  On the surface, Izgoev's treatment of the intelligentsia as student youth makes him a possible exception to my claim concerning the prominence of literary motifs in attempts to define them. Indeed, in 1904 he published an article entitled "The Intelligentsia as a Sociological Group." That said, just like the other contributors, Izgoev relies quite heavily on literary references in order to construct his portrait of the student-*intelligent*.

13  Bulgakov referred to Schiller's *Don Carlos*: "The intelligentsia's cosmopolitanism is also well-known. Brought up on the abstract formulas of the Enlightenment, the *intelligent* finds it perfectly normal to assume the role of a Marquis de Posa and regard himself as a *Weltburger*" (43).

14  It also seems reasonable to suggest that Bulgakov's portrait of Christian asceticism and genuine sacrifice, which he presents as the counterweight to the vain heroism he associates with the intelligentsia, took its inspiration from Max Weber's recent publication on the protestant ethic and ideal types. In 1906, Bulgakov had published an article entitled "Karl Marx as a Religious Type."

15  See Christopher Read, *Religion, Revolution and the Russian Intelligentsia 1900-1912: The* Vekhi *Debate and its Intellectual Background* (London: Macmillan, 1979), 117. Read mentions Chernyshevskii's protagonist Rakhmetov, the "rational egoist" in *Chto delat'?* (*What is to be Done?* 1863) as possibly one of the best-known examples in this

16  regard. See also Nahirny, *The Russian Intelligentsia*, ch. 5, "Men of Convictions: First Intelligenty," and Irina Paperno, *Chernyshevsky and the Age of Realism: A Study in the Semiotics of Behavior* (Stanford, CA: Stanford University Press, 1988).

16  Dmitrii Pisarev, "Bazarov" (1863), in D. I. Pisarev, *Bazarov. Realisty* (Moscow: Khudozhestvennaia literatura, 1974), 7.

17  Ibid., 12.

18  Dmitrii Pisarev, "Skholastika XIX veka" ("Scholasticism of the Nineteenth Century"), cited in P. Milioukov et al, *Histoire de Russie*, vol. III (Paris: Librairie Ernest Leroux, 1933), 894–95.

19  N. N. Strakhov, "Ottsy i deti" ("Fathers and Children"). Cited from N. N. Strakhov, *Literaturnaia kritika* (Moscow: Sovremennik, 1984), 191.

20  Ibid.

21  "Our Bazarov, too, was irrefutably logical when he refused to serve the interests of the *muzhik* and professed the most thorough indifference to the human prosperity that would ensue when 'burdocks would be growing' from him, Bazarov. We shall see later on that this contradiction finds quite palpable expression in the practical consequences of the intelligentsia's world-view" (135).

22  The majority of the *Vekhi* contributors played a major role as architects of the "new religious consciousness" that characterized the intellectual mood in the decade between revolutions. See, for example, Martha Bohachevsky-Chomiak and Bernice Glatzer Rosenthal, eds., *A Revolution of the Spirit: Crisis of Value in Russia, 1890-1918* (Newtonville, MA: Oriental Research Partners, 1982); Catherine Evtuhov, *The Cross and the Sickle: Sergei Bulgakov and the Fate of Russian Religious Philosophy* (Ithaca, NY: Cornell University Press, 1997); Philip Boobbyer, *S. L. Frank: The Life and Work of a Russian Philosopher, 1877-1950* (Athens, OH: Ohio University Press, 1995).

23  N. Berdiaev, "Specters of the Russian Revolution," in *Out of the Depths: A Collection of Articles on the Russian Revolution*, ed. and trans. W. F. Woehrlin (Irvine, CA: C. Schlacks Jnr., 1986), 35–36.

24  S. Trubetskoi, cited in Sokolov, *Rossiiskaia intelligentsiia*, 32. As Sokolov notes, the term "intelligentsia" appeared as a dictionary entry in the 1860s. See, however, Gary Hamburg, "Russian Intelligentsias," for a different account of the origins and uses of the term.

25  Also: "Theoretical, scientific truth, rigorous and pure knowledge for its own sake, and the disinterested search for a satisfactory intellectual [*intellektual'nyi*] image of the world and mastery over it were never able to take root in the intelligentsia's consciousness" (133).

26  Zygmunt Bauman, *Legislators and Interpreters: On Modernity, Post-modernity and Intellectuals* (Ithaca, NY: Cornell University Press, 1987), 1.

27  See, for example, Bulgakov: "It is remarkable how slight an impact people of profound education, intellect, and genius made on the Russian intelligentsia when they summoned it to look more deeply into religion, and to awaken from its dogmatic

Word Games? The Russian "Intelligentsia" as a Question of Semantics

stupor" (23). Or Izgoev: "Almost all the bright, mature boys with good and honest intentions, but who lack any outstanding creative talent, inevitably pass through the youthful revolutionary circles.... Somehow, the exceptionally gifted spirits—poets, artists, musicians, inventors, etc.—are not carried away by these circles" (76).

28   Struve was alluding here to Turgenev's "A Strange Story."

29   There is a definite echo of Berdiaev's pejorative neologism in Solzhenitsyn's use of the term *obrazovanshchina*, which he used to designate the Soviet-era "intelligentsia" in his main contribution to the collective volume *Iz-pod glyb* (*From Under the Rubble*, Moscow: Samizdat, 1974). In this essay, Solzhenitsyn ruthlessly attacked contemporaries for their cowardice and abject conformism.

30   Iakovlev, *Vekhi. Iz glubiny*, 12.

31   Similarly, in the English language the term "intellectual" has experienced mixed fortunes, connoting a cultural authority but also "the chattering classes" or even a "pub bore." See Stefan Collini, *Absent Minds: Intellectuals in Britain* (Oxford: Oxford University Press, 2006), Introduction and Part One.

32   Kistiakovskii echoed Struve's comment on Herzen's identity struggle, noting that he occasionally compromised the intellectual sobriety of his observations by the unguarded claims he made "as a true Russian *intelligent*" regarding Russia's future (94).

33   V. V-v, "Intelligentsiia," in *Novyi entsiklopedicheskii slovar'*, vol. 19 (St. Petersburg: Brokgaus i Efron, 1912), 537. Early surveys of the history of the Russian intelligentsia include those by: R. V. Ivanov-Razumnik, "Russkaia intelligentsiia," *Russkaia mysl'* 12 (1904); P. Miliukov, *Iz istorii russkoi intelligentsii: sbornik statei i etiudov* (St. Petersburg: A. E. Kolpinskii, 1902); and D. N. Ovsianiko-Kulikovskii, *Istoriia russkoi intelligentsii*, 3 vols. (St. Petersburg: Obshchestvennaia pol'za, 1906–11).

34   R. V. Ivanov-Razumnik, "Russkaia intelligentsiia," 80, as cited in Sokolov, *Rossiiskaia intelligentsiia*, 20.

35   The term was further refined as a social category through Russian Marxist responses to the Western Marxist debate on the role of the "bourgeois" intellectual in the socialist movement. See Nahirny, *The Russian Intelligentsia*, and Read, *Religion, Revolution, and the Russian Intelligentsia*.

36   On the functionalist and "culturalist" definitions, see Charle, *Les Intellectuels en Europe*, 19; Collini, *Absent Minds*, 46–48.

37   For a comprehensive discussion of the national versus universal characteristics of the intelligentsia, see Sokolov, *Rossiiskaia intelligentsiia*, 60–68.

38   P. Miliukov, "Intelligentsiia i istoricheskaia traditsiia," *Voprosy filosofii* 1 (1991): 108–09, cited in Sokolov, *Rossiiskaia intelligentsiia*, 26.

39   Collini, *Absent Minds*, 22.

40   Ibid., 36.

41   Ibid., 61.

42   Bauman, *Legislators and Interpreters*, 5.

43  Jane Burbank, *Intelligentsia and Revolution: Russian Views of Bolshevism, 1917–1922* (New York: Oxford University Press, 1986).

44  On the "academic intelligentsia," see James McClelland, *Autocrats and Academics: Education, Culture and Society in Tsarist Russia* (Chicago: University of Chicago Press, 1979).

45  Confino, cited in Collini, *Absent Minds*, 22. See also Michael Confino: "Ideologies et mentalités. Intelligentsia et intellectuals en Russie aux XVIIIe—XIXe siècles," in *Société et mentalités collectives en Russie sous l'Ancien Régime* (Paris: Institut d'Études Slaves, 1991), 389–422.

46  Nahirny, *The Russian Intelligentsia*, 6.

# 2

## Perversions and Transformations:
## A. S. Izgoev and the Intelligentsia Debates, 1904–22

*Stuart Finkel*

> The authors of *Vekhi* strove toward one thing only: to the transformation and rebirth [*pererozhdeniiu i vozrozhdeniiu*] of the intelligentsia, in order to make it fully prepared for the tasks standing ahead of it.
> —A. S. Izgoev, "The Intelligentsia and 'Vekhi,'"
> in *Russian Society and the Revolution*, 1910

> A knightly Rus'—this is the new, reborn Russian intelligentsia.
> —V. N. Murav'ev, "The Roar of the Tribe,"
> in *Out of the Depths*, 1918

*Vekhi* touched off a firestorm concerning the nature and mission of the intelligentsia that captivated educated Russians for several years after its initial publication in early 1909. Articles and lectures, volumes of rebuttal, and speaking tours featured supporters, and, far more often, opponents of the *Vekhi* contributors critiquing and condemning the pamphlet and denouncing its authors as anti-intellectual renegades. More subtly but lastingly, this acrimonious debate contributed to the reshaping of the ongoing self-conscious deliberation over the accursed question, "*Chto takoe intelligentsiia?*" (What is the intelligentsia?) which had already disturbed and puzzled Russia's intellectuals for quite some time. Among the *Vekhi* contributors, the Kadet (Constitutional Democrat) publicist Aleksandr Izgoev was especially involved in this debate, in a series of articles and polemics stretching over two decades.

While *Vekhi* represented a thorough and scathing critique of the contemporary Russian intelligentsia for what the authors believed to be its dangerous, hollow dogmatism, Izgoev and the other *Vekhi* contributors were taken aback by the strong censure it received from most *intelligenty*—which is to say, its targets—and they countered these rebukes with great vehemence. While the debate died down by late 1910, it resumed soon after the Revolution. With the events of 1917 having confirmed their direst warnings, five of the seven *Vekhi* contributors and six other authors penned their reproachful post mortem, *Iz glubiny* (*Out of the Depths*, 1918). The intelligentsia was charged with having paved the way for Bolshevism, and thus for having contributed to Russia's complete annihilation. The pointed warnings of *Vekhi* were now rephrased as bitter recriminations; the answer to "*Kto vinovat?*" (Who is to blame?) was clearer than ever: it was the intelligentsia.

But it is important to qualify this assertion immediately: while disgusted with the dogmatism and shallow materialism of the Russian intelligentsia, most of the *Vekhi* and *Out of the Depths* authors hardly questioned the broader conceits informing the general shared understanding of the intelligentsia's nature.[1] In particular, they held firmly to the notion that it had a special and critical role to play in the development of the Russian nation. They continued to assume without question that there was, in fact, a single entity with a moral-ethical dimension that could be called an "intelligentsia." Some of them even acknowledged the idea that the intelligentsia had a debt to pay before "the people," although they rejected revolutionary maximalism as the solution to this obligation.

In the storm of controversy following the publication of *Vekhi*, its authors were intensely irritated by, among other things, the repeated charge of anti-intellectual obscurantism levied against them. Izgoev, in particular, fought off such allegations with a great deal of exasperation. The *Vekhi* contributors, he insisted, were hardly motivated by hatred of the intelligentsia, as some of their critics charged. Rather, he wrote, "[we] all too clearly see the enormous role that the Russian intelligentsia has before it and are aware of how much needs to be done so that it is prepared for this role, so that it is able to resolve a problem of colossal difficulty: the transformation of Russia into a law-based and democratic state. [...] The authors of *Vekhi* strove toward one thing only: to the transformation and rebirth [*pererozhdeniiu i vozrozhdeniiu*] of the intelligentsia, in order to make it fully prepared for the tasks standing ahead of it."[2] Izgoev both shared the fundamental conviction that social forces needed to be mobilized in the transformation of Russia, and concurred that it was the intelligentsia, broadly conceived, that would spearhead this renaissance. Izgoev (and the other *Vekhi* contributors) therefore saw their task not as deposing the intelligentsia from its traditionally conceived leading role in guiding Russia's development, but as sounding the alarm regarding its current unfitness to do so.[3] This essay will analyze the contributions of Izgoev and other *Vekhi* and *Out of the Depths* authors to the extended intelligentsia debates of the early twentieth century, with a view to demonstrating that they aimed, in the end, not to displace the intelligentsia from its exalted role but rather to lament its current perversions, and to urge a root transformation that might enable it to lead Russia back from catastrophe.

Izgoev was no newcomer to debates over the definition, role, and function of the intelligentsia; his very first foray into polemical journalism had been an 1899 article entitled "Frantsuzskaia intelligentsiia" ("The French Intelligentsia").[4] But it was his article "Intelligentsiia kak sotsial'naia gruppa" ("The Intelligentsia as a Social Group"), which appeared in the journal *Obrazovanie* (*Education*) in 1904, that sparked an extended discussion over a period of several years.[5] In this lengthy sociological investigation, Izgoev attempted to demythologize the intelligentsia and to critique both previous and contemporary romanticizations of its role and place in Russian society. N. K. Mikhailovskii's well-known "subjective" declaration, that the intelligentsia proper consisted only of those thinkers whose "hearts and minds" were "with the people," explicitly excluding Aksakov and other Slavophiles, Izgoev found profoundly simplistic and utterly unsatisfactory.[6] However, he reserved his harshest reproofs for his future *Vekhi* collaborator Nikolai Berdiaev's idealistic conception that the true *intelligent* lived "above all for the interests of the mind, the intellect; spiritual hunger is his predominating passion."[7] Izgoev, still true to his pragmatic legal Marxist roots, found Berdiaev's lofty formulation highly implausible and even distasteful: "I don't know, perhaps this is very idealistic, elevated, eloquent, but for me it was extremely unpleasant to read this sentimental lie, striving to depict the *intelligent* as a person not of this world...." While explicitly acknowledging the "lofty mission [*vysshaia missiia*]" of the intelligentsia, Izgoev insisted that they must be understood as ordinary human actors in society, with normal material needs.[8]

At the same time, Izgoev rejected a purely "objective" approach to defining the intelligentsia, maintaining that attempting to describe it in simple "class" terms was equally problematic: Marx himself had never satisfactorily explained how this might be done, and his followers had made even more of a muddle of it.[9] Izgoev therefore eschewed purely material (economic) definitions of the intelligentsia as a class, and acknowledged that there could always be competing reasonable definitions.[10] Still, although denying that simple Marxist categories could be applied, Izgoev at least *began* his exploration via an exposition of broader economic classes on the basis of which the category of "intellectual workers [*intellektual'nye rabotniki*]" could be discerned. His own ultimate proposition, however, owed at least as much to an idealist perspective on intellectual activity as to a materialist one: the most crucial factor in uniting all those who belonged to the "social group of the intelligentsia" was "*the presence in the professional activities of these people of an element of pedagogy* [uchitel'stva], *in the broadest sense of the word*, the transmission to people of information and accumulated knowledge with the goal of teaching."[11]

While thus claiming to avoid the pitfalls of both an exclusively subjective and an impossibly objective understanding of *intelligenty*, in the end Izgoev still asserted that they had a pivotal role to play in Russian life. It was, among other things, their duty to press for those liberties, such as freedom of speech and religion, so needed by Russian society. "We might thus come to the general conclusion that the appearance in a society of the intelligentsia as a special social group leads to the establishment of spiritual freedom," he concluded.[12] Despite, then, his initial disdain toward Berdiaev, Izgoev too found a rather exalted goal for the intelligentsia: the promotion of freedom. "Only the intelligentsia social group strives toward full, multilateral, freedom, equal for everyone; only for this group is freedom both a means and an end in itself." Because of this, then, in the absence of liberty, the intelligentsia "stood on the highest pedestal in the country," was "the foremost element in society," and could play an "outstanding role in the life of the nation."¹³ Herein, in these glowing hopes, we find a rather stark difference between Izgoev (and, later, his *Vekhi* collaborators) and more strident critics of the intelligentsia, such as Jan Wacław Machajski and his followers.¹⁴ Among the flurry of articles and books on the intelligentsia that followed Izgoev's article, the Makhaevist Evgenii Lozinskii wryly complained in *Chto zhe takoe, nakonets, intelligentsiia?* (*What, Then, Finally, is the Intelligentsia?* 1907) that despite Izgoev's attempts to provide a more nuanced depiction of intellectual workers, "he then proceeded 'despite all logic' to single out the intelligentsia as a special group and surround it with 'a halo of ideological holiness.'"¹⁵

As Izgoev would insist in 1910 in "Intelligentsiia i 'Vekhi'" ("The Intelligentsia and 'Vekhi'"), the desire of the *Vekhi* authors to reform and improve the intelligentsia for its important tasks was radically different from the thoroughgoing scorn toward intellectuals displayed by resolutely anti-intelligentsia reactionaries (to whom *Vekhi*'s many critics, Izgoev grumbled, all too often compared the *Vekhi* contributors).¹⁶ So, too, did their aims differ from those of the iconoclastic and revered Lev Tolstoi, who offered a significantly more holistic critique of the intelligentsia's value to Russia. Tolstoi, although in agreement with the *Vekhi* contributors' entreaties that the intelligentsia abandon abstract theorizing about external forms and concentrate instead on internal self-improvement and the details of real lived life, was in the end disappointed that *Vekhi* could not let go of the intelligentsia, which he felt could "never enlighten the Russian people, [it could] only corrupt it."¹⁷ Indeed, the *Vekhi* contributors came not to bury the intelligentsia, but rather, as Izgoev insisted, to reform (or transform) it: to warn against the dangerous habits and pitfalls of the Russian intelligentsia tradition and its pernicious, mindless conformity, and redirect it instead toward internal spiritual development and humility.¹⁸

As Gary Saul Morson has argued, the *Vekhi* contributors were marked not so much by anti-intellectualism as by "anti-intelligentsialism"—a disgust for the dogmatic determinism of the intelligentsia as a caste.¹⁹ Berdiaev explicitly addressed this distinction in his *Vekhi* essay, "Filosofskaia istina i intelligentskaia pravda" ("Philosophical Verity and Intelligentsia Truth"), by contrasting the narrowness and utilitarianism of the contemporary Russian "*intelligentshchina*" with a true "intelligentsia" in the broader, historical sense of the word.[20] Berdiaev's prescription—now quite like Izgoev's, but very much unlike Tolstoi's—is not to abandon hope in the intelligentsia, but to attempt to revitalize it. "The intelligentsia's consciousness needs radical reform, and the purifying fire of philosophy will have no small role to play in this important task." When it had finally abandoned its attachments to the external and focused on internal development, "the new soul of the intelligentsia will be born."[21] Berdiaev's dramatic, strikingly poetic expression here, the essence of which would be reflected in Izgoev's more prosaic essay, "The Intelligentsia and 'Vekhi,'" also prefigures the mythos of destruction and rebirth that would find its full expression in its post-Revolutionary apocalyptic sequel, *Out of the Depths*.

When Berdiaev asserted in *Vekhi* that "political absolutism" had "crippled the soul of the progressive intelligentsia,"[22] he was echoing a concern that Izgoev had begun to elucidate several years before, in a series of articles in Petr Struve's journal *Russkaia mysl'* (*Russian Thought*), for which he was a recurring contributor. As Izgoev had already suggested in January 1907, not just the intelligentsia as narrowly defined, but all of Russia's social and spiritual life (*obshchestvennaia i dukhovnaia zhizn'*), had been warped by the need to combat the repressive autocracy. Literature and art, science and philosophy, the political ideologies imported from Europe, had all been stunted in Russia by having been valued only as they related to the goal of overthrowing absolutism. "The autocracy has thoroughly distorted our life of public ideas [*obshchestvenno-ideinuiu zhizn'*]."[23] In his *Vekhi* essay, Izgoev explored how this elemental corruption was inculcated in future Russian *intelligenty* by the distorted atmosphere and crippled morality of their student days.[24] Throughout, the goal remained the same: to imply not (as the conservatives and Tolstoi did) that the intelligentsia had nothing to offer Russia, but to the contrary that it must be salvaged precisely *because* only it could rescue the country. As Izgoev wrote in *Vekhi*: "But now there are only two alternatives: either all of Russia is condemned to death and there is no way to save her, or else there must be a radical change, an all-encompassing transformation [*vsestoronnii perevorot*] in this fundamental and, to my mind, most deeply rooted feature of the Russian intelligentsia's psychological structure. Instead of love of death, the basic motive force behind this activity must become love of life, life in common with its millions of compatriots."[25] While Izgoev denied neither the heroic achievements of the Russian intelligentsia (at least up until the proclamation of the October Manifesto) nor the fact that its "distortions" had been caused by the need to struggle single-mindedly against absolutism, he now felt it imperative, as he stressed in the polemics after the publication of *Vekhi*, to sound a clarion warning regarding the need to create new intelligentsia ideas.

What's more, even after they had effectively found the majority of the intelligentsia guilty of all charges after the Revolution, Izgoev and other *Out of the Depths* authors, in different ways and with different ends in mind, suggested a counter-image of a Russian intelligentsia that might have served (or might, perhaps, still serve) a far more effective and beneficent role in Russian society. Highlighting the critical nature of the intelligentsia, Izgoev began his *Out of the Depths* essay, "Sotsializm, kul'tura i bol'shevizm" ("Socialism, Culture and Bolshevism"), with the following questions: "Will the present events at least be a storm to clear the air and enlighten consciousness? Or will these days and months, so full of excruciating anxiety, pass, and those people who call themselves the Russian intelligentsia, those who teach the Russian masses by word and letter, return to their old ways? I believe that anyone who has not yet despaired of Russia, who still believes that 'Russia will live,' *is troubled most of all by this question*" (italics mine).[26] In this formulation, not only does the intelligentsia retain its central place in determining Russia's fate, but whether it will reform itself and abandon its former predilections becomes *the* central question facing Russia. If, as Izgoev and the other authors of *Out of the Depths* felt, it was the errors of the intelligentsia that had led Russia to its current catastrophic state, then it would have to be the intelligentsia that rescued it, that led it back out of the wilderness.

Izgoev asserts that there is a very straightforward, logical reason for this conundrum: "Experience has proven to us that without or apart from the intelligentsia, it is impossible to create a viable government. But, from the same experience, we know that the intelligentsia, raised on false and impracticable ideas, serves as a powerful weapon, not for the creation, but for the destruction of the state" (125). Since in Russia the intelligentsia had indeed demolished the state, it was through the intelligentsia that it must be restored—and although at present Izgoev had little faith that any lessons had been learned, it was nevertheless Russia's only eventual hope. The faceless Russian people, the *narod*, or any group within it, was neither to blame for what had happened nor the likely source of any future national rebirth. "The main cause of the present, unprecedented devastation of our state lies in the fact that the intelligentsia completely misunderstood the nature of man and the force of the motives that direct him, the nature of society and of the state, and the conditions necessary for their strengthening and development." The people, it seems, are simply the victims of these erroneous conceptions: the ideas of the intelligentsia "turned out to be false and fatal to the people" (125–26).

Similar assumptions grounded many of the other articles in *Out of the Depths* as well. It could even be said that the volume has as its shared foundational principle the sometimes explicit, sometimes implicit presupposition that Russia's historical fate depended primarily on the inner state and actions of the intelligentsia. If the intelligentsia was, as the *Out of the Depths* authors declared, to blame for most of what had happened, then it stood to reason that if there were any hope for revival there must first be a fundamental reconstitution of its ethos. Such, for example, was the conclusion of S. A. Kotliarevskii's essay, "Ozdrovlenie" ("Recovery"). Only a renewed, revitalized intelligentsia, Kotliarevskii suggested, the same group that had made so many mistakes and led to such destruction, could produce Russia's revival: "The Russian intelligentsia must seek to restore its strengths, now so cruelly broken, at the inexhaustible sources of life. And then, recovered from its longstanding intellectual perversions and spiritual diseases, it will find in itself both a willingness and an ability to begin the task of the creative restoration of Russia, which now seems like a heap of ruins, and which gives witness to the great sin committed, and to the great retribution already borne" (155). Needless to say, this quotation makes clear that Kotliarevskii shares the core *vekhovets* principle that reformation of the intelligentsia will occur only after a collective soul-searching, a turn from external causes to internal self-improvement. But after this has occurred, it is precisely the intelligentsia that will once again take the lead in restoring that which it is collectively to blame for having destroyed.

## Perversions and Transformations: A. S. Izgoev and the Intelligentsia Debates

Pavel Novgorodtsev's essay "O putiakh i zadachakh russkoi intelligentsii" ("On the Paths and Tasks of the Russian Intelligentsia") contains the most explicit contemplation of the role of intellectuals in *Out of the Depths*. He noted, in sympathy with the original *Vekhi* volume, that its authors had not aimed in any way at

> ... deflecting the intelligentsia from its distinctive task of consciously organizing life. They called upon it neither to reject work of creative consciousness, nor to deny faith in its vital calling. They only wanted to show that the path along which the mainstream of the intelligentsia had previously travelled was an incorrect and ruinous path, and that there was another possible and necessary path for it, one to which it had long been summoned by its greatest representatives (175).

Alas, the intelligentsia had not heeded this well-intended caution and instead had responded with almost unanimous condemnation of *Vekhi*. After the October Revolution, however, "even the blind can see. Now everyone is beginning to say what the few affirmed ten years ago" (183). But the more widespread criticisms of the intelligentsia for its abstractions and isolation still, according to Novgorodtsev, usually missed the mark in failing to understand the deep spiritual nature of the crisis (183–84). Only on recognizing the need to retain continuity with the organic course of history, and the holiness inherent in the objective state of human affairs, could the intelligentsia guide Russia to the restoration of its national life (184–85).[27] Like Izgoev, Novgorodtsev saw a concrete task for the intelligentsia in state-building, "for the intellectual principles of statehood are only worked out in the spiritual experience of the enlightened parts of society" (187).

This call to intellectual renewal can be seen even in the mystical, nationalist screed of V. N. Murav'ev ("Rev plemeni" ["The Roar of the Tribe"]), who, like Kireevskii and other nineteenth-century Slavophiles, lamented the disruption of the old Russian *sobornost'* from the time of Peter forward, and who saw the intelligentsia as the bearer of abstract thought, cut off from Russian nationhood. Having infected the Russian people with these abstractions, the intelligentisa itself had been destroyed in the conflagration of revolution. And yet even here, even in the seeming irredeemability of Murav'ev's intelligentsia, lies a call for its resurrection, and, moreover, a conviction that this renascence is a fundamental prerequisite for Russia's own recovery. "There cannot," Murav'ev averred, "be a renewal of Russia without the repentance of both the people and the intelligentsia,… the adoption of a new truth, its elevation above the old" (168). Murav'ev seems to part from his co-authors in what this entails—after its resurrection, the repentant *intelligenty* will no longer be an intelligentsia as such. "The ruin of the intelligentsia," he declares, "is the ruin of a world view constructed on thought alone" (169). In an almost Tolstoian manner, the wisdom of the intelligentsia is subordinated to the far greater (and more authentic) intuitive wisdom of the *narod*. For Murav'ev, even in its repentance the intelligentsia is not the primary force that will lead the way to renewal. "The Russia which thought, proved to be worthless. There remained only the whole, which acts. From its precious depths, it reconstructs the new cultural Russia" (171).

And yet, even here there is a place for the intelligentsia, a role for it to play, and quite an elevated role at that: "However much we would like to be mere observers and theorizing philosophers, we are forced, first of all, to be doers, apostles, and prophets." Thus for Murav'ev, the intelligentsia must serve (still!) as seers, discerning what is superficial from what is essential in the *narod* by submerging itself in "the roar of the tribe." "We are its messengers and heralds," he suggests, but only insofar as "[w]e sense it from within. We exist in its flow" (172). Like Semen Frank and Berdiaev, among other *Out of the Depths* co-authors, Murav'ev retained faith that such a prodigal return, a rebirth from the ashes, might well occur: "[F]rom the passionate torments of recognized sin, the saving Aeon is born. Sophia [the intelligentsia] returns, repentant, to the fatherly bosom. In the depository of the Russian spirit, she acquires once again the rejected wisdom." "A knightly Rus'—this is the reborn, new, Russian intelligentsia. Through it, the people's corn field will begin to form ears after the spring storm" (173). Even Murav'ev could not divest himself of the conviction that a new, reformed, authentic intelligentsia would be instrumental in leading the Russian people to renewal, to Russia's renascence.

As is often noted, *Out of the Depths* not only did not provoke the agonized public discussion that *Vekhi* had, it reached almost no immediate audience whatsoever. With its initial publication halted in late summer 1918 with the initiation of the Red Terror and the Civil War, and with an attempt to circulate it in Moscow at the time of the Kronstadt rebellion in March 1921 immediately forestalled, very few people in Russia or in the diaspora were able to read this volume at the time.[28] But it is not quite correct to say that there was no dissemination of the key *ideas* in *Out of the Depths*. Berdiaev's essay "Dukh russkoi revoliutsii" ("Specters of the Russian Revolution") had been printed in the final issue of *Russian Thought*, and Bulgakov's and Struve's would appear in emigration.[29] More broadly speaking, the authors of *Out of the Depths* managed to air their views not only in the burgeoning émigré press but also during the brief *babe leto* of intellectual activity in Moscow and Petrograd at the end of the Civil War.[30] Such views were vocalized both in the public lectures and discussions that occurred during 1920–22 and the briefly extant journals and almanacs of the time. In particular, Berdiaev and Frank in Moscow and Izgoev in Petrograd associated with the philosophical and literary organizations that flourished briefly and shared and traded views with both like-minded thinkers and opponents. To give just one prominent example, Berdiaev and Frank were key participants in the extended discussion of Oswald Spengler's much-celebrated *Der Untergang des Abendlandes* (*The Decline of the West*, 1918–22). A resulting volume of essays, *Osval'd Shpengler i zakat Evropy* (*Oswald Spengler and The Decline of Europe*, 1922), recapitulated several of the principal ideas in *Out of the Depths*, in particular the possibility (born of hoping against hope) that despite or even because of Russia's national catastrophe it was potentially uniquely positioned for a Phoenix-like rise from the ashes.[31]

The debate over the so-called "Changing Signposts" movement (*smenovekhovstvo*) also involved several of the original *Vekhi* contributors, especially Izgoev, who adamantly denied any connection between *Vekhi* and *Smena vekh* (*Change of Signposts*, 1921) in a series of public disputes in Petrograd.[32] Shortly thereafter, Izgoev and several other publicists issued a volume entitled *O smene vekh* (*On the Change of Signposts*, 1922), which denounced the attempt by the contributors to *Change of Signposts* to come to terms with the Soviet regime. "Beneath some external resemblances," Izgoev wrote, "there is an enormous difference in principles between the old and new 'Vekhi.'" Although the *Vekhi* contributors had advised intellectuals to rethink their categorical opposition to the old regime, "they were far from deifying the state. Their God was commensurate neither with social institutions nor with human establishments." The *Change of Signposts* authors, on the other hand, Izgoev claimed, effected precisely such a deification of the state, and they subordinated the "moral and spiritual character of the intelligentsia" to it. In so doing, they altered what for Izgoev remained the fundamental task of the intelligentsia. "The intelligentsia did not, does not, and will not have physical, material power.... The power of the intelligentsia is only moral, and spiritual. When a country does not sense the moral power of the intelligentsia, the harmony of life is drastically disturbed." Thus Izgoev reaffirmed the critical, even exclusive importance of the intelligentsia, and ascribed the tragedy of the current moment precisely to the fact that the intelligentsia had lost its moral authority.[33]

Following the *Change of Signposts* debates, Izgoev reiterated in an article called "O zadachakh intelligentsii" ("On the Tasks of the Intelligentsia," 1922) in the almanac *Parfenon* (*Parthenon*) that the intelligentsia retained a vital, central role in transforming Russia, and that its tasks were far from exhausted. He explicitly refuted those who, following Tolstoi, wondered "Who needed it?" [*A dlia kogo ona byla nuzhna?*] and believed that the intelligentsia's only real purpose was to demonstrate to Europe that Russia did indeed have a life of the mind.[34] Izgoev dismissed these doubters, noting that even if one did not value in the slightest the fruits of Russian culture, Pushkin, Dostoevskii, and Turgenev (and Tolstoi himself!), even if one did not recognize that millions of ordinary Russians were now familiar with them due to the expansion in education and literacy, it was impossible to ignore the fact that during the storm of the Revolution, it was precisely the slogans of the intelligentsia (in its narrower sense) that were taken up by the people.[35] The unmistakable importance of the intelligentsia had been confirmed, most unfortunately in Russia's case, by the course of events.

This was proof to Izgoev of the degree of influence that the intelligentsia could have (for good or ill), and it reinforced his own conviction that its energies needed to be not diffused but redirected. For Izgoev, the heart of the intelligentsia mission lay, simply enough, in its role as a "teaching element in the broadest sense of the word," just as he had articulated in his initial foray into intelligentsia studies, "The Intelligentsia as a Social Group," back in 1904.[36] Thus he once again did away with the narrower understanding, in his view much more subjective, proffered most famously by Mikhailovskii, which defined the intelligentsia on political grounds. More specifically, as R. V. Ivanov-Razumnik put it, "the intelligentsia ends on the right at the boundaries of the Kadet party."[37] Izgoev discarded this definition (which, arguably, was the definition assumed in the original *Vekhi* critique of the intelligentsia) in favor of his notion of a broad pedagogical mission, bringing to the people learning and knowledge in all of their forms. At the same time, therefore, in attempting to retain this quite broad idea of *uchitel'stvo*, Izgoev's reframed characterization was very much at odds with the simultaneous Bolshevik attempt to reframe "intelligentsia" sociologically as "*umstvennyi trud*," "mental laborers" divorced from any sense of mission (either political or pedagogical) whatsoever.

The authors of *Vekhi*, and even of the post-apocalyptic *Out of the Depths* and other volumes that followed, thoroughly reproached the Russian intelligentsia, but they did so almost entirely within the existing framework of debate concerning its tasks and its importance. Theirs represented not a rejection of the leading moral role of the intelligentsia in Russian society, but rather a methodical indictment of how poorly the intelligentsia had performed in that role. The prescription, especially in Izgoev's view, was not to banish *intelligenty* from a leading part in the construction of national life—this was neither possible nor desirable. Rather, it was to redirect them away from their former illusions and toward a more spiritual, holistic approach to larger questions, less obsessed with crude political solutions than with less tangible educative processes. Ironically, in the debate over *On the Change of Signposts*, it was now Bolshevik critics who accused Izgoev and the other *Vekhi* contributors of having attached too great an importance to the intelligentsia, even deifying it,[38] and it was the Bolsheviks who were simultaneously attempting to reduce the intelligentsia's role from that of moral arbiter to that of handmaiden of the state.

While Izgoev fiercely refuted the Bolshevik charge that he, for one, was looking to the intelligentsia for salvation—arguing that its role in his view was a modest, if important one, instructional rather than heroic[39]—we can see, in the poetic language of a number of the *Out of the Depths* essays, precisely the same heroicization that Sergei Bulgakov had criticized in *Vekhi* as characteristic of the delusions of the radical revolutionary intelligentsia.[40]

As Struve asserted in his passionate call for national revival, "Istoricheskii smysl russkoi revoliutsii i natsional'nye zadachi" ("The Historical Meaning of the Russian Revolution and National Tasks"),

> If there is a Russian "intelligentsia," as an aggregate of educated people, able to create ideals for itself and to act upon them, and if there is within this "intelligentsia" any kind of obligation before the people, then that obligation consists in bringing to the broad masses, with passion and persistence, the national idea, as a healing and organizing force, without which neither the regeneration of the people, nor the recreation of the state, is possible. This is the whole program of the spiritual, cultural, and political rebirth of Russia, which depends on the ideological education and reeducation of educated people and the masses.[41]

Thus this great collective sinner, the intelligentsia, which had brought Russia to apocalyptic ruin, might now, through a miraculous transformation, throwing off its atheist bravado for Christ-like humility, be reborn and help Russia rise up again from out of the depths.

## Notes

1. William F. Woehrlin makes a not dissimilar point in "Introduction: Voices from Out of the Depths," in *Out of the Depths (De Profundis): A Collection of Articles on the Russian Revolution*, trans. and ed. William F. Woehrlin (Irvine, CA: Charles Schlacks, 1986), xvii–xxxiii.

2. A. S. Izgoev, "Intelligentsiia i 'Vekhi' (Vmesto predisloviia)," in *Russkoe obshchestvo i revoliutsiia* (Moscow, 1910), 9–10. Reprinted in *Vekhi: pro et contra. Antologiia*, ed. V. V. Sapov (St. Petersburg: Russkii Khristianskii gumanitarnyi institut, 1998), 505–11.

3. Ibid., 3–11.

4. A.S. Izgoev, "Frantsuzskaia intelligentsiia," *Zhizn'*, no. 2 (1899). In this article, Izgoev, then a legal Marxist polemicizing against the populist N. Kudrin, sharply contested the notion that *intelligenty* were an "above-class" (*vneklassovaia*) phenomenon. (That this was his first published journal article is mentioned in "Intelligentsiia i 'Vekhi,'" 3.)

5. "Intelligentsiia kak sotsial'naia gruppa," *Obrazovanie*, no. 1 (January 1904): pt. 2: 72–94.

6   Ibid., 74.

7   Ibid., 78, quoting Berdiaev's "Kritika istoricheskogo materializma," *Mir bozhii*, no. 10 (October 1903): 1–30.

8   Ibid., 78–79. Izgoev held that while *intelligenty* might not be as directly focused on material needs, to pretend that they were entirely spiritual entities removed from ordinary concerns only obscured their true nature.

9   Echoing Weber's notion that sociological categories always amounted to ideal types, Izgoev here argues that social classes and groups were always a mental construct, an "idealized unity" that could not be said to match in any exact sense with the complexities of empirical reality. Ibid., 80–81.

10  Ibid., 82.

11  Ibid., 86. Italics in original.

12  Ibid., 87–88. Conversely, he added, "The necessity of spiritual freedom is the primary psychic quality of those subjects belonging to the intelligentsia social group." Ibid., 88.

13  Ibid., 93–94.

14  Machajski (1866–1926) was a Polish-born radical, known in Russian as Makhaev, who roundly critiqued the intelligentsia and sharply broke with contemporary Marxists over the idea that revolutionary intellectuals could or should lead a revolution for the working class.

15  Marshall S. Shatz, *Jan Wacław Machajski: A Radical Critic of the Russian Intelligentsia and Socialism* (Pittsburgh: University of Pittsburgh Press, 1989), 51, quoting from Evgenii Lozinskii, *Chto zhe takoe, nakonets, intelligentsiia. (Kritiko-sotsiologicheskii opyt)* (St. Petersburg: Novyi golos, 1907). Izgoev in turn, in reviewing Lozinskii's booklet for *Russian Thought,* declared it a total muddle, beneath contempt, an "abomination [*merzost*']." ("Publitsistika," *Russkaia mysl'*, no. 4 (April 1907), "Bibliograficheskii otdel": 78.)

16  Izgoev bitterly complained of the "blindness" and "dishonesty" (*nedobrosovestnost'*) of radical publicists who equated the essays in *Vekhi* with the "defamatory attacks on the intelligentsia" by "the Markeviches, the Diakovs, the Tsitoviches," and other reactionaries. ("Intelligentsiia i 'Vekhi,'" 8–9). On contemporary conservative criticisms of the intelligentsia, see Christopher Read, *Religion, Revolution and the Russian Intelligentsia, 1900–1912: The* Vekhi *Debate and its Intellectual Background* (London and Basingstoke: Macmillan, 1979), 98–106.

17  Nikolai P. Poltoratzky, "Lev Tolstoy and 'Vekhi,'" *Slavonic and East European Review* 42 (June 1964): 341. See also Gary Hamburg's essay in the current volume. As we will see, Izgoev would later explicitly counterpose Tolstoi's rejection of the intelligentsia with his own continued insistence that, despite all of its failures, it continued to have (potentially) a critical role to play in Russia's revival.

18  Woehrlin similarly notes that "when the authors of *Out of the Depths* tried to find some hope that could raise them out of despair, they looked once again to the very group that they had maligned. The intelligentsia, they argued, must experience a rebirth in

a new spirit, to become worthy of its traditional mission of leading the people." *Out of the Depths*, "Introduction," xxvii.

19  Gary Saul Morson, "Prosaic Bakhtin: *Landmarks*, Anti-Intelligentsialism, and the Russian Counter-Tradition," *Common Knowledge* 2, no. 1 (Spring 1993): 35–74. While I find Morson's characterization of the *Vekhi* contributors' views toward the intelligentsia useful, his insistence on the continuance of the traditional, narrow definition of the intelligentsia even at the time of *Vekhi* is problematic—this traditional understanding, even as it was utilized by the *Vekhi* authors, was already in the midst of fragmentation, and was already being challenged by other meanings.

20  Nikolai Berdiaev, "Filosofskaia istina i intelligentskaia pravda," *Vekhi. Iz glubiny*, ed. A. A. Iakovlev (Moscow: Pravda, 1991), 11. Berdiaev's play on words is, alas, lost in the translation by Marshall S. Shatz and Judith E. Zimmerman in *Vekhi/Landmarks: A Collection of Articles about the Russian Intelligentsia* (Armonk, NY: M. E. Sharpe, 1994), 1.

21  Shatz and Zimmerman, *Vekhi/Landmarks*, 15, 16.

22  Ibid., 2-3.

23  A. S. Izgoev, "Obshchestvennoe dvizhenie v Rossii. (Zametki publitsista)," *Russkaia mysl'*, no. 1 (January 1907): 161–66, 166.

24  A. S. Izgoev, "Ob intelligentnoi molodezhi. (Zametki ob eia byt' i nastroeniiakh)" ("On Educated Youth [Notes on its Life and Sentiments]"), Shatz and Zimmerman, *Vekhi/Landmarks*, 71-90. Izgoev's original intention was to write again more generally on the perversion of the intelligentsia, "the distortion of its knowledge as a consequence of the struggle with absolutism, and the reduction of knowledge to the level not of a weapon for life, but of a weapon for the attainment of a single political goal," as he wrote Gershenzon. (Izgoev to Gershenzon, undated [late 1908?] in V. Proskurina and V. Alloi, "K istorii sozdaniia 'Vekh,'" *Minuvshee: istoricheskii al'manakh* 11 [1991]: 266.) But Gershenzon insisted that Izgoev write on intelligentsia daily life (*byt*), despite the latter's protestations that he was entirely unqualified to do so, and Izgoev eventually chose to focus on the youth. The result was an essay with which neither Izgoev nor his collaborators were particularly satisfied. (See Izgoev's subsequent letters to Gershenzon in ibid., 266–78, as well as the quite critical remarks made by Gershenzon, quoted in ibid., 289.)

25  Shatz and Zimmerman, *Vekhi/Landmarks*, 86.

26  Woehrlin, *Out of the Depths*, 125. Further page references to essays in this volume are given in parentheses in the text.

27  Here Novgorodtsev quotes Edmund Burke at length and with a great deal of approval, even referring to him as a *liberal*—in the sense that he does not deny that progressive change is a positive constant in history, as long as it proceeds organically and without utterly destroying the foundations of what has been. Novgorodtsev proposes a liberal, inclusive, non-coercive vision of the nation-state, in which patriotism lies precisely in the understanding even of non-believers that the state represents the subordination of egoism to the greater whole, and thus constitutes the cause of God.

28   Woehrlin, *Out of the Depths*, "Introduction," xxiii.

29   An English translation of Bulgakov's essay even appeared in serial form in *The Slavonic Review* immediately before and after its author's expulsion. "On the Feast of the Gods: Contemporary Dialogues," *The Slavonic Review* 1, no. 1 (June 1922): 172–83; 1, no. 2 (Dec 1922): 391–400; 1, no. 3 (Mar 1923): 604–22.

30   See chapters 4 and 5 of my *On the Ideological Front: The Russian Intelligentsia and the Making of the Soviet Public Sphere* (New Haven, CT: Yale University Press, 2007), 89–150.

31   See my unpublished conference paper, "Russia's Spenglerites and the Revolution: Russia as Corpse or Phoenix?," American Association for the Advancement of Slavic Studies National Convention, Washington, DC, Nov. 2006. On Lenin's great irritation with the so-called "renaissance of bourgeois ideology," see inter alia Roger Pethybridge, "Concern for Bolshevik Ideological Predominance at the Start of NEP," *Russian Review* 44, no. 4 (1982): 445–53.

32   Finkel, *On the Ideological Front*, 133–37.

33   A. S. Izgoev, "'Vekhi' i 'Smena vekh,'" in *O smene vekh* (Petrograd: Izdatel'stvo "Logos" pri dome literatorov, 1922), 18, 21, 22–24. Izgoev's essay was subsequently republished by Struve in *Russkaia mysl'*, no. 3 (1922). See also Hilde Hardeman, *Coming to Terms with the Soviet Regime: The "Changing Signposts" Movement among Russian Émigrés in the Early 1920s* (DeKalb, IL: Northern Illinois University Press, 1994), 93, 106.

34   A. S. Izgoev, "O zadachakh intelligentsii," *Parfenon* 1 (1922): 32.

35   Ibid., 32–33.

36   Ibid., 34, quoting "Intelligentsiia kak sotsial'naia gruppa."

37   Izgoev, "O zadachakh intelligentsii," 34.

38   The two most prominent Bolshevik reviews of the debates over *Change of Signposts*, criticizing Izgoev in particular, were A. Voronskii, "Literaturnye otkliki," *Krasnaia nov'*, no. 2 (6) (March-April 1922): 262–63, and E. Preobrazhenskii, "Oblomki staroi Rossii," *Pod znamenem marksizma*, nos. 1–2 (January-February 1922): 33–35.

39   Izgoev, "O zadachakh intelligentsii," 37.

40   Sergei Bulgakov, "Geroizm i podvizhnichestvo. (Iz razmyshlenii o religioznoi prirode russkoi intelligentsii)," ("Heroism and Asceticism. [Reflections on the Religious Nature of the Russian Intelligentsia]," in Shatz and Zimmerman, *Vekhi/Landmarks*, 17–50.

41   Peter Berngardovich Struve, "The Historical Meaning of the Russian Revolution and National Tasks," in *Out of the Depths*, 217. Jane Burbank analyzes Struve's *Out of the Depths* essay in *Intelligentsia and Revolution: Russian Views of Bolshevism, 1917–1922* (New York: Oxford University Press, 1986), 132–37.

# 3

## THE INTELLIGENTSIA FIGHTS BACK:
The Left-wing Response to *Vekhi* and its Significance

*Christopher Read*

*Vekhi* has enjoyed at least three lives. Its original one, of course, came in 1909 and 1910, when it was the intellectual sensation of the age. Some of its admirers revived part of its spirit in *Iz glubiny* (*Out of the Depths*), written but not circulated in 1918.[1] The second life came in the 1960s. This was no accident; both collections were re-published in Paris as student rebellions and revolutionary movements spread around the world. *Vekhi* in this revival became something of a symbol of opposition to the *soixante-huitards* and was a marginal tool in the cultural Cold War. Revolution was in the air, in a variety of forms, from Berkeley to West Berlin and from Prague to Saigon. In the forefront were students, and polemics around their activities were increasingly intense as campus after campus exploded. Among those not sharing the ethos of exuberance and radicalization were Richard Pipes and Leonard Schapiro. Pipes was working on his excellent biography of Petr Struve and editing his collected works. Schapiro had already written one of the few articles of the time devoted to *Vekhi*, calling it "*Vekhi* and the Mystique of Revolution." In a limited way, *Vekhi* had become an "anti-sixties" manifesto. As the headiness of the sixties subsided, so too did the profile of *Vekhi*. For the best part of two more decades it sank deeper out of sight, into a half-life in which only a handful of people were working on or around it.[2] However, it was still known about, not only in the west but also among Soviet historians and specialists. Ironically, memory of it in its homeland had been preserved through Lenin having devoted an article to refuting it. In fact, *Vekhism* (*vekhovstvo*) was a more favored theme in Soviet journals of the seventies and early eighties than in western ones. It had become an intellectual peg on which Soviet ideologists could conveniently hang a whole array of their liberal critics. Interestingly, but not entirely accurately, by 1980 I. I. Mints was linking interest in *Vekhi* with the rise of the new right in Britain and the United States. In a review of Pipes's work on Struve, he claimed that Struve, in Pipes's view, was a forerunner of Ronald Reagan. There was some truth in that: Pipes, of course, was Reagan's National Security Advisor on the Soviet Union from 1981 to 1982. However, there is something here worth bringing to the fore: *Vekhi* had become a symbol, almost a brand name, a logo, for a certain kind of opposition to a loosely-defined leftism.

*Vekhi*'s third, present, life was generated by its having been "rediscovered" in the land of its birth, a rediscovery foreshadowed by that of Aleksander Solzhenitsyn and a handful of 1970s and '80s dissidents.[3] It gained a reputation for having, in some way, predicted the collapse of the revolutionary system, which eventually came about in 1991, a system that was deemed by many to embody the mechanistic, materialist, amoral, irreligious, unspiritual, anti-individualistic, and utilitarian principles that the *Vekhi* authors descried in the radical intelligentsia.

The present volume contains studies of numerous aspects of all these "lives." However, there is at least one intriguing difference between them: in its original life, *Vekhi* was largely reviled by the majority of its readers; in its second life it had admirers and critics; and in its third, post-Soviet, life it has largely been acclaimed, often uncritically. True, a volume of comments was entitled *"Vekhi": pro et contra ("Vekhi": For and Against)*,[4] but that was something of an exception. The aim of the present study is to re-examine some of the original criticisms of *Vekhi*, which are often overlooked amid the contemporary adulation. The questions pursued in this essay are: how did the defenders of the intelligentsia tradition react to *Vekhi*, and what does their response tell us? To answer them, the focus will be on the responses of leading liberals and populists, with a brief glance at social democrats. Particular attention will be paid to the Constitutional Democrats' (Kadet) *sbornik* entitled *Intelligentsiia v Rossii* (*The Intelligentsia in Russia*, 1910), the Socialist Revolutionaries' (SR) *"Vekhi" kak znamenie vremeni* (*"Vekhi" as a Sign of the Times*, 1910), and

Lenin's response, which, though short, did preserve memory of *Vekhi* in the way mentioned above. In the conclusion, a number of observations about these criticisms will be made.

## 1909: Reaction and Context

The publication of *Vekhi* in February 1909 set off a chain reaction. The contributors, mocked later by Merezhkovskii for their "false" modesty,[5] claimed to be saying nothing new.[6] However, the debate it set off was a defining event in early-twentieth-century intellectual history in Russia. Responses came from all parts of the intellectual spectrum. It was something like a spark falling in a box of fireworks: the ensuing explosion was colorful but chaotic. However, of all the comments one might make about the controversy around *Vekhi*, one of the few that is indisputable is that, as already mentioned, the overwhelming majority of reactions were hostile. This simple fact has not always been given its due. How do we account for the fierce reaction, and what did *Vekhi*'s opponents have to say?

The unexpected scale of its initial impact depended, not entirely but to a significant degree, on it appearing at a moment of gloom and despondency among the intelligentsia. Its impact was multiplied by its apparent renegade attack on people already reeling from the defeat of 1905–07. Today it is easy to underestimate the widespread contempt felt by ordinary, decent people within Russia and beyond for the anachronistic, apparently unreformable, and, in the hands of Nicholas II, antisemitic, backward-looking, and cruel autocracy. It was not necessary to be a radical to dislike tsarism intensely. Its violent repression of unarmed protest in January 1905 and on many other occasions through 1905–07 not only sowed the seeds of counter-violence from below but also made autocracy an object of contempt across western Europe. Russia was a pariah state. True, the impact of this international contempt was mitigated by the geopolitics of the period, which led to the somewhat hypocritical but "necessary" spectacle of Europe's two most democratic great powers, Britain and France, falling over themselves to ally with Russia, as a counterweight to their common enemy, a resurgent imperial Germany. Nonetheless, the depth of intellectual hostility remained great. Within Russia itself, though the worst of the armed repression had faded by 1909, there was still sufficient state violence to enable Tolstoi, in a famous essay on the death penalty, to complain about the continuation of "executions, executions, executions."[7] The ferocity of people's attitudes is shown by non-revolutionaries as well, like Leonid Andreev, who claimed that even moderates, including those who had a weak religious faith, hated government ministers so much that they would secretly pray for their deaths. Even so, when one of them—Lev Kasso, the Education Minister—did die of cancer, there was little satisfaction in it because, Andreev complained, his death had prevented him from being brought to justice.[8] It was not only the left that was horrified by the political situation. For quite different reasons, many on the right were sceptical of tsarism's ability to deliver stability. Its inefficiencies threatened to provoke revolution, which in turn would destroy the privileges of the landed and office-holding elite. Anachronistic elements, like antisemitism, were seen as particularly dangerous. In the most infamous antisemitic episode of the period, the 1911–13 investigation and trial of Mendel Beilis on a trumped-up charge of ritual murder of a Christian child in Kiev, Beilis's defense was undertaken by a center-right Duma deputy, Vasilii Maklakov. Even the elites were tired of being excluded from power and increasingly feared for their positions as tsarism stumbled blindly from crisis to crisis, culminating in the Lena goldfields shootings in 1912.[9] Perhaps one of the main reasons for the underestimation, decades later, of the atmosphere of the period is that, compared to an era like the 1930s, the degree of repression is *relatively* small. However, to cite French level-crossings, "[u]n train peut-en cacher un autre" (one train can hide another). More appropriately, in this case, *un mal peut-en cacher un autre*— one evil can hide another. Taking into account the fact that tsarism also has to bear a not-inconsiderable part of the blame for creating a culture in which extremism could not only survive but could break out into a mass movement, it is no defense of tsarism to say that Stalinism was worse. Obviously, no one knew in 1909 what lay in store for Russia. Setting aside the historian's advantage of hindsight, it is incontrovertible that there was a widespread opposition to and even visceral hatred of tsarism among elites, intellectuals, workers, and peasants. Only by recognizing this is it possible to comprehend why *Vekhi* was met with a massive volley of abuse. While historical parallels can be misleading, *Vekhi*'s, or at least Struve's, call for reconciliation with the autocracy had an impact comparable to, say, a former South African radical calling for co-operation with the apartheid regime a year or two after the Sharpeville massacre, or for a supporter of Allende calling for reconciliation with Pinochet shortly after the latter came to power over a football stadium of executed victims.

Does *Vekhi* deserve this reputation? It certainly did not see itself as crudely "right-wing" or conservative, and some of its contributors, notably Nikolai Berdiaev and Sergei Bulgakov, saw it as in its own way genuinely revolutionary, compared to what they saw as the false revolutionary commitment of those it criticized. That, too, opens up another question: which *Vekhi*? While Struve has, by and large, been the author most quoted by critics, his article was in no way "typical" of *Vekhi* as a whole. In truth, no article was. Berdiaev and Bulgakov were spiritual warriors; Mikhail Gershenzon, Bogdan Kistiakovskii, and Semen Frank were more stereotypical "liberal" intellectuals; and Struve, and to some extent Aleksandr Izgoev, were conservatives, at least in the making.

The two intellectual/political schools of the period which have attracted the most attention have been the liberals (Kadets) and the social-democratic Marxists (SDs). At one level this is completely absurd, because they were among the least influential and widespread schools at the time. Kadet liberalism only began to take on shape in 1905, and comprised only a small number of members, supporters, and natural voters (i.e., core supporters, not those who boosted its votes by using it as the only vehicle for supporters of banned or restricted parties). The Social Democrats, too, were highly aware of their vulnerable minority status at the time, which was an important consideration that caused many on both of its wings, in 1905 and after, to attempt reconciliation rather than deepen and widen the split between them, thereby making it permanent. To split an already tiny minority group was rightly considered to be insane, even at times by one of its chief proponents, Lenin. On the other hand, important groups like the Octobrists and the populist-based Socialist Revolutionaries (who were by far the most influential and widespread group of the era), have not been studied in anything like the same detail, especially in terms of their ideas and principles in the period from 1905 to 1917. The Octobrists, by almost all criteria, stand outside the intelligentsia and observed the controversy more

# The Intelligentsia Fights Back: Left-wing Response to *Vekhi* and its Significance

or less from without, but I will look more closely at the rather neglected SR response to *Vekhi*. First, however, an examination of some key responses from Kadet liberals.

## THE LIBERALS AND *VEKHI*

The official Kadet response to *Vekhi* came in the form of a *sbornik* entitled *The Intelligentsia in Russia*.[10] In it, many leading party members were wheeled out to refute the volume. The longest, and possibly most tedious, contribution came from the party leader Pavel Miliukov. In a rather ponderous, professorial tone, Miliukov defined the core of *Vekhi*'s criticism to be a charge of "apostasy" (*otshchepenstvo*) against the intelligentsia. The apostasy had three components—the intelligentsia's supposed irreligiousness; its hostility to the concept of the state; and its lack of national feeling, its cosmopolitanism (30). For Miliukov, it was in the nature of the intelligentsia to be cut off from the masses. The intelligentsia *should*, he said, be in the position of Socrates vis-à-vis the people (33). It *should* be proud to be separate from the people. As for the chief cause of its separation, religion, Miliukov said very little, not least, it seems, because he could scarcely believe the *Vekhi* authors were serious in bringing it back into intellectual debate.

Regarding the accusation by Struve in particular that the intelligentsia was characterized by an attitude of hostility to the state (*antigosudarstvennost'*), Miliukov was a little more comfortable. *Vekhi* was wrong, in his view, for several reasons. First, only extremists, maximalists—that is, largely anarchists—actually opposed the state. Though he does not mention it, he might have supported his argument by pointing out that all of the democratic parties—liberal, SR, and SD—made the calling of a constituent assembly their first programmatic demand. Second, he defended the need for society, and related institutions such as law, as a base for the defense of individual freedom. In an area which blends a critique of *Vekhi*'s stances on religion and on the state, Miliukov linked *Vekhi*'s granting primacy to inner life over outer restraints to counter-revolutionary romanticism of the early nineteenth century in western Europe, neglecting to note that this very romanticism also had links to support for the French revolution and indeed to early liberalism. In this sense, this particular accusation exploded, as it were, in Miliukov's own hands. He was, however, in a safer place when he also linked this trait to Slavophilism, though he greatly overstated the extent to which *Vekhi* shared the religious obscurantism that he, as an anticlerical, atheist, enlightened, westernizing intellectual, discerned at the heart of Slavophile thinking.

Finally, and sometimes surprisingly to those who are not familiar with the immediate context of the post-1905 years, Miliukov stoutly defended the Russian intelligentsia tradition and its combative and revolutionary acts and ambitions. The intelligentsia, which he defined not as the educated class but as a concentric circle of creative thinkers and activists within the educated class (94), was the pride of Russia. He recalled its achievements, notably its opposition to serfdom and hostility to autocracy, and failures. He did not himself closely define the tradition, but one of the other contributors, Ivan Petrunkevich, did, naming the familiar quartet of Belinskii, Herzen, Chernyshevskii, and Mikhailovskii as its spiritual sources (39). The claim, which put liberalism firmly within the Russian revolutionary tradition, remains a stark reminder that using identical terminology for Russian and western phenomena, in this case the concept of liberalism, can cause significant differences to be concealed. By and large, western liberals put a greater distance between themselves and revolution, at least in their own countries.

Where *The Intelligentsia in Russia* was frequently rather petty and pedantic, two other liberal responses were rather more engaging. Writing separately in the liberal journal *Russkaia mysl'* (*Russian Thought*), Aleksandr Kizevetter and Semen Lur'e gave a more imaginative set of reasons for liberal opposition to *Vekhi*'s project.[11] Both writers took the position that, in many ways, *Vekhi* had highlighted the problems of the intelligentsia correctly but had identified completely wrong solutions. In Kizevetter's opinion, as stated in his article focused on Bulgakov, Gershenzon, and Kistiakovskii, it was not necessary to withdraw into internal life; rather, one should do exactly the opposite. What was needed was "intensified and conscious participation in practical activity in society" (133). Gershenzon, he argued, was mistaken in seeing all *intelligenty* as leading superficial and neurotic lives. He was also very hostile to the religious aspect, stating that in *Vekhi*, "in place of the rattle of the gendarme's sabre I hear the clink of the censer" (129). Lur'e based his defense of the intelligentsia on the Latin proverb "*primum vivere, deinde philosophare*" (137). It was all very well for *Vekhi* to offer religious and philosophical nostrums, but there was practical work to be done first. Lur'e energetically defended the intelligentsia tradition for its focus on alleviating the suffering of the "humiliated and the injured," quoting the title of Dostoevskii's novel *Unizhennye i oskorblennye* (*The Humiliated and the Injured*). The intelligentsia should be praised, not blamed, for putting the interests of the people ahead of its own and for having chivalric qualities (143). The intelligentsia, Lur'e agreed, did have the people's welfare as its absolute value, but it was right to do so—certainly it is superior to *Vekhi*'s (or at least Frank's) placing of culture as its absolute value: one has to live first, only then can one engage in philosophy (146). Lur'e admitted that some groups of the intelligentsia were beyond defense—"to combat practical nihilism one does not need publicists but psychiatrists" (141)—but that was no reason to attack its healthier components. Like Kizevetter, Lur'e found the religious revivalism of *Vekhi* to be incomprehensible among educated, civilized people.

All in all, the liberals presented a robust defense of their social action, perhaps surprisingly robust when it's compared to that of their counterparts in the west, indicating, as we have already noted, how a term like "liberal" can be transformed in meaning when implanted in a new culture. True, they did stress the importance of institutions, a constitution, and law as necessary guarantors of individual freedom. However, they failed to exploit what could be seen as one of the greatest inconsistencies, even contradictions, within *Vekhi*. Berdiaev's (and Gershenzon's) insistence on the primacy of inner life over external forms could be seen as an excellent illustration of the truth of Kistiakovskii's accusation regarding a lack of awareness of law's importance among Russian intellectuals and also, perhaps, that of Struve's accusation of alienation from state and nation.

In his classic account of Russian liberalism, George Fischer pointed out that in a backward society (in the terminology of the time) liberals are caught between the tactics of collaborating with the oppressive authorities in the hope of gaining concessions and out-and-out revolutionary opposition.[12] In this situation, the Kadets were theoretically defending the latter course of action but were, in practice, getting closer and closer to adopting the former. In many ways, this moment of possible transition was central to the *Vekhi* debate, to the liberals themselves but also to their critics even further to the left. SR writers such as Viktor Chernov agreed: liberalism was doomed to be caught at the crossroads because of an "enormous disparity between its program and its tactics." The Kadets retained radical aims—for a constituent assembly and land reform—alongside a desire to work within the system as a kind of loyal opposition to His Majesty.[13] The remnants of the intelligentsia tradition interfered with this new posture, and Struve opened up a way of escape to enable them to reconcile with forces further to the right (20). Thus the intelligentsia was trapped. Any move to the right would discredit it with the left, but would risk being insufficient to earn the confidence of the right. Any step to the left would have the same impact in reverse, discrediting it with the right but not gaining credibility with the left (21). Fate had put the liberals in this position, which corresponded to Russian historical conditions. Russia lacked a strong, independent "liberal bourgeoisie prepared to fight courageously and decisively for political freedom" (20-21). The middle class, such as it was, was attempting to adapt the Kadet party to its own immediate interests and to throw out any superfluous remaining traces of "love of the people" and desires of the "third element" (22).

## Social Democratic Responses

Among Social Democrats, the embourgeoisement of the intelligentsia was the standard response, running through literary cultural criticism by Vladimir Friche, Vladimir Bazarov (Rudnev), and Nikolai Valentinov (Vol'skii) and more sociological analyses by Leon Trotskii and Aleksandr Bogdanov. These last were partially influenced by the theory of Jan Wacław Machajski, stating that socialism was the class ideology of the intelligentsia as a cover for its claim to be a ruling elite.[14] However, the Social Democratic position on *Vekhi* was pithily summed up by Lenin: *Vekhi* was "an encyclopaedia of liberal renegacy."[15] There was not much more to the SD position beyond, first, the embourgeoisement theory, which was partly true in the broad sense; second, the assumption that this led to compromise with the autocracy; and third, the more questionable assumption that *Vekhi* was simply supportive of the Kadets. The Kadet polemic against this was surely evidence of greater complexity, but Lenin did not acknowledge this. It could be instantly dismissed: "*Vekhi* is good because it discloses the whole spirit of the *real* policy of the Russian liberals and of the Russian Kadets included among them. That is why the Kadet polemic with *Vekhi* and the Kadet renunciation of *Vekhi* are nothing but hypocrisy, sheer idle talk, for, in reality the Kadets collectively, as a party, as a social force, have pursued and are pursuing the policy of *Vekhi* and *no other*."[16]

## THE SOCIALIST REVOLUTIONARIES RESPOND

One of the interesting features of the debate is how little influence the Social Democrats in general and Lenin in particular had on it. The great denunciations of *Vekhi* by liberals, populists, and others, not to mention *Vekhi* itself, paid little or no attention to the specifically SD school of thought. It was in fact the SRs who produced the most interesting, thoroughgoing, competent, and comprehensive reply to *Vekhi*, "*Vekhi*" as a Sign of the Times.[17] The collection consists of eight contributions but, although his name does not appear at all, three of them are by Chernov under the pseudonyms Iu. Gardenin, B. Iur'ev, and Ia. Vechev. With some justification, the contributors believed that they themselves, the SRs, were the chief target of *Vekhi*. "Yes! We stand at the centre of their attention and we should be proud" (10). "We are the sun in the planetary system of their opponents." (11)

In a hard-hitting overview from which the above quotations were taken, Chernov/Gardenin led the attack on *Vekhi* on behalf of the SRs. In a phrase which became the title of the collection, he identified *Vekhi* as "a sign of the times [*znamenie vremeni*]," or even better, he went on, as "a sign of stagnating times [*znamenie bezvremen'ia*]." Its success on the book market and as an intellectual phenomenon was a "*succès de scandale*" (1), a phrase used much later by Frank in his memoirs.[18] Nonetheless, he went on, it was "worth more serious attention than it had hitherto been given." This was, in Gardenin's view, nothing less than "the most reactionary book of the last decade. In this respect *Vekhi* defeated Pobedonostsev's

*Moskovskii sbornik* (*Memoirs of a Russian Statesman*).... The naive and direct 'old-style' reaction pales into insignificance compared to the subtle [*utonchennyi*] and out-and-out [*makhrovyi*] reaction in the modern style" (1). These were very large claims. Gardenin himself used thirty-seven large format pages to back them up, and the collection as a whole ran to 352 pages, nearly three times the length of *Vekhi* itself. What was it that the SRs found so despicable in *Vekhi*? For Gardenin, the first and fundamental point was that, as former members of the extreme left, the *Vekhi* contributors were, in the post-1905 atmosphere, the leading spokespeople of the turncoats and waverers. Quoting Jean Jaures' lofty denunciation of Georges Clemenceau, Aristide Briand, René Viviani, and others drifting to the right in France, he describes these renegades as demanding a "return ticket" from revolutionary socialism. In Russia, Gardenin said, the *Vekhi* authors were "the ideologues, theoreticians and philosophers of the 'return ticket'" (2). However, the real danger arose from the fact that they were not straightforward reactionaries. Quoting the witticism of the time that Struve was "the John the Baptist of all our rebirths," Gardenin pointed out that Struve was not antisemitic, like the traditional reactionaries, but was "a-Semitic": reactionaries wanted to restore the iron gauntlet, Struve wanted to strengthen the state system; reactionaries praised the idea of personal success, Struve supported the suitability (*godnost'*) of individuals; reactionaries roundly cursed the intelligentsia, Struve called on it to engage in self-denunciation and repentance (3). Chernov made much of the fact that the *Vekhi* authors themselves were, at heart, *intelligenty*, and had come through a typical intelligentsia formation, though they claimed to be outside it. Berdiaev, for instance, could be said to have once shared the primitive attitude to philosophy he denounced in others. They were, Chernov said, "inhabitants of Sodom but not Sodomites; *intelligenty* but alien to the intelligentsia; white, snow-white crows in a generally black flock" (10). The current period, Chernov continued, was one of revolutionary defeat and counter-revolutionary triumph. In an analysis many might see as having resonance today, Chernov pointed out that when the historical tide was ebbing, people ceased struggling for revolution and struggled off to wherever they could go. One turned to personal life, another into pure scholarship, a third into a caring profession, a fourth into eroticism;[19] a fifth, perhaps, may have entered into the auditorium of Struve and Gershenzon. But continued executions and exile meant that many would turn to renewed revolutionary activity (30). The *Vekhi* authors continually asked who was to blame for the failure of 1905, and constantly replied "the intelligentsia." Chernov refused absolutely to accept this. In any case, he argued, the so-called Octobrists, the liberals and their allies, were not people of 17 October but actually of 3 June.[20] *Vekhi* was a symbol of the general tragedy, or tragic comedy, of liberalism, of its illness, which he diagnosed as "complete impotence; senile degeneration of its substance, and its own distinctive kind of political arteriosclerosis" (35). *Vekhi* had no answer to the real needs of the time. It was not the intelligentsia which was doomed, it was the *Vekhi* authors. "They are doomed. They are cut off from the sharply greening stems of the liberation movement and there is no way back for them" (37). The other contributions to the collection were no less uncompromising. Under the name Iur'ev, Chernov defended "scientific philosophy" against "philosophising mysticism," claiming that *Vekhi* did not even remain true to Solov'ev. Instead, it came close to the old world of official religion. For instance, Solov'ev celebrated the Russian people as "fools in Christ," while Berdiaev and Frank simply denounced them as "Ivan-*durak*" (98–99). Their philosophizing was simply a cloak under which they smuggled socio-political contraband (101)—implicitly identified by Chernov as a restoration of the values of official Russia, namely Autocracy, Orthodoxy, and Nationality. Nikolai Avksent'ev energetically defended the record of socialism and the intelligentsia in terms of creating cultural values. Socialism, in particular, would establish the emancipation of the laboring classes, which was the only real base for the flourishing of human creativity (128). The *Vekhi* authors in general and Frank in particular did not understand that, for the intelligentsia, revolution was not a value but a condition. Socialism had various aims to establish new economic and other institutions in the real world, but "it does not see, does not know any concrete path to the realization of its demands other than through a revolutionary collision with the old order" (139). Nor did socialism assume that human nature was intrinsically good. Socialism, in its desire for the external transformation of institutions, also recognised the necessity of inner development of the personality (140). Frank and the others concentrated on the negative aspects of revolution without recognizing its potential for growth and renewal: "They hear only the rumblings of the collapse of the old edifice," but see nothing of its replacement and thereby "understand nothing" (141). Rather cheekily, Avksent'ev concluded by saying that Christ was the son of a poor carpenter who brought in a new teaching but died in ignominy, which is a proof for his pharisaic critics that his teachings were false, when in fact they were resurrected by numerous followers and became the basis for a universal religion. "Our" intelligentsia "now finds itself in the same position" (144). A final noteworthy response came from Leonid Shishko, in one of his last writings. Shishko attempted to refute the picture painted, especially by Struve, of the relationship between the intelligentsia and the inert, passive masses. Instead, Shishko argued, the previous half-century had seen the gradual rapprochement of two great historical forces—the social movement of the masses and the intelligentsia movement. From early naive encounters of the 1870s populism had learned that it would take longer than expected to achieve its aims, and it had been steadily attaining them, as time passed, though there had been many perturbations and problems. The events of 1905 certainly caused a serious setback, but it was not, as *Vekhi* assumed, "a complete and irremediable catastrophe" (278) which would destroy the process altogether. In fact, it was "the hopes which flared up in the light of October 17" which were proven to be fantasy "and ... have been destroyed, leaving the remnants of deep disillusion in many hearts" (278).

## Palpable Hits?

The response to *Vekhi* shows many things. Specific criticisms pointed out inconsistencies, contradictions, and perceived errors. For instance, several critics as diverse as Miliukov, Kizevetter, Chernov, and Lenin believed that the intelligentsia should be some kind of vanguard, or part of a vanguard, which educated and led the masses. It was not a weakness but a strength that the intelligentsia should be cut off from the benighted masses and should promote the interests of ordinary people above its own. Differences of emphasis in *Vekhi* between Berdiaev, Bulgakov, Gershenzon, and Struve over the role of the individual and the social in both the diagnosis of

## The Intelligentsia Fights Back: Left-wing Response to *Vekhi* and its Significance

the supposed ills of the intelligentsia and over the suggested cures were noted. Many specific points of disagreement emerged. However, above and beyond the individual points, some significant broader features can also be detected.

While at one level it is not surprising that hardly any of the defenders would admit to any serious failings in the intelligentsia, or to its bearing even partial responsibility for the collapse of the 1905 revolution, on another level it is somewhat disturbing. In fact, one of the main features of the debate is the strength and energy which the whole spectrum of the radical intelligentsia, from liberals to social democrats, put into the defense not only of the current intelligentsia but also of its revolutionary tradition. This also highlights the fact that, although we may translate deeply meaningful words like "liberal," "democratic," "populist," and so on from one language to another, the cultural framework around the terms, and their inner content, can engage in subtle and not-so-subtle shifts of meaning. All of them shared a more radical and even revolutionary meaning than is often associated with them in the United States or Western Europe. However, another key feature of the debate, about which the defenders of the intelligentsia were somewhat more divided, was the question of whether or not *Vekhi* was a sign of the growing transition of the intelligentsia from a radical, questioning group which challenged the autocracy into a more compliant and collaborative middle class hiding behind, as Gershenzon put it, the "bayonets and prisons" of the regime. Lenin was not the only one to be convinced that this was precisely what was happening. However, it is noteworthy that the portion of the intelligentsia most likely to be ripe for embourgoisement, the liberal professionals of the Kadet party, was among the stoutest critics of *Vekhi*, vigorously defending the social and the individual.

Not all of *Vekhi*'s critics were in agreement with one another—far from it, in fact. Two of the most effective responders, Kizevetter and Lur'e, were exceptions in that they did agree that *Vekhi* had diagnosed some serious weaknesses in the intelligentsia. Even so, they still did not think *Vekhi* had gotten all of its criticisms right. *Vekhi*, they felt, exaggerated the degree to which the intelligentsia was intellectually superficial and neurotic. It should praise rather than denigrate the intelligentsia's devotion to the interests of the *narod*, the people, the masses. Even more emphatically, however, they had no sympathy at all for *Vekhi*'s solutions. Kizevetter and Lur'e did not believe that the answer lay in mysticism, romanticism, inner development, and collaboration with the regime, as the *Vekhi* authors variously suggested, but in redoubling efforts to spread rationality and social engagement, not restrict them. They were also somewhat incredulous that *Vekhi* should be seriously suggesting a return to religion. For Lur'e particularly this was incomprehensible. It was not only the two of them who detected the "clink of the censer" in *Vekhi*. Almost all of *Vekhi*'s critics were of the same mind on this topic. Remarkably, perhaps, Miliukov was so contemptuous of the book's religious dimension that he did not even deem it worth refuting.

Finally, and this may be a point shared with many intellectual traditions, the debate showed that Russian intellectual life since the mid-nineteenth century was not a set of different "generations" which "succeeded" one another, but was rather a kind of palimpsest, or better, "layer-cake," with each segment adding to, rather than replacing, what had gone before. The debate showed not only a widespread devotion to a diverse set of revolutionary predecessors—Belinskii, Herzen, Chernyshevskii, Mikhailovskii, and others—but an important foundation of a kind of populism, in the sense of "serving the people," shared by liberals and socialists. Indeed, this observation leads to a broader speculation. As we have seen, Shishko, who was coming to the end of a long and fruitful life lived in the light of radical principles, believed that the intelligentsia and the masses were coming ever closer together. The tone of the debate bore this out at least in part. However, it was to be one of the tragic ironies of the October revolution that it was precisely the "natural" populism and the "natural" collectivism, even socialism, that were to be obliterated from Russian culture.

A close examination of the responses to *Vekhi* shows that, in the words of Hamlet, the rapiers of its critics made numerous palpable hits. The uncritical admiration often shown by *Vekhi*'s modern admirers needs to take this into account; its opponents are not to be dismissed simply as a group of narrow-minded, philistine fanatics. Many of *Vekhi*'s admirers take it to be a lone voice criticizing an intelligentsia all too ready to succumb to the perceived evils of post-revolutionary communism—in the forefront of which they identify intellectual superficiality; a flawed view of human nature; a contempt for the individual and a domineering view of the social; a crude utilitarianism; and a rejection of the rich cultural and artistic traditions of the past. The debate demonstrates the sophistication, complexity, and intellectual richness of the intelligentsia tradition. It shows that, while *Vekhi* did make many valid points and the intelligentsia was in some ways overly hostile, the final impression is one of passionate differences. The debate shows the traditional intelligentsia at its most developed, creative and diverse. The tragedy is not simply that it was destroyed by Bolshevik malevolence and fanaticism, but that the maelstrom of war and revolution made it almost impossible for it to have survived at all. In this sense, taking the range of the debate as a whole, the real significance is not in who "won" the argument. Rather, its significance lies in the fact that this debate is more or less the final exposition of the richness of late-nineteenth-century Russian intellectual life. It is the poignant swansong of a tragically doomed and much-missed group of talented, critical, and creative people.

### Notes

1   *Iz glubiny. Sbornik statei o russkoi revoliutsii* (Moscow/Petrograd, 1918; 2$^{nd}$ edition Paris: YMCA Press, 1967).

2   Those writing about *Vekhi* at this time included G. Öberlander, *Die Vechi-Diskussion (1909–1912)* (Cologne: Photostelle der Universität Köln, 1965); A. Kelly, "Attitudes to the Individual in Russian Thought and Literature with Special Reference to the *Vekhi* Controversy," (D.Phil. diss., Oxford, 1970); S. R. Tompkins, "*Vekhi* and the Russian Intelligentsia," *Canadian Slavonic Papers* 2 (1957): 11–25; and N. Poltoratzky, "The *Vekhi* Dispute and the Significance of *Vekhi*," *Canadian Slavonic Papers* 9, no. 1 (1967): 86–106.

3   *Iz-pod glyb. Sbornik statei* (Moscow: Samizdat, 1974; Paris: YMCA Press, 1974).

4   V. V. Sapov, ed., *"Vekhi": pro et contra. Antologiia* (St. Petersburg: Russkii Khristianskii gumanitarnyi institut, 1998).

5   D. S. Merezhkovskii, "Sem' smirennykh," *Rech'*, 9 May 1909.

6   M. I. Gershenzon, "Preface," *Vekhi: sbornik statei o russkoi intelligentsii* (Moscow : Tipografiia V. M. Sablina, 1909).

7. L. N. Tolstoi, "I Cannot be Silent," *New York Times*, 19 July 1908.

8. L. N. Andreev, *Pered zadachami vremeni* (Benson, VT: Chalidze Publications, 1985), 50.

9. R. Manning, *The Crisis of the Old Order in Russia: Gentry and Government* (Princeton, NJ: Princeton University Press, 1992); L. Haimson, *Russia's Revolutionary Experience: Two Essays* (New York: Columbia University Press, 2005).

10. *Intelligentsiia v Rossii: sbornik statei* (St. Petersburg, 1910). Page references are given in parentheses in the text.

11. "O sbornike *Vekhi*," *Russkaia mysl'* 5 (May 1909). A. A. Kizevetter: 127–37 and S. Lur'e: 137–46. Page references are given in parentheses in the text.

12. G. Fischer, *Russian Liberalism: From Gentry to Intelligentsia* (Cambridge, MA: Harvard University Press, 1958), 63.

13. *"Vekhi" kak znamenie vremeni* (Moscow: Zveno, 1910), 20. Subsequent page references are given in parentheses in the text.

14. Machajski (1866–1926) (real name A. Vol'skii and known as Makhaev in Russian) was best known for a three-volume pamphlet entitled *Umstvennyi rabochii* (*The Mental Laborer*, Geneva, 1905) in which he argued that socialism was the ideology which represented the class interests of the intelligentsia rather than the workers, because it accorded them the role of technocratic elite.

15. V. I. Lenin, *Polnoe sobranie sochinenii* (Moscow: Gospolizdat, 1958–65), vol.19, 168.

16. Ibid.

17. See footnote 13 for details.

18. S. L. Frank, *Smysl zhizni* (Paris: YMCA Press, 1925), 97.

19. "Saninism," a reference to a scandalous novel of the time. M. Artsybashev, *Sanin* (St. Petersburg, 1906).

20. 17 October was the date in 1905 on which the October Manifesto, a very limited proposal for reforms to be undertaken, was published over the signature of the tsar, mainly in order to divide and weaken the revolutionary movement of that year. 3 June was the day in 1907 when Prime Minister Stolypin dissolved the Second Duma and eventually replaced it with a Third Duma elected on a restrictive franchise.

Part II

# *VEKHI* and POLITICAL PHILOSOPHY

# 4

## The Rise of the People
## and the Political Philosophy of the *Vekhi* Authors*

*Evert van der Zweerde*

> ... Sem' vrachei sem'iu lekarstvami lechat bol'nogo.
>
> —Dmitrii S. Merezhkovskii, "Seven Humble Men," 1909

> Mais lorsqu'on lui pose la question: "Qui sont les *aristoi* qui doivent nous gouverner?", le démocrate se tourne vers le peuple pour lui laisser la décision.
>
> —Bernard Manin, *Principes du gouvernement représentatif*, 1996

Some argument is required to justify a discussion of the political philosophy of the *Vekhi* authors. This dimension received relatively little attention during the discussions immediately after the book's publication in 1909, which focused more on the *Vekhi* authors' perception of current affairs and, most of all, on the possible effects of their intervention.[1] It has also remained under-researched in later scholarly literature, which tends to concentrate on the religious philosophy of the authors, their conceptions of

---

* A Russian translation of a longer version of this essay, originally written in English, has appeared as "Narodnyi pod"em i politicheskaia filosofiia 'vekhovtsev,'" in *"Pravda." Diskursy spravedlivosti v russkoi intellektual'noi istorii*, ed. N. S. Plotnikov (Moscow: Institut "Spravedlivyi Mir," 2011), 276–319. The same version has appeared in German translation as "Der Aufstieg des Volkes und die politische Philosophie in den Vechi," in *Pravda: Diskurse der Gerechtigkeit in der russischen Geistesgeschichte*, ed. Holger Kuße and Nikolaj Plotnikov (Munich: Verlag Otto Sagner, 2011), 155–191.

religion, philosophy, and the intelligentsia, and, not least, on the question of whether, in a Russian tradition of prophecy (*prorochestvo*), they "saw it right." Finally, the *Vekhi* authors themselves suggested that "[I]n *Vekhi*, as is well known, politics occupies a relatively small place."[2] This may be true of politics in the *immediate* sense of parties, policies, and measures, although even there one may disagree: "*Signposts* claimed to stand above politics.... But the book's moral and cultural critique did in fact mask a predominantly political motive. [...] [T]he real political thrust of the book was an attempt to destroy the informal coalition of the liberals with the left which characterized Kadet [Constitutional Democrat] Party policy."[3]

At the time of writing of *Vekhi*, Europe was on the threshold of the age of democracy, and Russia was no exception in this respect: there was strong pressure to change the *politeia*, and some short-lived changes indeed took place after the 1905 revolution. In this situation, the pressure on intellectuals to engage in politics was strong. With the exception of Mikhail Gershenzon, the initiator of the project but an outsider in many respects (notably in his admiration of Tolstoi), all of the *Vekhi* authors were politically active, moving from Leftist positions (legal Marxism, social democracy) to liberal ones, and in some cases, for example that of Aleksandr Izgoev (Lande), remaining close to a non-orthodox Marxism.[4] With the exception of Izgoev, all had studied or lived in Germany. With the exception of Gershenzon, who later set up the Soviet *Soiuz pisatelei* and was its first president, all of them opposed the Soviet regime. Bogdan Kistiakovskii died in 1920 while a professor at Kiev University, but Petr Struve, after a brief membership in the "white" government of General Wrangel, left Russia after 1920, and Nikolai Berdiaev, Sergei Bulgakov, Semen Frank, and Izgoev were forced to emigrate in 1922 on the "Philosophy Steamer."[5] The chart on the next page illustrates their political activism and the gradual shift to liberal and "kadet" positions.[6]

The main reason, I suggest, why the book had the impact that it did have is its attempted intervention in the very foundation of any "politics": investigating the nature of the political, the relation between truth and power, and the role of the intelligentsia. This article, therefore, seeks to assess the political philosophy of the *Vekhi* authors, which is largely implicit in the seven articles that make up *Vekhi*. While *Vekhi* evidently neither is

|  | Politically active | Legal marxist | Social democrat | Soiuz osvobozhdeniia | Kadet party | Duma member |
|---|---|---|---|---|---|---|
| Berdiaev | yes | yes | yes | yes | member |  |
| Bulgakov | yes | yes | yes | — | member | 1905–07 |
| Frank | yes | yes | yes | — | close |  |
| Gershenzon | no | no | no | no | no |  |
| Izgoev | yes | yes | close | local leader | member |  |
| Kistiakovskii | yes | influenced | close | co-founder | member |  |
| Struve | yes | yes | ally | co-founder | leader | 1905–07 |

nor contains a treatise in political philosophy, a particular political philosophy is, I argue, taking shape on the pages of this famous, polemical, and highly contested symposium, which saw five editions within a year and began a second life in the late 1980s, when republication of this previously forbidden book became possible.[7]

The chapter consists of two parts. The first part focuses on a key issue at stake in *Vekhi*, namely the relation between democratic conditions and the idea of an integral worldview, and I introduce this topic by way of a discussion of the social and political philosophy of a major predecessor of and inspiration for Silver Age thought, Vladimir Solov'ev (1853–1900). The second part offers a systematic analysis of the overall political philosophy of the *Vekhi* authors (without ignoring their differences). To avoid misunderstanding: the expression "political philosophy" denotes not the *Vekhi* authors' political opinions or stances, but their overall conceptions of politics and the political.

A few preliminary remarks are appropriate. First of all, my objective is to understand, not to evaluate, let alone judge, the *Vekhi* authors. This is not without relevance, since *Vekhi*, whether in spite of or because of its "conciliatory" tendency, strongly invites the taking of a position even today, just as it is difficult to think about the first two decades of twentieth-century Russian history without developing strong opinions and emotions. Rather than concealing these behind the veil of scholarly objectivity, they should be pointed out. My overall intuition with respect to *Vekhi* is that the *Vekhi* authors were essentially fighting the already lost battle of an elite that had not even begun to play a major role. More generally, there is a prevailing sense of tragedy around *Vekhi*. Nonetheless, this should not stand in the way of sober analysis.

Second, it is important to note that the statement that the *Vekhi* authors were fighting a lost battle can only be made by virtue of the advantage of hindsight. It is difficult to avoid reading *Vekhi*, in the light of later developments, as a prophetic warning against "principled revolutionism" (Frank, 143; cf. Bulgakov, 30), against a peculiar combination of moral absolutism and nihilism, and against the dangers of any "instrumentalization" in politics—that is, against the notorious Jacobin justification of means by ends that would become the hallmark of the later Bolshevik regime.[8] In fact, however, we encounter here what I suggest one might call the *disadvantage* of hindsight, leading us to project later developments upon earlier events. A clear example of this is present in the review by Rüdiger Safranski of the German edition of *Vekhi*, published by Karl Schlögel in 1990: "Russian intellectuals of European reputation ... used *the calm before the great storm* after the failed revolution of 1905 to urge a radical self-scrutiny of the intelligentsia" (italics mine).[9] Obviously, to the *Vekhi* authors, the year 1909, in 1909 itself, was not an intermezzo: they were as ignorant of what would take place eight years from then as we are regarding what will take place eight years in our own future, even if they themselves, a decade later in *Iz glubiny* (*Out of the Depths*, 1918), recorded that "Russian educated society for the most part did not heed the warning addressed to it ...,"[10] thus contributing to the hindsight perspective.

Third, the use of words like democracy and aristocracy in this chapter calls for a terminological remark. Generally, I use the classical classification of six forms of *politeia*, three of them "virtuous" and three "corrupt."[11]

| Virtuous form | Number ruling | Corrupted form |
|---|---|---|
| Monarchy | One | Tyranny |
| Aristocracy | Some | Oligarchy |
| "Good democracy" | Many | Mob democracy / majority tyranny |

Other empirical forms, such as bureaucracy, gerontocracy, technocracy, expertocracy, hierocracy, and kleptocracy, are essentially variants of oligarchy. Corruption is possible in all three forms, but while the contrast between a good monarch and a tyrant is enormous, and an oligarchic elite can yield its place to a virtuous one which is truly oriented towards the common good, in the case of democracy the distance between "good" and "bad" democracy is relatively small. To the extent to which "the people" actually rules, it becomes difficult to find an alternative *demos*; corruption and amelioration can only come from the inside. The double meaning of *demos*, as denoting both the (political) people and the poor mob, is an indication of this. A *polity* with a virtuous *demos* could be qualified as "mass aristocracy,"[12] pointing to a political community that rests upon widespread civic education (*paideia*), an Aristotelian ideal that is strongly present in *Vekhi*.[13] Even Plato was not anti-democratic per se if *demos* meant a community of the virtuous.[14]

Conceptions of an *ideal politeia* contrast with the more realistic ideal of a *mixed polity*,[15] used by Cicero and before him Polybius to describe the Roman republic, and seen by them as a means to compensate for the flaws of *each* of the pure forms, prefiguring the idea of representative democratic government that runs from James Madison to Bernard Manin.[16] Empirically and historically, all regimes are compromises, and they are to a varying degree "corrupt"—they are somewhere on the scale of virtue, and engaged in the ongoing process of generation, corruption, and repair. This, however, is to be distinguished from the increase or decrease in political participation of members of the polity, in response to the actual development of society, as well as from the equalization of this participation, which historically led to universal suffrage on a one-(wo)man-one-vote basis. This increase and decrease of democratic participation is never smooth or uncontested—it tends to be rife with struggle and conflict.[17] *Vekhi* is seen, in this article, against the backdrop of a "rise of the people" with a claim to political participation on the one hand, and a call for virtue and "political quality" on the other.

Finally, I perceive three meanings of the expression "political philosophy." (i) In the most habitual meaning, political philosophy is a specialized branch of philosophy that focuses on "things political," that is, issues of government, justice, deliberation, political rights and liberties, party politics, and so forth. (ii) In a second, more properly philosophical meaning, it is a reflection on the question of why there are "political things" in the first place, and what makes them "political"—my position is that they are "political" insofar as they entail the possibility of "real conflict" (as opposed to mere disagreement or quarrel). This is, as Derrida has aptly labelled it, their *politicité* (politicity).[18] Here we are in the field of ontology, and my position, following Chantal Mouffe's interpretation of Carl Schmitt, is that *everything* social is always-already "political" in this precise sense. However, it is so to a varying degree, which can approach zero: some things are "politically neutral," some have been *neutralized*. Such neutralization itself is not neutral, but political; at the same time, they *are*, for all practical purposes, neutral—that is, they have *effectively* been neutralized.[19] That "everything is political" thus neither implies that anything is ever *purely* political nor that everything is *politics*—quite the contrary, it means that nothing is ever purely political *and* that nothing is ever purely a-political or un-political. Everything social has an inevitable political dimension: it is potentially conflictual and essentially contestable. (iii) If the previous is true, a reflexive notion of political philosophy is implied, which claims that political philosophy itself is always-already "political," and hence it makes sense to approach a book like *Vekhi* as a *politicum* (Gk: *politikon*) in its own right.

## THE BIG ISSUE: DEMOCRACY AND INTEGRAL WORLDVIEW

John Rawls has argued that under conditions of political freedom, there is likely to exist a plurality of comprehensive doctrines—that is, religious and non-religious worldviews, each of which offers a more or less elaborate conception of society, politics, the meaning of life, salvation of the soul (or lack thereof), and so forth.[20] Each of these "comprehensive doctrines" is a specimen in the category of what Berdiaev labelled "integral world-view" (*tselostnoe mirosozertsanie*), or "organic fusion of truth and goodness, knowledge and faith" (5, 13). One can connect the contrast that Aileen Kelly (thinking of Frank and Struve on the one hand, and Berdiaev and Bulgakov on the other) makes between doctrines that make a "clear distinction between religious and political tasks" and others that do not with Rawls's distinction between reasonable and unreasonable comprehensive doctrines.[21] A reasonable comprehensive doctrine recognizes the existence of a plurality of competing comprehensive doctrines and is capable of distinguishing its own comprehensiveness from its participation in an overlapping consensus with other comprehensive doctrines. While disagreeing with Rawls on the notion of reasonableness and sharing the critique of those who argue that it already presupposes a "modern autonomous self,"[22] I do agree with his idea of a plurality of comprehensive doctrines: under conditions of freedom, people will articulate their perceptions of the world in the form of contrasting worldviews which serve as each other's "constitutive outside" (*negierte Bestimmtheit*, one might turn Hegel inside out), and of which there hence have to be at least two.[23]

Under conditions of liberty, the elements of this plurality enjoy *prima facie* legitimacy. Consequently, what singles out a democratic polity, given a degree of freedom that allows for their development, is a plurality of integral worldviews, none of which can be a priori disqualified without undermining the very polity in which they exist. In other words, there is a plurality of *legitimate* mutually exclusive integral worldviews, none of which can lay exclusive claim to truth or justice, and which together express and reflect both the richness of human intellectual creativity and the conflicts that exist in the society that they relate to, and which they sustain through their interaction. At the same time, they demonstrate the differentiation and partition of that same society, and deny its organic nature unless this diversity of worldviews is sublated (*aufgehoben*) into a higher unity. Some of these integral worldviews (forms of liberalism and/or pluralism, for example) accommodate the very plurality just indicated, others do not; some appreciate it positively, others reject it or accept it as an inevitable evil.

The key point here is that there is a conflict between, on the one hand, this situation of "real existing plurality," and, on the other hand, the ideal situation that is part of the vision of the good society of at least some of the *Vekhi* authors. Upon Kelly's reading, *Vekhi* reflects precisely this conflict in its inner division and in its "two contradictory messages to the intelligentsia."[24] According to Kelly, the four main authors, all "former leading ideologists of

## The Rise of the People and the Political Philosophy of the *Vekhi* Authors

Russian Marxism," fall into two groups: the "maximalists" and "messianists" Berdiaev and Bulgakov, who stuck to an integral, Orthodox Christian worldview and hence viewed history in teleological terms, and political reality in apocalyptic ones, and the "pragmatics" or "humanists" Frank and Struve (joined by Izgoev and Kistiakovskii), who "were prepared to live with unpredictability as a consequence of openness to ideas (such as concepts of legal order and individual rights as preached and practiced in the West), which could extend the freedom of individuals in the present to determine their own destinies."[25]

The way in which thinkers address issues that are part of the "current affairs" of their time is determined, among others, by their philosophical background. Part of the background of the *Vekhi* authors was the massive figure of Vladimir Solov'ev, who represented the kind of thinker that the *Vekhi* authors were trying to be, and who had in his work pointed out a number of basic problems and questions that the *Vekhi* authors were also struggling with. This struggle becomes manifest on the pages of *Vekhi*. Solov'ev had not, in any direct or indirect sense, been the philosophical teacher or mentor of the *Vekhi* authors. As he himself famously asserted, he had not founded a doctrine or school of his own,[26] and even those who were philosophically closest to him—Berdiaev, Bulgakov, and Frank—cannot be considered his pupils. At the same time, however, he is mentioned several times in *Vekhi*, by Berdiaev, Bulgakov, Kistiakovskii (the only contributor who is critical of Solov'ev, and who is more generally an exception among the *Vekhi* authors), Gershenzon, and Struve, though not by Izgoev and Frank (who might, however, have referred to him in his analysis of Nietzsche, and who refers to him frequently in other works).[27] Apart from the well-known passage in Berdiaev's text in which he claims that "there seemed every reason to acknowledge Vladimir Solov'ev as our national philosopher and to create a national philosophical tradition around him," and that "the philosophy of any European country could take pride in a Solov'ev" (12), the most striking statement on the topic can be found in Struve, who claims that, in contradistinction to Mikhailovskii and Chernyshevskii, "Vladimir Solov'ev is not an *intelligent* at all" (121). Solov'ev was, for most *Vekhi* authors, a "role model" at this point, in the sense that they all identified, explicitly, as *intelligenty*, yet wanted to supersede this identity. Finally, and perhaps most importantly, it was Solov'ev who, in his philosophy of law and his attempts at a political philosophy, which was essentially an anti-political philosophy,[28] put key philosophical issues on the agenda. One such key issue concerns the relation between law and politics, and I will discuss this issue with the help of a recent analysis of Solov'ev's legal and moral philosophy by Alexander Haardt. In his commentary, Haardt situates Solov'ev's position in between those of Lev Tolstoi, who denied positive law in the name of Christian morality, and Boris Chicherin, who claimed the moral autonomy of the legal system. Solov'ev defends the position according to which positive law *does* have a moral dimension, which excludes out of hand any kind of legal positivism as well as its logical consequence, namely legal nihilism,[29] but also justifies the *legal* relations, guaranteed by the state, between members of a given society.[30] In his discussion of Kant, his main interlocutor in matters of moral and legal philosophy, Solov'ev concludes that the moral demand to treat each person always as an end in itself and never merely as a means founds the legal guarantee of personal rights and freedoms: "This right of the person [*pravo litsa*] is from its very nature *unconditional*, while the rights of the community with regard to the person are *conditioned* by the recognition of his individual rights [*lichnoe pravo*]."[31] However, while these individual rights do include, for Solov'ev, property rights, freedom of religion, and other personal rights, they do not include *political* rights: "While Solov'ev emphasized time and time again the rights that protect citizens against state power, he distanced himself from the rights to participation in political power of the individual, rights which are just as essential for a liberal conception of the state."[32] So if, on the one hand, we have good reasons to call Solov'ev a *liberal* at the level of individual rights and freedoms, he is neither a liberal nor a democrat at the level of *political* rights, that is, the right to participation. The shortest way to summarize his position is to say that if those who hold power in society, namely tsar, church, and civil society, act fully in accordance with the principles of Christian universal morality, as they obviously ought to do, in Solov'ev's view, the political participation of those who are ruled becomes superfluous. Given a just society with just rulers, democratic participation of substantial parts of the population can only lead to division and discord. Put differently, in a society fully determined by a Christian conception of justice, the difference between monarchic, aristocratic, and democratic *politeia* tends to become superfluous. To put it in Rousseauan terms: if the *volonté générale* is Christian in its essence, the *volonté de tous* becomes, if anything, a barrier to true justice.

As such, there is nothing particularly Solov'evian, Russian, Orthodox, or even Christian about this argument.[33] This position was embedded, however, in Solov'ev's case, in his conception of *Christian politics*, a position which, however liberal, rights-oriented and humanistic it may be, is not one that favors democracy.[34] The reason for this is the following: Christian politics, like Solov'ev's entire political project, relies on the idea of an *integral worldview* that not only comprises philosophy, religion, and science, but also answers all questions in the field of social and political philosophy.[35] By contrast, the acceptance of individual political rights, that is, the acceptance of the principle of legitimate free individuality, not only at the personal and the religious level, as with the adherents of Christian politics, and not only at the economic level, as with the liberals and to an extent Solov'ev, but also at the *political* level, means that *if* a single integral worldview is the shared conviction of the members of a given society, this is an accidental fact in the sense that *it happens to be the case* that people share the same integral worldview or, in Rawlsian terms, comprehensive doctrine. If, by contrast, a modernized church and a Christian intellectual elite manage to establish such an integral worldview at the level of society as a whole, it will not be accidental, but organically related to the very "idea" of that society.

This excursion into the social and political philosophy of Solov'ev serves to show that the *Vekhi* authors were situated between two positions: one which preferred a Christian society on the basis of liberal principles, and another which preferred a free society based on Christian principles. Even if the "net effect" of these two models can, in principle, be the same, their foundation is fundamentally different. Among the *Vekhi* authors, Kistiakovskii came closest to the first position, while Frank was the thinker who most clearly adhered to the second. What they all feared, however, was not simply the power of a mob that hated them, the *intelligenty*—though that fear was reflected in Gershenzon's much-loathed remark that "we must bless this government which alone, with its bayonets and prisons, still protects us from the people's wrath" (64). What they feared more, and with equally good reason, was that a democratic polity would not *automatically* yield a good or just society, let alone one that would fit the integral worldview that they, in different ways and to a varying extent, were endorsing. There is a general truth about democracy at play here: if a democratic polity is based on a liberal constitution that guarantees the citizens' rights and liberties, political rights included, it can surely yield a society that is considered just by the vast majority of its members, but the unity of such a society will be the contingent a posteriori outcome of law-based practices and procedures, and not part of the a priori make-up of that society as an organic whole: a democratic society, by definition—by virtue of its being democratic—does not necessarily yield a society that is considered just by any its members, except by those who equate democracy and justice.

The big issue, then, for the *Vekhi* authors and their contemporaries, was identical to one of the big issues of political philosophy today, one that divides, for example, "liberals" from "communitarians": how to accommodate the "democratic impulse," while retaining the possibility of a "substantive" integral worldview. The position of the *Vekhi* authors at this point was not simply that of an intellectual elite that wanted to take part in political power before they had to give it away to "the people"—their vision was *genuinely* aristocratic. At the same time, their effort to argue for such a perspective on the political reality of Russia after the 1905 revolution and its subsequent failure is itself squarely situated in that political reality. It is from this angle that we must try to assess the political philosophy that is present in *Vekhi*.

## *Vekhi* as Political Philosophy

If we start with the first, most habitual meaning of political philosophy (meaning [i], as indicated in the Introduction to this article), we ask how the *Vekhi* authors perceived polity and politics. For an assessment of the political philosophy that comes to the fore in *Vekhi*, it is appropriate, to begin with, to distinguish between preferred ends, acceptable means, and envisaged agents. Concerning *ends*, the *Vekhi* authors made their preferences clear. First of all, they wanted *order* in the sense of a society held together reliably and stably by a *politeia*. Secondly, they all desired *freedom*, at least in the sense of religious and intellectual freedom, which implied a break with the autocratic regime that had existed until 1905. In the third place, I think, they all desired social *justice*: throughout *Vekhi*, one senses genuine protest against the many forms of injustice in Russian society, and against the violation of elementary ethical norms. A fourth candidate, rule of law (*pravovoe gosudarstvo*) or legality (*zakonnost'*, which is rule *by* rather than *of* law), seems to be of less primary relevance to most *Vekhi* authors—at this point, Kistiakovskii comes across as a relative outsider,[36] while the others seem to perceive it as a means rather than as an end in itself.

As far as means are concerned, apart from rule of/by law, the *Vekhi* authors are crystal-clear on one point: revolution is to be avoided. Even if, standing in the tradition of legal Marxism, they did not exclude a strictly *political* revolution, they did reject revolution in the sense of a major social transformation.[37] Even if in some cases it might be inevitable, it is certainly not preferable, as its force is primarily destructive. Since the main alternative, reform, involving cooperation between the state and some form of representation of society, was not a serious possibility, as Bulgakov, Izgoev, and Kistiakovskii show with their critical assessment of the quality of political parties and Duma representatives, the question is what remains.[38] Revolution being rejected, and reform proving unrealistic, the overall answer that emerges from *Vekhi* is (political) education, an echo of the aristocratic ideal of *paideia* that we find in Aristotle, as opposed to mobilization of popular instinct: "The *Vekhi* authors saw one of the most serious accusations directed at the Russian intelligentsia in the fact that, instead of engaging in a systematic political education of the people in a spirit of reasonable compromise, it not only pandered to, but even fully consciously stirred up, the 'dark', 'destructive' instincts of the masses."[39]

Coming, finally, to agency or political subjectivity, the implicit position of the *Vekhi* authors is that, once cured and revitalized, the intelligentsia still would have to be the main vehicle of social and political change. There is a certain modesty at play here, since the intelligentsia is also held responsible for much of Russia's malady, but the basic position is that precisely because the intelligentsia has been profoundly wrong, it now really must do good. It is not difficult to see sincere intentions and genuine repentance here. However, at the same time, the "reborn intelligentsia" is again staged as the leading, if not exclusive, agent. If it does its job properly, there is no real need for the political participation of the people: in *Vekhi*, we find a profound critique of *what* the intelligentsia had been telling the *narod*—not, however, a critique of the fact *that* it was the intelligentsia that had assumed this role. This is not so much an anti-democratic as an a-democratic attitude, fully congruent with the Christian politics of Solov'ev. In Kelly's words—spoken of Berdiaev, but applicable more generally—the *Vekhi* authors showed "a reluctance to face the fact that in concrete situations choices frequently have to be made between equally desirable but conflicting values: democracy and aristocracy, equality and excellence, the demands of the flesh and the spirit."[40]

The primary agent of change, the intelligentsia, remains particularly vague in *Vekhi*. The *Vekhi* authors were criticized by, for example, Evgenii Trubetskoi, for the "extreme lack of definition of that concept which constitutes the fundamental theme of the reflections of *Vekhi*—the concept of the intelligentsia."[41] Schlögel, who subscribes to this critique of a lack of definition (*Ungenauigkeit*), forgives the *Vekhi* authors by arguing that the *intelligenty* as a matter of fact *were* unclear as a group.[42] This may be true, but there is something else at stake as well: the vagueness of this definition is productive in *Vekhi*'s key argument. The *Vekhi* authors were *intelligenty* themselves and they were identified as such by others.[43] Therefore they had to be, as Lenin might have put it, "*intelligenty drugogo tipa*" (*intelligenty* of a different kind), namely a kind that would be capable of properly diagnosing the crisis of the intelligentsia to which they themselves belonged, and to point a way out of this crisis. They were able to put themselves in this position by associating themselves with a number of people, such as Dostoevskii and Pushkin, who often were considered *intelligenty* but who, according to most *Vekhi* authors, were only wearing, like Herzen, the mask or the "uniform" of an *intelligent*—or even, like Solov'ev, were "not an *intelligent* at all" (Struve, 121). The *Vekhi* authors were those *intelligenty* who were capable of receiving the cure for the intelligentsia's ills as a whole *from the outside*, from non-*intelligenty* or from those who were merely apparent ones.

Proceeding to the second meaning of political philosophy (ii), namely a philosophy of the political understood as the possibility of conflict, we can state that the general perception of it by the *Vekhi* authors is negative. Political parties, for example, are explicitly defined as a necessary evil by Bulgakov: "The division into parties, based upon differences of political opinion, social position, and property interest, is a habitual and widespread phenomenon in countries with popular representation and, in a certain sense, is a necessary evil" (46). The fact that they are a *necessary* evil provides them with a certain legitimacy, but the fact remains that they are an *evil*. The persistence of this negative evaluation—which is by no means specifically Orthodox or Russian!—is shown by its presence in one of Aleksandr Solzhenitsyn's contributions to the 1974 *tamizdat*[44] publication *Iz-pod glyb* (*From Under the Rubble*), a book that saw *Vekhi* as one of its forerunners: "'Partiia' means a part. Every party known to history has always defended the interests of this one *part* against … the rest of the people. And in the struggle with other parties it disregards justice for its own advantage. […] In the world today, we doubtfully advance toward a dimly glimpsed goal: can we not, we wonder, rise above the two-party or multi-party parliamentary system? Are there no extra-party or strictly non-party paths of national development?"[45]

This protest against the partition of society, reflected by a multi-party system, is directly related to a predominantly organic conception of society as we find it in the thought of most of the *Vekhi* authors.[46] It is part of a particular type of worldview, again neither typical of nor limited to Christianity or to Orthodoxy, but widespread among late nineteenth-century and early twentieth-century thinkers (and not only in Russia). Struve later moved on to a nationalist position, which is indeed one of the possible vectors of development of the organic conception of society: "Contending that every state is an organism that needs to assert itself among its peers in order to maintain its health, he [Struve] argued that Russia could heal its internal wounds by pursuing an expansionist foreign policy based on a vigorous nationalism."[47]

Directly related to the idea of society as an *organism* is the predominance in *Vekhi* of the medical metaphor: if a society is a living organism, it can be ill, wounded, cured, killed, operated on, infected, contaminated, and so forth. The intelligentsia is described, by Gershenzon, as "a crowd of sick men quarantined in their own country" (63). When emphasis is on the spiritual dimension of Russian society, "psychotherapeutic" metaphors pop up with a vocabulary of crisis, healing (*ozdorovlenie*), self-searching, and similar notions. The *Vekhi* authors thus engage in anamnesis and diagnosis before suggesting a cure: "What follows from this diagnosis of the illness? First of all … it means that the ailment is deep-seated" (Struve, 127). A close reading of *Vekhi* shows that the metaphors of illness, diagnosis, and healing are present in all seven contributions except Kistiakovskii's.[48] As Dmitrii Merezhkovskii aptly, and sarcastically, put it: "Seven physicians are treating the patient with seven drugs."[49] Treating a patient with seven different medicines obviously has a strong risk of overkill, and this possibility catches the disagreement among the *Vekhi* authors, correctly highlighted by Merezhkovskii. More significant, however, is the political metaphysics at play here: if society is an organism, and one of its main limbs or organs, the intelligentsia, is ill, then it must receive proper treatment from that part of itself that is capable of providing it, namely, its *spiritual* part. This part can receive the remedy from the outside, because it is the *privileged* part of the social body.[50] Such metaphysics fits badly into a democratic society with matching polity: whatever unity or harmony there is under conditions of democracy is the *contingent* outcome of complex processes, not the manifestation of an underlying substance. This is not to say that the *Vekhi* authors were anti-democratic per se, in the sense of being opposed to elections (as Kadet party and Duma members, they would be performatively contradicting themselves if they were), but to argue that their perception of society, and of their own position in it, was essentially pre-modern and aristocratic.

Closely connected to the organic conception of society is the idea that the "body" of society consists of more or less clearly delineated "organs" and "members" (rather than of citizens or individuals). The two of these on which the *Vekhi* authors focus are, of course, the intelligentsia and the people (*narod*), the latter of which in Russian always has the connotation of "ordinary people," i.e., *demos* in the sense of the mob or *hoi polloi*. The relation between these two entities is stated and evaluated differently, but the pair itself is constant and goes unquestioned. Arguably, a belief in the central role of this pair is what the *Vekhi* authors have in common more than anything else, and it appears in all seven contributions (again, less prominently in Kistiakovskii's).⁵¹

Arriving, finally, at the third meaning of "political philosophy" (iii), we should address the *politicity* of *Vekhi*, that is, the fact that the book's very appearance and existence are political. First of all, the book itself, not so much as a physical object but as an event, as something that was there, is a "thing political." It was a *politicum* in 1909, when it saw five editions within a year and became the object of heated debate. It was a *politicum* during the Soviet period, when it "survived as a negative" in the polemical works of Lenin, in Stalin's *Kratkii kurs istorii KPSS* (*Short Course on the History of the Soviet Union Communist Party*), one of the key ideological texts of the Stalin era, and in the official Soviet renderings of the history of philosophy in Russia, for example in the *History of Philosophy* that appeared in six hefty volumes between 1957 and 1965 (in a chapter entitled "Critique of the Bourgeois-Landowner Idealistic Philosophy and Sociology in Russia in the Epoch of Imperialism" *Vekhi* is discussed as "maliciously attacking [*zlobno napadaia na*]" Marxism, materialism, and natural science while invoking "the Slavophiles, Iurkevich, Solov'ev and other mystics," and Lenin's "O 'Vekhakh'" is repeatedly quoted to disqualify *Vekhi* as "an encyclopaedia of liberal renegacy.")⁵² And it was a *politicum*, once again, around the end of the Soviet regime, when it was republished in large numbers (the edition used for this article appeared in 75,000 copies),⁵³ and played a key role in the reassessment of the intelligentsia and of the role it claimed it could or should play.⁵⁴

In terms of *what* it did, secondly, *Vekhi*'s nature as a *politicum* comes to the fore in the decisions it takes at the level of theory.⁵⁵ The sustained juxtaposition of intelligentsia and *narod* as not only historical or sociological categories but also as political agents and non-agents respectively is a first case in point. The nascent nationalism of the *Vekhi* authors, in opposition to both proletarian internationalism and the "Christian cosmopolitanism" of Tolstoi, is a second example. It appears in several places, for example at the end of Izgoev's contribution, where he ascribes the political success of the Young Turks to their emphasis on the nation-state and contrasts it with the failure of the Russian intelligentsia (90).⁵⁶ A third example is the renouncement of revolution as a viable strategy for political change, and the choice for a combination of reform and conciliation, highlighted by Merezhkovskii, among others.[57] All three examples point to political decisions at the level of theoretical discourse, and they are part of the polemics that *Vekhi* engages in.

Finally, and perhaps most interestingly, *Vekhi* is political in its *formal* aspects, that is, in *how* it develops its positions and polemics and thus in how it "engages in politics" itself. To avoid misunderstanding, it should be clarified that this is not a matter of doubting the sincerity of the *Vekhi* authors (as if they were "politicians cloaked as philosophers"), but a matter of highlighting the *inevitable* political nature of their endeavor, and of laying bare the logic of things (a logic which implies that philosophers always *are* "politicians" in the precise sense that they, too, have to deal with "the political" that is present in their text). To start with, the polemics of *Vekhi* are anti-polemical, with their emphasis on "reconciliation" (*smirenie*), a feature noted by many commentators, including Merezhkovskii, whose critical commentary bore the title of "Sem' smirennykh" ("Seven Reconciled Men").[58] To be anti-polemical, however, is to be polemical in a different way: the original opponents are those who continue the struggle, who *refuse* to reconcile, and a plea for conciliation is a form of self-concealing polemics. In this sense, *no* position or perspective can ever escape the logic of polemics.

Crucially important is the use of one key word of political philosophy, "we":[59] a conciliatory word par excellence, it is also, as Frank emphasized elsewhere, oppositional: "... 'we' is fundamentally limitless. It is true that, empirically, 'we' is always limited: every 'we' ... is opposed by ... some 'you' and 'they.' But, along with this, 'we' in another, projected unity can embrace and include all 'you' and 'they' ..."[60] This is the case with the "we" formed by the *Vekhi* authors too. Apart from the differences within this "we," it is also always constitutive of its "other." A close analysis of the use of "we" (*my*) and its derivatives such as "our" (*nash*) serves to show that while its *meaning* (in the Fregean sense of *Sinn*) remains constant, namely, "this group of which I as locutor am part and in the name of which I speak," its *reference* (Fregean *Bedeutung*) shifts between *three* positions: sometimes "we" stands for the Russian nation, sometimes "we" stands for the intelligentsia as a whole, and sometimes, finally, it stands for those *intelligenty* who, unlike the vast majority but including the *Vekhi* authors themselves, perceive the real causes of the crisis and have the proper remedy.

In the three cases mentioned, "we" stands in opposition to, respectively, people other than Russian nationals, non-*intelligenty*, and, most importantly, the "you" that is addressed directly and has the choice between becoming part of a reborn "we" or remaining stubbornly "ill," thus risking becoming part of "they." This shifting use of "we" is what enables the *Vekhi* authors to turn their criticism of the intelligentsia into a *samokritika* (self-critique) by the intelligentsia as a whole, in which case they themselves are the agents of this *samokritika*.[61] A cured intelligentsia will be capable of becoming the agent of change of the "big we" of the Russian nation. The shifting reference of "we" thus is the precondition for the *Vekhi* authors to distance themselves from the intelligentsia while remaining part of it, and thus both to "remove themselves from the ranks of the accused,"[62] and to turn the intelligentsia into, to put it in present-day terms, a self-help group.

In sum, *Vekhi* is political with respect to its very existence—its *that*; with respect to its content—its *what*; and with respect to its form—its *how*.

From this analysis of *Vekhi* as a specimen of political philosophy, three conclusions can be drawn. First of all, it has been demonstrated that the largely implicit political philosophy (distinct from their political stances) of the *Vekhi* authors was aristocratic, not so much in terms of their own social background (which was rather mixed in this respect),[63] but in terms of their perception of political agency. This conception is clearly at odds with the *first* model of democracy that I have distinguished, that is the Jacobin model of direct or pure democracy in the tradition of thinkers from Rousseau to Lenin and Schmitt. But it could be made compatible with the *second* model, or representative democracy as a mixed polity with aristocratic elements, if the *Vekhi* authors could have accepted the idea of a plurality of radically different, yet all a priori legitimate, "comprehensive doctrines" and, perhaps more importantly, the intrinsically political nature of things political, including their own endeavor. Their organicist social ontology, however, precluded this: it held no place for conflict, division, and plurality other than as an ailment to be cured or, at best, as a necessary evil.

Connected to this is a second conclusion: the *Vekhi* authors have been qualified as reactionaries and mocked as *renegaty* and *nazadniki* (literally, "backwarders"),[64] and they have objected to this misqualification.[65] They were partly right: they did not support autocracy, they did favor constitutional and democratic reform, they were "liberals" in such issues as freedom of religion, opinion, and movement, and they were certainly progressive. Still, their qualification as reactionaries does make sense: their position was not only and explicitly a reaction to the failed revolution of 1905 and to the ensuing crisis of the intelligentsia; it was also, and more profoundly, a reaction against the actual democratization of Russian society. This reaction comes to the fore most clearly in their persistent use of the opposition: intelligentsia-*narod*. One can link this to a conservative position, aiming at the preservation of the worldview monopoly of the intelligentsia, but it is, in fact, reactionary, because this monopoly *already* belonged to the past. Shelokhaev rightly states that, while the *Vekhi* authors accepted the idea of a *political* revolution (and thus could approve of the February revolution of 1917), they were opposed to the idea of a social revolution.[66] They ignored, however, the social revolution that was already taking place, and to which the February and October revolutions were the *alternative* reactions. In *Vekhi*, we see a partial recognition of this new situation when, for example, Kistiakovskii points to the legitimate existence of a plurality of political parties (99),[67] or when Gershenzon, in the last section of his contribution, displays an almost visionary awareness of the coming-to-be of a society of individuals who decide for themselves (66–69). Such insights, however, remain relatively rare on the pages of *Vekhi*.

Finally, when Shatz and Zimmerman, in the Introduction to the English edition, state that "contemporary Western political thought and practice can also be illuminated by *Signposts*," they claim that *Vekhi* shows that "the need for political and social justice" should be placed "within the larger perspective of the need for a creative and productive culture" (xxiv–xxv). Safranski, in reviewing the German edition, adds that *Vekhi* shows "how from the struggle against a political tyranny emerges the *tyranny of the political*."[68] Shelokhaev, finally, in the preface to a 1991 post-Soviet edition, states that when the *Vekhi* authors demonstrated the poverty of political culture in Russia, they were overstating their case.[69] All three may have a point. The main conclusion from the *Vekhi* case, however, is that it shows that a democratic *politeia*, whatever its details, that matches a democratizing, individualizing, and differentiating society, does not rely on, and no longer *can* rely on, an integral worldview that is monopolized by intellectuals or *intelligenty*. Instead, it relies on the contingent and hence unpredictable dynamic interplay between a plurality of worldviews and a society as it actually exists and develops. The *Vekhi* authors saw this situation approaching and rejected it, and in doing so they demonstrated the conflict between a Platonic-Christian *ideal politeia* on the one hand and the unpredictable plurality of a democratic society under *mixed polity* on the other. This is not an exclusively Russian problem. On the contrary, it was and is also a European and global problem. Karl Schlögel, in the concluding remark of his Introduction, points to an open question rather than to an achieved answer: "To be able to live without *Vekhi*, leaving them behind as signs on a road which at last leads Russia out of the time of catastrophe—that would be 'New *Vekhi*.'"[70] This, again, is not an exclusively Russian issue. At this point, *Vekhi* and the *Vekhi* authors continue to be highly instructive indeed. We see seven intellectuals playing doctor, struggling to keep up the idea of an organic society-cum-polity that has a single integral worldview as its "spiritual foundation,"[71] while the world, Russia included, had already developed beyond that point.[72]

## Notes

1 See V. V. Sapov, ed., *Vekhi: pro et contra. Antologiia* (St. Petersburg: Izdatel'stvo Russkogo Khristianskogo gumanitarnogo instituta, 1998).

2 A. S. Izgoev, "Sol' zemli," in Sapov, *Vekhi: pro et contra*, 485.

3 Marshall S. Shatz and Judith E. Zimmerman, eds. and trans., *Vekhi/Landmarks: A Collection of Articles about the Russian Intelligentsia* (Armonk, NY: M.E. Sharpe, 1994), xvii. Henceforth references to this edition are in parentheses in the text.

4 See A. S. Izgoev, "Intelligentsiia i 'Vekhi,'" in Sapov, *Vekhi: pro et contra*, 505, where he writes: "As far as 'Marxism' is concerned, I both was and remain a Marxist. But I never considered myself an orthodox 'Marxist.'"

5   For details on this involuntary trip and on some of the *Vekhi* authors, see Evert van der Zweerde, "La place de la philosophie russe dans l'histoire de la philosophie mondiale," *Diogène* 224 (Juillet 2008): 121–23.

6   The scheme is based on the biographical information that is contained in the Russian, English, and German editions used for this article (see note 7, below), as well as B. V. Emel'ianov, ed., *"Zheleznyi vek" russkoi mysli: pamiati repressirovannykh* (Ekaterinburg: Izdatel'stvo Ural'skogo universiteta, 2004).

7   Shatz and Zimmerman, *Vekhi/Landmarks*, vii; V. Shelokhaev, "Predislovie," in *Vekhi: sbornik statei*, ed. N. Kazakova (Moscow: Molodaia gvardiia, 1991), 5; Karl Schlögel, ed., *Wegzeichen: Zur Krise der russischen Intelligenz* (Frankfurt am Main: Eichborn Verlag, 1990), 6; Aileen M. Kelly, "Which Signposts?," in Kelly, *Toward Another Shore: Russian Thinkers Between Necessity and Chance* (New Haven, CT: Yale University Press, 1998), 155.

8   See Julien Freund, *L'essence du politique* (Paris: Sirey, [1965] 1986), 299; Michael Oakeshott, "The Masses in Representative Democracy," in Oakeshott, *Rationalism in Politics and Other Essays* (Indianapolis: Liberty Fund, 1991), 377, who distinguishes between parliamentary and popular government, the latter meaning "jacobinism"; cf. also Alain Besançon, *Les origines intellectuelles du léninisme* (Paris: Calmann-Lévy, 1977).

9   Rüdiger Safranski, "Tauben Ohren gepredigt; Russische Intellektuelle vor der Oktoberrevolution," *Die Zeit*, 8 March 1991, 48.

10  P. B. Struve, "Predislovie," *Iz glubiny: sbornik statei o russkoi revoliutsii* (1918), quoted in Shatz and Zimmerman, *Vekhi/Landmarks*, xix.

11  The scheme is essentially based on Plato, *Politikos* 302c-e and Cicero, *De re publica*, I 26-27.

12  Far-fetched as this may seem, it is in fact what is currently put forward in, for example, Benjamin Barber's notion of strong democracy. See Benjamin Barber, *Strong Democracy* (Berkeley, CA: University of California Press, [1984] 2003).

13  See M. I. Gershenzon, "Creative Self-Consciousness," in Shatz and Zimmerman, *Vekhi/Landmarks*, 68.

14  See Thom Brooks, "Is Plato's Political Philosophy Anti-Democratic?," in *Anti-Democratic Thought*, ed. Erich Kofmel (Exeter, VA: Imprint Academic, 2008), and Leo Strauss, "What is Political Philosophy?," in Strauss, *What is Political Philosophy? and Other Studies* (Chicago: University of Chicago Press, [1959] 1988), 36.

15  At this point, I propose to distinguish a mixed *polity*, i.e., a mixture of monarchic, aristocratic, and democratic elements, from mixed *government*, i.e., the balanced configuration of different powers as in the *trias politica*, a notion already present in antiquity (Aristotle, *Politika*, Book IV, xi.1 / 1297b, 37 - 1298a, 3).

16  Cicero, *De re publica*, II-29 and II-39, James Madison, "The Federalist No. 10" (1937), in *The Federalist Papers*, ed. Charles R. Kesler and Clinton Rossiter (New York: New American Library, 2003), 71–79, and Bernard Manin, *Principes du gouvernement représentatif* (Paris: Flammarion, [1995] 1996), 66–67, 198–99.

17  Cf. Chantal Mouffe, *The Democratic Paradox* (London: Verso, 2000), 3, as well as Charles Tilly, *Contention and Democracy in Europe* (Cambridge: Cambridge University Press, 2004) and *Democracy* (Cambridge: Cambridge University Press, 2007).

18  Jacques Derrida, *Politiques de l'amitié* (Paris: Galilée, 1994), 137; the English translation renders *politicité* as "politicity": J. Derrida, *The Politics of Friendship* (London: Verso, 2005), 117.

19  See Carl Schmitt, *Der Begriff des Politischen* (Berlin: Duncker & Humblot, [1929] 1987), esp. "Das Zeitalter der Neutralisierungen und Entpolitisierungen" (79–95); for Mouffe's project "to think with Schmitt against Schmitt" (*The Democratic Paradox*, 2), see Chantal Mouffe, *The Return of the Political* (London: Verso, [1993] 1997), Mouffe, *The Democratic Paradox*, and Chantal Mouffe, ed., *The Challenge of Carl Schmitt* (London: Verso, 1999).

20  John Rawls, *Political Liberalism* (New York: Columbia University Press, [1993] 2005), 3ff., 133ff., and passim.

21  Kelly, "Which Signposts?," 196.

22  See, e.g., Mouffe, *The Democratic Paradox*.

23  The notion of "constitutive outside" is adopted from Henry Staten, *Wittgenstein and Derrida* (Lincoln, NE: University of Nebraska Press, 1984), 23; cf. also Chantal Mouffe, *On the Political* (London: Routledge, 2005), 15.

24  Kelly, "Which Signposts?,"167–68.

25  Ibid., 156, 164–66, and 198–99; a clear example of Berdiaev's apocalyptic vision of history is his influential *The End of Our Time* (London: Sheed & Ward, [1933] 1935).

26  Cf. V. S. Solov'ev, "O poddelkakh," in *Sochineniia v dvukh tomakh* (Moscow: Pravda, 1989), vol. 2, 316, and "Pis'mo k redaktoru V.V. Lesevich," *Voprosy filosofii i psikhologii* 1, no. 5 (1890), also in *Sobranie sochinenii* (Brussels: 1966–69), vol. 6, 269–75.

27  Shatz and Zimmerman, *Vekhi/Landmarks*, xxviii, 5, 12 ff., 23, 44, 93, 119, 121.

28  See Evert van der Zweerde, "Zlo i politika: ob anti-politicheskoi politicheskoi filosofii Vl. Solov'eva," in *Vladimir Solov'ev i kul'tura serebrianogo veka*, ed. A. A. Takho-Godi and E. A. Takho-Godi (Moscow: Nauka, 2005), and "La place de la philosophie russe."

29  See Andrzej Walicki, *Legal Philosophies of Russian Liberalism* (Notre Dame: University of Notre Dame Press, [1967] 1992).

30  Alexander Haardt, "Personalität in Recht und Moral: Vl. Solov'evs Begegnung mit Kant," in *Diskurse der Personalität: die Begriffsgeschichte der "Person" aus deutscher und russischer Perspektive*, ed. Alexander Haardt and Nikolaj Plotnikov (Munich: Wilhelm Fink, 2008), 171.

31  Vladimir Solovyov, *The Justification of the Good: An Essay on Moral Philosophy*, trans. Nathalie A. Duddington (first publication 1918), ed. and annotated Boris Jakim (Grand Rapids, MI: William B. Eerdmans Publishing Company, 2005), 229; in Russian, *Opravdanie dobra*, in V. S. Solov'ev, *Sochineniia v dvukh tomakh* (Moscow: Mysl', 1988), vol. 2, 346.

32 Haardt, "Vl. Solov'evs Begegnung mit Kant," 181.

33 One can construct a similar position departing from Islamic principles, for example.

34 See Pauline W. Schrooyen, *Vladimir Solovëv in the Rising Public Sphere* (Nijmegen: Ipskamp, 2006), 69–89.

35 See Evert van der Zweerde, "Vladimir Solovjov: een levend denkwerk," *Tijdschrift voor Filosofie* 65 (2003), 715–35, for a concise rendering.

36 This impression is strongly confirmed by Vanessa Rampton's contribution to this volume.

37 Shelokhaev, "Predislovie," 8–9.

38 Shatz and Zimmerman, *Vekhi/Landmarks*, 46, 89, 101–02.

39 Shelokhaev, "Predislovie," 15. The translation from the Russian is my own.

40 Kelly, "Which Signposts?," 173.

41 Evgenii Trubetskoi, "'Vekhi' i ikh kritiki," in Sapov, *Vekhi: pro et contra*, 324.

42 Schlögel, *Wegzeichen*, 12–13.

43 Ibid., 7, and D. I. Shakhovskoi, "Slepye vozhdi/vozhdi slepykh," in Sapov, *Vekhi: pro et contra*, 48.

44 *Tamizdat*, consisting of the words "*tam*" (there) and "*izdat*'" (to publish), refers to publications by Soviet dissident authors in the West; it is a counterpart to the better-known expression of *samizdat*, from "*sam*" (self) and the same "*izdat*'."

45 Alexander Solzhenitsyn, "As Breathing and Consciousness Return," in A. Solzhenitsyn et al., *From Under the Rubble* (London: Collins & Harvill Press, 1975), 19. Originally published as Aleksandr Solzhenitsyn i dr., *Iz-pod glyb* (Paris: YMCA Press, 1974).

46 Shatz and Zimmerman, *Vekhi/Landmarks*, 13, 33, 48, 63, 88; in all these places, the ideas of an organic whole and organic activity take center stage.

47 Kelly, "Which Signposts?," 178.

48 Shatz and Zimmerman, *Vekhi/Landmarks*, 5, 15, 45, 49, 63, 65, 78, 86, 127, 133, 153.

49 D. S. Merezhkovskii, "Sem' smirennykh," in Sapov, *Vekhi: pro et contra*, 103. Originally published in *Rech'*, 26 April [9 May], 1909.

50 Note the parallel here, despite all the differences, to the self-perception of the Bolsheviks as the privileged part of the proletariat.

51 Shatz and Zimmerman, *Vekhi/Landmarks*, 2, 7, 21, 43–44, 57, 64, 80, 94–95, 104, 124–125, 140–41.

52 M. A. Dynnik et al., eds., *Istoriia filosofii v 6-i tomakh*, vol. 5 (Moscow: izd. Akademii Nauk SSSR, 1961), 342.

53 Kazakova, *Vekhi*, 464.

54 See Jutta Scherrer, *Requiem für den Roten Oktober: Rußlands Intelligenzija im Umbruch 1986-1990* (Leipzig: Universitätsverlag, 1996), 44–51 and 159–65, and my review of it in *Symposium: A Journal of Russian Thought* 2 (1997): 167–69.

55  That Louis Althusser was arguably wrong when qualifying philosophy as *class* struggle at the level of theory does not mean that philosophy is not always-already struggle, i.e., that it always, and necessarily, has a polemical side to it.

56  In a footnote to the second edition, he even reinforced this point (Shatz and Zimmerman, *Vekhi/Landmarks*, 90 and note 17); I am grateful to Catherine Evtuhov for drawing my attention to this point.

57  Sapov, *Vekhi: pro et contra*, 103.

58  See note 49.

59  Also discussed by Stuart Finkel in his contribution to this volume.

60  S. L. Frank, *The Spiritual Foundations of Society* (Athens, OH: Ohio University Press, 1987), 50. Originally published as *Dukhovnye osnovy obshchestva* (Paris: YMCA Press, 1930).

61  Cf. Nikolai Berdiaev, "Philosophical Verity and Intelligentsia Truth," in Shatz and Zimmerman, *Vekhi/Landmarks*, 5; Sergei Bulgakov, "Heroism and Asceticism (Reflections on the Religious Nature of the Russian Intelligentsia"), ibid., 18.

62  Shelokhaev, "Predislovie," 11.

63  The only real aristocrat was Berdiaev; the others had their roots in the academic elite (Struve, Kistiakovskii), clergy (Bulgakov), professional middle class (Frank), and business milieu (Gershenzon). Data about the Jewish family in Odessa that Izgoev grew up in are hard to find.

64  Cf. V. Il'in [V. I. Lenin], "O 'Vekhakh,'" in Sapov, *Vekhi: pro et contra*, 488, and Schlögel, *Wegzeichen*, 12.

65  See, e.g., Izgoev, "'Sol' zemli," in Sapov, *Vekhi: pro et contra*, 485–87.

66  Shelokhaev, "Predislovie," 8–9.

67  See Schlögel, *Wegzeichen*, 16.

68  Safranski, "Tauben Ohren gepredigt," 48.

69  Shelokhaev, "Predislovie," 15.

70  Schlögel, *Wegzeichen*, 44.

71  The expression "spiritual foundation" is taken from Frank's main work in social philosophy, *Dukhovnye osnovy obshchestva* (see note 60 for details).

72  From this perspective, the Bolshevik revolution of 1917 and the regime that it led to, far from being "progressive," were even more reactionary.

# 5

## INDIVIDUAL FREEDOM AND SOCIAL JUSTICE:
Bogdan Kistiakovskii's Defense of the Law

*Vanessa Rampton*

In his introduction to the *Vekhi* symposium, Mikhail Gershenzon describes the contributors' "common platform" as their "recognition of the theoretical and practical primacy of spiritual life over the external forms of community. They mean by this that the individual's inner life is the sole creative force in human existence, and that this inner life ... constitutes the only solid basis on which a society can be built."[1] Bogdan Kistiakovskii's article "V zashchitu prava (Intelligentsiia i pravosoznanie)" ("In Defense of Law [The Intelligentsia and Legal Consciousness]") constitutes an obvious exception to this "common platform." Instead of exploring how society could be regenerated via internal moral renewal, Kistiakovskii focused precisely on the significance of the rule of law, an *external* means of shaping new cultural values. His article stressed that there was no opposition between external freedom guaranteed by law and internal spiritual development: "Inner, more absolute spiritual freedom is possible only when external freedom is present," he wrote, "and the latter is the best school for the former" (91). Consciously or unconsciously, Kistiakovskii's piece was devoted to proving that the opposition Gershenzon set up between law and individual self-realization was false.

Kistiakovskii's decision to focus on the normative value of law was prompted by his concern at how thoroughly disregard for the idea of the rule of law had permeated Russian society. He deplored the arbitrary nature of tsarist legal practices, but also the intelligentsia's legal nihilism and refusal to acknowledge the links between a legal order and both individual and collective morality. Rather than approaching law as a living process embodied in social convictions and ideals, the intelligentsia saw it as "faith in the omnipotence of statutes and the force of binding rules" (107). And it was not only the intelligentsia that presented a false ethics on which to rebuild Russian society: Kistiakovskii was also wary of attempts, some of which were offered by *Vekhi* collaborators, to refashion society based on idealist personalism, which neglected what he saw as the unique advantages offered by the idea of law.

The extent to which different strands within *Vekhi* figure in its opposition to the revolutionary intelligentsia has attracted much scholarly interest over the years. The problem of *Vekhi*'s place within the philosophical tradition of Russian liberalism has been examined particularly by Aileen Kelly, Leonard Schapiro, and Andrzej Walicki in separate though related arguments.[2] The present essay seeks to address the issue from a slightly different point of view, namely that of how Kistiakovskii's convictions concerning the rule of law were grounded in an ethical theory and politics that differed substantially from those of his co-contributors.[3] The difference between Kistiakovskii and his fellow contributors was noticed long ago, but rarely pursued further. The leader of the Kadet Party Pavel Miliukov, for example, devoted a lecture tour to criticizing *Vekhi*, yet found "one essay [Kistiakovskii's] in *Vekhi* with which one could fully agree, except for its terminology and a few sentences at the beginning and end, by which it is stitched on, rather artificially, to the rest of the book."[4] Viktor Chernov of the Socialist Revolutionary party (writing under the pseudonym of Ia. Vechev) went even further, arguing that "Kistiakovskii's essay, 'In Defense of Law,' differs favorably from the reactionary noise of *Vekhi* by its pithiness, correctness of style, and serious tone."[5]

The contradiction implicit in Kistiakovskii's affinity with *Vekhi* and the cautiously positive reception of his article among the book's opponents raises questions about the points of intersection between his theory and that of his fellow contributors. My aim is therefore to explore to what extent Kistiakovskii's philosophy and politics differed from the theories of freedom and selfhood commonly associated with the *Vekhi* symposium. Kistiakovskii was a neo-idealist, but by retaining a resolutely neo-Kantian, "scientific" approach to ethics, he distanced himself from the metaphysical assumptions of the predominant strain in Russian neo-idealism. His resistance to the idea that idealism necessarily implies a transcendent metaphysical reality, and the corresponding focus on inner, personal aspects of freedom, led him to emphasize the concept of justice, a moral principle that is social by its very nature. In turn, his ethics fed into a progressive politics that focused on embodying the absolute ideal of justice in the more prosaic value of law.

## Scientific-Philosophical Idealism and Social Ethics

The neo-Kantian ethics underpinning Kistiakovskii's *Vekhi* article were the product of a philosophical outlook he had devoted much of the previous decade to refining. Kistiakovskii's intellectual path developed in the broader context of the emergence of neo-idealism in Russia, and shares many characteristics of the better-known transition "from Marxism to idealism" of his fellow *Vekhi* authors Nikolai Berdiaev, Sergei Bulgakov, Semen Frank, and Petr Struve. Kistiakovskii (1868–1920) was from a prominent Ukrainian family in Kyiv, and was exposed from a young age to the study of law (his father was a renowned criminal lawyer) as well as to the Ukrainian national movement.[6] Interested in Marxism at university, Kistiakovskii gradually was drawn to the description of individual freedom and dignity in neo-Kantian thought. His five years of graduate work in Germany, where he studied first in Berlin under the neo-Kantian Georg Simmel and then in Strasbourg under the supervision of Wilhelm Windelband, consolidated his sense that idealism provided a firmer basis for the scientific study of society than Marxism.

Like other neo-idealists, Kistiakovskii drew on Kant's thought to articulate a response to pervasive positivist claims that everything intellectual can be reduced to the natural, and that moral consciousness is simply a derivative of the sensible or psychological.[7] In 1907 he described the following propositions as irrefutable: since ethical problems exist independently of tangible reality and cannot be subordinated to it, individuals benefit from the "incontrovertible ability to evaluate reality independently and autonomously," which presupposes their freedom.[8] Individual freedom has important implications: on the one hand, it indicates the "principle of the intrinsic value of the individual person and the equal value of persons among themselves"; on the other, freedom constitutes the basis of moral behavior: "an individual [is free to] create ideals for him/herself and demand their fulfillment in reality."[9]

Yet what led Kistiakovskii to reject Marxism in favour of neo-Kantianism was also what distinguished him from Berdiaev, Bulgakov, Frank, and Struve. Kistiakovskii found in idealism a rigorous method for the scientific study of society as well as a defense of the autonomous value of the personality and individuals' moral equality. But he also repudiated the reduction of all processes and structures to a single governing principle, a reductionism that led many neo-idealists to formulate metaphysical postulates about a moral world order and religious belief. "All monisms," he wrote in the preface to his dissertation, *Gesellschaft und Einzelwesen: Eine methodologische Studie* (*Society and the Individual: A Methodological Study*, 1899), "both materialist and idealist must necessarily be metaphysical. They construct a final objective for scientific development instead of beginning with their starting point."[10] Kistiakovskii prided himself on a more inductive approach, concerned not so much with the origins (metaphysical or not) of a moral world order, but rather with what the scientific study of moral behavior can reveal about social processes.

In his own work, Kistiakovskii sought to make Kantian principles relevant for social life while maintaining Kant's methodological rigor. He argued that the study of society should be approached as a science (*Naturwissenschaft*) with a correspondingly stringent methodology, and in light of the Kantian categories of understanding. As in the natural sciences, social phenomena should be broken down into isolated instances; only then can one determine the causal relations between them and the general laws that govern social relations.[11] In ethics, Kistiakovskii took as his starting point the idealist notion that the form of "ought" is permanent but its content changes with progress, and that moral principles represent common reference points for all individuals without exception.[12] Yet he was particularly interested in linking Kantian practical reason and broader social processes. In various publications of the period, he explored the ramifications of individual freedom and morality for social well-being.

Kistiakovskii sought to bridge the social and personal implications of Kantian thought by designating the category of justice (*spravedlivost'*), an objective and universally valid category for understanding social processes, even if it only applies to the social world and not the natural one.[13] In his reading, justice, a moral yet inherently social principle, is one of the innate and incontrovertible attributes of the human condition. In particular, individuals' equal moral worth validates universal aspirations for respect and recognition. Kistiakovskii claims that the moral commitment to improving the life of the individual within society has traditionally been expressed in the creation of legal norms.[14] Law, therefore, takes on the historically and scientifically necessary task of expressing social justice: the generalized social feelings and aspirations that encourage us to form legal norms (*pravovye normy*) are also characterized by categorical necessity (*bezuslovnaia neobkhodimost'*).[15]

Kistiakovskii's views of the tasks of neo-idealism were further fleshed out in his contribution to the collection *Problemy idealizma* (*Problems of Idealism*, 1902). His article "'Russkaia sotsiologicheskaia shkola' i kategoriia vozmozhnosti pri reshenii eticheskikh problem" ("The 'Russian Sociological School' and the Category of Possibility in the Solution of Social-Ethical Problems") criticizes the ethical theories of the Russian subjective sociologists (associated with the thought of N. K. Mikhailovskii and P. L. Lavrov) for denying both the objectivity and necessity of values. Rather than attempting to clarify universal moral principles that stem from human conscience, the "subjective sociologists" emphasized the socially determined aspects of human knowledge. Kistiakovskii denounces this ethical relativism, in which phenomena are approached not in light of the Kantian category of "causal necessity" but rather in terms of "possibility."[16] The false assumptions of the subjective sociologists result in a misleading account of the relationship between what is socially desirable and what is historically possible, allowing them to identify the "possible" with the "potentially desirable"—in short, allowing them to justify "anything at all."[17] Kistiakovskii concludes his article with the remark, "We strive for the realization of our ideals not because they are possible, but because our conscious duty imperatively demands it of us and everyone around us."[18] Eventually, he came to associate this "consciousness of duty," which has its own type of objectivity or necessity, with a realm he defined as transcendental-normative.[19] Yet in 1902, Kistiakovskii was already adamant that ethics must remain within the realm of pure science and that ethical problems could be approached (and solved) scientifically, without reliance on metaphysics.

At the time of *Problems of Idealism*'s publication, this position contrasted with those of other neo-idealists, including Berdiaev, Bulgakov, Pavel Novgorodtsev, and Struve. In his contribution, Struve frames the transition from positivism to idealism in terms of a "metaphysical need."[20] The problem of uniting "what is" and "what ought to be," Struve declares, "belongs by its essence to metaphysics."[21] He describes his personal transition from Marxism to idealism as follows: once we acknowledge "the objective nature of ethics as a problem, [we] arrive at a metaphysical postulate of a moral world-order, independent of subjective consciousness."[22] Echoing Struve, Novgorodtsev, the editor of *Problems of Idealism*, confirmed that the objectivity of ethics demonstrates the existence of a trans-empirical level of reality in which the self and morals are grounded: "affirmation of the relative nature of empirical knowledge means for me also the admission of free, creative, uncaused being."[23] Bulgakov as well associates the solutions of the most primordial questions—"questions about our world as a whole, about its substance, about whether it has some meaning or rational end, about whether our life and deeds have any value, about the nature of good and evil, and so on and so forth"—with "the sphere of metaphysical thought."[24]

In 1904, Berdiaev distinguished between two neo-idealist approaches in Russia, based on the above-mentioned distinction regarding metaphysics: "One is decisively metaphysical, and attracted to a religion of the transcendent, the other is ethical-epistemological, drifting in the channel of Kantian transcendental idealism."[25] In 1907, Kistiakovskii further clarified his aspiration to be associated with a separate branch of "ethical-epistemological" idealism in his article "V zashchitu nauchno-filosofskogo idealizma" ("In Defense of Scientific-Philosophical Idealism"). A strict scientific development of the implications of the autonomy of the personality and individuals' equal moral capacities would lead to a proper understanding of the role and significance of moral problems in all their forms and manifestations. The fact that the ethical world is independent from reality and cannot be subordinated to it, Kistiakovskii wrote, need not lead to metaphysics: only a "scientific-philosophical" solution to the problem of ethics can be thoroughly convincing.[26]

Kistiakovskii's reluctance to ground the self and ideals in a higher, ontological reality is, I think, linked with his desire to expand the Kantian idealist project beyond the private, individual sphere.[27] Rather than focusing on the origins of Kant's description of individual autonomy (speculations that led many other neo-idealists in the direction of metaphysics and religion), Kistiakovskii concentrated on the implications of individual moral consciousness for life in society. The affinity he suggests between individual autonomy and individuals' moral worth led him to consider social justice a universal moral imperative. In turn, this dovetails with his interest in the idea (elaborated in more detail in his political writings) that we necessarily pursue self-perfection in a social context, and that therefore our individual goals are inextricably bound up with how we relate to others. Because he refrained from adopting an exclusively personalist approach to freedom and morality, Kistiakovskii was naturally drawn to a conceptual apparatus in which justice, law, and civic consciousness each played a fundamental part.

## From Social Ethics to Socialism

Much recent work has been devoted to the power of idealist philosophy to promote and reinforce liberal values in tsarist Russia.[28] Notwithstanding the concern of turn-of-the-century Russian neo-idealists with regard to separating the tasks of philosophy and politics, idealist claims concerning the autonomy of moral consciousness, individual dignity, and the perfectibility of individuals meshed well with liberal approaches to freedom and selfhood.[29] It is no coincidence, then, that the majority of *Vekhi* contributors were also actively engaged in the reform movement and the emergence of liberalism as a social philosophy.[30] Kistiakovskii was in this case no exception: his early acquaintance with Struve during his student years in Germany spurred his participation in the Liberation Movement, in which Struve played a key organizational role.[31] Together with many other neo-idealist thinkers, Kistiakovskii took part in the meeting in Schaffhausen, Switzerland, in July 1903 that laid the groundwork for the

Russian constitutional movement.[32] Later on, he became a member of the Kadet party and was actively involved in its activities.[33]

Like his neo-idealist colleagues, Kistiakovskii defined the ideal state as a constitutional democracy with legal guarantees of rights. He emphasized that a rule-of-law state is founded on the recognition of a sphere of negative liberty, that is the inviolable, indestructible rights of individuals, and his insistence on this point is what aligns his political theory most obviously with classical liberalism.[34] Moreover, his conviction that the possession of rights and the ability to enjoy them is crucial for another aspect of freedom, namely the striving toward moral self-perfection, fits into a recognizable liberal tradition. The possibilities of self-development in a sphere of freedom can be traced back to John Stuart Mill's *On Liberty*, with its description of "man as a progressive being," and its romantic notion of the "absolute and essential importance of human development in its richest diversity."[35] Thus conceived, the limits law places on state power and the power of one person over another ensure that each person retains the ability to develop and work out his or her individuality to its full potential. "Legal norms [are] rules that regulate people's external conduct," Kistiakovskii wrote, while "their internal conduct [is] governed by ethics," and the former is a condition of the development of the latter (104).

Much of Kistiakovskii's discussion of law and personhood is informed by his Kantian premises. He identified his view of "internal" and "external" freedom (what we might call moral and political freedom, respectively) with Kant's, and, like the German philosopher, developed an account of law as the basis of civil society.[36] Yet Kistiakovskii went further than Kant in assigning law a crucial role in fostering social discipline.[37] In particular, he argued that the external discipline provided by law helps further individual awareness of moral duty: "Legal convictions [provide] internal discipline," and thereby facilitate the development of a civil society founded on respect for the rights of all (107).[38] Thus law, and political institutions generally, play a crucial role in the process whereby individual awareness of duty translates into active citizenship.[39] As we have seen, the gradual expression of value judgments in legal norms slowly engenders a freer, more equal society. In essence, legal and political institutions have the power to instantiate the neo-idealist ideal of community, in which individual desires work toward the realization of the collective good. In this reading, state institutions play a crucial didactic role, one that involves making their citizens aware of their rights and shared interests, as well as allowing them to develop their full potential: the state "ennobles and elevates the individual. It gives [her/him] the opportunity to develop the best part of [her/his] nature and implement ideal goals."[40]

Despite his emphasis on law and "negative freedoms" as the foundations of a viable state, Kistiakovskii went further than most Russian liberals in arguing that a socialist political order was best able to both protect individual rights and promote self-realization.[41] In particular, he stressed that individual and political liberties lose their value unless their affinity with economic and social aims is acknowledged. Negative liberties cannot be authentically realized if one class has a dominant position in relation to another, and similarly cannot be realized unless certain positive measures designed to attenuate social inequality are introduced.[42] These positive measures necessary for individual self-development (the rights Kistiakovskii referred to as socialist [*sotsialisticheskie prava*]) include the right to work, the right to receive care in the event of illness, old age, and inability to work, the right to develop one's capacities fully, the right to a proper education, and the right to a dignified human existence.[43] The willingness of a socialist state to enshrine this last right in law was what led Kistiakovskii to consider this political order superior to a rule-of-law state.[44] "A legal order," he wrote in *Vekhi*, "is a system of relationships whereby all members of a given society possess the greatest freedom of action and self-determination. But a legal order defined in this way cannot be contrasted to a socialist order. Quite the contrary, a more profound understanding of both leads to the conclusion that they are closely related, and that from the juridical point of view a socialist order is simply a more rigorously implemented legal order" (99).

Kistiakovskii perceived the main threat to his Kantian-inspired socialism as stemming from the lack of conviction—particularly widespread in turn-of-the-century Russia—that law has the ability to guarantee personal autonomy and to effect social and political change. Historically, Slavophile thinkers popularized the idea that there was something positive in the absence of legal forms in Russian life, feeling that the dictates of inner consciousness and ethics were sufficient guides for individual self-

## Individual Freedom and Social Justice: B. Kistiakovskii's Defense of the Law

development (95). Following the revolution of 1905, a number of thinkers in their tradition argued that constitutionalism and the rule of law were foreign Western imports and emphasized the superiority of spiritual forces over law as the potential foundation of social life.[45] While Kistiakovskii singled out the intelligentsia's attitude toward the law in his *Vekhi* article for particular scorn, a significant number of Russian intellectuals—including several *Vekhi* contributors—resisted assigning the rule of law primary significance in the constitution of personhood.

As a rule, the other *Vekhi* contributors drew different conclusions than Kistiakovskii from the Kantian postulates concerning individual autonomy and moral equality. We have seen how, for Kistiakovskii, the notion of individuals as ends in themselves remained meaningless unless it was translated into social and economic spheres and guaranteed by law. For many of his colleagues, however, the existence of a metaphysical world order in which absolute values are grounded informed their view of the method for drawing nearer to eternal, spiritual ideals such as truth, holiness, and goodness at the individual level. Thus conceived, spiritual freedom is to be found within individuals, and exists in potential tension with systemic changes at the level of society designed to further political, economic, and social reform. Notwithstanding the different political agendas represented in *Vekhi*, the authors' focus on inner, spiritual freedom made them wary of political doctrines such as socialism, doctrines that they felt placed excessive emphasis on the idea of society. In the words of Leonard Schapiro, the *Vekhi* authors "emphasise again and again the need for moral self-perfection, for repentance, and the incompatibility of materialistic socialism and egalitarianism with the Christian way of life."[46]

Of the *Vekhi* authors, Gershenzon presents perhaps the most extreme example of the rejection of politics.[47] Berdiaev as well repudiated the "bourgeois" qualities of his previous liberalism in favor of a libertarian philosophy which considered relative values such as law and politics oppressive for the human spirit.[48] Yet even among those authors who did believe in the rule of law, Kistiakovskii's presentation of the mutual reinforcement of individual freedom and social justice stands out.[49] Struve's article in *Vekhi*, "Intelligentsiia i revoliutsiia" ("The Intelligentsia and Revolution"), makes explicit his view of the tension between individual freedom and egalitarian aims: "Our concept of education has nothing to do with the 'organization' of the social environment and its pedagogical effect on the personality. This is the 'socialist' idea of education, and it has nothing in common with the idea of education in the religious sense. The latter is completely alien to socialist optimism. It believes not in organization but only in creation, in a person's positive labor on himself, in his inner struggle for the sake of creative tasks" (127).[50] For Struve and others, the idea of humanity had undeniably religious implications and, in their holistic account of reality, personal self-fulfillment took on a metaphysical significance.[51] While law could serve to guarantee the freedom necessary for personal development, the more didactic aspects of socialism, concerned with the value of egalitarianism and the socialization of individuals, posed a risk for individual freedom. Novgorodtsev, a legal scholar close to the *Vekhi* authors, remarked that by believing that socialism was fully compatible with a rule-of-law-state, Kistiakovskii was "confused as to the real goals of socialism."[52]

Kistiakovskii defended his view of a potential harmony between negative liberties and the achievement of social and economic equality by pointing to European history, where he found evidence of the progressive expansion of citizens' rights and freedoms as well as the widening of the spheres of activity of the state and increase of its sovereign rights.[53] In the Russian case, Kistiakovskii advocated the construction of a new society informed by both political and philosophical theory as well as Russia's own resources and traditions. Professing cautious optimism regarding what he refers to as the "intuitive" consciousness of right and non-right in Russian society, he pointed to the forms of redistributive justice in Russia's communal social structures (the agrarian commune and *artel'*, for example) as examples of the externalization of moral rules (104). Russians' legal consciousness could be developed both by formalizing the elements of customary morality and by performing inner soul searching: in order to reconnect with the legal convictions that were part of its spiritual make-up, the intelligentsia "must withdraw into itself and plunge deeply into its own inner world in order to bring fresh air and health to it" (112). Both respect for the law and personal self-development would help promote a legal order and a socialist state.

# Individual Freedom and Social Justice: B. Kistiakovskii's Defense of the Law

## FREEDOM AND JUSTICE

Kistiakovskii's "In Defense of Law" is frequently cited as the "classic" article in the Russian tradition on the need to enlist law in the preservation of liberal values.[54] To be sure, his understanding of the development of personhood within a sphere of negative liberty guaranteed by law taps into one of the most established strands of liberal thinking. Yet Kistiakovskii kept his distance from the individualistic, abstract, rights-centred approach to law often associated with mainstream liberalism. For him, law was the means by which the imperatives of Kantian moral philosophy were embodied in reality, thereby guaranteeing individuals their innate autonomy and moral equality. Because law represents a formal expression of the moral duty of individuals to promote certain common ends, it has both an individual and a social significance: law enables the self-realization of *all*. In this way, a viable legal order is also the foundation of a progressive social politics, in which the state assumes a broad range of tasks, including the guarantee of the right to a dignified existence.

By placing the values of justice and law at the centre of his political and philosophical concerns, Kistiakovskii both overlaps with and stands out from the Christian and humanist traditions to which his *Vekhi* co-authors belonged. The distinctiveness of his legal and social theory is firmly located in his resistance to giving it any religious or metaphysical foundations, and to approaching human nature as part of a holistic explanation of reality. It seems plausible that, because Kistiakovskii rejected a metaphysical approach to freedom as the point of connection between the individual and the absolute, he was especially concerned with linking individual rights to social duties, and to attribute to them their own type of objectivity or validity. In his account, justice is a category as universally valid as freedom; rather than turning inward to find authentic liberation, individuals should embrace their common humanity and externalize shared values in the rule of law.

This conception of positive liberty is what makes Kistiakovskii able to bridge the gap between liberalism and socialism without denying his liberal heritage. And perhaps his blurring of these two political traditions works towards the liberal label after all: as Waldron notes, liberals are liberals because they acknowledge a tension between order and justice, between negative and positive freedom.⁵⁵ Of all the *Vekhi* authors, Kistiakovskii was the most concerned with the question of what valid limits could be placed on individuals in order to enable the self-realization of all. His argument in favor of law thus presents an attempt to reconcile principles that are at the heart of both liberalism and socialism, while acknowledging that because they exist in constant interaction there can never be a final balance between them.

## Notes

[1] Marshall S. Shatz and Judith E. Zimmerman, eds. and trans., *Vekhi/Landmarks: A Collection of Articles about the Russian Intelligentsia* (Armonk, NY: M. E. Sharpe, 1994), xxxvii. Henceforth references to this edition are in parentheses in the text.

[2] See Aileen Kelly, "Which Signposts?," in *Toward Another Shore: Russian Thinkers between Necessity and Chance* (New Haven, CT: Yale University Press, 1998); Leonard Schapiro, "The 'Vekhi' Group and the Mystique of Revolution," in *Russian Studies*, ed. Ellen Dahrendorf (New York: Viking Penguin, 1987); Andrzej Walicki, "Bogdan Kistiakovskii and the Debate about the Intelligentsia," in *Legal Philosophies of Russian Liberalism* (Oxford: Clarendon Press, 1987; Notre Dame: University of Notre Dame Press, 1992).

[3] For a study of Kistiakovskii's thought in the context of the *Vekhi* debate, see Anita Schlüchter, "Zashchita prava B. A. Kistiakovskogo v kontekste filosofskikh diskussii nachala XX v. v Rossii," in *Sbornik "Vekhi" v kontekste russkoi kul'tury*, ed. A. A. Takho-Godi and E. A. Takho-Godi (Moscow: Nauka, 2007), 125–32.

[4] P. Miliukov, "Intelligentsiia i istoricheskaia traditsiia" (1910), in *Vekhi. Intelligentsiia v Rossii: Sborniki statei. 1909–1910gg.* (Moscow: Molodaia gvardiia, 1991), 134–35.

[5] Ia. Vechev, "Pravovye idei v russkoi literature," in *"Vekhi" kak znamenie vremeni* (Moscow: Zveno, 1910), 174.

[6] For example, his uncle, Volodymyr Antonovich, collaborated with one of the leaders of the Ukrainian intellectual movement, Mykhailo Drahomanov, on an important text on Ukrainian ethnography. M. Drahomanov and V. Antonovich, eds., *Istoricheskie pesni malorusskogo naroda* (Kyiv: Tipografiia M. P. Fritsa, 1874–75).

7   With the exception of Izgoev, all *Vekhi* contributors were interested in idealist thought.

8   B. A. Kistiakovskii, "V zashchitu nauchno-filosofskogo idealizma," *Voprosy filosofii i psikhologii* 86 (1907): 57–109, reprinted in slightly modified version in B. A. Kistiakovskii, *Filosofiia i sotsiologiia prava*, ed. Iu. N. Davydov and V. V. Sapov (St. Petersburg: Izdatel'stvo Russkogo Khristianskogo gumanitarnogo instituta, 1998), 116–53 (118).

9   Ibid.

10  B. A. Kistiakovskii, "Vorwort," *Gesellschaft und Einzelwesen: Eine methodologische Studie* (Berlin: O. Liebmann, 1899). Beginning with this insight, Kistiakovskii criticized both organicist and Marxist models of society for considering that one basic substance or principle is the basis of reality and for conflating ethical questions and those of positive science into one comprehensive worldview.

11  See, for example, Kistiakovskii, *Gesellschaft und Einzelwesen*, 42: "Gleich den anderen Wissenschaften aus dieser Kategorie [Kosmologie, Geologie, Biologie] untersucht die Soziologie einen zeitlich ununterbrochenen Entwickelungsprozess in einem abgeschlossenen Kreise von Erscheinungen."

12  Ibid., 155.

13  B. A. Kistiakovskii, "Kategorii neobkhodimosti i spravedlivosti pri issledovanii sotsial'nykh iavlenii," reprinted in B. A. Kistiakovskii, *Sotsial'nye nauki i pravo* (Moscow: M. and S. Sabashnikov, 1916), 176, 186. Justice benefits from "inalienability and universal validity, Allgemeingültigkeit." It is important to note that, for Kistiakovskii, assigning social justice an a priori value did not compromise in any way the attempt to study society in a scientific fashion.

14  Ibid., 187: "The ultimate link in any social process generally and in the social-psychological process in particular is the clarification of some or other moral demand or the definition of some or other legal norm."

15  Ibid., 167. Elsewhere, Kistiakovskii argued that the state can be considered a Kantian subject that makes sense of the world by matching its categories of understanding with those of nature. As Kant taught, "die Synthese nicht in den Dingen selbst oder in den Beziehungen und Verhältnissen zwischen ihnen enthalten, sondern im menschlichen Bewusstsein als deren spontane Funktion begründet ist. Es giebt jedoch noch ein Subjekt, dem die Synthese als von ihm erzeugt und nur ihm angehörig zukommt, und das ist der Staat," *Gesellschaft und Einzelwesen*, 199–200.

16  See Randall A. Poole, ed. and trans., *Problems of Idealism* (New Haven, CT: Yale University Press, 2003), 330.

17  Ibid., 337.

18  Ibid., 352.

19  Kistiakovskii's position is associated with the axiological approach of the Southwest German school of neo-Kantianism. Wilhelm Windelband, the school's initiator and Kistiakovskii's doctoral supervisor, suggested that the problem of the objectivity of values can be solved transcendentally, without resorting to metaphysics. For an

overview, see Hans-Ludwig Ollig, "Neo-Kantianism," in *The Routledge Encyclopedia of Philosophy*, ed. E. Craig (London: Routledge, 1998), 776–92.

20  P. B. Struve, "Toward Characterization of our Philosophical Development," in Poole, *Problems of Idealism*, 154.

21  Ibid., 151.

22  P. B. Struve, "Predislovie," in N. A. Berdiaev, *Sub"ektivizm i individualizm v obshchestvennoi filosofii: Kriticheskii etiud o N. K. Mikhailovskom* (Moscow: Kanon, 1999 [1900]), 51.

23  P. I. Novgorodtsev, "K voprosu o sovremennykh filosofskikh iskaniiakh. (Otvet L. I. Petrazhitskomu)," *Voprosy filosofii i psikhologii* 66 (1903): 138. Berdiaev's intellectual development represents yet another example of the attempt to solve ethical problems using metaphysics. He concluded that the substantiality of the spirit (spiritualism) was the answer to the problem that absolute moral perfection cannot be realized in experience.

24  S. N. Bulgakov, "Basic Problems of the Theory of Progress," in Poole, *Problems of Idealism*, 87.

25  N. A. Berdiaev, "O novom russkom idealizme," *Voprosy filosofii i psikhologii* 75 (1904): 684.

26  B. A. Kistiakovskii, "V zashchitu nauchno-filosofskogo idealizma," *Filosofiia i sotsiologiia prava*, 117. Kistiakovskii maintained that metaphysical idealists had negated Kant's distinction in *The Critique of Pure Reason* between the transcendental forms and the content of knowledge, and thereby broken the link between philosophy and universal truths. The desire of thinkers such as Struve for "wholeness, finality, and completeness" had led them in the direction of metaphysics, and resulted in their mistaken refusal to maintain a separation between the absolute and the relative, between "ought" (*dolzhenstvovanie*) and "is" (*bytie*).

27  One could also note Kistiakovskii's religious differences with other neo-idealists: while most were believers, Kistiakovskii's religion is not known.

28  See, in particular, the masterly work of Randall A. Poole in this regard. See also Patrick Lally Michelson's doctoral dissertation, "'The First and Most Sacred Right:' Religious Freedom and the Liberation of the Russian Nation, 1825–1905" (PhD diss., UW-Madison, 2007), particularly Chapter 5; and Laurent Cauderay's doctoral dissertation, *Die Partei der konstitutionellen Demokraten und das liberale Weltbild von Pavel Ivanovic Novgorodcev* (St. Gallen: D-Druck-Spescha, 2004).

29  Consider, for example, Novgorodtsev's introduction to *Problems of Idealism*, in which he writes: "New forms of [social and political] life now no longer represent the simple demand of expediency, but the categorical imperative of morality, which gives primary importance to the principle of the absolute significance of personhood [*lichnost'*]." "Foreword, Russian Edition," in Poole, *Problems of Idealism*, 83.

30  See Judith Zimmerman, "The Political Views of the *Vekhi* Authors," *Canadian-American Slavic Studies* 10 (1976): 306–27, for an overview of their political activities.

31  The movement was supported by the launch of the émigré journal *Osvobozhdenie* (*Liberation*) in 1902 with Struve as editor and the establishment of *Druz'ia osvobozhdeniia* circles, around which the radical-constitutional movement crystallized. For details, see Shmuel Galai, *The Liberation Movement in Russia 1900-1905* (Cambridge: Cambridge University Press, 1973), and Kornelii Shatsillo, *Russkii liberalizm nakanune revoliutsii, 1905-1907gg: Organizatsiia, programmy, taktika* (Moscow: Nauka, 1985).

32  The conference planned both the establishment of the Union of Liberation and the Union of Zemstvo Constitutionalists.

33  For details, see Susan Heuman, *Kistiakovsky: The Struggle for National and Constitutional Rights in the Last Years of Tsarism* (Cambridge, MA: Harvard University Press, 1998).

34  See, for example, B. A. Kistiakovskii, "Gosudarstvo pravovoe i sotsialisticheskoe," *Voprosy filosofii i psikhologii* 85 (1906): 469-507, reprinted in *Voprosy filosofii* 6 (1990): 141-59 (144).

35  J. S. Mill, Epigraph to *On Liberty* (Harmondsworth: Penguin, 1974); for clarification of the epigraph, see ibid., 120-22.

36  Kant's notion of Right is based on his concept of external freedom. See his *The Metaphysics of Morals*, trans. Mary Gregor (Cambridge: Cambridge University Press, 1991); Paul Guyer, "Kantian Foundations for Liberalism," in his *Kant on Freedom, Law, and Happiness* (Cambridge: Cambridge University Press, 2000); and Peter Benson, "External Freedom According to Kant," *Columbia Law Review* 87 (1987): 559-79.

37  Kant was also extremely interested in the idea of discipline (see, for example, his *Vorlesung über Pädagogik* [1803] in *Schriften zur Ethik und Religionsphilosophie* [Darmstadt: Wissenschaftliche Buchgesellschaft, 1983], 699, where he writes that "Der Mensch kann nur Mensch werden durch Erziehung. Er ist nichts, als was Erziehung aus ihm macht"). Kistiakovskii, however, made the link between discipline and law more explicit, claiming that law "disciplines a person much more than does logic or scientific method or any systematic exercise of the will." Shatz and Zimmerman, *Vekhi/Landmarks*, 91.

38  In her chapter "Combined Underdevelopment: Discipline and Law in Imperial and Soviet Russia," Laura Engelstein contrasts Kistiakovskii's understanding of the role of discipline in a legal order with that of Foucault. See her *Slavophile Empire: Imperial Russia's Illiberal Path* (Ithaca, NY: Cornell University Press, 2009), 13-32.

39  B. A. Kistiakovskii, "Prava cheloveka i grazhdanina," *Voprosy zhizni* 1 (1905): 142.

40  Kistiakovskii, "Gosudarstvo pravovoe i sotsialisticheskoe," 142.

41  Ibid., 155. The numerous points of connection between Kistiakovskii's concept of an ethical socialism and that of German neo-Kantians—particularly Herman Cohen and the Marburg school—are evident but have yet to be fully explored. For an overview of neo-Kantian socialism in Germany see Timothy Keck, "The Marburg School and Ethical Socialism," *The Social Science Journal* 14 (1977): 105-19; Thomas Willey, *Back to Kant: The Revival of Kantianism in German Social and Historical Thought,*

42  Kistiakovskii, "Prava cheloveka i grazhdanina," 121.

43  Ibid., 125. The "right to a dignified existence" was formulated by the Russian philosopher Vladimir Solov'ev as follows: "Everybody should have the means of existence and sufficient physical rest secured to him, and he should also be able to enjoy leisure for the sake of his spiritual development." Cited in Walicki, *Legal Philosophies of Russian Liberalism*, 195. Solov'ev's ideas exerted considerable influence on Kistiakovskii, even though the latter distanced himself from the former's philosophical views as a whole.

44  Kistiakovskii, "Gosudarstvo pravovoe i sotsialisticheskoe," 157: "In a socialist society the right to a dignified human existence will not be merely the realization of social justice, something analogous to charity for the poor, but the fully valid personal right of each citizen and person." For a contemporary account of the legal significance of the right to a dignified existence in a rule-of-law state, see P. I. Novgorodtsev, "Pravo na dostoinoe chelovecheskoe sushchestvovanie" (1905), reprinted in *Obshchestvennye nauki i sovremennost'* 5 (1993): 127–32.

45  The resurgence of religious thought in this period is associated with the work of Nikolai Berdiaev (1874–1948), Aleksandr Bogdanov (1873–1928), Anatolii Lunacharskii (1875–1933), and Dmitrii Merezhkovskii (1865–1941), among others. See G. M. Hamburg and Randall A. Poole, eds., *A History of Russian Philosophy 1830–1930* (Cambridge: Cambridge University Press, 2010), particularly chapters 11 and 13.

46  Schapiro, "The Vekhi Group and the Mystique of Revolution," 83.

47  Gershenzon warned, for example, against "the tyranny of civic activism." Shatz and Zimmerman, *Vekhi/Landmarks*, 68. See also Zimmerman, "Political Views of the Vekhi Authors," 308.

48  Berdiaev called for "not only political liberation but also liberation from the oppressive power of politics," Shatz and Zimmerman, *Vekhi/Landmarks*, 15. On Berdiaev's political views see Poole, *Problems of Idealism*, 77, n. 230.

49  Bulgakov advocated a "Christian socialism," but approached socialism as a means of realizing the metaphysical principle of Christian love for one's fellows. On his political views, see Catherine Evtuhov, *The Cross and the Sickle: Sergei Bulgakov and the Fate of Russian Religious Philosophy* (Ithaca, NY: Cornell University Press, 1997).

50  Cited in Frances Nethercott, "Russian Liberalism and the Philosophy of Law," in Hamburg and Poole, *History of Russian Philosophy*, 260–61.

51  Struve's position in *Vekhi* retains a certain affinity with Kistiakovskii's, due to his liberalism and assertion that an effective state authority is necessary to safeguard liberty. Eventually his theory took the form of a conservatism that emphasized national unity, a strong state, and Russian cultural imperialism. See, for example, "Velikaia Rossiia. Iz razmyshlenii o russkoi revoliutsii," *Russkaia mysl'* 1 (1908): 143–57. Struve and Kistiakovskii also disagreed profoundly on the question of national self-determination, with Kistiakovskii advocating a moderate Ukrainian nationalism.

See B. A. Kistiakovskii, "K voprosu o samostoiatel'noi ukrainskoi kul'ture. Pis'mo v redaktsiiu," *Russkaia mysl'* 32 (1911): 133, 142.

52  Pavel Novgorodtsev, "Ob obshchestvennom ideale," *Voprosy filosofii i psikhologii* (1911-1916), n. 376 in *Filosofskii portal* <http://www.philosophy.ru/library/vehi/ideal.html> [accessed 4 November 2010].

53  In various instances, the reduction of the sphere of individual liberties was compensated for by a marked increase in the participatory rights of individuals. See Kistiakovskii, "Prava cheloveka i grazhdanina" and "Gosudarstvo pravovoe i sotsialisticheskoe." Kistiakovskii strongly criticized both socialists and liberals who held that individual liberties and constitutional governments are necessarily bourgeois or liberal. As support for his theory, he pointed to the behavior of socialist parties in contemporary constitutional states in which state laws are a compromise worked out by different parties, including socialists.

54  See, for example, Poole, "Editor's Introduction," *Problems of Idealism*, 52, and Walicki, *Legal Philosophies of Russian Liberalism*, 13.

55  Jeremy Waldron, "Theoretical Foundations of Liberalism," *Philosophical Quarterly* 37 (1987): 131.

# 6

## Russian Political Theology in an Age of Revolution
*Randall A. Poole*

### I

One of the most important directions in religion today is political theology.[1] It is not a new concept, but it has taken on a new meaning within the past fifty years, so much so that scholars now distinguish between the old and the new political theology.[2] The old goes back to the ancient empires of the Near East, and refers to the use of religion to sanction or legitimate a given political order. Augustine of Hippo, in the *City of God*, criticized the old Roman political theologies and opposed the sacralization of any earthly political order, but his pessimistic conception of human nature, with its emphasis on human depravity and original sin, formed the basis for its own type of old political theology: for him, salvation largely meant salvation from ourselves, by the external action of grace and the church acting as its earthly instrument. Accordingly, Augustine condoned the use of state power against heretics who challenged church dogma and threatened salvation. In general, the old political theology was premised on an external approach to salvation, with external (i.e., political) power being seen as a necessary means to salvation—the salvation of those subject to such power. After Augustine, political theology fell into long disuse as a theoretical concept, though certainly not as a political practice. It was reintroduced into modern discourse by Carl Schmitt in his 1922 essay *Politische Theologie* (*Political Theology*). (Schmitt later served as "crown jurist" of the Third Reich.) Despite some new theoretical content, Schmitt basically perpetuated the old meaning of the term, that is, the subordination or instrumentalization of religion for political purposes, which purposes were, for Schmitt, the only absolute ones.

The new form of political theology was founded in the 1960s and 1970s by a very different German thinker, the Catholic theologian Johann Baptist Metz. It refers not to the ideological legitimization of political power but to the theological analysis, criticism, and justification of politics, society, and history. In Metz's conception, political theology is a "practical fundamental theology" that seeks to ground politics in a theological anthropology and to elaborate a theological or normative framework for political and social praxis.[3] The old political theology was more about politics than theology, and tended to reduce theology to political purposes. The new political theology, by contrast, is first and foremost about theology. It conceives politics in relation to the absolute values and ends of theology, which means re-conceiving politics as the ways human beings work and struggle together in history and society to realize ever more fully their personhood (or, as Metz often puts it, "to become subjects before God"[4]), to build a just society befitting them as persons or subjects, and to take responsibility—as autonomous, self-determining moral subjects or agents—for their salvation. The very idea of God, according to Metz, is an "ineluctably political one," because it expresses an *option*: "opting for a state of affairs in which all people are able to be subjects and ought to become subjects" (76). In this way Metz directly relates the idea of God to the *human* capacity for self-determination, self-realization, and subjecthood. Here is the profound humanism of the new political theology, in stark contrast to the old.

II

In 1999 Rowan Williams published a fine edition of the writings of twentieth-century Russia's most important theologian, Sergei Bulgakov.[5] Williams chose as the subtitle for his book, "Towards a Russian Political Theology," clearly referring to the new political theology.[6] He writes that Bulgakov's thought "could well be read as a systematic attempt to work out the basis on which political action and policy could be seen as philosophically—and, eventually, theologically—legitimate" (7). In this article I shall argue, following Williams's lead, that the Russian religious-philosophical tradition, as represented by Bulgakov and other members of the *Vekhi* group, is both a remarkable anticipation of the new political theology and a trenchant critique of the old.

The Williams collection includes one of Bulgakov's lesser-known texts, "Dusha sotsializma" ("The Soul of Socialism," 1932–33). This essay offers perhaps the best succinct justification of Williams's subtitle. Bulgakov's main themes here are human personhood, human work, and human history. Socialism, in his account, misunderstands all of them. Its anthropology or conception of human nature is based on two doctrines, "sociologism" and "economism," which together make up the impoverished soul of socialism. Sociologism dissolves the individual human person in the social whole and denies its independent reality, freedom, and creativity. Economism debases human work and economic activity. In Marxism it is materialistic and even "zoological" (240). Bulgakov commends instead the sophiological approach to economy that he developed in his 1912 treatise *Filosofiia khoziaistva* (*Philosophy of Economy*),[7] which understands that through free, creative work man humanizes the world and transforms it in his own image. This sophianic work takes place in history, and with this Bulgakov turns to his conception of human history, his most important theme. He advances an activist, humanist understanding of eschatology, one that is strikingly similar to Metz's new political theology some forty years later.

Bulgakov's main burden is to reconcile eschatology, the transcendent fulfillment and end of history, with human responsibility for it within history. History and eschatology have, according to him, been too long separated and set in opposition to each other, the link between them denied. He calls this separation "eschatological transcendentalism," whereby "all earthly illumination is quenched and all earthly values destroyed: all that remains is personal merit and personal sin, with their equivalents of reward or punishment, which each individual receives for himself alone, without any regard to the collective work of humanity in history" (244). Such eschatological transcendentalism leads to historical nihilism: in order for history to have meaning and value, people must believe that they are responsible for it and are working toward its culmination. In this sense, "history has its own *inner* apocalypse, which makes history itself already eschatology fulfilling itself in time"—though the fulfillment remains ultimately transcendent (244). Thus Bulgakov tries to preserve the idea of a transcendent eschaton with an immanent goal of human aspiration.

He links his philosophy of history with a critical "sense of an orientation towards the future, with consciousness of obligatory tasks to be performed and of continuing historical labour" (253). This "orientation towards the future" is a type of utopianism, in the positive sense of the human capacity to imagine the future and to work toward it as an ideal. Bulgakov describes utopia—"an object of social faith, hope and love"—in terms of the biblical definition of faith, "the assurance of things hoped for, the conviction of things not seen" (Heb. 11:1). Utopia, he writes, is "an ideal with a changing content," depending on the specific historical circumstances.[8] In his conception, utopian ideals are the driving force behind historical progress; they take us ever beyond present historical reality and constantly into the future. But such ideals must remain rooted in religious consciousness; otherwise they collapse into the "tired positivism" that is inimical to the very concept of the ideal (248–49).

The supreme ideal is the Kingdom of God. It cannot remain a "purely passively understood prophecy" but must become "an active utopian ideal, a hope"—in short, a human task. "Naturally this symbol in itself is abstract," Bulgakov writes, "but it is constantly being filled out with concrete content, in terms of actual advances or achievements in history, of the summons directed by the future towards the present" (257–58). He contrasts this activist and progressive philosophy of history to "pseudo-eschatologism," which resigns before the eschaton and shuns historical responsibility. He extols the Hebrew (Old Testament) prophetic tradition, with its sweeping utopian vision ("in the positive sense of 'utopian,' of course") and demand for social justice. The New Testament brought a definite shift, as expectations of the imminent end of the world brought about a certain indifference to history, social quietism, and "a peculiar kind of apolitical vision" (254). From this come Bulgakov's efforts to historicize the Apocalypse. He calls hopefully for a *Christian reformism*, inspired by the active utopian ideal of the Kingdom of God.

"The Soul of Socialism" is a landmark essay. In Williams's estimation, it "draws together a remarkable range of Bulgakov's ideas, and displays some of the deepest continuities in his thought" (235). A year later, in his "Social

Teaching in Modern Russian Orthodox Theology," which was delivered as a lecture at the Seabury-Western Theological Seminary in Evanston, Illinois, Bulgakov used a simple but apt term to describe the main direction of his theology and of modern Russian theology as a whole: "Christian humanism." Its distinctiveness, again simply and aptly put, is that "it includes the creativity of man in the means of his salvation" (283). This type of religious humanism, with its faith in the efficacy of human work and progress toward salvation, is also the distinctive feature of the new political theology and of its antecedents and correlates, such as nineteenth-century Kantian liberal theology, the social gospel movement, and liberation theology.

### III

"The Soul of Socialism" was published in German translation in 1977,[9] the same year that Johann Baptist Metz's most important work, *Glaube in Geschichte und Gesellschaft* (*Faith in History and Society: Toward a Practical Fundamental Theology*), appeared.[10] Metz describes his theology as "the struggle for the subject—or, practical fundamental theology as the political theology of the subject" (70). This is a meaningful formulation. First, the term "practical" signals not only Kant's moral philosophy but also the humanist dimension of Marxism, both of which have decisively shaped Metz's thought.[11] Second, Metz's term "subject" indicates his focus on human personhood. He prefers "subject" to emphasize human autonomy, agency, and responsibility, but those qualities can, of course, be emphasized in the term "person" as well, as they were by Bulgakov and other Russian neo-idealist philosophers. Metz has had an abiding preoccupation with theological anthropology; his first major work was *Christliche Anthropozentrik* (*Christian Anthropocentrism*, 1962).[12]

The thesis of *Faith in History and Society* is that people are called to become subjects in the presence of, and through their relationship to, God. This idea has a dual meaning: first, God wants us to be subjects; second, God wants us to be subjects *even* in his presence, that is, he wants us to preserve our autonomy and responsibility in his presence rather than to be overwhelmed by it. As Metz writes, "the relationship to God does not become the expression of a slavish subjection and enervated devotion; it does not humiliate persons as subjects" (71).[13] Human beings can become subjects before God only in history and society. This is necessarily a struggle—Metz refers to the "historical struggle for humanity"—and human beings are subjects most when they struggle to help others become subjects. The implication, Metz stresses, is that people struggle to become subjects in solidarity with each other. The historical struggles for all human beings to be subjects, and by which they become subjects, is the main theme of Metz's political theology.

This theme is an eschatological one. In his 1968 book *Zur Theologie der Welt* (*Theology of the World*),[14] Metz wrote, "The universal existential-anthropological viewpoint in Christian theology depends on the eschatological viewpoint. This is true, because only in the eschatological horizon of hope does the world appear as a reality *coming into being*, whose development and process is handed over to the free action of man."[15] The "eschatological horizon of hope" is a telling expression. It makes clear the humanism of Metz's understanding of eschatology. For him, as for Bulgakov earlier, eschatology stands for human freedom in history. History is the sphere of human freedom, because unlike the natural world, its future is open and undetermined. In his conception of history, especially the notion that history is the coming into being of that which has not yet existed, the *Noch-nicht-gewesene*, Metz drew on the Marxist thinker Ernst Bloch, who for a Marxist was uncharacteristically interested in religion. In the words of one Metz scholar, "the uniquely human capacity, which is the ground of genuinely free activity, is the capacity to envision this *Noch-nicht-gewesene* and orient one's activity by it. For Bloch this is the sensorium for Utopia. The power of utopia is what pulls history forward."[16] Metz himself, in a famous passage, writes of utopia: "The name 'God' stands for the fact that the utopia of all human beings being liberated to become subjects possessed of human dignity is not a pure projection—which is certainly what it would be if there were only utopia and no God" (76).

The "struggle for the subject" is a theme that, given human nature and history, is full of suffering. Suffering in history, the theodicy problem, redemptive eschatology, and the meaning of progress in light of past suffering are all among the main concerns of Metz's new political theology.

They are perennial Russian themes. Metz prefers to call them by the name "Auschwitz,"[17] but Dostoevskii's treatment of them also helped to shape his thought. They are powerfully dealt with in Bulgakov's 1902 essay "Osnovnye problemy teorii progressa" ("Basic Problems of the Theory of Progress").[18] Earlier that year Bulgakov published his famous Dostoevskii essay "Ivan Karamazov kak filosofskii tip" ("Ivan Karamazov as a Philosophical Type").[19] Both Bulgakov and Metz level the same critique against the secular idea of progress, namely that it makes the suffering of past generations the "manure" (in Dostoevsky's expression) for the harmony of future ones.[20] Contrary to its secular conception, they believe that progress needs to be reconceived as eschatology.[21]

## IV

Metz insists on separating his new political theology from the old, Carl Schmitt's in particular, for good reason. In the preface to *Faith in History and Society*, he writes that unlike "the classical 'political theology,' ... the new political theology was never guided by the intention of exalting a politics that was already in force or on the increase anyway, and of simply copying theologically the way it operates" (xi). Other scholars agree. According to the authors of a recent short history of the concept, "The current positive *theological* use of political theology has to be understood as a reinvention of the term."[22]

Schmitt's use of the term was political rather than properly theological. In 1933 Erik Peterson formulated an influential critique of Schmitt, the so-called "Peterson thesis": "Political theology," he wrote, "is not really an element of theology but rather of political thought," and is in truth a political theory of a "particularly heretical nature."[23] Peterson thought it particularly heretical because the political was the only absolute for Schmitt. In 1934, in his preface to the second edition of *Political Theology*, Schmitt wrote that "the political is the total."[24] In that banal sense, Schmitt's idea of politics is "theological" (or "metaphysical"). Banal but dangerous: Schmitt recognized no limits on state power and endorsed the idea of the "total state." For him, "the specific political distinction to which political actions and motives can be reduced is that between friend and enemy," as he put it in his 1927 essay

*Der Begriff des Politischen* (*The Concept of the Political*).²⁵ The sovereign makes the distinction on the basis of nothing but arbitrary, raw power. There is no higher framework of morality or natural law.²⁶

The title chapter of *Political Theology* opens with the following well-known lines: "All significant concepts of the modern theory of the state are secularized theological concepts" (36). After Schmitt, a number of remarkable central European thinkers developed this insight into the powerful concept of "political religions," another variant of political theology. Among these scholars were Schmitt's disillusioned protégé Waldemar Gurian as well as Karl Löwith and Eric Voegelin.²⁷ They saw contemporary totalitarian ideologies as secular forms of millenarianism and eschatology, which purported to offer collective terrestrial salvation by external political means. The link between political religions and the old political theology was their common illiberal, pessimistic view of human nature with their corresponding emphasis on external salvation (whether by church or party-state); this is also what separates them from the basic humanism of the new political theology, with its "faith in history and society"—its faith that human beings can work toward, and must take responsibility for, their salvation. (In contrast to the new political theology, conservative political philosophers such as Voegelin, on the basis of their analysis of political religions, reemphasized the radical distinction between the transcendent divine realm and the immanent realm of human existence in history. Their theological and anthropological presuppositions were rather different than those of thinkers such as Bulgakov and Metz. Bulgakov would have criticized Voegelin for "eschatological transcendentalism.")

V

Here as well, with the idea of political religions, Bulgakov and other Russian idealist philosophers were prescient. Even before the Russian Revolution, they interpreted positivism and socialism as secular religions, whose promise of salvation was based on a claim to knowledge of the laws and teleology of history, unfolding independently of human will but leading inexorably to the promised age.²⁸ As early as 1878 Vladimir Solov'ev wrote, in his *Chteniia o bogochelovechestve* (*Lectures on Godmanhood*), that socialism and positivism were substitutes for "rejected gods."[29] Bulgakov, as we shall see further, developed this approach in a number of his writings, including his essays "Basic Problems of the Theory of Progress" (1902), "Karl Marks kak religioznyi tip" ("Karl Marx as a Religious Type," 1906), and "Geroizm i podvizhnichestvo (Iz razmyshlenii o religioznoi prirode russkoi intelligentsii)" ("Heroism and Asceticism [Reflections on the Religious Nature of the Russian Intelligentsia]," 1909).[30] Pavel Novgorodtsev also took up the theme. His 1917 book *Ob obshchestvennom ideale* (*On the Social Ideal*) includes a long, seminal analysis of Marxism as a pseudo-religion of coerced collective salvation in history.[31]

Perhaps the most influential Russian proponent of the "socialism as religion" theme was Nikolai Berdiaev.[32] He addressed it in several of his pre-revolutionary writings and in his widely read book *Istoki i smysl russkogo kommunizma* (*The Origin of Russian Communism*, 1937), where he depicts the Soviet state as an "inverted theocracy" in which everything assumes the character of orthodoxy or heresy. "The Soviet communist realm," he wrote, "has in its spiritual structure a great likeness to the Muscovite Orthodox Tsardom"—that is, to the old political theology of tsarist Russia.[33] In his account, both the tsarist and communist autocracies were premised on the denial of freedom of conscience, because for them salvation was not a matter of inner self-determination and individual striving but of collective, external determination. The political religions approach remains influential among historians of totalitarianism today.[34]

What made the Russian neo-idealists such early and perceptive critics of twentieth-century political religions, and of the old political theology more generally, was their essential humanism, their belief, as Bulgakov put it, in the idea that human creativity is included in the means of salvation. For them, salvation was not something purely external (again, whether through grace, church, or party-state); rather, it depended on human self-determination and human self-realization, both individually and collectively. This is how the founder of modern Russian theology, Vladimir Solov'ev, understood salvation: the self-realization of humanity's intrinsic divine potential, or of Godmanhood (*bogochelovechestvo*), ultimately culminating in deification (*theosis*).[35] The type of humanism expounded by Solov'ev and his followers is what distinguishes the new political theology from the old, then and now.[36] Solov'ev even coined the term "Christian politics" to champion the consistent application of Christian moral principles to all spheres of human life (public as well as private) in the project of building of the Kingdom of God on earth.[37]

## VI

This is the tradition, broadly, of *Vekhi* and of its predecessor volume, *Problemy idealizma* (*Problems of Idealism*, 1902). These two landmarks of the Russian Silver Age can be read, first, as powerful implicit critiques of the old political theology of the Russian autocracy; second, as critiques of the political religions of the Russian intelligentsia; and third, as classic texts of the new Russian political theology. *Problems of Idealism* is probably the most significant text in the first and third respects, while *Vekhi* focuses more on the salvific ethos of the intelligentsia and its belief in revolution as salvation.

*Problems of Idealism* was conceived at the beginning of the Russian Liberation Movement as a defense of freedom of conscience and its importance in liberalism.[38] The volume's architects, Petr Struve and Novgorodtsev, understood freedom of conscience in two interrelated senses. First, it meant the inalienable right of the individual to determine his or her religious beliefs, a right not recognized by the tsarist government until the October Manifesto of 1905. Second, they understood freedom of conscience in the even more fundamental, Kantian sense as inner autonomy or self-determination according to freely recognized absolute ideals, which capacity Kant held to be the essence of morality, human dignity, and personhood itself. In their understanding of the dual meaning of the concept, Struve and Novgorodtsev followed the two greatest philosophers of nineteenth-century Russia, Boris Chicherin and Solov'ev.[39]

In its Kantian, liberal defense of self-determination and freedom of conscience, *Problems of Idealism* was a powerful critique of the old political theology in autocratic Russia. Almost fifty years ago Michael Cherniavsky described this political theology in his book *Tsar and People*, basing his comparative historical framework in part on Ernst Kantorowicz's classic work *The King's Two Bodies: A Study in Mediaeval Political Theology*. "The myth of the pious ruler drew its strength from the eschatology of Russian political theory," Cherniavsky wrote. "From its beginning around 1500, the Third Rome, Moscow, was the chief fact in the economy of salvation. Upon the orthodoxy and personal piety of the tsar depended the salvation of Russia as a state and thereby the salvation of the whole world."[40] Beginning with Peter the Great, the ideology of Russian autocracy was partly Westernized and secularized, but after the assassination of Alexander II in 1881 there was a return to a religious image of monarchy. Richard Wortman has shown that Alexander III and Nicholas II both projected "scenarios of power," showing themselves as pious Muscovite rulers who believed themselves responsible for their people's salvation.[41]

Against the old political theology of autocracy, *Problems of Idealism* advanced a new political theology of personhood (cf. Metz's "political theology of the subject"). Following Kant, Russian neo-idealists defined the essence of personhood as the human capacity for morality or for self-determination—which capacity was the anthropological basis, in turn, for freedom of conscience as a natural right. Recognition of the absolute value of personhood and of its natural rights was incompatible in principle with autocracy, and stipulated, for nearly all the volume's contributors, the constitutional limitation of political power and the rule of law. At the beginning of Russia's long age of revolution, the new political theology of personhood thus took the practical form of liberalism. This was a type of liberalism that, in contrast to prevailing positivist conceptions (e.g., in Pavel Miliukov), was self-consciously idealist and, for most of its proponents, ultimately theological. While the old Russian political theology made religion an instrument of state power, the new political theology made it a limit of such power.

## VII

The clearest formulations of the new Russian political theology of personhood can be found in what are surely the two best essays in *Problems of Idealism*: Bulgakov's "Basic Problems of the Theory of Progress" and Novgorodtsev's "Nravstvennyi idealizm v filosofii prava" ("Ethical Idealism in the Philosophy of Law").[42] Bulgakov's essay, which opens the volume, is one of his finest. He begins with a straightforward refutation of positivism: the idea or category of the absolute (whether in the form of morality, religion, or metaphysics) cannot be derived from the positive data of sense experience (the positivist criterion of reality), and yet it is intrinsic to human consciousness and cannot be eradicated.[43] Positivist attempts to deny the presence of the absolute lead only to unconscious metaphysics, since it then enters into thought as "contraband"—it is smuggled in under the guise of scientific, historical, social or other concepts, rather than being openly recognized and justified before reason (96, 107). The result is that the relative and absolute are distorted and conflated with each other.

Bulgakov's brilliant case study of this type of conflation is the positivist theory of progress (under which he includes both Comte's and Marx's version). "For humanity today," he writes, "the significance of the theory of progress is that it is called upon to replace lost metaphysics and religion, or, more precisely, it takes the form of both" (91). In Bulgakov's analysis, the theory of progress turns out to be a pseudo-scientific, secular "religion of progress" because it posits a perfect human future—a future like nothing that could be positively extrapolated from the human past, but rather one that has overcome worldly contingency as such and achieved absolute perfection (97). Here the theory of progress betrays its debt to traditional religious faith in salvation, which obviously is not "positively given" but reflects human longing for the absolute. At the same time, "it wants to inspire confidence in the certain advent of this future kingdom through science," with its alleged ability to identify the laws of history and predict their necessary course (92–93). Thus the theory of progress not only promises a perfect (though utterly unverifiable) future, but also promises that it will come about "externally" through historical necessity, not through human self-determination and striving toward a transcendent, absolute ideal.

Bulgakov holds that ultimately the theory of progress fails because positivism cannot contend with the problem of personhood, which must rest on idealist and theistic foundations. The very concept of the person contradicts positivism's premises: it is a moral and metaphysical concept derived from the will's self-determination by the law or ideal of "ought"—which is of "supra-empirical origin" (105–06). "Ought," as a moral demand directed toward the will, is an ideal of action; it can autonomously motivate us, despite the claims of historical determinism to the contrary.

With this Bulgakov turns directly to the theme that would still occupy him thirty years later in "The Soul of Socialism"—the philosophy of history, or, as he prefers to call it here, the metaphysics of history, defined as "the discovery of the absolute in the relative" (108). "And if the absolute is a synonym for freedom," he writes, "then the metaphysics of history is the revelation of the principle of freedom in history, its victory over mechanical causation" (109). The metaphysics of history is not some abstract, impersonal schema: the absolute is recognized by *persons* in conscience as the moral law or categorical imperative, and persons are responsible for progressively realizing the absolute in history.

The moral law, according to Bulgakov, commands us "to want *progress*. From this point of view, progress is not a law of historical development," as it is in positivism, "but a moral task." In this idealist conception of it, progress requires inner strength. By contrast, "the positivist theory of progress flatters our weakness; it … promises the external support of the natural course of things to that which does not find adequate support internally. In this, the positivist theory of progress represents its own type of eschatology, invoked to inspire warriors and sustain religious faith in the final triumph of the good. But another type of eschatology is needed before man can find in it real support for his moral activity" (111). This second type of eschatology is the one that Bulgakov will later call "Christian humanist." It respects human autonomy and dignity and recognizes that salvation or the Kingdom of God can be achieved only through what Kant called the kingdom of ends, which Bulgakov mentions in this context (112).[44] "This is the true theory of progress—is any other needed!" Remarkably, Bulgakov has shown that this theory of progress (idealist and theistic) is consistently humanist, while the purported humanism of positivism (materialist and atheistic) actually shares the external, misanthropic approach to salvation of the old political theology.

## VIII

Novgorodtsev, in his chapter of *Problems of Idealism*, is less explicitly theological than Bulgakov and more political. His topic is the revival of natural law, and he is more specifically interested than Bulgakov in developing neo-idealism as a theory of liberalism. Nonetheless, there is broad and impressive philosophical agreement between them. Their common themes are personhood, progress, the critique of positivism, and the philosophy of history. Both philosophers are centrally concerned with rescuing history from positivist determinism and restoring it as the sphere of human freedom.

For Novgorodtsev, the openness of history defines the very task and importance of natural law. According to him, natural law reveals a constant human need: "This is the need consciously to go forward to meet the future, as yet undetermined and still within our power, as it were, and to realize in it our ideal strivings and hopes" (283). In another formulation, he writes: "Human thought has this quality of living not only in the present, but also in the future, of bringing to the future its ideals and aspirations, and in this sense natural-law constructions are an integral property of our spirit and testimony to its higher calling" (284). Decades later, Bulgakov would write of the "sense of an orientation toward the future," and Metz, in terms even more strikingly similar than those of Novgorodtsev, of the *Noch-nicht-gewesene*. Like them, Novgorodtsev relates the openness of history to the power of utopian ideals to shape the future (292).

The task of natural law, as he understands it, is to order ideal paths of progressive development. Natural law is about the future of law, and in this its guide is the moral ideal of "what ought to be" (286). The ideal nature of natural law (in contrast to positive law) makes it "a norm and principle of personhood" (303). This is an intricate connection: the moral ideals that take juridical form in natural law are the same ideals that make self-determination and therefore personhood itself possible. The idea of personhood was the center of Novgorodtsev's philosophical liberalism, from its treatment of ethics to its treatments of law and public policy. His ultimate social ideal was the "kingdom of ends." "The self-determining person," he writes, "is the ground on which is raised the supreme good of the moral world, 'the kingdom of persons as ends,' in Kant's expression"

(305). This "supreme good" is not only a moral one but also a broadly theological one; it fits squarely within the humanist tradition of the new political theology.

Novgorodtsev stressed the core liberal implication of his theory of natural law and of personhood: the inalienable rights of the person solidly mark the limits of state power. In the modern conception, he writes, "natural law is the expression of the autonomous, absolute significance of the person, a significance that must belong to it in any political system. In this respect natural law is more than a demand for better legislation: it represents the protest of the person against state absolutism, reminding us of the unconditional moral basis that is the only proper foundation of society and the state" (313). Novgorodtsev thought that the absolute value of the person held theistic implications—though in his *Problems of Idealism* essay he points only rather obliquely to a "higher metaphysical synthesis" (314)—so that his idealist liberal theory incorporates, indeed rests on, a political theology of personhood. In tsarist Russia, where in 1902 Konstantin Pobedonostsev had starkly symbolized the old political theology of autocracy for over twenty years, his ideas must have resonated.

## IX

The great divide between *Problems of Idealism* and *Vekhi* was, of course, the 1905 revolution. The *Vekhi* authors blamed the radical intelligentsia and its positivist ideology for the failure of Russian liberalism in the aftermath of the revolution. *Vekhi*'s criticisms of the intelligentsia drew heavily on *Problems of Idealism*, in particular on its critique of positivism, its defense of neo-idealism, and its political theology of personhood. Five of the seven *Vekhi* authors had contributed to *Problems of Idealism*. The initiative for the earlier volume came from Struve, who was also an important inspiration behind *Vekhi*.

Struve's *Vekhi* essay, "Intelligentsiia i revoliutsiia" ("The Intelligentsia and Revolution"), highlights a central philosophical continuity between the two volumes, namely their religious-philosophical humanism. In 1905 Struve wrote an essay with Semen Frank on the philosophy of culture. In it they offer a defense of humanism, "by which we mean idealism, a faith in absolute values which is linked with faith in humanity and its creative tasks on earth."[45] Pipes suggests that their philosophy of culture drew directly on Kant's idea of human self-determination.[46] "Culture is creativity," they wrote, "the conscious and deliberate transformation of reality in accord with ideals."[47] In *Vekhi*, Struve applies this same idealistic humanism to religion, writing that any true religion must rest on "faith in the redemptive power and decisive importance of personal creation, or, more truly, of personal achievement [*podvig*] in conformity with the will of God."[48] Like Lev Tolstoi, whom he greatly admired, Struve believed that "the Kingdom of God is within you," and that "for the religious mind, therefore, nothing can be more important than a person's individual self-perfection" (120). The atheistic intelligentsia, in denying the existence of ideals (as its positivism stipulated), also denied itself the possibility of self-determination and self-perfection, of personal achievement and responsibility.

Despite his impressive formulation of important tenets of Russian religious humanism, Struve seems to reject the "political religions" approach to understanding the intelligentsia's psychology, as advanced by Solov'ev, Bulgakov, and others. His argument refuting this approach is that the alleged religiosity of the intelligentsia's outlook and ideologies was purely a matter of form, not content (119, 124)—but this is precisely what proponents of the "political religions" approach claim. He also rejected the idea of "Christian politics."[49]

## X

In his famous *Vekhi* essay, "Heroism and Asceticism: Reflections on the Religious Nature of the Russian Intelligentsia," Bulgakov applies his 1902 critique of the theory of progress more specifically to the Russian intelligentsia. The essay is a classic analysis of the intelligentsia's political religions. According to Bulgakov, an eschatological "striving for the salvation of mankind" was the intelligentsia's distinctive trait (21). In this external sense of the concept, eschatology captures the "heroism" that was central to the intelligentsia's "entire spiritual economy" (27). "The very essence of heroism," he writes, "presupposes a passive object of activity, the nation or humanity that is being saved" (29). The intelligentsia's heroic mission was the "external salvation of mankind"; it rested on "an arrogant view of the people as an object of salvation" (39, 43). The intelligentsia's salvific heroism can be traced, Bulgakov argues, to the circumstances under which the radical intelligentsia emerged—to persecution, suffering, and a type of martyrdom under the tsarist police regime. He leaves unstated an interesting paradox: the Russian autocracy's political theology thus gave rise to the intelligentsia's political religions, both premised on the idea that they were responsible for the people's salvation.

The external means by which the intelligentsia hoped to bring about the salvation of Russia and humanity was the positivist theory of progress that Bulgakov analyzed in *Problems of Idealism*. The intelligentsia took the atheism of this theory as an article of faith. In *Vekhi*, Bulgakov is highly critical of "humanism," here associating the term (despite the real humanism of his own religious philosophy) with atheism and with the intelligentsia's faith in humanity's natural goodness, corrupted only by irrational or defective external circumstances (such as religion). In the "humanistic intelligentsia church" (22), salvation is understood as something that will take place automatically through rational, necessary historical development toward socialism. With this belief, "the intelligentsia lives in an atmosphere of expectation, awaiting the social miracle, the universal cataclysm—it lives in an eschatological frame of mind" (30).

Bulgakov draws a crucial implication from this "heroic" type of eschatology: it cannot provide a real basis for personhood because (to put it somewhat more philosophically than he does) it cannot sustain an ideal, which is a necessary condition for self-determination and self-development. Self-determination (which capacity defines personhood) requires an ideal by which the will can be self-determining. "Heroic" eschatology collapses the ideal to an immanent process of automatic historical development. Salvation happens through historical necessity, not through the self-determination of persons acting in history according to higher, ultimately transcendent ideals. These considerations explain why "the absence of a correct doctrine of personhood is the intelligentsia's chief weakness" (34).

Bulgakov commends not heroism but asceticism (*podvizhnichestvo*) or humility, which he considers to be self-discipline, self-mastery, and self-perfection—in short, as the religious cultivation of personhood. In its recognition of "absolute norms and values," asceticism can serve "as an inner structuring of personhood" (36, 38). It is oriented not toward external salvation, the salvation of others, but toward inner salvation, the salvation of oneself. In opposition to Enlightenment notions of the natural goodness and (mechanical) perfection of human nature, asceticism requires recognition of sin and a willingness to struggle against it, first of all within oneself. Despite the inward emphasis of asceticism, Bulgakov argues that the same ideals that make self-determination (and personhood) possible are also culturally and economically creative. Ascetic obedience to one's duty can be applied to any field of "external" activity: the discipline of obedience or "worldly asceticism" cultivates the self through work in the world (39). Though some of Bulgakov's language sounds archaic and though he opposes the term "humanism," his overall case for asceticism directly anticipates his later "Christian humanism." Asceticism is already the new political theology, while heroism is the old.

## XI

In his *Vekhi* essay, "Etika nigilizma: k kharakteristike nravstvennogo mirovozzreniia russkoi intelligentsii" ("The Ethic of Nihilism: A Characterization of the Russian Intelligentsia's Moral Outlook"), Frank does use the term "humanism" to describe his philosophical worldview, one which bears striking similarities not only to Struve's but also to Bulgakov's. All three thinkers were concerned perhaps above all with the role of objective ideals and of absolute values in the constitution of personhood and in cultural creativity. The concepts of "heroism" and "nihilism" are different ways of describing the loss of the ideal and the consequences of that loss. Bulgakov emphasizes the consequences for personhood, while Frank emphasizes those for culture. Frank defines nihilism as "the denial or non-recognition of absolute (objective) values" (136). The inevitable result is the creation of false absolutes or idols, the ascribing of absolute significance to one or another relative value or interest (fanaticism). A good example, according to Frank, is the intelligentsia's "moralism," by which everything is judged according to the utilitarian criterion (and false absolute) of the people's happiness. The intelligentsia's faith in the inevitability of universal human happiness drove its "theory of progress," its "religion of socialism," and its belief that it held the key to "the universal salvation of mankind" (142–43). On this point Frank's analysis is very similar to Bulgakov's.

In *Vekhi* Frank devotes relatively more attention than Bulgakov to outlining an idealist theory of culture. Clearly drawing on his 1905 essay written with Struve, he defines culture as "the aggregate of objective values which have been actualized by the historical development of social life" (139, italics removed). In this conception, culture is the ever-richer embodiment and ever-greater realization of ideals and values in life through human self-determination and aspiration. This is the real dynamic of progress. It also underlies what Frank calls the "metaphysical concept of wealth" and the intelligentsia's aversion to it: "*The Russian intelligentsia does not love wealth.* In the first place, it does not value spiritual wealth, or culture—the ideal force and creative activity of the human spirit that impels it to master and humanize the world and to enrich its life with the values of science, art, religion and ethics. What is more remarkable, it even extends this dislike to material wealth, instinctively recognizing its symbolic connection with the general idea of culture" (148). It is clear that the nihilist (and more broadly positivist) denial of the ideal—without which there is no object for the will's self-determination and nothing to be embodied in life—cannot but impoverish personhood, culture, and economy. By contrast, recognition of the ideal—which ultimately meant metaphysical theism for Bulgakov, Frank, Novgorodtsev, and Struve—enriches them. This is why Frank concludes his article (and *Vekhi*) with the following call: "We must pass from unproductive, anti-cultural *nihilistic moralism* to creative, culturally constructive *religious humanism*" (155).

## XII

Within ten years and in the midst of another Russian revolution, *Iz glubiny* (*Out of the Depths*, 1918) appeared as a type of sequel to *Problems of Idealism* and *Vekhi*.[50] Some of its essays also pursue the critique of the old political theology, whether in the form of the old regime's appropriation of religion for its own ideological purposes or in the form of the intelligentsia's political religions. By 1918, however, the Great War had radically undermined the premises of liberal theology all over Europe. In 1919 Karl Barth published his *Der Römerbrief* (*Epistle to the Romans*), one of the most important theological works of the twentieth century. "The book's adversary was every form of liberal theological humanism," in Mark Lilla's recent estimation.[51] The point of all its rich metaphors and images "is to show that there can never be a fusion of the human and divine, either in morality or in history," Lilla writes. "The God of *Romans* could not be further from ... Kant's moral lawgiver."[52] Barth and other Weimar-era theologians cast Kant aside and returned to Augustine, with his emphasis on original sin—the depravity of human nature—and our need for total redemption. Their new theology was the old one of the need for salvation from ourselves.

The theological currents of Weimar Germany may seem worlds apart from the Marxism-Leninism of the Soviet Union during this era. In fact, they shared certain presuppositions about human nature. Lenin created Leninism when he pronounced the proletariat incapable of developing its own true class consciousness—which was the precondition of communism. As a result, such consciousness would have to be brought to the proletariat from without, by a vanguard party of professional revolutionaries. In other words, the workers had to be saved from themselves, and the external agent of salvation was the party. Lenin's contempt for humanity had much in common with Carl Schmitt's. It is for good reason that one recent scholar writes that Schmitt's thought suggests "a kind of right-wing Leninism."[53]

Europe's theological despair, in its various forms, began to lift with the post-1945 appearance of the new political theology, representing as it does a revival of earlier traditions of liberal theological humanism. Its further development has much to gain from the rich resources of Russia's tradition of religious-philosophical humanism.

## Notes

1. See two recent large anthologies: Peter Scott and William T. Cavanaugh, eds., *The Blackwell Companion to Political Theology* (Malden, MA: Blackwell, 2004); and Hent de Vries and Lawrence E. Sullivan, eds., *Political Theologies: Public Religions in a Post-Secular World* (New York: Fordham University Press, 2006).

2. Bernd Wacker and Jürgen Manemann, "Political Theology: History of a Concept," in *Missing God? Cultural Amnesia and Political Theology*, ed. John K. Downey, Jürgen Manemann, and Steven T. Ostovich (Berlin: LIT Verlag, 2006), 170–81.

3. Johann Baptist Metz, *Faith in History and Society: Toward a Practical Fundamental Theology*, ed. and trans. J. Matthew Ashley (New York: Crossroad, 2007).

4. Ibid., 70–84.

5. Rowan Williams, ed. and intro., *Sergii Bulgakov: Towards a Russian Political Theology* (Edinburgh: T&T Clark, 1999). Further references to this edition are given in parentheses in the text.

6. He does not refer to Metz, but suggests that Bulgakov's political theology might be compared to the ideas of John Milbank, Stanley Hauerwas, and William Stringfellow (Ibid., 233–34).

7. Sergei Bulgakov, *Philosophy of Economy: The World as Household*, ed. and trans. Catherine Evtuhov (New Haven, CT: Yale University Press, 2000).

8. This definition recalls Rudolf Stammler's formula for natural law. On Bulgakov and Stammler, see Catherine Evtuhov, *The Cross and the Sickle: Sergei Bulgakov and the Fate of Russian Religious Philosophy, 1890-1920* (Ithaca, NY: Cornell University Press, 1997), 30, 40.

9. Sergej N. Bulgakov, *Sozialismus in Christentum?*, ed. and trans. Hans Jürgen Ruppert (Göttingen: Vandenhoeck und Ruprecht, 1977).

10. J. B. Metz, *Glaube in Geschichte und Gesellschaft: Studien zu einer praktischen Fundamentaltheologie* (Mainz: Matthias-Grünewald Verlag, 1977). Parenthetical page references are to the English edition cited in note 3 above.

11. For a fine, succinct presentation of Metz's thought, with due attention to the Kantian and Marxian influences, see J. Matthew Ashley, "Johann Baptist Metz," in Scott and Cavanaugh, *Blackwell Companion to Political Theology*, 241–55.

12. J. B. Metz, *Christliche Anthropozentrik: Über die Denkform des Thomas von Aquin* (Munich: Kösel-Verlag, 1962).

13. Eighty years earlier Vladimir Solov'ev, Russia's greatest religious philosopher, wrote, "In man's consciousness and his freedom is the inner possibility for each human being to stand in an independent relation to God." Vladimir Solovyov, *The Justification of the Good: An Essay on Moral Philosophy*, trans. Nathalie A. Duddington, ed. and annotated Boris Jakim (Grand Rapids, MI: William B. Eerdmans Publishing Company, 2005), 149–50.

14. J. B. Metz, *Zur Theologie der Welt* (Mainz: Matthias-Grünewald, 1968); *Theology of the World*, trans. William Glen-Doepel (New York: Herder, 1969). The title echoes

that of Lev Zander's massive study of Bulgakov' *God and World*: L. A. Zander, *Bog i mir (Mirosozertsanie ottsa Sergiia Bulgakova)*, 2 vols. (Paris: YMCA Press, 1948). In this connection see Paul Valliere, "A Russian Cosmodicy: Sergei Bulgakov's Religious Philosophy," in *A History of Russian Philosophy, 1830–1930: Faith, Reason, and the Defense of Human Dignity*, ed. G. M. Hamburg and Randall A. Poole (Cambridge: Cambridge University Press, 2010), 171–89.

15  As quoted by J. Matthew Ashley in his introduction to Metz, *Faith in History and Society*, 15.

16  Ibid.

17  Steven T. Ostovich, "Melancholy History," in Downey, Manemann, and Ostovich, *Missing God?*, 93–101.

18  S. N. Bulgakov, "Basic Problems of the Theory of Progress," in *Problems of Idealism: Essays in Russian Social Philosophy*, trans. and ed. Randall A. Poole (New Haven, CT: Yale University Press, 2003), 85–123.

19  S. N. Bulgakov, "Ivan Karamazov kak filosofskii tip," *Voprosy filosofii i psikhologii* 13: 1, kn. 61 (1902): 826–63; reprinted in his collection *Ot marksizma k idealizmu. Sbornik statei (1896-1903)* (St. Petersburg: Tovarishchestvo "Obshchestvennaia literatura", 1903), 83–112.

20  Bulgakov, "Basic Problems of the Theory of Progress," 103; Metz, *Faith in History and Society*, 123.

21  See Metz, *Faith in History and Society*, ch. 6, "The Future Seen from the Memory of Suffering: On the Dialectic of Progress," 97–113. I do not know if Metz had any familiarity with Bulgakov. He need not have in order to have arrived at a similar theology: they both drew on a common philosophical and theological discourse that awaited fuller development into powerful humanist theologies. That both thinkers pursued this direction attests to their caliber as theologians, not necessarily to Bulgakov's influence on Metz.

22  Wacker and Manemann, "Political Theology: History of a Concept," 177.

23  Ibid., 174.

24  Carl Schmitt, *Political Theology: Four Chapters on the Concept of Sovereignty*, trans. George Schwab, foreword Tracy B. Strong (Chicago: University of Chicago Press, 2005), 2.

25  Carl Schmitt, *The Concept of the Political*, trans. George Schwab (Chicago: University of Chicago Press, 1996), 26.

26  For three excellent accounts of Schmitt's illiberalism and its dangers, see Michael Hollerich, "Carl Schmitt," in Scott and Cavanaugh, *Blackwell Companion to Political Theology*, 107–22; Mark Lilla, *The Reckless Mind: Intellectuals in Politics* (New York: New York Review Books, 2001), 47–76; and Steven Ostovich, "Carl Schmitt, Political Theology, and Eschatology," *KronoScope* 7 (2007): 49–66.

27  Among their many relevant works, see W. Gurian, *Bolshevism: An Introduction to Soviet Communism* (Notre Dame: University of Notre Dame Press, 1953), the first chapter of which is "Bolshevism as Social and Political Religion"; K. Löwith, *Meaning in*

*History* (Chicago: University of Chicago Press, 1949); and E. Voegelin, *Die politischen Religionen* (Vienna: Bermann-Fischer, 1938).

28  See Andrzej Walicki, "Russian Philosophers of the Silver Age as Critics of Marxism," in *Russian Thought after Communism: The Recovery of a Philosophical Heritage*, ed. James P. Scanlan (Armonk, NY: M. E. Sharpe, 1994), 81–103.

29  V. S. Solovyov, *Lectures on Divine Humanity*, trans. Boris Jakim (Hudson, NY: Lindisfarne Press, 1995), 2.

30  All three are available in English: the first in *Problems of Idealism* (see note 18 above); the second as *Karl Marx as a Religious Type: His Relation to the Religion of Anthropotheism of L. Feuerbach*, trans. Luba Barna, ed. Virgil R. Lang, and intro. Donald W. Treadgold (Belmont, MA: Nordland, 1979); and the third in *Vekhi/Landmarks: A Collection of Articles about the Russian Intelligentsia*, trans. and ed. Marshall S. Shatz and Judith E. Zimmerman (Armonk, NY: M. E. Sharpe, 1994), 17–49, as well as in the Williams collection.

31  P. I. Novgorodtsev, *Ob obshchestvennom ideale*, ed. A. V. Sobolev (Moscow: Pressa, 1991). This work was first serialized in *Voprosy filosofii i psikhologii*, 1911–16, and then published in three editions (Moscow, 1917; Kiev, 1918; and Berlin, 1921). For analysis see Andrzej Walicki, *Legal Philosophies of Russian Liberalism* (Oxford: Clarendon Press, 1987), 328–41.

32  An English translation of his 1906 essay "Socialism as Religion" can be found in Bernice Glatzer Rosenthal and Martha Bohachevsky-Chomiak, eds., *A Revolution of the Spirit: Crisis of Value in Russia, 1890-1924* (New York: Fordham University Press, 1990), 107–33.

33  Nicolas Berdyaev, *The Origin of Russian Communism*, trans. R. M. French (Ann Arbor: University of Michigan Press, 1960), 143–44.

34  For example, Stephen Kotkin, *Magnetic Mountain: Stalinism as a Civilization* (Berkeley: University of California Press, 1995), esp. chapter 7. Kotkin calls his own comparison of the Stalinist party-state to a theocracy a "revisionist characterization." See also Igal Halfin, *From Darkness to Light: Class, Consciousness, and Salvation in Revolutionary Russia* (Pittsburgh: University of Pittsburgh Press, 2000). For a recent powerful interpretation of Nazism as a political religion, see Michael Burleigh, *The Third Reich: A New History* (New York: Hill and Wang, 2000).

35  Richard F. Gustafson, "Soloviev's Doctrine of Salvation," in *Russian Religious Thought*, ed. Judith Deutsch Kornblatt and Richard F. Gustafson (Madison: University of Wisconsin Press, 1996), 31–48; and Randall A. Poole, "Solov'ëv's Philosophical Anthropology: Autonomy, Dignity, Perfectibility," in Hamburg and Poole, *History of Russian Philosophy*, 131–49.

36  The humanism of modern Russian theology has been treated most recently and systematically by Paul Valliere, *Modern Russian Theology: Bukharev, Soloviev, Bulgakov: Orthodox Theology in a New Key* (Grand Rapids, MI: William B. Eerdmans Publishing Company, 2000).

37  See Greg Gaut, "Christian Politics: Vladimir Solovyov's Social Gospel Theology," *Modern Greek Studies Yearbook* 10/11 (1994–95): 653–74; and Gaut, "Can a Christian

38  Be a Nationalist? Vladimir Solov'ev's Critique of Nationalism," *Slavic Review* 57, no. 1 (Spring 1998): 77–94.

38  For the project's conception and history, see my introduction to *Problems of Idealism*.

39  See my essay "Religious Toleration, Freedom of Conscience, and Russian Liberalism," *Kritika: Explorations in Russian and Eurasian History* 13, no. 3 (Summer 2012): 611–34.

40  Michael Cherniavsky, *Tsar and People: A Historical Study of Russian National and Social Myths* (New Haven, CT: Yale University Press, 1961), 71. Isabel de Madariaga agrees. In her recent study *Ivan the Terrible* (New Haven, CT: Yale University Press, 2005), she writes that "fundamental to Ivan's conception of his role as Tsar was his responsibility for the eternal salvation of his people" (378).

41  Richard S. Wortman, *Scenarios of Power: Myth and Ceremony in Russian Monarchy*, vol. 2 (Princeton: Princeton University Press, 2000), ch. 7.

42  Berdiaev's essay "Eticheskaia problema v svete filosofskogo idealizma" ("The Ethical Problem in the Light of Philosophical Idealism") is also directly relevant, but beyond the scope of this article.

43  Poole, *Problems of Idealism*, 85–89. Subsequent parenthetical pages references are to this edition.

44  In *Justification of the Good*, Solov'ev explicitly argues that the Kingdom of God can be achieved only through the kingdom of ends (149–50). Bulgakov could hardly have had higher regard for Solov'ev, writing that his "philosophy is so far the last word in world philosophical thought, its highest synthesis" (116).

45  P. B. Struve and S. L. Frank, "Ocherki filosofii kul'tury," pt. 1, "Chto takoe kul'tura?," *Poliarnaia zvezda* no. 2 (1905): 115. As quoted and cited in Aileen M. Kelly, "Which Signposts?," in her *Toward Another Shore: Russian Thinkers between Necessity and Chance* (New Haven, CT: Yale University Press, 1998), 175. In this essay Kelly contrasts the humanism of Struve and Frank to what she understands as the illiberal religious and national messianism of Berdiaev and Bulgakov. I think Bulgakov's position is more complicated.

46  Richard Pipes, *Struve: Liberal on the Right, 1905-1944* (Cambridge, MA: Harvard University Press, 1980), 85–86.

47  P. B. Struve and S. L. Frank, "Ocherki filosofii kul'tury," pt. 2, "Kul'tura i lichnost'," *Poliarnaia zvezda* no. 3 (1905): 174–75. As quoted and cited in Pipes, 86.

48  Shatz and Zimmerman, *Vekhi/Landmarks*, 119. Subsequent parenthetical page references to *Vekhi* are to this edition.

49  Pipes, *Struve*, 99.

50  *Out of the Depths (De Profundis): A Collection of Articles on the Russian Revolution*, trans. and ed. William F. Woehrlin (Irvine, CA: Charles Schlacks, 1986).

51  Mark Lilla, *The Stillborn God: Religion, Politics, and the Modern West* (New York: Alfred A. Knopf, 2007), 261.

52  Ibid., 263.

53  Tracy B. Strong, "Foreword" to Schmitt, *Political Theology*, xxviii.

# Part III

# *Vekhi* and the RUSSIAN INTELLECTUAL TRADITION

7

# CHAADAEV AND *VEKHI*
Robin Aizlewood

Anyone choosing the original landmark critique of the state of intellectual affairs in Russia in the nineteenth century would most likely identify it as Petr Chaadaev's *Lettres philosophiques/Filosoficheskie pis'ma* (*Philosophical Letters*, 1828–30), and in particular the "First Letter," written some 80 years before *Vekhi*.[1] In the "First Letter" Chaadaev describes Russia as a lacuna in the "intellectual order" (330); Russia lacks historical consciousness and does not participate in the "wondrous connection of human ideas in the succession of generations" (323). This leads Chaadaev to the direst of conclusions: "We belong to those [peoples] which do not as it were form a component part of the human race and exist only to teach a great lesson to the world" (326). The contemporary reception of both *Vekhi* and Chaadaev's "First Letter," when it was eventually published due to a censor's error in 1836, has marked them as "scandals."[2] In both cases the intemperate nature of contemporary responses was not without a certain provocation, and in this respect, while none of the *Vekhi* authors pull their punches, Mikhail Gershenzon—the original instigator and compiler of the *Vekhi* collection, as well as the publisher of Chaadaev's *Philosophical Letters* at the same time—may in particular be thought to have taken on the mantle of what Chaadaev called his "exaggeration" and Viazemskii called his "splendid and masterly satire."[3]

The publication history of Chaadaev's work was marked by severe disruption, at the time and subsequently (disruption in the case of *Vekhi* took place only subsequently). Yet *Vekhi* and Chaadaev come together in the period 1904–09, through the republication of Chaadaev's work made possible at long last in 1905 (though the *Philosophical Letters* in its entirety still remained unpublished), and especially, of course, through Gershenzon, who was at the center of this republication, as he was of *Vekhi*. He began work on Chaadaev in 1904, publishing him in *Voprosy filosofii i psikhologii* (*Questions of Philosophy and Psychology*) in 1906 and again as an appendix to his own 1908 study *P. Ia. Chaadaev. Zhizn' i myshlenie* (*P. Ia. Chaadaev: Life and Thought*).[4] The supposition that Chaadaev has a presence which informs the *Vekhi* project, first of all in Gershenzon but to a greater or lesser extent throughout, can be taken, I would suggest, as granted.[5] There may be archival material of interest here, although there is no mention of Chaadaev in the "Commentary" to the 1991 edition of *Vekhi*, which traces in some detail the background formation of the project, or in the letters from the participants to Gershenzon published in *Minuvshee* (*The Past*), also in 1991.[6] He is, however, prominently there in Gershenzon's "Preface," in the final paragraph: "Our warnings are not new: all of our most profound thinkers, from Chaadaev to Solov'ev and Tolstoi, said the same things again and again."[7]

Indeed, the connection in Gershenzon's thinking between Chaadaev and *Vekhi* is clearly apparent from the opening sentences of the "Preface" to his 1908 book, in which he exposes the widespread "misconception" of what Chaadaev stands for:

> A lot has been written about Chaadaev and his name is familiar to almost every educated Russian; but it is only now that we are learning how to go about understanding his thought. For various reasons, in part of a general kind, in part personal, his name has become the preserve of legend: despite being someone who was an unambiguous critic of all that our vanguard intelligentsia held most dear about itself—its exclusively positivist orientation and its revolutionary politics—he was enlisted in the synod of Russian liberalism as one of the glorious figures of our liberation movement. This misconception began already in his own lifetime...[8]

In the second paragraph, Gershenzon goes on to speak of the "eternal truth" to be found in Chaadaev concerning "that internal freedom, for which external and hence political freedom is only the footstool," and of Chaadaev's focus on the "highest tasks of the spirit."[9] Consider the following sentence from the "Preface" to *Vekhi*: "Their [the authors'] common platform is a recognition of the theoretical and practical primacy of spiritual life over the external forms of community. They mean by this that the individual's inner life is the sole creative force of human existence, and that this inner life, not the self-sufficient principles of the political realm, constitutes the only solid basis on which a society can be built" (xxxvii). The fourth and final paragraph of Gershenzon's "Preface" to his book on Chaadaev begins with the question, "Is now the time to remind Russian society of Chaadaev? I think it is—indeed more so than ever." The reason for this is not so much Chaadaev's particular opinions, such as his "negative attitude to revolutions," but the "general spirit of his teaching": "Through the entirety of his thought he tells us that the political life of peoples, directed towards temporary and material aims, in reality is only realizing in part an eternal moral idea, i.e., that any social cause is in essence no less religious than the ardent prayer of the believer. He tells us the following about the life of society: enter in, and God is here: but he adds: and remember that God is here and that you serve *Him*."[10]

All in all, then, this "Preface" of 1908 reads like something of a blueprint for *Vekhi*, and it is apparent that Chaadaev, through Gershenzon, has served as a catalyst in its conception. It is a curious turn of events that this is a reprise of his role in stimulating philosophical enquiry and intellectual debate in his own time, which was memorably described by Herzen as having the awakening effect of a "shot ringing out in the dark of night."[11] At the same time it is one of the paradoxes of Chaadaev that, despite this role, his philosophical project itself is in a way a "failure" in its immediate context. Or, to put it another way, its impact lay less in its content, which was not taken up, than in its meta-content, its formulation of key questions and problematics, including the very problem of philosophy; and in longer perspective, as in *Vekhi*, Chaadaev's project has an enduring resonance through the nineteenth and early twentieth centuries, with reverberations thereafter.[12]

Thus, in exploring the presence of Chaadaev in *Vekhi*, I do not mean only to assert a direct influence, although in the case of Gershenzon there clearly is one. The aim of my study is to trace continuities and tropes, as well as genealogies, in Russian intellectual history. In this respect, parallels—whether they are typological similarities, common themes, or direct affinities—between Chaadaev and *Vekhi* provide an interesting perspective on some of the overarching problematics in the tradition of Russian philosophical thought, as well as on the individual thinkers concerned. In addition, approaching *Vekhi* through the prism of Chaadaev, and vice versa, can pose questions for how we conceptualize that tradition. In what follows I will concentrate on two main lines of enquiry: first, an analysis of how we may juxtapose or transpose the framework of the Chaadaevan critique to *Vekhi*; and second, an exploration of the conception of the person in both Chaadaev and *Vekhi* that illuminates tensions and divergences as well as continuities in Russian thought. A key aspect of Chaadaev's resonance in Russian culture, which comes to the fore in the second part of my study and its conclusion, lies precisely in the Chaadaevan image, championed by Gershenzon, of the person of moral intellect.

I

Typically, the transposition of Chaadaev's framework to *Vekhi* involves a shift in the object/address of the critique from Russia/Russians as a whole in Chaadaev to the intelligentsia in particular in *Vekhi*. However, such a shift immediately begs the question—pertinently asked in contemporary responses to *Vekhi*—of whether and how the contributors to *Vekhi* may themselves display at least some of the characteristics they criticize in the intelligentsia. In the same way, the response to Chaadaev of the Slavophiles and others—including Dostoevskii—was to shift the address of his critique from Russia/Russians in general to the small part of society that was the alienated, westernized elite (which on a rather partial, limited understanding could include Chaadaev himself and which, with appropriate qualification, may offer a closer parallel to the object of the *Vekhi* critique).[13] In this connection, by way of a prelude, it is worth briefly noting a couple of distinctive tropes in Russian culture which receive a protean formulation in Chaadaev and have lost none of their currency in the *Vekhi* critique. Two such tropes are the alienation of Russians/the intelligentsia, and the juvenility of Russians/the intelligentsia. In Chaadaev, these two features are in effect aspects of the lack of historical consciousness and lack of continuity of ideas among Russians, which will be considered in greater detail below. This is why Russia has never progressed beyond its youth (324–25) and why "we are as it were alien to ourselves" (326). The juvenility of Russia and/

or of the intelligentsia had acquired considerable cultural baggage by the time of *Vekhi*, where it concentrated around the image of the "student" (in Sergei Bulgakov, Semen Frank, and Aleksandr Izgoev's contributions, for example). The same applies even more, of course, to alienation—from the incorporation of Hegelian (and later Marxian) ideas, on the one hand, to the Dostoevskian notion of the educated elite's alienation from the Russian "soil," on the other. A variation on Hegelian/Marxian alienation may be found in Petr Struve's central diagnosis of the intelligentsia's "alienation" or "dissociation" (*otschchepenstvo*) from state and religion (118), while a reiteration of Dostoevskii's motif is found in Bulgakov's and Gershenzon's essays (27, 52), identically worded in the original as being "torn from the soil" (an echo of this may conceivably be seen in Struve as well).[14]

The central question in the transposition of Chaadaev's critique to *Vekhi* concerns not these tropes, important as they are, but the intelligentsia's "attitude to philosophy," as highlighted by Nikolai Berdiaev in the opening sentence of the collection's opening essay (1). At the outset, it is worth reiterating the fundamental ground that Chaadaev and *Vekhi* have in common: the insistence throughout *Vekhi* by all the contributors on absolute values, on consciousness, and on the link between the absolute and consciousness is in essence fully shared—and equally emphasized—by Chaadaev. That said, for the most part the Chaadaev-*Vekhi* intertext can be traced more especially through Berdiaev, Bulgakov, Frank, and Gershenzon, with the latter—as has already been demonstrated—taken as something of a special case. Gershenzon, as we shall see throughout, may indeed be interpreted in certain respects (though not wholly and solely) as not only reproducing but even ventriloquizing the Chaadaevan critique. Nor is it surprising that the main connections are otherwise to be explored through Berdiaev, Bulgakov, and Frank, since it is these three thinkers who primarily occupy the same religious-philosophical disciplinary territory as Chaadaev.

There are three main, closely related Chaadaevan themes that can be traced in the critique of the intelligentsia's "attitude to philosophy" in *Vekhi*: these are the truth, philosophical culture, and the borrowing of ideas. At the centre of Chaadaev's philosophy lies the idea that the truth resides in the unity and historical continuity of thought in human,

Christian consciousness, that "wondrous connection of human ideas in the succession of generations" (323), as he calls it. Russia, however, lies "as it were outside time" (323) and has not contributed "a single thought to the mass of human ideas" (330). In rhetorical affirmation, the "First Letter" plays out continuous variations on the theme, such as, for example, in the following passage:

> As we move forwards in time, our past experience disappears without return. This is the natural consequence of a culture which is entirely borrowed and imitative. We have absolutely no internal development, no natural progress; former ideas are swept away by new ones because the latter do not arise out of the former, they just appear from nowhere. We only take in ideas that are completely ready-made, therefore those ineradicable traces which are laid down in the mind through the consecutive development of thought, and which create intellectual strength, do not leave furrows in our consciousness. (326)

Alongside the lack of continuity of ideas, therefore, comes a weak philosophical culture, the absence of rigorous method or "consecutive [logical] development" (*posledovatel'noe razvitie*) in the process of thinking. The same point, lamenting both the "blind, superficial, very often senseless borrowing" of ideas and the corresponding lack of "some kind of stability and rigor [*posledovatel'nost'*] in the mind, some kind of logic" is reiterated a page later (327–28). Throughout the *Philosophical Letters*, Chaadaev's essential point of reference is the higher, absolute truth—*istina*—of Providence. Indeed, while he changes to a more optimistic assessment of Russia's future in the "Apology of a Madman" (a shift already apparent in letters written in 1833–35), he still proceeds from an assertion of the primacy of "love for the truth" over "love for one's country," "fine thing" though that may be (523): "The way to heaven is via the truth [*istina*], not via one's country," he states, and then adds: "It's true [*pravda*] that we Russians have always been little interested in what's true [*istinno*] and what's false" (523–24).

So let us now move on to the critique of the intelligentsia's "attitude to philosophy" in *Vekhi*, concentrated as it is—just as it is in Chaadaev—around the priority of truth as an absolute value, the need for a strong philosophical culture and rigor in the exposition of thought, and the borrowing and continuity of ideas. The affinities with Chaadaev will become readily apparent, and indeed it may be assumed that the essays of Berdiaev, Bulgakov, and Frank (as well as Gershenzon) are at least to some extent directly or indirectly informed by Chaadaev's thought. A reasonable supposition would be that the affinity is more direct in the case of Berdiaev than in those of Bulgakov and Frank: in the paragraph in which Berdiaev introduces his account of "original Russian philosophy" and the "philosophical content" of Russian literature, the first person he mentions is Chaadaev, followed by Solov'ev, Dostoevskii, and Tolstoi (12). Neither Bulgakov nor Frank foregrounds Chaadaev in this way.

The title of Berdiaev's essay, "Filosofskaia istina i intelligentskaia pravda" ("Philosophical Verity and Intelligentsia Truth"), draws on the distinction in Russian between higher truth (*istina*) and truth as justice (*pravda*) and so, as one might expect, the priority of truth—*istina*—is a major theme of his essay. In a formulation that echoes Chaadaev's as noted above, he notes that "the intelligentsia does not care whether Mach's theory of knowledge, to take one example, is true or false," and laments a "feeble awareness of the unconditional value of the truth" (4–5). He goes on to emphasize, again echoing Chaadaev—this time, I would say, explicitly—that "love for egalitarian justice, for social good, for the people's welfare, paralyzed love for the truth and almost destroyed any interest in truth" (6). Chaadaev's love for one's country has here mutated into a populist love for the people. The theme of truth—"love for the truth" as an "absolute value" (6), "love of objective, ecumenical truth" (7), the intelligentsia as "unreceptive to objective truth" (12), "humility before the truth" (15) and so on—continues through the rest of his essay. As a corollary, there is the related theme of philosophical thinking. At the outset, Berdiaev laments a "very low level of philosophical culture" and a "temperament" and "values" antipathetic to philosophy (1); he comments that "our intelligentsia was always interested in questions of a philosophical nature, though not in their philosophical formulation" (3). He notes a "weak appreciation of intellectual life as an autonomous value" (7), indifference to a scientific, scholarly approach (20), "hostility to philosophical endeavor" (14; in the original, "hostility to the philosophical work of thought").[15] He finds this weakness in the new mysticism (which Berdiaev identifies with Ivanov, Merezhkovskii, and Rozanov) as much as in the thought of the radical intelligentsia, and calls for such mysticism, with its "dionysian principle," to combine with the "apollonian principle of philosophy" (14–15). Bearing in mind Berdiaev's later self-confessed or even self-proclaimed antipathy to systematic exposition,[16] it is interesting to find such a strand in his critique, but also to note that it is couched in the rather general terms of "philosophical culture" and "apollonian principle." Indeed, compared with the attention to methodological rigor in some subsequent contributions, particularly those of Bogdan Kistiakovskii and Frank, Berdiaev's essay is easier on itself in this respect.

While Gershenzon, Bulgakov, and Frank all take up the themes of the intelligentsia's indifference to the truth and lack of philosophical culture, there are some interesting differences of emphasis. In Gershenzon, for example, the theme of the truth is presented in terms very close to those of Chaadaev: it is described as the "one and indivisible Divine truth" which "out of the millennia of its life experience mankind is slowly assembling" (53); he talks of "mankind's universal consciousness" (53) and of "suprapersonal ideas" (55), and of the "content of thought-truth" directing the will (58). It is this understanding of the truth that can redirect the crippled consciousness of the individual *intelligent*; the corollary need for rigorous philosophical thinking is nowhere stated, although it may perhaps be inferred. Bulgakov's main theme is the intelligentsia's attitude to religion, but to this he adds their "suspicious attitude toward philosophy" (22). It is interesting that Bulgakov, whose thought at this time was turning more to the theme of history, is the one author to stress the breaking of "intellectual" and "historical" "continuity" in Russia (25, 26)—echoing Chaadaev—which manifests itself in the intelligentsia's "historical impatience" instead of the proper "feeling of connection with and gratitude to the past" (39). Frank, whose topic is the intelligentsia's nihilistic moralism, adopts an approach that seeks to clarify the "foundations of the prevailing ideas in morality and religious philosophy" of this outlook (154). He notes that the intelligentsia's mind-set has no place for "ideals of truth, beauty and Divinity," "theoretical, aesthetic and religious values," and "theoretical, scientific truth, rigorous and pure knowledge for its own sake" (133). When he states that "perhaps the most remarkable trait of the recent Russian social movement ... is its *lack of philosophical reflection and understanding*" (154;

in the original, perhaps more precisely, "how poorly thought through and articulated it is in philosophical terms [*ego filosofskaia neprodumannost' i nedogovorennost'*]"),[17] Frank shows himself to be the author who most keenly feels the need for rigorous philosophical thinking, some 80 years after Chaadaev.

The third "Chaadaevan" theme covered by all four authors is the problem of the superficial borrowing of European ideas, and on this they all write in similarly eloquent and pained terms. Gershenzon is dismayed that the periodization of Russian thought is not defined by its own "internal development" but by the dominance of "one or another foreign doctrine." He decries the fact that "our collective consciousness failed to work out its own life values," that it did not have its "own national evolution of thought," but "simply seized on what Western thought had created for itself" until a "gift" that was "new and better" came along; on the other hand, "we did not value the truth that *our* best minds—Chaadaev, the Slavophiles, Dostoevskii—had attained" (59). Compared with Chaadaev, there is more emphasis on the distortion that marks such borrowing. Berdiaev spends several pages on the topic (7–12), covering, for example, positivism, Marxism, and empiriocriticism before ending on the "especially sad fate" of Nietzsche (11), which leads him to exclaim: "Poor Nietzsche, and poor Russian thought!" (12) Neo-Kantianism, on the other hand, suffered less distortion, and he commends the way that an interest in Kant and Fichte, for example, has "raised our philosophical level" (10). Bearing in mind the broadly or more narrowly Kantian framework to which the *Vekhi* authors have subscribed or do subscribe, there is a touch of self-approbation here—Berdiaev is never shy in this respect. In similar terms, Bulgakov writes that the intelligentsia "did not go beyond external appropriation" of Western ideas, and Frank's penultimate paragraph (already quoted from above) offers an extended critique linking the absence of "independent intellectual activity" to the "philosophical mindlessness" that comes from superficial borrowing (154). It is notable too that all four writers, like Chaadaev before them, present European thought and culture, for all its competing trends, as, in Bulgakov's words, an "organic whole" (25).

The continuities with Chaadaev that we have seen are, I would suggest, striking in both range and depth; and they are important—whether as influence, affinity or typological similarity—for our understanding of the larger narrative of Russian intellectual history as well as the particular places of Chaadaev and *Vekhi* in that narrative. It is significant for a reading of *Vekhi* that Chaadaev is not located in the distant intellectual background—as is more or less the case for other Russian thinkers from before the 1860s—but, through the publication of his work in the few years leading up to *Vekhi*, is present in the synchronic foreground, less prominently than Dostoevskii and Solov'ev, for sure, but there all the same. To this must be added his role, via Gershenzon, as a catalyst in the very conception of the collection, and his highlighted presence in the text. One might even interpret the state of affairs 80 years on as worse than that described by Chaadaev. Certainly it seems more than likely that, with Chaadaev's work newly republished, a recognition by the *Vekhi* authors that they were repeating his words about the borrowing of ideas—and about attitudes to truth and to philosophy—can only have heightened the sense of dismay in their critique of the intelligentsia.

## II

Having explored the convergence of *Vekhi* and Chaadaev, I would now like to turn to the conception of the person, a thematic field in which the picture that emerges is more complex (and where, as noted earlier, the image of the Chaadaevan persona has a striking—and contested—resonance). Russian thought has often been characterized as being especially concerned with the person, for example in Zen'kovskii's formulation that it is "anthropocentric,"[18] and recent scholarly attention and analysis have continued to advance the investigation of this aspect of Russian philosophy.[19]

I will begin by bringing another of the iconic texts of nineteenth-century Russian culture into the frame, namely Dostoevskii's 1880 "Pushkin Speech" (delivered on the occasion of the unveiling of the monument to Pushkin in Moscow). Dostoevskii has an overtly influential presence in *Vekhi*, especially in the first three essays, those of Berdiaev, Bulgakov, and Gershenzon. Dostoevskii's exploration of mangodhood and Godmanhood, his portrayal of intelligentsia types in Raskol'nikov, Verkhovenskii, Stavrogin, Ivan Karamazov, et al., his call for personal moral responsibility and repentance—all this has a weight informing *Vekhi* which for Berdiaev, Bulgakov, and Gershenzon, at any rate, would be hard to exaggerate. Dostoevskii clearly informs Frank's searching analysis of the intelligentsia's atheism and moral nihilism too (and, covering a whole range of themes from the intelligentsia's mores to the Russian state, one might also construct a dialogue between Dostoevskii and Izgoev, Kistiakovskii and Struve).

Dostoevskii's "Pushkin Speech" distills a portrait of the intellectual type—proud, rootless, destructive but truth-seeking—from the presentations of Pushkin's characters Aleko and Onegin as initial archetypes of the "superfluous man." Bulgakov in fact twice draws on the "Speech" in support of his critique of the intelligentsia, first to quote Dostoevskii's rewording of Pushkin on the need for the proud intellectual to "humble" himself (35) and then to refer to the rootless "wanderer" type identified by Dostoevskii in Pushkin's heroes (43). However, while Chaadaev, as we have seen, has been lined up by Gershenzon and Berdiaev on the side of the *Vekhi* critique (and so far we can say the same, at least implicitly, for the other authors), the Dostoevskian perspective places him on the other side. This is because the figure of Chaadaev is for Dostoevskii none other than the epitome of the "European Russian," the proud intellectual "torn from his native soil,"[20] which is exactly how Bulgakov and Gershenzon, following Dostoevskii, describe the intelligentsia, as we have seen. Chaadaev is indeed one of the sources of the "superfluous man," in the particular case of Pushkin's Onegin (referred to in the novel as "a second Chaadaev") and more generally, though this does not of course mean that Dostoevskii's interpretation of Chaadaev is the only valid one. That said, while the interpretation may be contested or qualified, it is not a wholesale mis-representation. Certainly, in respect to pride and humility as integral to such conceptions of the person, Chaadaev is a key figure, both in his own construction of his persona based on aristocratic pride of the intellect and in the image of him that is projected in Russian culture.[21]

The presence of Chaadaev in *Vekhi* is thus a problematic one, notwithstanding Gershenzon's wished-for triumvirate of "*our* best minds—Chaadaev, the Slavophiles, Dostoevskii" (59). It serves as a prism through which to illuminate not only complexities and competing lines in the intellectual origins or genealogy of *Vekhi*, but also underlying tensions and differences in the *Vekhi* authors' conception of the person. This may be gathered around the notion of the primacy of the "inner life of the person," but, as has been apparent from the moment of the collection's appearance, if one looks past the (more or less) converged application of this notion when directed against a common object of critique, divergences emerge, whether fully-fledged, implied, or nascent. At a more general level, this has to do with what happens when an attempt to elaborate and embed in Russian culture a liberal, Kantian conception of the autonomous value of the person—one of the primary goals of *Vekhi*'s predecessor volume, *Problemy idealizma* (*Problems of Idealism*, 1902)[22]—interacts with the rich and diverse thinking on the person that had developed in Russian thought over the nineteenth century and continues into the twentieth century. The Russian scholar Nikolai Plotnikov has recently observed that Russian thought concentrates on the conception of a person's distinctive individuality, much more so than on the Kantian autonomous person or the Lockean conception of the person as locus of an identity formed over time.[23] Such an overarching framework nevertheless has to accommodate radical conceptual differences between, say, an Orthodox-oriented conception of the integral person in Slavophilism, on the one hand, and Herzen's free individual, with an admixture of the autonomous person, on the other. Similarly, any account of the person in Russian thought will focus, for example, on the concept of Godmanhood as elaborated upon by Solov'ev and a pleiad of subsequent thinkers; it will dwell on the interpersonal, dialogic conceptualization of the person in Bakhtin; and it will engage with Dostoevskii's extraordinary exploration of consciousness and the subject, intuitively informed by philosophy from Descartes onwards, in texts such as *Zapiski iz podpol'ia* (*Notes from Underground*, 1863) and "Son smeshnogo cheloveka" ("Dream of a Ridiculous Man," 1876).[24]

Within this large area of thought, the image or conception of the person that can be associated with Chaadaev—the aristocratic person of the intellect, of religious/moral intellect—has a specific interest, in the contexts of *Vekhi*, Chaadaev's own thought, and Russian philosophy and culture more generally.[25] There are two related but distinct phenomena here: the image of Chaadaev as a person or persona, in—as already noted—his own construction and its construction in Russian culture; and the conception of the person in Chaadaev's thought. The emphasis in Chaadaev's thought is on the supra-personal and the role of special thinkers or prophets as being the media between Providence and people; he also stresses the subordination of the individual person to the higher principle. His concern for continuity of ideas and memory, at the supra-personal level and also in terms of the individual, has implications for a conception of the person in Lockean terms of identity. It is interesting to consider how one aspect of the "failure" of Chaadaev's philosophical project may be the marginalization of this conception in the Russian tradition.

While Chaadaev's persona may have aspired to the role of special thinker, it is important to recognize that this vision is grounded in a conception of the individual life of the person, down to the level of daily routine. In this connection, the concentration in *Vekhi* on the individual life of the person also draws us retrospectively to consider the generally ignored passages in the *Philosophical Letters* in which Chaadaev talks to his female addressee about just this. The passages concerned are found in the first three Letters: in the opening of the "First Letter" (320–23), at some length in the "Second Letter" (339–46) and, very briefly, at the start of the "Third Letter" (355–56) (of these only the first was known and published at the time of *Vekhi*). Moreover, these passages, though more or less discrete, contain sentences that articulate key aspects of his overall philosophy, and the passages as a whole reinforce—and are reinforced by—that overall philosophy. They constitute a particular, but not extraneous, strand in the work.

In comparing the conception of the person in Chaadaev and *Vekhi*, the reader finds generic Christian elements as well as more specific points of similarity and contrast. Among the former we could note, for example, Chaadaev's assertion of the need for the "regeneration of our being" following Christ at the start of the "Third Letter" (356) and his prescription in the "Sixth Letter" for both peoples and individuals to "know and evaluate themselves" and to "repent of their mistakes" as a condition for moving forward on the path of perfection (398). Regeneration and repentance are much more insistent themes in *Vekhi*, perhaps because of the sheer urgency of the national predicament and/or because of the intelligentsia's nihilistic and destructive atheism, whereas atheism is not a concern in Chaadaev's work, and the trauma of the Decembrist uprising is deep but not threatening in the same way as the revolution of 1905 and its aftermath were. More specific parallels—though they are still at a level of generality of idea—could include, for example, Struve's statement that "human goodness depends entirely on a person's free submission to a higher principle" (120), where the emphasis on "free submission" echoes Chaadaev, or Gershenzon's closely Chaadaevan formulation of the personality's active transformation in accordance with "supra-personal ideas" (55).

A more revealing and multi-faceted comparison can be explored through the question of the inner and the external life of the person (which was invoked at the outset when juxtaposing Gershenzon's "Prefaces" to his book on Chaadaev and to *Vekhi*). Chaadaev, in keeping with his overall philosophy, does not see the individual person as isolated from society and the outside world. Indeed, his ultimate aim is the transformation of society. However, in a formulation that accords with *Vekhi*, the first obligation placed on the individual is to live a "concentrated life dedicated in the main to a religious mind-set and exercises," although, as this "First Letter" notes with a gendered interpretation, "what could be more natural for a woman?" (322). In a further parallel with *Vekhi*, the dire state of Russian society makes attention to this bedrock of the individual life even more crucial. Chaadaev elaborates on this at some length in the "Second Letter" (which was not known to the *Vekhi* authors). Here he moves from the need to redirect ourselves at the level of ideas to the arrangement of the individual's personal life, including attention to the aesthetic aspect of oneself, one's home and one's surroundings (339–41); indeed, Chaadaev was legendary in his attention to dress. Overall he calls for a "methodical way of life" since, in words that directly echo what he has to say about intellectual life, "we all lack the spirit of order and method" (341). Such a way of life—implicitly aristocratic, as far as Chaadaev was concerned—extends to the organization of the day, in which it is important to set aside hours for oneself to allow for "concentrated thought"; all this will train one in resisting the allure of superficial "novelties" (345), a strain familiar from his general critique that appears in *Vekhi* as well. It is interesting to compare this with what Gershenzon and Bulgakov have to say about the intelligentsia's life-style, which they link to an overall inadequacy in attention to the person. Bulgakov notes the absence of "disciplined work habits and a measured pace of life" and a "lack of principle in everyday life" (20, 33). Gershenzon, twice using a notion favored, as we have seen, in Chaadaev—*(ne)posledovatel'nost'*: "logic/order/consistency" or the lack thereof (52, 58)[26]—decries this lifestyle as "horrible," and comments that for the intelligentsia "a day passes, and who knows why; today things are one way, and tomorrow a sudden fancy will turn everything upside down" (58). Izgoev's whole article carries a critique of the intelligentsia's woeful lifestyle, in the family, sexual, educational, and professional arenas. In this context, it is striking to return to Chaadaev's conclusion that "the closer you tie the external with the internal, the visible with the invisible, the more pleasant will the path ahead of you be," which is followed in the same paragraph by a familiar rhetorical lament, culminating: "Has anyone here dedicated themselves to the cult of the truth?" (345–46). As for Chaadaev himself, not only does this conception of the life of the individual fit directly into his overall philosophy, as already noted, but the biographical evidence also suggests that he practised what he preached in the performance of his persona.[27] Moreover, his model is grounded in both religious practice and everyday reality in a way that demonstrates its superiority to the fragile basis of calls in *Vekhi* for a spiritual reorientation of lifestyle. On the other hand, his aristocratic nature undoubtedly relates to a similar undercurrent in *Vekhi* (especially, but not only, in Berdiaev).

It has long been argued that the differences among the *Vekhi* authors concerning the "common platform" of "primacy of the inner life of the person" may be construed not just as a matter of emphasis but as differences of a fundamental order. Such arguments relate, for example, to Kistiakovskii's notion that the external reality of a law-governed society will serve to cultivate the inner life, not the other way round, and they may also relate—perhaps as a matter of emphasis, but significantly nevertheless—to Struve's call for political education and Frank's concern for cultural creativity and positive evaluation of wealth-creation, in the broadest sense. Here, one has to say that Chaadaev's unequivocal concern for the external forms of life, from the individual to society, could draw him toward Kistiakovskii and Struve, as well as Frank. That is, in addition to the specific parallels to Gershenzon and Bulgakov that have been noted, there are grounds for a qualified linking of Chaadaev with the *Vekhi* authors whom we have had less reason to consider so far, while the one author who does not figure in this comparison (except in terms of his aristocratic nature) is the one who, apart from Gershenzon, has otherwise shown the closest affinity to Chaadaev: Berdiaev.

In summary, then, starting from the problematic juxtaposition of Chaadaev and Dostoevskii in the genealogy of *Vekhi* and continuing to a detailed comparison of conceptions of the person, the Chaadaevan perspective casts an interesting and revealing light across the complex strands that constitute *Vekhi*, both synchronically and diachronically. In addition, it highlights important aspects for study—Lockean identity, aristocratism, the external as well as the inner, and the intellect, among others—in the conceptualization and representation of the person across the Russian philosophical tradition and Russian culture.

In conclusion, I would like to return to the particular, definitive image of Chaadaev as a person of the intellect. Indeed, the person of the intellect is one of the underlying themes of *Vekhi*. As such, it constitutes an aspect of the ongoing consideration—by Russian thinkers and scholars of Russian thought alike—of the pursuit of reason in the Russian philosophical tradition, which ranges from the advocacy of a reductionist scientific reason in Chernyshevskii through the apogee of attempted integration of reason and faith in Solov'ev to Shestov's life-long assault on the pretensions of rationalist philosophy. As we have seen, the call to acquire a proper philosophical culture and rigorous intellectual method is a call to become a person of the intellect, to reorient the intelligentsia toward the root notion of the "intellect." As we have also seen, the Chaadaevan presence in *Vekhi* has revolved around his conception of thought and idea in the life of mankind and the individual person. Gershenzon's description of the kind of person that Russia has needed, which none of the *Vekhi* authors would disown even if they might phrase it differently, comes close to a portrait of Chaadaev as an aristocratic person of the intellect—of religious/moral intellect: "Had there been a handful of whole, fully conscious people in Russia, people whose high intellectual level [*vysokii stroi myslei*] was organically rooted in their personality, despotism would have been inconceivable" (57). This is remarkably close to the portrait put forward by Osip Mandel'shtam in his 1913 essay "Petr Chaadaev." Mandel'shtam writes:

> The trace left by Chaadaev in the consciousness of Russian society is so deep and ineradicable that the question involuntarily arises: is this not the trace left by a diamond passing over glass? [...]
>
> All those qualities, of which Russian life was deprived, about which it did not even have a suspicion, came together as if deliberately in the personality of Chaadaev: huge inner discipline, lofty intellectualism, moral architectonics. [...]
>
> What is the famed "mind" of Chaadaev, that "proud" mind, respectfully sung by Pushkin, denigrated by the tiresome Iazykov, other than a fusion of the moral and intellectual principles—a fusion which is so characteristic for Chaadaev and which directed the growth of his personality towards perfection?[28]

Mandel'shtam's words provide an eloquent statement as to how the image of Chaadaev, as constructed by both himself and Russian culture, has a resonance in the Russian Silver Age and beyond, and *Vekhi*—as I hope to have shown—is one of the texts that conveys and refracts that resonance.

### Notes

1. All references to Chaadaev are taken from P. Ia. Chaadaev, *Polnoe sobranie sochinenii i izbrannye pis'ma*, ed. Z. A. Kamenskii et al. (Moscow: Pravda, 1991), 2 vols, and are given in the text, citing page number (all quotations are from the first volume). Translations of Chaadaev and other Russian texts are my own, except where the reference is to a translated source; translations of Chaadaev are from the Russian version of the *Philosophical Letters* in this edition, with consultation of the original French.

2. Sapov, in the opening paragraph of his Introduction to the collection *Vekhi: pro et contra*, makes just this comparison: "Neither before nor after *Vekhi* did a book in Russia provoke such a storm of reaction in society and in such a short space of time.... Perhaps only Chaadaev's "Philosophical Letter," which appeared more than 70 years before *Vekhi*, had stirred up such a 'heated discussion' in Russian society." See V. V. Sapov, "Vokrug 'Vekh.' (Polemika 1909–1910 godov)," in *Vekhi: pro et contra*.

3   In "Apologie d'un fou"/"Apologiia sumasshedshego" ("Apology of a Madman," 1837), Chaadaev admits somewhat archly, in an extended rhetorical sentence, that there was "exaggeration" (four times repeated) in his "idiosyncratic accusatory act" (536–37). The clever characterization of the "First Letter" as "satire" comes in a letter from Viazemskii to A. I. Turgenev (28 October 1836), quoted in V. A. Mil'china and A. L. Ospovat, "O Chaadaeve i ego filosofii istorii," introductory article in P. Ia. Chaadaev, *Sochineniia*, ed. V. Iu. Proskurina (Moscow: Pravda, 1989), 3–12 (9).

4   M. Gershenzon, *P. Ia. Chaadaev. Zhizn' i myshlenie* (1908; reprint: The Hague, Paris: Mouton, 1968). Concerning the publication history of Chaadaev, including Gershenzon's role in it, see Z. A. Kamenskii and M. I. Lepekhin, "Sud'ba literaturnogo nasledstva," in Chaadaev, *Polnoe sobranie sochinenii*, 678–81.

5   The juxtaposition of Chaadaev and *Vekhi* is found as a passing mention in the scholarship, with a rare headlining by Sapov (see Note 2 above), but, as far as I am aware, the closer connection between them has not been explored in detail before.

6   Concerning the pre-history and publication history of *Vekhi*, see M. A. Kolerov and N. S. Plotnikov, "Primechaniia," in *Vekhi. Iz glubiny*, ed. A. A. Iakovlev (Moscow: Pravda, 1991), 500–48 (500–08). See also V. Proskurina and V. Alloi, "K istorii sozdaniia 'Vekh,'" *Minuvshee. Istoricheskii al'manakh* 11 (1991): 249–91.

7   Mikhail Gershenzon, "Preface to the First Edition," in *Vekhi/Landmarks: A Collection of Articles about the Russian Intelligentsia*, trans. and ed. Marshall S. Shatz and Judith E. Zimmerman (Armonk, NY: M. E. Sharpe, 1994), xxxvii–xxxviii (xxxviii). Subsequent references are given in parentheses in the main text. References to the Russian text are taken from *Vekhi. Iz glubiny* (see Note 6 above). Gershenzon originally listed just Chaadaev and Solov'ev, Tolstoi was added at the suggestion of Struve. See Kolerov and Plotnikov, "Primechaniia," 508.

8   Gershenzon, *Chaadaev*, iii.

9   Ibid., iii–iv.

10  Ibid., iv.

11  A. I. Gertsen, *Byloe i dumy* (Moscow: Khudozhestvennaia literatura, 1967), parts 4–5, 103. Sapov continues his comparison of *Vekhi* and Chaadaev (see Note 2 above) by suggesting the appropriateness of Herzen's words to *Vekhi* ("Vokrug 'Vekh,'" 7). In connection to Herzen's words, it is worth noting that Chaadaev and *Vekhi* share an analogous historical context, namely writing in the shadow of a national political trauma—the Decembrist uprising of 1825 and the 1905 revolution, respectively. Sergei Bulgakov's description at the start of his essay in *Vekhi*—"Russian society … is in a state of torpor, apathy, spiritual malaise, and despondency" (17)—could equally well apply to the mood in Russia after 1825, as evoked *inter alia* by Chaadaev's designation of his place of writing as "Necropolis" (339). While both the *Philosophical Letters* and *Vekhi* are revisited some 10 years later in, respectively, Chaadaev's "Apology of a Madman" (1837) and *Iz glubiny* (*Out of the Depths*, 1918), in this case we see more

divergence than parallel, or perhaps an inverted parallel: Chaadaev's "Apology" carries a changed, more optimistic prognosis for Russia, while *Out of the Depths* contemplates in horror the worst outcome possible from the malaise analyzed in *Vekhi*.

12   It is interesting to note that Chaadaev's ouevre and *Vekhi* are interwoven, whether explicitly or not, in the context that informs later ponderings on the intelligentsia and Russia, especially in the 1960s and 1970s, and again in the heady days of mass republication of Russian thinkers at the end of the Soviet period. Concerning the reading and interpretation of Chaadaev's thought in the later Soviet period, see Julia Brun-Zejmis, "Messianic Consciousness as an Expression of National Inferiority: Chaadaev and Some Samizdat Writings of the 1970s," *Slavic Review* 50 (1991): 646–58. For a narrative of the wider phenomenon, see Stanislav Bemovich Dzhimbinov, "The Return of Russian Philosophy," in *Russian Thought after Communism: The Recovery of a Philosophical Heritage*, ed. James Scanlan (Armonk, NY: M. E. Sharpe, 1994), 11–22; for an analytical commentary on trends in the philosophical scene over the Soviet period, see Galin Tihanov, "Continuities in the Soviet period," in *A History of Russian Thought*, ed. William Leatherbarrow and Derek Offord (Cambridge: Cambridge University Press, 2010), 311–39.

13   In this connection, it is worth commenting that both the writings of Chaadaev and *Vekhi* reveal an ambiguity in respect of reflexivity or auto-reflexivity in the rhetoric of critique: this relates to the scope and rhetorical use of the first person plural pronoun and possessive, "we" and "our." Chaadaev uses these throughout the "First Letter," taking in the whole of Russian society and history in the broad sweep of his critique. While, on the one hand, he no doubt has himself in mind in ready answer to his rhetorical question "where are our wise men, where are our thinkers? Who of us has ever thought, who thinks for us today?" (329) and so implicitly distinguishes himself from the object of his critique, he does not, on the other hand, differentiate himself in his discourse from the "we" that is Russia. While one might conclude that Chaadaev dissembles in his use of "we," there are no other indications to this effect; there is thus a tension in his rhetoric that intimates a consciously ambivalent self-awareness. In *Vekhi*, meanwhile, there is no common discursive strategy in this respect and, one is inclined to think, less self-awareness. Gershenzon, whether at times imitating Chaadaev, or out of a peculiar sense of belonging to the intelligentsia, or out of uncertainty, is variable in his use of the first person "we." Having introduced the pronoun as it were from a perspective outside the intelligentsia ("The one thing we can and must tell the Russian *intelligent* is: try to become a human being"), he then carries on to say, "We are not people, but cripples" (51). But Gershenzon is not subsequently consistent: at times he uses the neutral phrasing "our intelligentsia," as do other authors; at times he refers to the intelligentsia in the third person; at times "we" returns. Curiously, the other author who may have a closer affinity to Chaadaev, Berdiaev, occasionally also adopts a more inclusive and ambiguous first person plural reference, as in his very opening sentence, when he refers to "our attitude to philosophy," or in the rhetorical flourish of his finale: "We will be freed from external oppression only when we are freed from internal bondage" (1, 16). The remaining authors, however, avoid any first person plural alignment with the object of their critique. When considering both Chaadaev's writings and *Vekhi*, therefore, it transpires—as one might expect—that auto-reflexivity of critique, its acceptance or denial, is a complicated affair.

14 Iakovlev, *Vekhi*, 44, 74.

15 Ibid., 28.

16 For an extended disquisition on his philosophical "creativity" and aversion to system and logic, see Nikolai Berdiaev, *Sobranie sochinenii*, ed. N. A. Struve, vol. 1, *Samopoznanie (opyt filosofskoi avtobiografii)* (Paris: YMCA Press, 1989), 253–59. For a fascinating encounter between Berdiaev and a highly trained logical mind, see Frederick C. Copleston, *Philosophy in Russia: From Herzen to Lenin and Berdyaev* (Tunbridge Wells: Search Press and University of Notre Dame Press, 1986), 371–89.

17 Iakovlev, *Vekhi*, 197.

18 V. V. Zenkovsky, *A History of Russian Philosophy*, trans. George L. Kline (London: Routledge and Kegan Paul, 1953), 6.

19 See, for example, *Studies in East European Thought* 61, 2–3 (2009), "Special Issue: The Discourse of Personality in the Russian Intellectual Tradition," ed. Nikolaj Plotnikov. See also many of the articles in G. M. Hamburg and Randall A. Poole, eds., *A History of Russian Philosophy 1830–1930: Faith, Reason, and the Defense of Human Dignity* (Cambridge: Cambridge University Press, 2010).

20 For an overview of Chaadaev in Dostoevskii's thought and work, see A. S. Dolinin, *Poslednie romany Dostoevskogo. Kak sozdavalis' "Podrostok" i "Brat'ia Karamazovy"* (Moscow-Leningrad: Nauka, 1963), 112–24; A. S. Dolinin, "F. M. Dostoevskii v rabote nad romanom 'Podrostok.' Kommentarii," *Literaturnoe nasledstvo* 77 (1965): 435–507 (455–60).

21 Chaadaev's persona as an aspect of the study of his thought is an underlying theme I have traced in three previous articles (the third of which concerns Chaadaev and Dostoevskii): see my "Revisiting Russian Identity in Russian Thought: From Chaadaev to the Early Twentieth Century," *Slavonic and East European Review* 78 (2000): 20–43; "Berdiaev and Chaadaev, Russia and Feminine Passivity," in *Gender and Sexuality in Russian Civilisation*, ed. Peter I. Barta (London: Routledge, 2001), 121–39; "To Europe and Back: Chaadaev and Dostoevskii," in *Convergence and Divergence: Russia and Eastern Europe into the Twenty-First Century*, ed. Peter J. S. Duncan (London: School of Slavonic and East European Studies, UCL, 2007), 121–37.

22 For a thorough introduction to *Problems of Idealism*, including its neo-Kantian foundations, see Randall A. Poole, "Editor's Introduction: Philosophy and Politics in the Russian Liberation Movement," in *Problems of Idealism: Essays in Russian Social Philosophy*, ed. and trans. Randall A. Poole (New Haven, CT: Yale University Press, 2003), 1–78.

23 Nikolaj Plotnikov, "Preface," *Studies in East European Thought* 61 (2009): 71–75 (72–73).

24 Among studies in the two collections mentioned in Note 19 above, see, for example, Derek Offord, "Alexander Herzen," in Hamburg and Poole, *A History of Russian Philosophy 1830–1930*, 52–68; A. Alyoshin, "The Slavophile Lexicon of *Personality*," *Studies in East European Thought* 61 (2009): 77–88; Randall A. Poole, "Vladimir Solov'ëv's Philosophical Anthropology: Autonomy, Dignity, Perfectibility," in Hamburg and Poole, *A History of Russian Philosophy 1830–1930*, 131–49; see also G. M. Hamburg

and Randall A. Poole, "Introduction: The Humanist Tradition in Russian Philosophy," and Caryl Emerson, "Afterword: On Persons as Open-Ended Ends-in-Themselves (The View from Two Novelists and Two Critics)," in Hamburg and Poole, *A History of Russian Philosophy 1830–1930*, 1–23, and 381–89 (Emerson's novelists are Dostoevskii and Tolstoi, her critics are Bakhtin and Lidiia Ginzburg). For a philosophical approach to Dostoevskii, important methodologically and conceptually, see James P. Scanlan, *Dostoevsky the Thinker* (Ithaca, NY: Cornell University Press, 2002).

25  Two illuminating approaches to Chaadaev, which address his persona, his philosophy, and questions of Russian philosophy and culture, are K. G. Isupov, "Pushkinskii analiz istoricheskogo protsessa i sinteticheskaia istoriosofiia P. Ia. Chaadaeva," *Pushkin: Issledovaniia i materialy* 15 (1995): 5–24, and P. V. Kuznetsov, "Metafizicheskii nartsiss i russkoe molchanie: P. Ia. Chaadaev i sud'ba filosofii," in *P. Ia. Chaadaev: pro et contra. Lichnost' i tvorchestvo Petra Chaadaeva v otsenke russkikh myslitelei i issledovatelei. Antologiia*, comp. A. A. Ermichev and A. A. Zlatopol'skaia (St. Petersburg: Izdatel'stvo Russkogo Khristianskogo gumanitarnogo instituta, 1998), 731–52.

26  Iakovlev, *Vekhi*, 74, 82.

27  For accounts of Chaadaev's life, in addition to Gershenzon's study of Chaadaev (see Note 4 above), see also Boris Tarasov, *Chaadaev*, 2nd edition (Moscow: Molodaia gvardiia, 1990), and the still valuable Charles Quénet, *Tchaadaev et les Lettres philosophiques: contribution à l'étude du movement des idées en Russie* (Paris: Librairie ancienne Honoré Champion, 1931).

28  Osip Mandel'shtam, "Petr Chaadaev," in Mandel'shtam, *Sochineniia v dvukh tomakh*, ed. S. S. Averintsev and P. M. Nerler (Moscow: Khudozhestvennaia literatura, 1990), vol. 2, 151–56 (151–52); on Mandel'shtam and Chaadaev, see Clare Cavanagh, "Synthetic Nationality: Mandel'shtam and Chaadaev," *Slavic Review* 49 (1990): 597–610.

# 8

# Lev Tolstoi, Petr Struve and the "Afterlife" of *Vekhi*

G. M. Hamburg

When did Tolstoi first read *Vekhi*, and how did he react to the anthology? According to the great literary critic Boris Eikhenbaum, Tolstoi read the volume in late April 1909—a month after the book's publication—and immediately began to write a response to it. This response, the draft article "On *Vekhi*," was never published in Tolstoi's lifetime: it appeared in print only in 1936, in volume 38 of his collected works.[1]

The draft article, "O Vekhakh" ("On *Vekhi*"), consisted of four parts: a pair of epigrams on the role of teaching and scholarship in society; criticisms of *Vekhi*; a long excerpt from a letter written to Tolstoi by the "illiterate" peasant Ivan Vasil'evich Kolesnikov; and a final commentary on the role of educated Russians in contemporary life. The argument of "On *Vekhi*" was straightforward: the authors of the *Vekhi* anthology had proven themselves unable to teach the Russian people how to live. Tolstoi suggested that the *Vekhi* anthology was badly written, its style being an awkward mixture of un-Russian neologisms and fashionable political jargon. This bad writing, he argued, was proof of the *Vekhi* authors' intellectual obtuseness and of their incompetence as teachers. Furthermore, according to Tolstoi, the authors had shown themselves to be unforgivably arrogant in assuming that the fate of Russia lay in the intelligentsia's hands, yet nowhere in the anthology had they explained the "one necessary thing": namely, of what the "inner" or "spiritual work" of individuals should consist. True, Nikolai Berdiaev had demanded that educated Russians show humility before the truth, but he had not explained the precise nature of this truth. Sergei Bulgakov had called upon the intelligentsia to return to the Church, but Tolstoi considered Bulgakov's "solution" to Russia's problems "strange" and unrealistic. According to Tolstoi, there was more wisdom in the peasant Kolesnikov's call for Christian love than in the entirety of *Vekhi*. Tolstoi concluded his draft article by describing *Vekhi* as a symptom of the intelligentsia's "increasing confusion and perversion."[2]

According to Eikhenbaum, Tolstoi probably finished writing "On *Vekhi*" on 8 May 1909. Although Tolstoi was very unhappy about the content of *Vekhi*, he decided not to publish his response to the anthology: he told his secretary Nikolai Gusev that he did not want to offend the "young intelligentsia" and did not want to contribute to the public debate which *Vekhi* had stirred up.[3] Nevertheless, on 20 May 1909, Tolstoi gave an interview to Sergei Spiro, correspondent for the newspaper *Russkoe slovo* (*Russian Word*), in which he summarized his unpublished draft article, telling Spiro that the intelligentsia had lost its way and had lost the capacity to formulate the main questions of life.[4]

Unfortunately, Eikhenbaum's "canonical" account of Tolstoi's reaction to *Vekhi* is both inaccurate and seriously oversimplified, for three reasons.

First, Eikhenbaum's commentary underestimates the importance of Tolstoi's contacts with the *Vekhi* authors before the anthology's publication. Both Mikhail Gershenzon and Bulgakov had met Tolstoi personally on more than one occasion: Gershenzon at Iasnaia Poliana in July 1904 and again in January 1909; Bulgakov at Iasnaia Poliana in January 1897 and at Gaspra in May and June 1902. Tolstoi had read Petr Struve's journal *Osvobozhdenie* (*Liberation*) since its initial publication in 1902,[5] and he was familiar with Struve's Great Russian nationalism. It goes without saying that the *Vekhi* authors had read Tolstoi's great novels and his religious writings. Berdiaev had studied Tolstoi from childhood and had internalized the master's literary characters as intellectual reference points.[6] Bulgakov had written about Tolstoi's religious conversion in his 1901 lecture "Ivan Karamazov kak filosofskii tip," ("Ivan Karamazov as a Philosophical Type"),[7] in his 1903 article on Vladimir Solov'ev's philosophy,[8] in his 1903 inaugural lecture at Kiev University on political economy,[9] in his article "O sotsial'nom ideale" ("On the Social Ideal") for the journal *Voprosy filosofii i psikhologii* (*Questions of Philosophy and Psychology*),[10] and in his essay on Thomas Carlyle in the anthology *Dva grada* (*Two Cities*).[11] The young

Semen Frank was keenly interested in Tolstoi's moral teaching, especially Tolstoi's idea that moral authority and political power are independent phenomena—which he criticized in a 1905 essay, "Problema vlasti" ("The Problem of Power").[12] Frank analyzed Tolstoi's ethical teachings in two 1908 articles which also explored the intelligentsia's attitude to Tolstoi.[13] Tolstoi's familiarity with the intellectual position staked out by the *Vekhi* authors before 1909, and their knowledge of his works, suggests that his reaction to *Vekhi* was to some degree already determined before he actually read the anthology.

Second, Eikhenbaum's account of Tolstoi's reaction to *Vekhi* was based in part on an error in dating. In fact, Tolstoi had acquired *Vekhi* not in mid-April 1909, but on 18 March 1909—a month earlier. We know this from the diaries of Tolstoi's physician Dushan Makovitskii, who summarized Tolstoi's initial response to the anthology.[14] After beginning to read *Vekhi* in mid-March, Tolstoi planned an essay or manifesto in which he would reformulate his philosophy of non-resistance to evil. This essay/manifesto took shape in Tolstoi's long draft article, "Neizbezhnyi perevorot" ("The Inevitable Revolution"), which was written between March and 2 June 1909. This essay/manifesto was published in abridged form in *Russkie vedomosti* (*Russian News*) in September 1909, and in unabridged form in Tolstoi's collected works in 1936.[15]

Tolstoi's "The Inevitable Revolution" summoned readers to follow the "law of love" instead of the "law of violence." If they did so, he predicted a "universal, sweeping revolution [*vsemirnyi velikii perevorot*]," a new joyous life for humanity.[16] In Tolstoi's opinion, the chief obstacles to the coming of the new era were governments and their revolutionary opponents, who engaged in absurd violence in the pursuit of mistaken objectives. In addition, however, two groups of intellectuals also constituted obstacles to the new order: the "so-called scholars" who studied "sciences" that excluded ethical questions bearing on how people should live, and members of educated society who did address ethical questions but nevertheless lived in a conformist fashion that actually supported the "superstition" of violence. In this latter group Tolstoi placed nationalist patriots and supporters of the institutional Russian Orthodox Church. In chapter eight of "The Inevitable Revolution," Tolstoi argued that most intellectuals translated the question

"What is to be done?" as "How shall I arrange the lives of others?" rather than as "What must I do to change myself?" This erroneous translation bespoke arrogance, for it placed intellectuals above others and imputed to these intellectuals the right to transform the supposedly benighted common people. In effect, Tolstoi contended, the "superstition" that one group of people can and must organize the lives of others was nothing but a summons to violence. Tolstoi claimed that the alternative to participation in such coercion could be found in a simple set of rules: 1. Do no violence; 2. Take no part in the violence being done by others; 3. Do not approve of violence in any form. Tolstoi regarded these rules for non-violent living as manifestations of self-restraint, a virtue that could be practiced by anyone who wished to escape "slavery" to church and state. His criticism of the Russian intelligentsia, including the *Vekhi* authors, was clear: the "old" and "young" *intelligenty* imagined themselves to be opponents of the existing order, but they were actually defenders of violence, secretly attached to the worst abuses of the existing system. To escape the way of violence, they would have to recognize the law of love.

Third, Eikhenbaum's account of Tolstoi's response to *Vekhi* neglected the most interesting episode in that response: Tolstoi's conversation with Struve at Iasnaia Poliana on 12 August 1909. In the remainder of this essay I intend to examine in detail that conversation and its aftermath. The essay will be divided into four parts: a description of the primary sources from which we can reconstruct Tolstoi's conversation with Struve on 12 August 1909; a reconstruction of the conversation; an analysis of one of Struve's late 1909 articles criticizing Tolstoi; and a reflection on the significance of the Tolstoi-Struve conversation as an indicator of the "afterlife" of *Vekhi*.

I

On 4 July 1909, the same day that Tolstoi gave the manuscript of "The Inevitable Revolution" to his editor Nikolaev, Makovitskii reports that he discussed with his family the fact that "everyone is reading *Vekhi*, because the intelligentsia has [just] discovered that God exists." During this discussion Tolstoi agreed to meet the following month with Struve and the politician Aleksandr Stakhovich. His comment, "It would be better to allow

Struve [and Stakhovich] to visit," indicates that his family was of divided opinion about the wisdom of such a visit, for one result would surely be a dispute between Tolstoi and Struve over *Vekhi*.[17] For his part, Struve was anxious to meet Tolstoi. Stakhovich had solicited his company on a trip to Iasnaia Poliana in a curious letter, which stated that, "I want very much to visit Tolstoi, although I'm anxious about it. This [Tolstoi] is a grand and terrible being who has lived not one, but several human lives of the sort that for a single human being to endure would be strange and terrible." Struve, who had never seen Tolstoi before 1909, claimed to have "sensed that I must meet him. I understood that soon it would be too late to do so."[18] Struve accepted Stakhovich's invitation to accompany him to Iasnaia Poliana.

From the two principals we have terse written reactions to the meeting, which occurred at Iasnaia Poliana on 12 August 1909. In an article written after Tolstoi's death the next year, Struve reported his "strongest impression [of the meeting]" as being that "Tolstoi lives by the thought of God alone, by the idea of his proximity to God." According to Struve, Tolstoi was physically present in August 1909, but "psychologically and spiritually he had already gone to that place across the grave where the majority of human beings go, unseen and unknown to the living. But he had already gone there and I *saw* this." Struve's sole allusion to the conversation's content came when he recalled Tolstoi's statement, "It is not surprising that we disagree, since I am more than twice your age." At this, Struve had nodded assent, "for I felt that into these words Tolstoi himself packed not just a reference to his age, but to the very feeling of having lived several lives."[19]

Perhaps, in retrospect, the meeting was more significant to Struve than it had been to Tolstoi, who recorded his reaction in his diary on 13 August. "Stakh[ovich] A[leksan]dr and Struve visited [yesterday]. They were little interesting and were ponderous, especially Struve. I read them 'On Science' to no effect and spoke to them to no effect."[20] Tolstoi's muted response to the conversation in his diary was perhaps not entirely faithful to his mood, as perceived by others, immediately after the meeting. Makovitskii, who had listened to the conversation, reported: "On parting, Lev Nikolaevich told Struve he would always be happy to be in communication with him. It seems he [Tolstoi] even kissed him [Struve]. Struve was somewhat confused; he listened, did not argue and sought explanation [from Tolstoi] and [he sought] the truth rather than [to justify] his own correctness. Lev Nikolaevich obviously liked him."[21]

Besides the short reactions from the principals, we have two eyewitness accounts of the conversation between Tolstoi and Struve—one from Tolstoi's physician Makovitskii and the other from his friend, the musician Aleksandr Gol'denveizer. Of the two, Makovitskii's account was the fuller, since he was present from the conversation's beginning, at 1:30 p.m. on the terrace, to its end late at night in the manor house. Gol'denveizer heard the latter portions of the conversation; however, his account was perhaps more astute, because he had a clearer grasp of the issues at stake.[22] Both Makovitskii and Gol'denveizer understood that the conversation was an important intellectual event, and so both allotted considerable space in their diaries to its recording. By comparing these two accounts, we can reconstitute the flow of the conversation, and at moments we can even "hear" the two participants.

II

According to Makovitskii, Tolstoi asked Struve from which direction he had traveled to Iasnaia Poliana. Struve's answer—that he had come from the White Lake district in Iaroslavl' province where there were many famous monasteries—provoked Tolstoi to observe that a monastery is a "useful and essential haven [from the world]." Struve then noted that, in Kazan', he had once seen Vasilii Polenov's "wonderful" series of paintings on the life of Christ. Tolstoi apparently let this remark drop without comment; at least Makovitskii did not record a response on this point.[23] Unbeknownst to Struve, however, Polenov's paintings had been the subject of extended conversations in Tolstoi's household. On 17 March 1909, Makovitskii reports, Tolstoi recalled seeing the paintings at an exhibit in St. Petersburg: he had not been impressed.[24] But the next day, he had expressed interest in seeing them again.[25] In late April, Sofiia Andreevna and Tolstoi's son Sergei had seen Polenov's exhibit, and they had praised the paintings for their naturalism and "avoidance of the mystical."[26] Tolstoi himself had studied the album of the exhibition, pronouncing the reproductions of *Mysterious*

*Evening* and *Crucifixion* "good," and the entire series "in general, good."[27] In November 1909, nearly three months after the conversations with Struve, Sofiia Tolstaia and Sofiia Stakhovich again discussed Polenov's paintings in Tolstoi's presence, prompting him to say, "[The life of Christ] is so dear to us, that it is better not to touch on it [*etogo ne trogat'*]."[28] Thus, the first exchanges between Struve and Tolstoi dealt with the phenomenon of religion: Struve established his credentials as a "new" *intelligent* interested in the subject; Tolstoi acknowledged that interest but without opening up his own emotions on the subject.

Tolstoi then turned to the theme of the intelligentsia and *Vekhi*, asserting that of the vast number of books now being published, "not a single one is useful." He told Struve that he agreed with the chief point made in *Vekhi*. "On your main idea ["inner work" in preference to political action], I am *plus royaliste que le roi*," but, he added, "I find *Vekhi* too superficial." He told Struve, "There are more profound reasons for this" that he would discuss later, after a walk. Struve also lamented that journals had "lost their former significance and now played to the common denominator." Tolstoi complained that he had said many times that one should write for the people, but "everyone persists in writing for the intelligentsia."[29] By this second stage of the conversation, Tolstoi had indirectly reproached Struve twice—once for his superficiality and again for his failure to write "for the people." Struve read these reproaches as opening gambits in Tolstoi's attack on *Vekhi* and awaited further developments. Tolstoi promised to speak himself out: "The word is an important thing, so one must say everything, not just half of it."[30] For Struve, the prospect of hearing Tolstoi "speak himself out" must have been thrilling but also daunting.

Tolstoi excused himself to ride in the forest with his daughter Aleksandra. After returning from the forest, he rejoined Struve for a late afternoon/early evening meal. The group, now including Gol'denveizer, adjourned to the balcony for continued conversation. Makovitskii recorded an observation of Tolstoi: "When I ride in the forest, the feeling is very Christian. I want others to exalt in nature, and I regret that we alone do so."[31] Tolstoi's "very Christian feeling" was probably the result of two impulses: his belief that God is in everyone and everything, and his Christian desire to share with the less fortunate (in this case, city dwellers) his sense of religious unity with creation. The effect of this observation was to reconnect the collocutors to the subject of religion.

Makovitskii and Gol'denveizer agreed that the conversation then turned quickly to the religious views and intellectual significance of the "old" intelligentsia, specifically to Aleksandr Herzen, Nikolai Ogarev, and Mikhail Bakunin. Tolstoi compared Herzen to the German philosopher Arthur Schopenhauer. According to Tolstoi, "[Herzen,] in spite of his philosophical-political beliefs, enunciated religious truths of universal human significance," whereas in the thought of Schopenhauer, an atheist, "one can find more propositions about the unavoidability of religion than in [the catechism of Metropolitan] Filaret."[32] In praising Herzen's religiosity, Tolstoi probably had in mind two epigrams he had quoted in "The Inevitable Revolution," in chapters seven and nine. In the latter, Tolstoi quoted Herzen as writing, "If only people wanted, instead of saving the world, to save themselves; instead of liberating humanity, to liberate themselves—how much they could do to save the world and to liberate humanity."[33] Under questioning by Struve, Tolstoi pronounced Ogarev "an insignificant man." He described Bakunin as "some sort of crazy man [*kakoi-to shal'noi*]," but conceded that "much in him [Bakunin] was attractive."[34] At this moment in the conversation, Struve was trying to draw Tolstoi out on one of *Vekhi*'s subjects, the irreligion of the "old" intelligentsia, but Tolstoi was refusing to play along: rather than indict Bakunin and company for their shallowness and militant atheism, Tolstoi pointed toward Herzen's spiritual sensibility and Bakunin's charisma. He hinted that the difference between the "old" and "new" intelligentsia was perhaps not so dramatic as Struve and the other *Vekhi* authors had imagined. Tolstoi's allusion to Filaret's catechism also alerted Struve to Tolstoi's hostility toward the institutional church and to Tolstoi's assessment of the costs of churchliness [*tserkovnost'*]. Behind this barb was Tolstoi's criticism of two *Vekhi* authors, Berdiaev and Bulgakov, whose essays in *Vekhi* had espoused a return to the Orthodox Church.

From 8:30 to 10:00 p.m., Tolstoi read to Struve and eight others his draft article "O nauke" ("On Science.")[35] We know from Gol'denveizer's diary entry of 10 August that Tolstoi had contemplated this step in advance. He had told Gol'denveizer that the conclusions of "On Science" needed to be widely known, and he admitted his pride over having written the essay:

"It suddenly struck me how deeply I feel this ... If you assign grades [to articles], you sometimes see a 'two' or a 'three,' but then you run across a 'five plus.' That is what I think about the article 'On Science.'"[36] Tolstoi apparently believed that reading the article to Struve would demonstrate why the educational mission of the "new" intelligentsia was suspect.

"On Science" made the point that science as usually defined by intellectuals is "the knowledge of everything in the world except the one thing necessary to each individual to live a good life."[37] In contrast, Tolstoi believed that genuine science "is knowledge of what every individual must do to live better in this world during the short time allotted him by God, by fate or by the laws of nature—whatever you wish to call it."[38] The experimental sciences are flawed, according to Tolstoi, because the meaning of experiments depends on subjective interpretation of the data by observers. Even if one were to eliminate subjectivity in reporting experimental results, Tolstoi thought, scientists would remain unable to interpret the meaning of experiments for human life properly, because each experiment yields only a discrete result, a description of a certain causal sequence that, in principle, is only a finite portion of an infinitely long sequence of causes that constitute the natural world.[39] He regarded applied sciences like physics and medicine as instruments whereby "the rich increase their power over enslaved workers and intensify the horrors of warfare."[40] Tolstoi emphasized the harm done to the people not only by theological and "quasi-philosophical" deceptions, but also by "military-patriotic lies."[41] He compared "what is now called science" to a handbook for vandals and thieves, aimed at defining "the best scientific way to assault and rob the people."[42] Tolstoi saw the false sciences as profoundly anti-human: they were based neither on love nor on respect for others, and thus "nothing good can come from them, only harm."[43] Those who embraced the false sciences would only survive "as long as the falsity of their science remains hidden." Tolstoi called on common people to "place no trust in science introduced by coercion [from above] and by government grants."[44]

Tolstoi sought to put Struve on the defensive with the force of this article, and to damn the entire mission of the Russian intelligentsia, whose self-selected mission was "to serve our unhappy Russian people" through scientific education.[45]

Struve offered two objections to Tolstoi's article. First, he argued that the division of society into two "castes"—the educated and the uneducated—"exists only in Russia"; in the West, this division did not obtain. According to Struve, "in America the labor of a teacher and of a factory worker ... are identically compensated."[46] In Germany, he said, "A train conductor earns more money than a *Privatdozent*." Second, Struve argued, medicine does not aim to harm or to enslave people: "The preservation of human life might be posited as its goal."[47] Struve insisted on the utility of crutches in helping the lame and of chemical remedies for curing the ill. He pointedly asked Tolstoi: "Don't you value science aiming at the prolongation of human life?"[48] Struve's intention was to vindicate science by denying any necessary link between scientific research and violence or social exploitation, and by showing its value to common laborers. In the process, he sought to blunt Tolstoi's insinuation that the intelligentsia's "arrogant" *kul'turtregerstvo*, bringing of culture to the masses, is harmful.

The two collocutors had now arrived at the heart of their disagreement over *Vekhi*. In Tolstoi's opinion, the disagreement over science was a manifestation of a deeper dispute about action in the world. According to Gol'denveizer, Tolstoi told Struve: "Of course, 'thou shalt not kill' is the first moral law in relationship to others. But if I set myself the goal of preserving human life, then I must kill a person who wants to throw a bomb, so as to prevent the death of a hundred others, and from this [postulate] one can derive all the sophisms on which the current violent order is based."[49] According to Makovitskii's account, Tolstoi said the following:

> So by your reckoning, if one wants to save a hundred people, it is permissible to kill one of them. [But] the sense of moral law cannot be made contingent on the presumed utility of actions, but [must derive] only from the imperative of conscience. The goal of actions undertaken by a religious person is the observance of the moral law. [On the other hand,] the scientific superstition holds that, in the future, in a better-ordered society, the people's welfare can be secured, just as the Church superstition holds that one will receive one's reward in the next life. Your mission is action; you seek to transform the lives of people by external means, but by what methods? By socialistic methods? By anarchistic methods? I think that change occurs entirely in the realm of ideas, that an individual obeys an inner law, conscience, God.[50]

Tolstoi maintained that in the "simple non-violent life of the future," there would be no science of the currently existing type. "What sort of science will exist I don't know, but the current kind will not exist."[51]

After a (very late) tea, Tolstoi returned to the subject of *Vekhi*. He told Struve apropos of Berdiaev's and Bulgakov's articles: "I will never succeed in understanding the Orthodoxy of people such as [Vladimir] Solov'ev and those like him."[52] According to Makovitskii's account, Tolstoi said, "One has to choose between two possibilities: either to believe in the [institutional] Church's teaching, or to accept as Christian what is taught in common by all religions."[53] In Tolstoi's opinion, the modernist Orthodoxy espoused by Solov'ev, Berdiaev, and Bulgakov was a false third option—*ne ryba, ne miaso*. According to Makovitskii, Tolstoi told Struve: "I understand the Orthodoxy of my sister [Mariia Nikolaevna] … She has a relationship to God who is the foundation of everything—that is, [she renders] loyalty and obedience to him."[54] According to Gol'denveizer, Tolstoi sympathized with his sister's brand of Orthodoxy because "here is a person whose highest need is the religious posture toward life, but who does not have the capacity to regard critically the existing religious creeds, who simply takes them on faith, and thus satisfies her religious requirements. But when a person who has once succumbed to doubt then resorts to sophisms to justify the Church faith in which he was raised—that I cannot understand. As Kant said, having once assimilated certain views, a man then becomes a sophistic apologist for his mistaken ideas."[55]

Struve attempted to parry this attack on *Vekhi* by saying that only Berdiaev and Bulgakov deserved the reproach of Orthodox *tserkovnost'*: "Of the other contributors, two for example are Jews [Gershenzon and Frank], who are completely innocent of ascribing themselves to any sort of Orthodoxy."[56] Significantly, Struve was silent about his own belief. Frank, in his biography of Struve, described Struve's faith *circa* 1909 as a generalized, non-dogmatic belief in God. According to Frank, Struve acknowledged the mystical side of religion without subjecting it to searching analysis. Indeed, although Struve considered religious faith a natural impulse, "he never studied religious questions nor did he discuss the problems and concepts of religion." In Frank's opinion, Struve's belief system corresponded to "the spirit of liberal Protestant theology."[57]

In May 1909, Struve had published an article in *Russkaia mysl'* (*Russian Thought*) attacking religious dogmatism. In it he wrote that "[d]ogmatism is the pretension of a finite consciousness to complete possession of an infinite or final truth. And as paradoxical as it may sound, I claim that for contemporary consciousness the only way to strengthen genuine *religiosity* is the gradual overcoming of dogmatism."[58] Struve took as an example of religious anti-dogmatism none other than Tolstoi, in whose teaching Struve could find "not a single dogma." However, in the same article, Struve classified Tolstoi as "genuinely dogmatic in the sphere of morals." He accused Tolstoi of issuing absolute prescriptions for new ways of living based on religion, yet of refusing responsibility for the implementation of those prescriptions.[59] At the same time, Struve criticized Tolstoi for inconsistently taking a gradualist approach to social change and for pretending that this social change could occur suddenly, "in the blink of an eye."[60] By these obscure formulas Struve apparently sought to indict Tolstoi for absolutely rejecting violence, for laying on individuals the responsibility of refraining from violence, and for assuming that the non-violent movement might change Russia virtually overnight.

Struve himself embraced a faith based on personal responsibility and gradual change. In his March 1909 lecture on "Religiia i sotsializm" ("Religion and Socialism"), he endorsed a "genuinely religious worldview in which old religious motives growing out of Christianity, and out of liberalism, would combine with the idea of personal religious mission [*podvig*] and personal responsibility, compounded of a new motive—the motive of the freedom of the individual understood as *creative* autonomy."[61] This vague formula amounted to an endorsement of the intelligentsia's mission of gradual cultural enlightenment of the masses, and also to the privileging of intellectual freedom as a prerequisite for cultural progress.

Given this personal religious perspective, which was alien both to traditional Orthodoxy and to Tolstoi's brand of Christianity, Struve's choice in August 1909 to keep quiet about his own religious beliefs made sense. However, Tolstoi had not yet said all that was on his mind concerning the *Vekhi* authors' religiosity. According to Gol'denveizer, Tolstoi said to Struve: "Yes, but I don't see [in *Vekhi*] any well-defined religious foundation of any kind. Your reproaches to the intelligentsia for irreligion are justified, and

I would add that they [the *intelligenty*] should also be reproached for their appalling arrogance [*v uzhasaiushchei samouverennosti*]. But, in any case, I don't see the religious foundation in the name of which all this [in *Vekhi*] is being said, and that is the main thing."[62] In Makovitskii's diary, Tolstoi's account was more pointed: "I see here [in *Vekhi*] a kind of superficial attitude [toward religion]. [You] don't want to say everything [about your faith]. But this is not religiosity: it is appalling arrogance. 'We don't need this Christianity.' But you should have a more precise position [*nado bolee tochnuiu tochku*] from which to attack the intelligentsia."[63]

According to Makovitskii, Struve then began to speak about social progress, about how in the future a well-ordered society would appear. He may have hinted at his doubt about whether Tolstoi's own variety of Christianity would produce positive results: Makovitskii's diary is opaque on this matter, and Gol'denveizer did not mention Struve's commentary on social progress. However, if we believe Makovitskii, Tolstoi cut off Struve's train of thought by asserting that "I am not talking about the consequences [of belief], but rather about genuine knowledge of how I can obey the will of Him who sent me [into the world]."[64]

Gol'denveizer and Makovitskii agreed that the conversation ended with a discussion by Tolstoi of a critical letter he had just received from Petr Velikanov. According to Makovitskii, Tolstoi informed Struve that "there are people who know how to write belligerently and poisonously, and who take advantage of that ability. When they criticize me, I rejoice because I see that I do not live in God when I catch myself becoming angry."[65] According to Gol'denveizer, Tolstoi observed that Velikanov "was always writing me nasty letters [*rugatel'nye pis'ma*]." "I wanted to tell him not to write again so as not to stir up negative emotion in himself.... He writes caustically apropos [Nikolai] Gusev's exile that I hide behind the backs of my friends and that, just as behind [Prime Minister Petr] Stolypin there is Nicholas II, so behind my friends there is Lev I, and so on. My prayer is: 'Rejoice when they slander you. When you are alone and in a good mood that suffices,... but when you are in a bad frame of mind, it becomes depressing."[66]

At first glance, this closing episode in the Tolstoi-Struve conversations seems unrelated to the matter at hand. At the end of a very long day, the old man could not help complaining about an unpleasant letter, perhaps because he sought Struve's sympathy, perhaps because he wanted to remind Struve that his religious dissent carried heavy personal costs (such as Gusev's exile and his own exposure to "poisonous" correspondence). But we might contemplate at least one other explanation for Tolstoi's comment at the end of the conversation. Tolstoi was disappointed with *Vekhi* and exasperated with Struve, whom he found a "ponderous" or "heavy" passenger. Of course, Tolstoi, ever the *barin*, hid that exasperation beneath a polite visage. He told Struve he would be "always glad" to see him and to hear from him.[67] As we noted above, he even kissed Struve on the latter's departure from Iasnaia Poliana.

However, for Tolstoi the conversation had indeed been futile. Recall his diary entry of 13 August: "I read them 'On Science' to no effect and spoke to them to no effect."[68] Perhaps this futile conversation reminded Tolstoi of the pointlessness of corresponding with the "poisonous" Velikanov. We have on record three unsent letters from Tolstoi to Velikanov, drafted on 12 August 1909. In the third variant, Tolstoi wrote: "Each person has his own convictions, and therefore I think it completely useless to write poisonous letters to people holding opposed views. Besides being a waste of time, it only produces negative emotions, one of the most harmful things in life."[69] The conversation with Struve had not been exactly poisonous—Struve had conducted himself tactfully enough—but it had obviously stirred in Tolstoi "negative emotion."

In general, the conversation with Struve on 12 August 1909 followed the intellectual line on *Vekhi* set down by Tolstoi in the draft article "On *Vekhi*" and in the unpublished "The Inevitable Revolution." In Struve's presence Tolstoi attacked the "terrible arrogance" of the *Vekhi* authors, the "strangeness" of Berdiaev's and Bulgakov's modernist Orthodoxy, and the absence of a well-defined religious perspective in *Vekhi*. Tolstoi strongly implied that Struve's failure to accept non-violent Christianity indicated acceptance of "all the sophisms on which the current violent order is based." Tolstoi pressed Struve not to calculate the external consequences of genuine Christian belief in advance of adopting it, and warned Struve that the *Vekhi* authors had actually assumed the same posture as the "old" intelligentsia: "Your mission is action; you seek to transform the lives of the people by external means." Tolstoi tried to persuade Struve that *Vekhi*, which had ostensibly justified "inner" work over political activism, actually showed its authors to be enemies of the "inner law, of conscience, of God," as Tolstoi understood those things. In sum, Tolstoi accused Struve and the other *Vekhi* authors of contributing to the "illusion" of the necessity of violence rather than to the dissipation of that illusion. They had said "half a word" about religion in criticizing the intelligentsia's godlessness. Tolstoi wanted them to "say everything."

## III

An excerpt from Tolstoi's "The Inevitable Revolution" appeared in *Russian News* on 10 September 1909, less than a month after Tolstoi's meeting with Struve at Iasnaia Poliana. Struve responded to the excerpt with a short analysis in *Russian Thought* under the title "Rokovye voprosy" ("Fateful Questions").[70] Although Struve characterized his response "not as a 'polemic' in the usual sense of the term," his commentary on Tolstoi's thinking was a continuation of the conversation at Iasnaia Poliana, this time in a forum Struve could control.

Struve credited Tolstoi for raising fundamental questions, questions of a "fateful character," that deserved the intelligentsia's attention. At the same time, he underlined what he took to be the "illogic" and "contradictoriness" of Tolstoi's thinking. On the one hand, Struve observed, Tolstoi insisted on personal responsibility for one's actions and on the primacy of "inner work" over external action. On the other hand, Struve contended, Tolstoi argued that "the cause of the evil from which we all suffer [i.e. violence] is not within people, but in a false order of life based on violence, which people consider necessary."[71] Struve considered these two propositions contradictory. He saw Tolstoi's emphasis on personal responsibility for actions as incompatible with the notion that people bear no responsibility for structural violence stemming from social arrangements into which they are born.

Struve suggested that there are two possible explanations for the corrupt social order in which people live. Either they live badly because they themselves are bad or corrupt, or they live badly because they *do not know how* to organize their lives properly. Struve asserted that, from a religious perspective, only the first possibility makes sense. Tolstoi had written repeatedly that the "kingdom of God is within you"; Struve wrote that the "kingdom of the devil or of evil is also within us in an organic sense."[72] In other words, Struve argued, "If human beings are not 'evil' or 'guilty [of vice],' they are certainly [morally] weak."[73]

For Struve, the implication of the fact that human nature is neither wholly good nor innocent was that "the perfection of life and the improvement of human character cannot be accomplished through mere 'education,'" or by "a simple sermon" of the sort Tolstoi routinely delivered. Human perfectibility, the overcoming of evil, required instead "a complicated, multi-front effort encompassing all of life and the strengthening of an individual's entire character." According to Struve, the problem with *tolstovstvo* lay not in Tolstoi's ultimate goal of avoiding violence, but rather in a "more difficult, and damnably puzzling problem: how to make human beings *strong* enough for 'love excluding violence'?"[74]

Struve's contention—that Tolstoi had failed to understand evil or to fathom the weakness inherent in human nature—had been levelled at Tolstoi by Solov'ev in *Tri razgovora* (*Three Conversations*, 1899), as Struve surely knew. Here, in "Fateful Questions," Struve alluded both to Solov'ev's critique of Tolstoi and to what Struve regarded as a universally accepted religious proposition—that evil is part of human nature. The idea was to rebut Tolstoi's assertion of 12 August that there was "no religious foundation whatsoever" behind *Vekhi,* while simultaneously defending Berdiaev, Bulgakov, and himself against the charge of modernist superficiality in matters of faith. The charge that Tolstoi's concept of personal moral responsibility contradicted his critique of violence enabled Struve to pose as a "realist" sympathizing with Tolstoi's long-term objective of a violence-free society while wondering whether "weak" human beings could ever be "*strong* enough for 'love excluding violence.'" Although Struve did not say so, his doubts about the "strength" of human nature implied the need for coercive measures against criminals of every sort, at least until humanity showed itself morally worthy of a non-violent society. This was Struve's answer to Tolstoi's accusation that licensing the killing of one person "to save a hundred others" was a "sophism" on which the entire violent social order rests. Struve was telling Tolstoi that, in view of the evil within human beings, it was a "sophism" to pretend that a non-violent social order could easily be established.

Struve did not realize that Tolstoi had repeatedly pointed in "The Inevitable Revolution" to those people—workers, government officials, *intelligenty*—whose beliefs and actions sustained the "illusion" that violence is a necessary component of the social order. Surely this proposition indicated Tolstoi's awareness that the evil of violence is a product of human volition, and that this evil "illusion" and its manifold justifications come from *within* human beings. Tolstoi's profoundest idea was perhaps that, since this element of the external social order sprang from within human beings, those same individuals might, by exerting spiritual self-discipline, extricate it from their characters by refusing to do violence and by refusing to approve of its being done. Tolstoi knew from personal experience that exercising spiritual discipline is not easy, but he also knew that it is possible to exercise such discipline. His far-flung network of correspondents told him that even common people could manage such discipline.

In Struve's "Fateful Questions" there was an unbecoming arrogance that manifested itself in condescension toward Tolstoi as a thinker and toward human nature itself. In Struve's pleas to take cognizance of human *weakness*, one hears the echoes of Dostoevskii's Grand Inquisitor, for whom pity toward human weakness served as a justification of coercion. The article "Fateful Questions," like Tolstoi's early reactions to *Vekhi*, showed why no full meeting of minds between Tolstoi and the *Vekhi* authors was possible. Tolstoi was a resolute opponent of not only the "old" intelligentsia but also the "new" one. Being "*plus royaliste que le roi*" in advocating inner work did not make Tolstoi amenable to Struve's political "realism." Struve was right to acknowledge that, alongside the Russian public's "idol-worship" of Tolstoi, there was on the educated public's part a "lamentable absence of interest in his thinking."[75] Struve should have admitted that, even among the *Vekhi* authors, there was little real *sympathy* for Tolstoi's spiritual worldview.

## IV

One might have predicted that Struve's 1909 visit to Iasnaia Poliana would come to naught, or worse, that it would set off an unpleasant polemic between himself and Tolstoi. After all, the two men were very different creatures: Tolstoi was an autodidact, a literary artist turned religious radical, the most distinguished survivor of Russia's "golden age," and Struve was a radical political economist turned conservative, a religious *naif*, a figure embodying the contradictoriness of Russia's on-going "silver age." Aside from these stark personal differences, Struve appeared at Tolstoi's estate as representative of a cohort of intellectuals with whom Tolstoi had uneasy relations. Tolstoi had met Bulgakov in 1897, but had offended him mortally in 1902; he had helped Gershenzon by providing materials for the latter's books on the intelligentsia, but had quarrelled with him in early 1909, before the publication of *Vekhi*. Tolstoi had never met Berdiaev, but, as we have seen, he found his brand of modernist Orthodoxy preposterous. Thus, Struve was not only personally disagreeable to Tolstoi, he was guilty by association.

Intellectually, the differences between Tolstoi and Struve could not have been greater. Because Struve was a true believer, perhaps the last and most eloquent one, in the manifest destiny of the Russian empire, he believed in the kind of strong government that Tolstoi felt to be a practical disaster and a moral abomination. Struve's nationalism, which combined reverence for the "creative process of national life" with an elitist condescension toward the uncultured *narod*, struck Tolstoi as not only a false posture typical of the "old" intelligentsia but as an attitude likely to perpetuate the structural violence then afflicting Russia and the world. Struve's deeply held faith in science seemed to Tolstoi both naive and unexamined; it was also repellent to him because, in the thought of Struve and other *Vekhi* authors, it was linked to a contradictory philosophy of life that justified killing under the banner of avoiding killing. On the other hand, in Tolstoi Struve saw a creative artist of the first rank and a religious thinker who had upheld the spirit's banner in trying times; however, by 1909, Tolstoi was also, in Struve's view, an old man with one foot in the grave, an intellectual curiosity because, while physically alive, he had nonetheless already passed into the afterlife. Moreover, Tolstoi's spiritual outlook, as Struve understood it, was flawed by dogmatic moralism and hyper-rationalism. Tolstoi's political views seemed to Struve pitifully naive about the realities of human evil and the imperatives of power, which Struve and his liberal friends fancied that they understood. In Struve's eyes, Tolstoi's opinions about science and about the uses of technology seemed obscurantist, even hopelessly anti-modern. In Struve's view, Tolstoi wanted to lead the Russian people backward, rather than forward toward a more civilized and radiant future. Therefore, Struve's August 1909 polemics with Tolstoi only demonstrated why, despite the *Vekhi* authors' support for "inner work" over political action, no agreement between his group and Tolstoi concerning the means of transforming Russia was in principle possible.

By attacking the intelligentsia's obsession with external political change, the *Vekhi* anthology recalled to Russians' attention the very different ethical assumptions held by the intelligentsia and by its nineteenth-century critics. On the one hand, as the outpouring of newspaper and journal articles on *Vekhi* after its publication in March 1909 had shown, the *Vekhi* authors' condemnation of the intelligentsia elicited strong defensive reactions from those committed to political change through violence. Yet, as the Struve-Tolstoi polemics demonstrated, *Vekhi* also evoked from Tolstoi, Russia's leading proponent of non-violence, an attempt to restate his own criticisms of the intelligentsia and to apply these same criticisms to its authors. The history of the debate over *Vekhi*, of which the Struve-Tolstoi debate was an important part, therefore suggests that the "afterlife" of *Vekhi* was a recapitulation, in a shorter time frame, of the nineteenth-century Russian debate about the ends of life and about the means of achieving a just society. It was as if all the fury of the preceding century were suddenly concentrated within a few months and focused on a single document.

## Notes

1 B. M. Eikhenbaum, "Kommentarii. O *Vekhakh*," in L. N. Tolstoi, *Polnoe sobranie sochinenii*, vol. 38 (Moscow: Gosudarstvennoe izdatel'stvo khudozhestvennoi literatury, 1936), 571–73. The Western historian Nikolai Poltoratzky has argued that Tolstoi obtained and read *Vekhi* "no earlier than 15 April [1909]." See Poltoratzky, "Lev Tolstoi and *Vekhi*," *Slavonic and East European Review* 42, no. 99 (June 1964): 334. For a longer, more systematic analysis of Tolstoi's immediate reaction to *Vekhi*, see G. M. Hamburg, "Tolstoy and *Vekhi*," *Tolstoy Studies Journal* XXII (2010): 1–16.

2   Tolstoi, "O Vekhakh," PSS 38, 285–90.

3   N. N. Gusev, *Dva goda s Tolstym* (Moscow: Khudozhestvennaia literatura, 1973), 253: entry of 8 May 1909.

4   Gusev, *Dva goda s Tolstym*, 256: entry of 20 May 1909.

5   Tolstoi, *PSS* 73, 252: letter to M. L. Oblonskaia, 31 May 1902.

6   See N. A. Berdiaev, *Samopoznanie: opyt filosofskoi avtobiografii* (Paris: YMCA, 1949), passim.

7   S. N. Bulgakov, "Ivan Karamazov kak filosofskii tip," in *Ot marksizma k idealizmu. Sbornik statei (1896–1903)* (St. Petersburg: Tovarishchestvo "Obshchestvennaia literatura", 1903), 83–112, especially 84, 110.

8   S. N. Bulgakov, "Chto daet sovremennomu soznaniiu filosofiia Vladimira Solov'eva?," *Ot marksizma k idealizmu*, 259–62.

9   S. N. Bulgakov, "Ob ekonomicheskom ideale," *Ot marksizma k idealizmu*, 273, 286

10  S. N. Bulgakov, "O sotsial'nom ideale," *Ot marksizma k idealizmu*, 288–316, especially 297–98.

11  See S. N. Bulgakov, "O sotsial'nom moralizme (T. Karleil')," *Dva grada. Issledovaniia o prirode obshchestvennykh idealov*, vol. 1 (Moscow: Tovarishchestvo tipografii A. I. Mamontova, 1911), 106–49.

12  See S. L. Frank, "Problema vlasti (Sotsial'no-psikhologicheskii etiud)," *Voprosy zhizni* no. 3 (March 1905): 205–50.

13  See S. L. Frank, "Nravstvennoe uchenie L'va Tolstogo," *Filosofiia i zhizn'. Etiudy i nabroski po filosofii kul'tury* (St. Petersburg: Izdatel'stvo D. E. Zhukovskogo, 1910), 289–302, and "Lev Tolstoi i russkaia intelligentsiia," *Filosofiia i zhizn'*, 303–11. Frank's attitude toward Tolstoi has been analyzed by Inessa Medzhibovskaya, "Dogmatism or Moral Logic? Simon Frank Confronts Tolstoy's Ethical Thought," *Tolstoy Studies Journal* XVI (2004): 18–32.

14  D. P. Makovitskii, *U Tolstogo 1904–1910. "Iasnopolianskie zapiski" D. P. Makovitskogo. Kniga tret'ia. 1908–1909 (ianvar'–iiun')*, *Literaturnoe nasledstvo* 90 (Moscow: Nauka, 1979), 362, entry of 19 March 1909.

15  L. N. Tolstoi, "Neizbezhnyi perevorot," *PSS* 38, 72–99.

16  Ibid., 98–99.

17  See D. P. Makovitskii, *U Tolstogo 1904–1910, "Iasnopolianskie zapiski" D. P. Makovitskogo. Kniga chetvertaia. 1909 (iiul'–dekabr')–1910*, *Literaturnoe nasledstvo* 90, 10: entry of 4 July 1909.

18  P. B. Struve, "Smysl smerti Tolstogo," in *Patriotica: politika, kul'tura, religiia, sotsializm*, ed. V. N. Zhukov (Moscow: Respublika, 1997), 303. Volume originally published in 1911.

19  Ibid.

20  L. N. Tolstoi, "Dnevniki," *PSS* 57, 115: entry of 13 August 1909.

21  Makovitskii, *U Tolstogo. Kniga chetvertaia*, 10: entry of 12 August 1909.
22  Ibid., 37–40; A. B. Gol'denveizer, *Vblizi Tolstogo* (Moscow: Khudozhestvennaia literatura, 1959), 287–93.
23  Makovitskii, *U Tolstogo. Kniga chetvertaia*, 37: entry of 12 August 1909.
24  Makovitskii, *U Tolstogo. Kniga tret'ia*, 360: entry of 18 March 1909.
25  Ibid., 363: entry of 19 March 1909.
26  Ibid., 397: entry of 1 May 1909.
27  Ibid., 418: entry of 24 May 1909.
28  Makovitskii, *U Tolstogo. Kniga chetvertaia*, 94: entry of 2 November 1909.
29  Ibid., 38: entry of 12 August 1909.
30  Ibid.
31  Ibid.
32  Ibid.; Gol'denveizer reported Tolstoi saying: "Both, thanks to their intelligence and sensitivity, enunciated universal truths," *Vblizi Tolstogo*, 287: entry of 12 August 1909.
33  Tolstoi, "Neizbezhnyi perevorot," 86, 95: here, 95.
34  Gol'denveizer, *Vblizi Tolstogo*, 287: entry of 13 August 1909.
35  Makovitskii, *U Tolstogo. Kniga chetvertaia*, 38–39: entry of 12 August 1909.
36  Gol'denveizer, *Vblizi Tolstogo*, 284: entry of 10 August 1909.
37  Tolstoi, "O nauke," *PSS* 38, 137.
38  Ibid., 135.
39  Ibid., 140–41.
40  Ibid., 141–42.
41  Ibid., 144.
42  Ibid., 144–45.
43  Ibid., 147.
44  Ibid., 148–49.
45  Ibid., 138.
46  Makovitskii, *U Tolstogo. Kniga chetvertaia*, 39: entry of 12 August 1909.
47  Gol'denveizer, *Vblizi Tolstogo*, 288: entry of 13 August 1909.
48  Makovitskii, *U Tolstogo. Kniga chetvertaia*, 39: entry of 12 August 1909.
49  Gol'denveizer, *Vblizi Tolstogo*, 288: entry of 13 August 1909.
50  Makovitskii, *U Tolstogo. Kniga chetvertaia*, 39: entry of 12 August 1909.
51  Ibid., 39–40: entry of 12 August 1909.

| | |
|---|---|
| 52 | Gol'denveizer, *Vblizi Tolstogo,* 289: entry of 13 August 1909. |
| 53 | Makovitskii, *U Tolstogo. Kniga chetvertaia,* 40: entry of 12 August 1909. |
| 54 | Ibid. |
| 55 | Gol'denveizer, *Vblizi Tolstogo,* 289: entry of 13 August 1909. |
| 56 | Ibid. |
| 57 | S. L. Frank, *Biografiia P. B. Struve* (New York: Izdatel'stvo im. Chekhova, 1956), 225-26. |
| 58 | P. B. Struve, "'Vekhi' i 'Pis'ma' A. I. Ertelia. Po povodu stat'i Kn. D. I. Shakhovskogo," *Patriotica,* 247. |
| 59 | Ibid., 247–48. |
| 60 | Ibid., 249–50. |
| 61 | P. B. Struve, "Religiia i sotsializm," *Patriotica,* 333. |
| 62 | Gol'denveizer, *Vblizi Tolstogo,* 290: entry of 13 August 1909. |
| 63 | Makovitskii, *U Tolstogo. Kniga chetvertaia,* 40: entry of 12 August 1909. |
| 64 | Ibid. |
| 65 | Ibid. |
| 66 | Gol'denveizer, *Vblizi Tolstogo,* 290: entry of 13 August 1909. |
| 67 | Ibid.; Makovitskii, *U Tolstogo. Kniga chetvertaia,* 40: entry of 12 August 1909. |
| 68 | Tolstoi, "Dnevniki," 115 (see note 20). |
| 69 | Tolstoi, "Pis'ma," *PSS* 80, 282. |
| 70 | Struve's article was reprinted as "Rokovye voprosy. Po povodu stat'i L. N. Tolstogo 'Neizbezhnyi perevot,'" *Patriotica,* 304-08. |
| 71 | Ibid., 305–06. |
| 72 | Ibid., 308. |
| 73 | Ibid. |
| 74 | Ibid. |
| 75 | Ibid., 304. |

# 9

## ALEKSEI LOSEV AND *VEKHI*:
## Strategic Traditions in Social Philosophy

*Elena Takho-Godi*[1]

Aleksei Fedorovich Losev, one of the last representatives of nineteenth- and early twentieth-century Russian religious philosophy, did not take part in the *Vekhi* project: when *Vekhi* was published he was still at school. We might then ask whether it is legitimate to speak of Losev's connection to *Vekhi*. In my view it is indeed both legitimate and interesting to do so, first because Losev became personally acquainted with several of the *Vekhi* contributors not long after it was published, and second (and more importantly) because he inherited the social-philosophical strategy of *Vekhi*, which may be defined as opposition to the cause of revolution by means of the word or creative activity (the word—*slovo*—is here placed in opposition to the deed—*delo*). This position is most explicitly formulated in Mikhail Gershenzon's essay "Tvorcheskoe samosoznanie" ("Creative Self-Consciousness") and Semen Frank's essay "Etika nigilizma" ("The Ethics of Nihilism"), both of which explain the difference between what Frank calls creative "cultural production" and "principled revolutionism" (184), with its emphasis on social struggle and the destruction of existing social forms.[2] This leitmotif can also be discerned in the works of other *Vekhi* contributors. Thus Petr Struve, in his essay "Intelligentsiia i revoliutsiia" ("The Intelligentsia and Revolution"), stresses that the liberal intelligentsia which led the revolution has never been able to comprehend the field of Russian literature, that is, precisely the sphere of the word (156). In this context, the accentuation of the merits of the literary and artistic spheres that is typical for Russian philosophy acquires a special meaning. The *Vekhi* authors wanted to transform the inner nature of the Russian intelligentsia through the word, through their social-philosophical public discourse, to arouse its creative self-consciousness. It was the "creative struggle of ideas" (166), as Struve put it, spiritual opposition, and the ascetic struggle (*podvizhnichestvo*) that were important to them, not the "heroism" or titanism of the social struggle of the revolutionary superman who had taken upon himself the task of destroying those with differing views in order to create a new social order.

## ALEKSEI LOSEV (1893-1988): LIFE AND WORKS

Aleksei Losev was born in Novocherkassk, in southern Russia.[3] In 1911, after finishing his secondary education at a classical gymnasium and graduating from the Italian F. Stadzhi's music school, he matriculated at Moscow University in both the department of philosophy and the department of classical philology. An interest in psychology led him to the Psychological Institute founded by Professor Georgii Chelpanov. Thanks to Chelpanov's support, in the 1910s Losev became a participant in the famous Religious-Philosophical Society, which was established in memory of Vladimir Solov'ev in 1905. In 1915 Viacheslav Ivanov, the symbolist poet and classical philologist, read Losev's graduation thesis on Aeschylus. Losev was retained at the University to train for the academic profession, and his first publications appeared in 1916: articles on eros in Plato and the operas of Verdi and Rimskii-Korsakov. In the revolutionary year of 1919 he was a professor at the University of Nizhegorod. In the 1920s he was a full member of the State Academy of Artistic Sciences and a professor at the Moscow Conservatory and the State Institute of Musical Science. During this time Losev wrote and published no fewer than eight books, which were received by his contemporaries as "a new Russian philosophical system":[4] *Antichnyi kosmos i sovremennaia nauka* (*The Ancient Cosmos and Modern Science*), *Filosofiia imeni* (*The Philosophy of the Name*), *Dialektika khudozhestvennoi formy* (*The Dialectics of Artistic Form*), and *Musyka kak predmet logiki* (*Music as an Object of Logic*), all in 1927; and *Dialektika chisla u Plotina* (*The Dialectics of Number in Plotinus*, 1928); *Kritika platonizma u Aristotelia* (*Aristotle's Critique of Platonism*, 1929); and *Ocherki antichnogo simvolizma i mifologii* (*Essays on Classical Symbolism and Mythology*) and *Dialektika mifa* (*The Dialectics of Myth*), both in 1930.

The poet Andrei Belyi recorded in his diary his first impressions of *Essays on Classical Symbolism and Mythology* on 12 February 1930:

> An enormous volume, more than 800 pages, it leaves a splendid impression. One can be proud that such a book has appeared in Russia at such a time. It is principally devoted to Plato. On a cursory reading (I'll give it proper attention later) you can see that this is not Frank, Berdiaev, or the like: genuine, original thought, extremely valuable material, and simple and modest in tone. I consider that at another time Losev's book would have created the same reaction in Russia as Spengler's did in Germany, but Losev's thought, so it seems to me, is more monumental. Losev is a genuine philosopher in the good sense of the word, and as a living philosopher he doesn't "philosophize" or "terminologize," but thinks. For now I write this in anticipation, because I've just sniffed at the book: I'll read it properly, but I have a good sense of smell.[5]

Although *Essays on Classical Symbolism and Mythology*, which had so impressed Belyi, went generally unnoticed, *The Dialectics of Myth* created quite a stir.[6] Here Losev set himself an impossible task in the Soviet context: namely that of writing a philosophical-theological treatise on absolute mythology—on the Holy Trinity, the concept of the angel, the symbolism of immaterial powers, and so forth.[7] Moreover, Losev's understanding of myth itself, as "the essential ontological identity of being and consciousness, whereby all being is fundamentally one or another manifestation of consciousness (not according to its arbitrary appearance, but in its ultimate substance) and whereby all consciousness is being (in the same way)," became the particular key to Losev's analysis of the socio-political system and mass psychology of the time.[8] Losev demonstrated how socialism, that new relativist mythology with its cult of the material, its idea of the intensification of class struggle, and so forth, distorts personal and social consciousness. It is unsurprising that after the appearance of *The Dialectics of Myth* Losev was not only subjected to persecution in the press (a campaign in which Maksim Gor'kii participated) and condemned at the 16th Party Congress as an enemy of the people, but was also arrested on 18 April 1930, and subsequently sent to a concentration camp for the construction of the White Sea-Baltic canal. In 1931, Nathalie Duddington, in a review of Russian philosophy for the English *Journal of Philosophical Studies*, informed the European public of the "bad news" concerning the philosopher Losev, "of whom Russia could be proud" and whose profound works of metaphysics had been declared counter-revolutionary.[9] Losev himself, however, pondering on what had happened, wrote to his wife from the camp on 11 March 1932 that, suffocating "from the impossibility of expressing myself and speaking my mind," he had no longer felt able "to confine myself within the iron bands of Soviet censorship": "I knew that it was dangerous, but for a philosopher and writer the desire to express oneself, to let's one's individuality speak out, surmounts all consideration of danger."[10]

In 1933, following the completion of the canal, Losev's sentence was lifted, along with those of hundreds of other prisoners involved in the construction. He returned to Moscow, but was forbidden from engaging in philosophy: access to publication was completely blocked for him until 1953 and the death of Stalin. Under the conditions of the spiritual underground, in this quarter-century of enforced silence, Losev continued to write. Drawing on the doctrine of the Divine Energies formulated in the fourteenth century by Gregory Palamas (the knowledge of God through His energy) and on the religious-philosophical name-worshipping movement (*onomatodoxia*) of the early twentieth century (among the adherents of which was Pavel Florenskii), Losev developed a doctrine of the name that he had first begun in his book *The Philosophy of the Name*, in the essays "Veshch' i imia" ("The Thing and the Name") and "Samoe Samo" ("Self Itself"). Losev's basic concepts come to the fore in these works: thing, being, meaning, the depths of the *eidos*, "selfness" (*samost'*), and "self itself" (*samoe samo*), which should be understood as "the essence of the very essence of being,"[11] "the most genuine, most insuperable, most terrible and potent reality that can possibly exist,"[12] which engenders "innumerable interpretations."[13] During the same period Losev wrote works on the philosophy of mathematics (he had received a professional mathematical education in the 1920s from the prominent professor of mathematics Dmitrii Fedorovich Egorov, and through his correspondence with Nikolai Luzin, another outstanding mathematician). Among the themes most important to him were the analysis of the infinitesimal, the theory of multiples, and the theory of the complex variable.[14] He translated Plato, Plotinus, Sextus Empiricus, Proclus, and Nicholas of Cusa, and studied

Classical mythology. He created an original philosophical literary prose, displayed in his novel *Zhenshchina-myslitel'* (*The Woman-Philosopher*), in which the ideas of Solov'ev and the traditions of Dostoevskii are refracted in a distinctive way,[15] and earned a living teaching Classical literature in provincial universities. Only during the war years (1942–44) was he allowed to read lectures in Moscow University's faculty of philosophy, and he was soon forced out after being denounced as an idealist. From this time until his death Losev worked in the Moscow State Pedagogical Institute in the departments of Russian language and general linguistics.

In the 1960s, 1970s, and 1980s Losev turned once more to the philosophy of symbol and myth, in *Problema simvola i realisticheskoe iskusstvo* (*The Problem of the Symbol and Realistic Art*, 1976), and *Znak. Simvol. Mif* (*Sign. Symbol. Myth*, 1982), and to language, in *Vvedenie v obshchuiu teoriiu iazykovykh modelei* (*Introduction to the General Theory of Linguistic Models*, 1968), and *Iazykovaia struktura* (*Linguistic Structure*, 1983). His works on language raised the question of the possibility of a strict axiomatics in linguistics, and foregrounded communicative and interpretative acts. The author of *The Philosophy of the Name*, having traced the ladder of "naming" (*imenitsvo*) from the Divine Name down to the sound that is not yet illuminated by meaning, was convinced that two spheres of thought exist. The first was that of pure thought, the realm of "ideas," or "thought in general," while the second was its earthly realization in language, or in "the unmediated actuality of thought."[16] Reality as it is developed mentally, according to Losev, always has "*communicative directionality*," because "language does not repeat the pure and abstract element [*stikhiia*] of thought, but gives it concrete substance, realizes it and *interprets* it anew, in order to become closer to reality in its original and, for thought, primary existence."[17] The American linguist Sebastian Shaumyan has commented that "Losev's law of polysemy is the most important discovery since the 1930s, when the basic concepts and principles of the classical semiotic paradigm were formulated."[18]

Nevertheless, Losev's main work of these decades was the writing of the monumental eight-volume *Istoriia antichnoi estetiki* (*History of Classical Aesthetics*, 1963–94), in which a thousand years of Classical thought is analyzed, from the birth of aesthetics and the aesthetic terminology of the Homeric era to early Christian neo-Platonism and the Gnostics. The books *Estetika Vozrozhdeniia* (*The Aesthetics of the Renaissance*, 1978) and *Ellinisticheski-rimskaia estetika I–II vv. n.e.* (*Hellenic-Roman Aesthetics of the First and Second Centuries*, 1979) are thematically related to this work. If we take into account his unfinished work of the 1960s, "Srednevekovaia filosofiia" ("Medieval Philosophy"), Losev's design for the recreation of an historical panorama of European aesthetics and philosophy, in all its fullness, becomes obvious.

The symbolic conclusion of Losev's life's work was his book on Solov'ev, the first on this philosopher to be written in the entire Soviet period. Losev considered Solov'ev to be his spiritual teacher: his extraordinary encyclopaedic interests are rooted in Solov'ev's concept of pan-unity. The book had a complicated fate: a shorter version, printed in 1983, was published but subject to a confiscation order, and the entire print run was exiled to remote regions of the north, central Asia, and the far east,[19] while the full version, *Vl. Solov'ev i ego vremia* (*V. Solov'ev and his Time*) only came out after the author's death.

In 2004 the State Library of the History of Russian Philosophy and Culture was opened in Losev's house, in which he had lived for the last fifty of his ninety-five years, on the Old Arbat in Moscow. The "House of A. F. Losev" is a memorial not only to the philosopher himself, but to the whole of Russian philosophy, including the thought of those who took part in the *Vekhi* symposium. It is fitting that an international conference entitled "The *Vekhi* Symposium in the Context of Russian Culture" was held in the "House of A. F. Losev" to mark the centenary of *Vekhi*'s publication.[20]

## LOSEV AND THE *VEKHI* AUTHORS: BIOGRAPHICAL CONNECTIONS

Losev is often referred to as the last representative of the Silver Age of Russian culture. However, there have still been no studies made of the personal connections between Losev and his older colleagues in philosophy. It is difficult to fill this gap in our knowledge, because Losev's entire personal archive, and his correspondence from the middle of the 1910s until the end of the 1920s, were lost upon his arrest in 1930. The main venue for meetings between Losev and the philosophers of the early twentieth century, including the *Vekhi* contributors, was the Vladimir Solov'ev Religious-Philosophical Society in Moscow. There Losev was able to exchange views with Nikolai Berdiaev, Sergei Bulgakov, S. N. Durylin, Ivanov, I. A. Il'in, G. A. Rachinskii, E. N. Trubetskoi, Frank, and Florenskii (Father Pavel was the priest who married Losev and V. M. Sokolova in 1922).[21] Losev related how he was often present at meetings of the Religious-Philosophical Society, and how he used to receive notifications of and invitations to meetings.[22] He states that he went to a meeting of the Society for the first time at the house of Margarita Kirillovna Morozova to hear Ivanov give a paper entitled "On the Margins of Art," on 14 November 1913.[23] "Grigorii Alekseevich Rachinskii presided at the meeting. ... The speaker, Ivanov, sat next to him, then Evgenii Trubetskoi, and Berdiaev was there too."[24] It appears that the young Losev, who was in raptures over Ivanov's speech, was not as swayed by Berdiaev's contribution to the discussion: "Berdiaev endorsed Viacheslav Ivanov's aesthetics, but he said that one should make art accessible to a wide audience and to do that one had to write simply, although it is absurd to say such things to Ivanov: clearly he can't write like Pushkin."[25] Nonetheless other contributions by Berdiaev had a lasting and "enormous impact" on him: "A brilliant orator. He had one flaw that he suffered from all his life, a facial tic ... a terrible tic: his face would regularly distort into a grimace and he would stick his tongue out. But this did not prevent him from speaking. He spoke beautifully"[26] and "loved to speak. It was a basic need for him, such that on one occasion he remarked: I haven't spoken today yet! How can this be? He usually spoke with restraint, in a considered way. Not passionately, as he does in *The Meaning of the Creative Act* [*Smysl tvorchestva*, 1916]. Berdiaev is a writer-orator. He writes absolutely brilliantly. But his speech was calm, unprovocative, and accessible."[27]

Losev first encountered another *Vekhi* contributor, Bulgakov, a year earlier, on 21 September 1912, at the latter's defense of his doctoral dissertation *Filosofiia khoziaistva* (*The Philosophy of Economy*) at Moscow University. For Losev, Bulgakov was "a genuine scholar," "a theologian who is equally a philosopher."[28] In the five intervening years before the closure of the Religious-Philosophical Society in the summer of 1918, Losev may have been present at papers given by Bulgakov on "Russian Tragedy," about Dostoevskii's novel *Besy* (*The Devils*, 1872) (2 February 1914), "The Sophianicity of the World" (17 January 1916), "The Conquered Conqueror (the fate of Leont'ev)" (13 November 1916), his contributions on the subjects of the new Russia (15 April 1917) and Vladimir Ern (19 May 1917, at an evening commemorating Ern at which Berdiaev also spoke), and the paper "At the Feast of the Gods (Contemporary Dialogues)" (3 June 1918).[29] In 1918 Losev, Bulgakov, and Ivanov attempted to publish a religious-philosophical series called *Dukhovnaia Rus'* (*Spiritual Rus'*, see the next section, below). Neither Bulgakov nor Losev could have predicted that in 1930 Bulgakov's son Fedor would be arrested in connection with the Losev affair, and that in the 1960s Fedor would invite Losev to pose for a sculpture.[30]

Losev did not restrict himself to the role of silent listener in the Religious-Philosophical Society. He presented a paper on "The Question of the Fundamental Unity of Plato's Dialogues *Parmenides* and *Timaeus*," which elicited responses from Rachinskii and Florenskii.[31] When the Society ceased to exist, Losev began to attend meetings in Berdiaev's apartment and at his Free Academy of Spiritual Culture.

Of all the contributors to *Vekhi*, Losev enjoyed the closest relationship with Frank. Since his youth Losev had been a dedicated reader of the journal *Russkaia mysl'* (*Russian Thought*), where Frank was chief editor of the philosophy and literature sections, and of the journal *Logos*, in which Frank regularly published.[32] He would recall his special relationship with Frank all his life, and in the mid-1970s noted that "Frank valued me highly."[33] And in 1930, in the notes to *Essays on Classical Symbolism and Mythology*, he relates how his research into Plato's use of the terms "eidos" and "idea" was discussed in various Moscow academic societies: in the Lopatin Philosophical Society in June 1921, in Berdiaev's Free Academy in April 1922, in the Moscow Psychological Society in June 1922, and also in the Institute of Scientific Philosophy; in this connection he recalls that Frank "fully took on board my work on 'eidos' and 'idea' and told me personally that '[a] new understanding of Platonism has been in the air in Europe for a long time now. You have discerned and articulated it.'"[34]

As Losev recollected in 1975, Frank was the reason he ended up attending the sessions held at Berdiaev's home: "Frank and Il'in told me about them. So I went."³⁵ On 5 April 1922 the Free Academy, where Frank delivered a course of lectures entitled "Introduction to Philosophy,"³⁶ reported on Losev's presentation of the paper "Greek Linguistic Ontology in Plato." Among the respondents were B. A. Griftsov, Rachinskii, P. S. Popov, B. P. Vysheslavtsev, and Frank.³⁷

Frank participated in the discussion of Losev's work not only at the Free Academy and the Institute of Scientific Philosophy: we know that in the Lopatin Philosophical Society, too, when Losev gave a paper on Aristotle, Frank took part in the debate along with Griftsov, Rachinskii, and Vysheslavtsev.³⁸ According to the notes to *Music as an Object of Logic*, Frank was also present at Losev's talk at the State Institute of Musical Science on 24 December 1921.³⁹ In *Music as an Object of Logic*, Losev mentions exchanging views with Frank not only on the subject of his own definition of the number (in his view Frank's thinking about the number in *Predmet znaniia* [*The Object of Knowledge*, 1915] "sets out the meaning of my definition of the number in a more precise form"),⁴⁰ but also on the coincidence of Frank's ideas with those of Plotinus.⁴¹

A common interest in Platonism and neo-Platonism informed their mutual attention to the philosophy of Nicholas of Cusa. Frank considered Cusa to be one of his greatest teachers (not for nothing did one of the outstanding philosophers of the Russian emigration, V. N. Il'in, devote an article to the relationship between Nicholas of Cusa and Frank). For his part, Losev wrote a book about Cusa in the 1920s, which was lost after his arrest, and in the 1930s he translated three of Cusa's treatises: "On the Not-other," "On the Mind," and "On the Possible-actual."⁴² It appears he held conversations of some kind with Bulgakov about Cusa as well, or else how could he have known that Bulgakov possessed a sixteenth-century "copy of Nicholas of Cusa published in Lyons"?⁴³

We can form an opinion about Frank's attitude to Losev from a review of his *The Philosophy of the Name* and *The Ancient Cosmos and Modern Science* which was published in the journal *Put'* (*The Way*) in 1928. When he was preparing his review, Frank well understood the consequences that praise for Losev in the press of the White emigration would have for the Soviet philosopher. In an unpublished letter from Frank to the journal's editor, Berdiaev, dated 8 November 1927 and accompanying his review of

Losev's books, we find the following lines: "Dear Nikolai Aleksandrovich … I have been cautious and have not said everything that should have been said, but have confined myself to allusions in order not to cause Losev trouble."[44] Aware of the obligatory concessions to the Soviet censorship in Losev's books, Frank writes that "the isolated irritating passages in which the author pays tribute, as it were, to the ruling 'spirit of the age' … are organically quite unrelated to the rest of the content of his ideas," and that "there is no need to dwell on these; the 'tribute' is clearly an unwilling one."[45] For Frank what is important is that "with his books the author has undoubtedly joined the ranks of the foremost Russian philosophers and … has borne witness to the fact that even inside Russia the spirit of true philosophical creativity is alive, the pathos of pure thought, directed towards the absolute: a pathos which itself is, in its turn, a witness to spiritual life and spiritual fire."[46]

According to Frank, *The Ancient Cosmos and Modern Science*, which is devoted to the dialectics of being, represents a detailed analysis of just one of the aspects of *The Philosophy of the Name*, in which "the author's own philosophical system is set out." "Briefly and in popular language" summarising Losev's "infinitely complex and abstract construction," Frank conveys the essence of Losev's philosophical conception as follows:

> For the author, the *name*, as the place where the "meaning" of human thought and the immanent "meaning" of the object world itself meet, is in its ultimate completion the expression of the essence of being itself. Everything in the world, including dead nature, is "meaning," and therefore the philosophy of nature and the philosophy of spirit unite in the philosophy of the "name" as the self-disclosure of meaning. The name in its completion is the "idea," capturing and expressing the "eidos," the essence of the object. The name acquires ultimate fullness and depth when it also embraces the precious "apophatic" layer of being: it then reveals itself as "myth," which is not an invention but, on the contrary, the ultimate plenitude, self-revelation, and self-understanding of reality. The philosophy of the name thus coincides with the dialectic of the self-understanding of being and by the same token with philosophy itself, for the "name," understood ontologically, is the highest pinnacle of being, reached through its immanent self-revelation.[47]

At the same time, Frank considers it essential to draw attention to the traditions whose development, continuation, or re-conceptualization are most apparent in *The Philosophy of the Name*. The first of these is Classical dialectics—Plato's *Parmenides* and the further development of its constructions in Plotinus and Proclus. The second is the phenomenology of Edmund Husserl, transformed by Losev, drawing on Plato and the neo-Platonists, "into a universal 'dialectics,' which for him is identical with philosophy as such." The third comprises "the obvious points of contact with the ideas of Florenskii and his 'magic of the word.'" Fourth, "the many pages of *The Philosophy of the Name* in which categories dialectically give rise to one another are extraordinarily reminiscent of Hegel, and indeed in terms of difficulty, complexity, but at the same time subtlety in the working of abstract thought, there can hardly be many examples since Hegel's *Phenomenology of Spirit* of philosophical systems on a par with that of Losev."[48]

It is curious that Losev knew about this review by Frank, which had been published in Paris: the Foreword to his *Dialectical Foundations of Mathematics*, dated 29 April 1936, makes reference to it.[49] It is likely that in the 1920s Losev was still able to maintain links with émigrés and to access émigré publications, something that was harshly punished by the Soviet authorities.[50] We know that in 1923 he read Berdiaev's *Filosofiia neravenstva* (*Philosophy of Inequality*), which contained sharp criticism of the Soviet regime, and that Berdiaev's "inspired words" made a huge impression on him—such that in the 1970s he could quote from this work from memory: "What have you done to my country!"[51] Thus it was no accident that in 1930, in the course of Losev's interrogation, he was reminded of his acquaintance with Berdiaev. It is not impossible that the link between Paris and Losev was the well-known botanist Professor V. V. Markovich (arrested in 1932 in connection with the affair of Leningrad's Aleksandr Nevskii Brotherhood),[52] or the Dane M. M. Brensted, who appears in the memoirs of Lidiia Berdiaeva and who lived in Russia in the 1920s, but left for Paris in the year of Losev's arrest, subsequently collaborating on Berdiaev's journal *The Way*.[53]

Even in his old age Losev preserved a special piety in regard to the older philosophers with whom he had had the good fortune to engage. "I have retained not just a bright, but a dazzling impression of them all,"[54] he confessed, not attempting to count himself their equal. "As people, they were real giants of their kind, so that I would hardly dare to shake their hand, just say 'how do you do.' At most I had some insignificant conversations with just one or two of them."[55] In a documentary film made at the end of his life, Losev speaks in the same spirit:

> I was a student just starting out, but these were very important people. All those Bulgakovs, Berdiaevs, and Trubetskois, they were already giant figures, so to speak. I even used to greet them formally and they would shake me by the hand, but I didn't really manage to get close to any of them. ... And anyway, the revolution was on its way: I graduated from university in 1915, and in 1917—revolution! So just when I was rather more grown-up and could make my presence felt more strongly and get properly close to them, it was all broken off by events, mechanically ... only Frank, perhaps, he was somehow enthused by my research on Platonism and understood me more sensitively and deeply. But the rest were too far above me, at too far a remove from this young lad who had just shown up in Moscow and didn't know anything or anyone, and anyway what contribution could he bring and what could he say.[56]

However, the story of Losev's intellectual and spiritual opposition (in particular his collaboration on the *Spiritual Rus'* series, described below) is testament to the fact that in his oral reminiscences, whether on purpose or not, he downplayed the degree of his real and actual proximity to the *Vekhi* authors.

## Losev's Opposition to the Revolutionary "Cause" ("Delo")

Several key stages in the history of Losev's opposition to the revolutionary "cause" by means of the "word" can be distinguished, and they serve to illuminate his relationship to the *Vekhi* tradition.

The first stage that we know about was a project to publish a series of books devoted to Russian national identity under the general title *Spiritual Rus'*.[57] The plan for the project was conceived by Ivanov, Bulgakov (by now Father Sergii Bulgakov), and Losev in the spring of 1918: Losev was to be general editor. Losev informed the publisher, M. Sabashnikov, that the series "exclude[d] the remotest possibility of any party viewpoint," but he made no secret of the fact that the authors' views were anti-Marxist, although "the approach [was always to be] that of a free, non-confessional religious consciousness."⁵⁸ The series was to include works by Berdiaev, Bulgakov, the poet Georgii Chulkov, Sergei Durylin, secretary of the Vladimir Solov'ev Religious-Philosophical Society, the critic and publicist A. S. Glinka-Volzhskii, Ivanov, Evgenii Trubetskoi, and Losev himself. The project was never realized, but analysis of the proposal indicates that Berdiaev's essay "Ghosts of the Russian Revolution (Gogol', Dostoevskii, Tolstoi)," along with the articles by Bulgakov and Ivanov that were similarly included in Struve's symposium *Iz glubiny* (*Out of the Depths*), were originally intended for Losev's *Spiritual Rus'* also. The chronology of the preparation of both publications is the same, running from March to August 1918; the parallelism of their ideas is quite evident as well. *Spiritual Rus'*, like *Out of the Depths*, was intended as a sui generis continuation of *Vekhi*.

In the first half of 1918, Losev published his work in the newspaper *Zhizn'* (*Life*),⁵⁹ which was opposed to the Soviet authorities from an anarchist standpoint, that is, from a standpoint exactly opposite to that of *Vekhi* and *Out of the Depths*—hence the polemical attacks on the newspaper by the weekly *Nakanune* (*On the Eve*), which published the work of the *Vekhi* authors Berdiaev, Bulgakov, and Struve. The appearance of Losev in such a publication may seem strange, but in the context of a rapidly contracting space for free discourse uncontrolled by the Bolshevik censorship, the newspaper attracted people of various political persuasions, including well-known writers like Anna Akhmatova, Belyi, Aleksandr Blok, and Osip Mandel'shtam.

Of the three articles published by Losev in *Life*, "The Crisis of the Private Secondary School" and the review article "Russian Philosophical Literature in 1917–18" are of the most interest to us.⁶⁰ In the first the author describes, with emotional restraint and relying only on facts and figures, the catastrophic situation in private schools, the last "islets" not to be exposed to the pernicious influence of the new ideology. The article on Russian philosophy, for its part, only at first sight appears removed from social problems and the debate about the Russian intelligentsia and revolution that was conducted in *Vekhi* in 1909. It seems that the twenty-four-year-old Losev deemed the position of his older colleagues from *Spiritual Rus'* to be too passive. Losev was convinced that "from of old Russian philosophy, which is in essence social and frequently mystical at base, has always reacted strongly to social and political phenomena, describing them from the point of view of its more profound conception of the world."[61] As he himself put it, Losev was looking to philosophy for a spiritual "weapon for the fight,"[62] and he was unhappy that "despite the horrifying course of events Russian philosophy is silent, and we do not know what it has to say about everything that is happening."[63] This is why he writes with a certain reticence about the works of the "Slavophiles," Bulgakov's *Svet nevechernii* (*The Unfading Light*, 1917) and *Tikhie dumy* (*Quiet Thoughts*, 1918), Ivanov's *Rodnoe i vselenskoe* (*The Native and the Universal*, 1917), and Evgenii Trubetskoi's *Metafizicheskie predpolozheniia poznaniia. Opyt preodoleniia Kanta i kantianstva* (*The Metaphysical Presuppositions of Knowledge. An Essay in Overcoming Kant and Kantianism*, 1917). Thus, after paying tribute to Bulgakov's "sincere, profoundly Orthodox mysticism," "the religion of the Russian Christ that is the final and longed-for end of Bulgakov's entire work," he concludes that there is "little that is new and fiery" in *The Unfading Light*.[64]

Losev's intellectual affinities made him closer to the "western" wing of Russian thinkers at the time, among whom Losev classed Gershenzon (*Mudrost' Pushkina* [*The Wisdom of Pushkin*, 1917], *Troistvennyi obraz sovershenstva* [*The Trinitarian Image of Perfection*, 1918]), Frank (*Dusha cheloveka. Opyt vvedeniia v filosofskuiu psikhologiiu* [*The Soul of Man: Introduction to Philosophical Psychology*, 1917]), Il'in (*Filosofiia Gegelia kak uchenie o konkretnosti Boga i cheloveka* [*The Philosophy of Hegel as a Doctrine on the Concreteness of God and Man*, 1918]), and P. I. Novgorodtsev (*Ob obshchestvennom ideale* [*On the Social Ideal*, 1917]). Losev welcomed Il'in's "ardent affirmation of eternal truths" and Novgorodtsev's "objective critique of Marxism." He warmly recommended Frank's book as "a superb weapon in the fight against the outmoded and crude conventions of sensualism and materialism,"[65] while in Gershenzon's *Trinitarian Image of Perfection* he valued a "precise and clear ... sense of the vital antinomies of which everything consists," "a feeling for the contradictions and lamentable chaos of life," which "are also an essential stage on the way to ultimate affirmations."[66]

The second landmark in Losev's opposition to the revolutionary "cause" is his participation in the Swiss collection *Russland* (*Russia*), in which his article "Russian Philosophy" was published.⁶⁷ According to the table of contents, the first part of *Russia* was to include a second article by Losev, "Die Ideologie der orthodox-russischen Religion" ("The Ideology of Russian Orthodoxy"). This article was listed as appearing in *Russia* but for unknown reasons it never did so. Losev apparently intended to submit it, since an essay in German, "Die Onomatodoxie" ("Onomatodoxy"), survives, devoted to "one of the oldest and most typical trends in the Orthodox east," the name-worship that attracted numerous apologists among Russian religious thinkers of the early twentieth century.⁶⁸

*Russia* was edited by Vera Erismann-Stepanova, Theodor Erismann, and Jean Matthieu, and was published in Zürich in 1919.⁶⁹ Matthieu was an active Swiss social democrat, while Erismann-Stepanova was a graduate in philosophy from the University of Zürich who was married to the psychologist Theodor Erismann.⁷⁰ Family tradition has it that the initiative for *Russia* came from the Erismanns,⁷¹ but be that as it may, it seems that the ideological platform was the idea of Erismann-Stepanova's brother-in-law, the well-known historian Sergei Mel'gunov, who was exiled from Russia in 1922 on the famous "philosophical steamship." Mel'gunov's atheistic, liberal-populist position, which informed his attacks on *Vekhi* in 1909,⁷² changed to a certain extent when the Bolsheviks came to power. Mel'gunov started to look for allies in various political circles, and this brought him to the *Soiuz vozrozhdeniia Rossii* (Union for the Revival of Russia, established in 1918), which aimed to restore Russian statehood. It was probably only for tactical reasons that Mel'gunov's name was not included in the list of editors of *Russia*. The collection contains an article by him on church and state in Russia, and another by his wife, Erismann-Stepanova's sister, Praskov'ia, and the majority of *Russia*'s other contributors (the publicist Ivan Belokonskii, the pedagogue Nikolai Rumiantsev, the historian Konstantin Sivkov, and the folklorist Boris Sokolov) had actively published their works in Mel'gunov's co-operative publishing house, Zadruga. It is likely that the project aimed to provide the western reader with detailed information about Russia and its culture, and that aim was in conformity with the ideas of Mel'gunov as a member of the Union for the Revival of Russia.

In this context one thing remains unclear, and that is how Losev's article "Russian Philosophy" came to be included in this publication.⁷³ There is no evidence that Losev and Mel'gunov were acquainted, but we know that Losev became a member of Zadruga at some point between 1918 and 15 May 1919:[74] his name appears in the membership list until 15 May 1919,[75] and in 1919 he considered publishing his *Genesis of Greek Tragedy* with Zadruga. Several hypotheses can be advanced. The most persuasive is that Losev's friend from university days, Pavel Popov, acted as an intermediary between Losev and Mel'gunov between 1917 and 1919. Popov had become acquainted with Mel'gunov in the late 1910s, and was an active member of Zadruga.

Like the review of philosophical literature in *Life*, Losev's article for *Russia* is only superficially unrelated to the problems debated in *Vekhi*. For a start, albeit unsurprisingly, Losev includes Berdiaev, Bulgakov, and Frank in his list of the representatives of contemporary Russian philosophy. He offers a brief description of Berdiaev's *The Meaning of the Creative Act* and Bulgakov's *The Unfading Light*. He also quotes copiously from Berdiaev's book on Khomiakov because, as he himself explains, Berdiaev "is one of the most significant representatives of contemporary Russian philosophy," and it is evident from his book that "in our time Russian philosophy has become aware of its own essence, and that, as a rule, it is true to this essence in only setting itself the tasks that have always been associated with genuine Russian philosophy."[76] Losev believes that, beginning with Solov'ev, "a new Russian apocalyptic conception of the world"[77] had come into being; it is therefore unsurprising that Berdiaev and Bulgakov seem to him to be "Slavophiles with the addition of apocalyptic mysticism."[78] Additionally (and in the context of *Vekhi* this is particularly noteworthy), Losev underlines the publicistic principle present in Russian philosophy. He states that Russian philosophy, with its characteristic "mystical-ontological realism,"[79] has always been "intricately connected with real life, and for this reason often appears in polemical and publicistic guise, drawing its vitality from the general spirit of the age, with all its positive and negative aspects, with all its joys and sufferings, with all its order and chaos."[80]

Losev did not choose to write about the history of Russian thought only out of a desire to inform his western readership about a world with which it was unfamiliar. He highlights the philosophical character of Russian literature, the philosophy of the Slavophiles, and above all the philosophy of

Solov'ev, that is, the creative endeavors of precisely those Russian thinkers "the Russian intelligentsia does not want to know," according to Berdiaev's essay for *Vekhi*, "Filosofskaia istina i intelligentskaia pravda" ("Philosophical Verity and Intelligentsia Truth"). Losev develops Berdiaev's thinking on the "concrete idealism" or "ontological realism" of Russian philosophy, and on its religious foundations as reflected in the striving for a "synthesis of knowledge and faith." At the same time, Losev's assertion that "Russian philosophy has never dealt with anything other than the soul, the person, and inner asceticism"[81] also invites comparison with Bulgakov's essay for *Vekhi*, "Geroizm i podvizhnichestvo" ("Heroism and Asceticism"), in which the spiritual act and Christian asceticism are opposed to the intelligentsia's heroism and anthropotheism. In his texts from 1918, Losev agrees with Bulgakov on the need to form a "national self-consciousness" on "religious-cultural foundations."

Although *Vekhi* is neither directly quoted nor mentioned in Losev's article, one can nevertheless see here a continuation of the conversation begun in *Vekhi* by Berdiaev, who thought that "the purifying fire of philosophy" was to play a significant role in the radical reformation of the intelligentsia's consciousness. Subsequently, Losev would make further discreet reference to Berdiaev's *Vekhi* essay. For example, in the late 1930s allusions to this essay appear in Losev's novel *Vstrecha* (*The Meeting*), which is the closest of his works to the set of problems discussed in *Vekhi*. Meanwhile, Berdiaev's reference to a special "proletarian class mysticism" is recalled in *The Philosophy of the Name* and *The Dialectics of Myth*, in which Losev writes about the mysticism of materialists, the communist and proletarian mythology. A telling example is the grotesquely ironic apology for "a world without end or limit, without form or bounds," a blind and dead material world that true materialists fanatically believe in: "We have our own mythology, and we love it, cherish it, we have spilled and will again spill our living and warm blood for it."[82]

Whatever the interest—considerable as it is—of Losev's attempts in the years 1917–19 to express his social-philosophical position, it was *The Dialectics of Myth* (1930), the last anti-Marxist book to be published in the Soviet Union, that marked the culmination of his intellectual and spiritual opposition to the Soviet order.[83] This work is not about ancient myths.

It is about a different kind of mythology: the ideas of the public sphere that possess individuals as well as entire social groups. *The Dialectics of Myth* is at once a religious-philosophical treatise exploring the dialectics of the mythology of the Absolute and a sui generis sociological study of the psychology of mass thinking, an attempt to define the basic ideological units that pre-determine the behavior of specific social groups or whole nations.

The polemical, almost publicistic, tone that, unusually for a work of philosophy, permeates Losev's text, is confirmation that this work continues the tradition of social-philosophical (typically journal) writing of the *Vekhi* authors, and indeed of *Vekhi* itself, and, in a broader sense, of a classical Russian philosophy that (as Losev himself declared in "Russian Philosophy") is notable for its vitality, its involvement in real social life, and its interest in pre-logical, mythological thinking. It is not without reason that *The Dialectics of Myth* developed many of the themes of *Vekhi*: atheism as a peculiar religious faith, the idolization of science and progress by the intelligentsia, and the rejection of positivism and rationalism in philosophy. Echoing/repeating Frank's article "The Ethics of Nihilism,"[84] Losev stresses the real spiritual and religious foundations of social and political events by demonstrating how spiritual nihilism—the negation of both the Absolute and the mythology of the Absolute—transform man into nothing and plunge him into a spiritual and social hell where various relative mythologies, including Marxism, reign:

> From the point of view of Communist mythology, not only [is it the case that] "a *specter* wanders in Europe, the specter of Communism" ([as stated at] the beginning of the *Communist Manifesto*), but also [that] "the vermin of counterrevolution are swarming," "the jackals of imperialism are howling," "the hydra of the bourgeoisie is baring its teeth," and "the jaws of financial sharks are gaping." Here we also find scurrying about such figures as "bandits in tail-coats," "monocled brigands," "crowned blood-letters," "cannibals in mitres," and "cassocked *jaw-shatterers*." In addition, everywhere there are "*dark* forces," "*gloomy* reaction," "the *black* army of *obscurantists*"; and in this darkness there is "the *red* dawn" of "global fire," "the *red* flag" of rebellion. What a picture! And they say there is no mythology here.[85]

The opposition Losev constructs between proponents of the mythology of the Absolute and adherents of relativist mythologies such as socialism in many aspects mirrors the opposition in *Vekhi* between two social-philosophical types: the opponents and the advocates of revolution.

Contemporary readers may share the view of some that Losev's attacks on socialism and communism get lost in the theoretical analysis of the nature of myth and mythological thinking, but even these sporadic passages were enough to have their author sent to one of the forced labor camps organized for the construction of the White Sea-Baltic canal, and to have him condemned as a class enemy at the 16th Party Congress. After his release his works were not published until after Stalin's death, but his intellectual and spiritual opposition to the regime did not cease. In the 1930s and 1940s, Losev's opposition to Soviet reality is expressed in his literary works, in which one can also find allusions to *Vekhi* and the problems addressed therein. In *Meeting*, mentioned above, the problem treated is that of the intelligentsia and revolution. In the story "Iz razgovorov na Belomoro-Baltiiskom kanale" ("From Talks at the White Sea-Baltic Canal"), Losev addresses the question of production under socialism that so greatly troubled the *Vekhi* authors, above all Frank. The main subject of debate for the interlocutors in the story is the question of the correct attitude to technology. For the author, this question is closely related to the problem of civilization as the last stage of human history, when the human spirit is subjugated to the spirit of the thing, the machine. Such a "neo-Luddite" orientation was typical for the turn of the twentieth century, when "it was as if literature became the site of a pitched battle between the 'mechanizers' and the 'anti-mechanizers,'" as reflected in the novels of H. G. Wells and the dystopias of E. M. Forster or Aldous Huxley. In their "brave new world," power has also been usurped by a new and humanly improved "Lord our Ford, or Freud" (Huxley). Man himself prays to the machine because the Bible has long since been replaced by the "Book of the Machine" (Forster).[86] At the same time this idea of Losev's is in complete agreement with the general outlook of Russian religious philosophical thought. Thus, for Berdiaev, socialism is "civilization, but not culture" because "culture is organic" while "civilization is mechanical."[87]

## Aleksei Losev and *Vekhi*: Strategic Traditions in Social Philosophy

In a world in which animated being has been replaced by the inanimate, God and the idea of the Absolute are squeezed out by matter, and the logic of the absurd comes into play such that, as the central protagonist of *Meeting*, Nikolai Vershinin, says, "they want to base morality and self-sacrifice for the sake of society on the natural sciences, on biology," or when a person who has been deprived of his personhood and soul has it explained to him that "they say you are descended from the apes. *Therefore* you should love one another."[88] Vershinin's words are a veiled quotation from Berdiaev's *Vekhi* article: "Vladimir Solov'ev very wittily observed that the Russian intelligentsia always reasons from the same syllogism: man is descended from the apes, therefore we ought to love one another. The intelligentsia perceived scientific positivism wholly in terms of this syllogism; positivism was merely an instrument for affirming the reign of social justice and for utterly destroying those metaphysical and religious ideas which, the intelligentsia dogmatically assumed, support the reign of evil" (21). Only in this context can the direction of Losev's thinking be properly understood. Losev is persuaded that the triumph of materialism and the extirpation of metaphysical and religious ideas distort morality and transform man into an ape and the world into a prison. As he says through his mouthpiece Vershinin, all his abstract talk about philosophy or music is but "an analysis of the Russian revolution."[89]

Beginning in the mid-1950s, Losev worked on his *History of Classical Aesthetics* in eight volumes. His withdrawal to the history of philosophy was a forced step, but it gave him the opportunity to realize at least partially his plan of the 1920s to create a general typology of cultures that presupposed their present condition. By plunging into antiquity, Losev seemed to abandon the burning social problems of *Vekhi*, but his mood was quite different. Allegorically, in Aesopian language, he continued to develop ideas similar to those of the *Vekhi* authors. For example, in 1985 the Party newspaper *Pravda* published a conversation with Losev entitled "Derzanie dukha" ("The Daring of the Spirit").[90] Is it an accident that the title reminds us of Berdiaev's words in *Vekhi* about "the love of truth and the daring of thought [*derznovenie mysli*]" that are being extinguished by the reigning demagogy? It is unlikely. This is confirmed by Losev's argument, expressed during the interview, that as a counterweight to an irrational technologism aimed at the destruction of the human person and humanity there should be a correct worldview, "a secret or open striving for freedom,"[91] and that there was a need to educate young people in "love for the profundity and beauty of thought for its own sake."[92] It is not without reason that Losev makes the reservation that he may be considered "a bad idealist for preaching a quiet, conciliatory and sober way of thinking,"[93] given that his words are a paraphrase of Gershenzon's argumentation about "creative self-consciousness."

## Conclusion

Of all the participants in *Vekhi*, three figures—Berdiaev, Bulgakov, and Frank—attracted Losev's attention throughout his life. In Gershenzon he saw "a profound critic" with a "beautiful style," but toward the end of his life he was rather critical of his philosophy in general.[94] Losev's special relationship with Frank has already been discussed in detail. As far as Berdiaev and Bulgakov are concerned, there are many positive references to them in Losev's work. In the 1970s Losev had in his field of vision Bulgakov's books *The Unfading Light* (1917), *Lestvitsa Iakovlia* (*Jacob's Ladder*, 1929), and *Nevesta Agntsa* (*Bride of the Lamb*, 1945), and Berdiaev's *The Meaning of the Creative Act, Opyt opravdaniia cheloveka* (*Essay in Religious Anthropology*, 1916), *O naznachenii cheloveka* (*On the Destiny of Man*, 1931),[95] *Samopoznanie* (*Self-Knowledge*, 1949)[96] and *Ekzistentsial'naia dialektika chelovecheskogo i bozhestvennogo* (*The Dialectic of the Human and the Divine in Existentialism*, 1952). If Bulgakov's books delighted him with their marvelous titles,[97] Berdiaev's did so by their style: "Sometimes in Berdiaev every phrase is an aphorism. 'The personality is the sacrament of one, marriage is the sacrament of two, the church is the sacrament of three.' Or, 'Two types of Satanism, fascism and communism.' But this is not politics, it is a meticulously worked out philosophy."[98] To Losev, it is important that Bulgakov, and Berdiaev too, are "Solov'evians," although "touched by the twentieth century."[99] Not for nothing does he devote a special paragraph to describing Bulgakov's relationship to Solov'ev's philosophy in his book on the latter.[100] In the documentary film "Losev" he speaks with no less enthusiasm about Berdiaev's philosophy, and calls him "an apostle of freedom." According to Losev, Berdiaev "senses the divinity of his freedom like Angelus Silesius, who said: 'Without me God could not make the tiniest movement.'"[101] It is interesting that in one private conversation Losev aligned himself precisely with Berdiaev: "Like Berdiaev I call myself a child of freedom."[102] All the more, then, did he suffer from not being able to work openly in conditions of unfreedom, not being able to study his favourite thinkers and own their books: "Once I saw that someone was selling six or seven of Berdiaev's works for fifty rubles. But I was afraid of political provocation. Moscow would find out immediately who that man sold his books to."[103] He recommends reading Berdiaev: "Even if you don't share all his views, it is always useful to commune with a genius," but at the same time acknowledges that this is dangerous since "it's dangerous not even to read, but simply to keep the books. You get persecuted for that [...] They lock you up, there's been the trial of Daniel', Siniavskii, Ginzburg."[104] It seemed demeaning to him to study his favorite philosophers in secret: "No, I don't like it when you have to hide. I say what I think; I'd repeat it in front of an audience of two hundred. Let everyone see what Losev thinks. I like to do things openly. But to study Berdiaev by reading him in snatches at night—that's not interesting. You have to study seriously so as to think things through, you have to become absorbed."[105]

Of course, seventy years of the Soviet system trained Losev to write in Aesopian style. But as soon as perestroika began in the Soviet Union, the philosopher began to speak openly about *Vekhi*. This is evident in the documentary filmed in 1987, toward the end of Losev's life, by V. Kosakovskii. "Today *Vekhi* is deemed to be a dreadful book, you can't read or own or discuss it," he declares, and admits at the same time that "[w]hen I read it I was excited by its profound thought. Very profound thought! They saw that the revolution suppressed the person too much. That's why the cry went up, 'Where is man?' Well, production—production is good. Progress, the public. ... But where is man? He isn't there."[106]

The philosopher had to spend the major part of his life in a depersonalized, dehumanized society, suffer many catastrophes, and make various sacrifices, but inwardly he remained faithful to the social-philosophical strategy of resisting evil with the word and with creative activity in the field of culture. In the days of his youth this strategy had also guided his older colleagues, the *Vekhi* authors, in their philosophical endeavor.

## NOTES

1. This article was written as part of the project RGNF 11 - 03 - 00408a.

2. *Vekhi. Iz glubiny*, ed. A. A. Iakovlev (Moscow: Pravda, 1991). Page references to this edition appear in parentheses in the text.

3. See A. Haardt, *Husserl in Russland: Phänomenologie der Sprache und Kunst bei G. Spet und Aleksej Losev* (Munich: Wilhelm Fink Verlag, 1993); *The Life and Thought of Aleksei Losev*, special edition, *Russian Studies in Philosophy* 35: 1 (1996); A. Jubara, *Die Philosophie des Mythos von Aleksej Losev im Kontext "Russischen Philosophie"* (Wiesbaden: Harrassowitz Verlag, 2000); *The Dialectic in A. F. Losev's Thought*, special edition, *Russian Studies in Philosophy* 40: 3 (2002); *Aleksej Fedorovich Losev: Philosophy and the Human Sciences*, ed. Robert Bird, *Studies in East European Thought* 56: 2–3 (2004); H. Kuße, *Metadiskursive Argumentation. Linguistische Untersuchungen zum russischen Diskurs von Lomonosov bis Losev* (Munich: Otto Sagner, 2004); *A. F. Losev and Twentieth-Century Human Sciences*, *Russian Studies in Philosophy* 44: 1 (summer 2005); A. A. Takho-Godi, *Losev*, 2nd ed. (Moscow: Molodaia gvardiia, 2007) ("Zhizn' zamechatel'nykh liudei" series); M. Dennes, ed., *L'Œuvre d'Aleksei Losev dans le contexte de la culture européenne*, *Slavica Occitania* 31 (2010).

4. S. L. Frank, "Novaia russkaia filosofskaia sistema," *Put'* 9 (1928).

5. The reference is to the police investigation of Andrei Belyi's wife and was given to me by M. L. Spivak.

6. *The Dialectics of Myth* has been translated into Bulgarian, Czech, English, German, Japanese, Serbian, and Spanish. The most reliable edition of Losev's book in Russian is: A.F. Losev, *Dialektika mifa. Dopolnenie k Diakektike mifa* (Moscow, 2001), *Filosofskoe nasledie* series, vol. 130). The English edition is A. F. Losev, *The Dialectics of Myth*, trans. V. Marchenkov (London: Routledge, 2003).

7. A similar idea for the second part of *The Dialectics of Myth*, partly lost as a consequence of his arrest, is a further argument in favor of the idea that Losev was one of the prototypes for the central protagonist of Mikhail Bulgakov's novel of the 1930s, *Master i Margarita* (*The Master and Margarita*), the "thrice romantic" master, with his idea to write a novel—in the Soviet period—about Christ and Pontius Pilate. See V. P. Troitskii, "Chernaia shapochka mastera," in V. P. Troitskii, *Razyskaniia o zhizni i tvorchestve A. F. Loseva* (Moscow: Agraf, 2007), 87–105.

## Aleksei Losev and *Vekhi*: Strategic Traditions in Social Philosophy

8   Unpublished fragment of Losev's work on Nicholas of Cusa and ancient-medieval dialectics.

9   Nathalie Duddington, "Philosophy in Russia," *Journal of Philosophical Studies* 6: 22 (1931): 226.

10  A. F. Losev and V. M. Loseva, *"Radost' na veki": Perepiska lagernykh vremen* (Moscow: Russkii put', 2005), 57.

11  Unpublished commentary on Nicholas of Cusa's "De non aliud," composed in the 1930s.

12  A. F. Losev, *Mif. Chislo. Sushchnost'* (Moscow: Mysl', 1994), 334.

13  Ibid., 352.

14  Losev's essays on mathematics are collected in A. F. Losev, *Khaos i struktura* (Moscow: Mysl', 1997).

15  A. F. Losev, *"Ia soslan v XX vek ..."* (Moscow: Vremia, 2002). On Losev's literary prose, see E. W. Clowes, *Fiction's Overcoat. Russian Literary Culture and the Question of Philosophy* (Ithaca, NY: Cornell University Press, 2004), my book about Losev as a writer *Khudozhestvennyi mir prozy A. F. Loseva* (Moscow: Bolshaia rossiiskaia entsiklopediia, 2007), and my article "Alexey Losev's Philosophical Novel 'The Woman Thinker' and the Problem of the Eternal Feminine," *Transcultural Studies: A Series in Interdisciplinary Research. Special Issue on Sophia Across Culture: From the Old Testament to Postmodernity*, vol. 4 (2008): 131–39.

16  A. F. Losev, *Iazykovaia struktura* (Moscow: MGPI, 1983), 150.

17  Ibid., 148.

18  S. Shaumyan, "Dialekticheskie idei A. F. Loseva v lingvistike," in *Obraz mira—struktura i tseloe* (Moscow: Logos, 1999), 376.

19  See A. A. Takho-Godi, "K 20-letiiu vykhoda knigi A. F. Loseva *Vl. Solov'ev* v izdatel'stve Mysl': Delo o knige A. F. Loseva *Vl. Solov'ev*," in *Vladimir Solov'ev i kul'tura Serebriannogo veka: K 150-letiiu Vl. Solov'eva i 110-letiiu A. F. Loseva* (Moscow: Nauka, 2007).

20  See A. A. Takho-Godi and E. A. Takho-Godi, eds., *Sbornik "Vekhi" v kontekste russkoi kul'tury* (Moscow: Nauka, 2007).

21  See my article "Zum gegenseitigen Verhältnis von A. F. Losev und S. L. Frank," in *Kultur als Dialog und Meinung. Beiträge zu Fedor A. Stepun und Semen L. Frank*, in *Specimina philologiae slavicae*, ed. H. Kuße, Bd. 153 (Munich: Verlag Otto Sagner, 2008), 219–37.

22  V. V. Bibikhin, *Aleksei Fedorovich Losev. Sergei Sergeevich Averintsev* (Moscow: Institut filosofii, teologii i istorii sv. Fomy, 2004), 225.

23  A. F. Losev, "Iz poslednikh vospominanii o Viacheslave Ivanove," in *Eskhil. Tragedii: V perevode Viacheslava Ivanova* (Moscow: Nauka, 1989), 464.

24  Bibikhin, *Aleksei Fedorovich Losev*, 242.

25  Ibid.

26  Ibid., 29.

27  Ibid., 242–43.

28  Ibid., 161.

29  See "Moskovskoe religiozno-filosofskoe obshchestvo pamiati Vl. Solov'eva: Khronika russkoi dukhovnoi zhizni," ed. and intro. O. T. Ermishin, *Literaturovedcheskii zhurnal* 28 (2011): 711.

30  Takho-Godi, *Losev*, 158, 244.

31  A. F. Losev, "V poiskakh smysla," *Voprosy literatury* 10 (1985): 212. The interview was conducted by Viktor Erofeev.

32  A. A. Takho-Godi and V. P. Troitskii, eds., *Aleksei Fiodorovich Losev. Iz tvorcheskogo naslediia. Sovremenniki o myslitele* (Moscow: Russkii mir, 2007), 711.

33  Bibikhin, *Aleksei Fedorovich Losev*, 242.

34  A. F. Losev, *Ocherki antichnogo simvolizma i mifologii* (Moscow: Mysl', 1993), 698.

35  Bibikhin, *Aleksei Fedorovich Losev*, 243.

36  S. M. Polovinkin, "Vol'naia akademiia dukhovnoi kul'tury," *Pravoslavnaia entsiklopediia* (Moscow: Tserkovno-nauchnyi tsentr "Pravoslavnaia entsiklopediia," 2005), vol. 9, 284–86.

37  Takho-Godi and Troitskii, *Iz tvorcheskogo naslediia*, 711.

38  A. A. Takho-Godi, E. A. Takho-Godi, V. P. Troitskii, *A. F. Losev—filosof i pisatel'* (Moscow: Nauka, 2003), 24.

39  A. F. Losev, *Forma. Stil'. Vyrazhenie* (Moscow: Mysl', 1995), 586.

40  Ibid., 594.

41  Ibid.

42  E. Takho-Godi, "Nicolaus Cusanus in the perception of A.F. Losev," in *Nicolaus Cusanus: ein bewundernswerter historischer Brennpunkt: Philosophische Tradition und wissenschaftliche Rezeption*, ed. K. Reinhardt and H. Schwaetzer with O. Dushin (Regensburg, 2008), 255–79.

43  Bibikhin, *Aleksei Fedorovich Losev*, 161.

44  Related by A. A. Gaponenkov.

45  Frank, "Novaia russkaia religioznaia sistema," 90.

46  Ibid.

47  Ibid.

48  Ibid., 89.

49  A. F. Losev, *Khaos i struktura*, 11.

50  For example, in 1928–29 members of the religious-philosophical circle *Voskresenie* were accused of reading and distributing White émigré publications. See *Zvezda* 11 (2006).

51  Bibikhin, *Aleksei Fedorovich Losev*, 245, 247.

52  See: www.sobornoedelo.ru/book.php?mode=get_glava&glavaID=1107.

53  A. A. Takho-Godi, *Losev*, 150–51.

54  Bibikhin, *Aleksei Fedorovich Losev*, 245. Losev is here referring specifically to Berdiaev and Stepun.

55  Ibid., 225.

56  The documentary "Losev" was filmed by V. Kosakovskii in the last two years of Losev's life. The transcription is the author's.

57  The history of the planned series *Spiritual Rus'* is expounded in detail in my book *Velikie i bezvestnye. Ocherki po russkoi literature i kul'ture XIX–XX vekov* (St. Petersburg: Nestor-Istoriia, 2008), 425–42.

58  Ibid., 434.

59  For a detailed discussion of Losev's participation in *Life*, see Takho-Godi, *Velikie i bezvestnye*, 443–92.

60  All three texts are reprinted in Takho-Godi and Takho-Godi, *Sbornik "Vekhi" v kontekste russkoi kul'tury*, 403–09. The article "Russian Philosophical Literature in 1917–18" is reprinted in Takho-Godi, *Velikie i bezvestnye*, 493–96.

61  E. A. Takho-Godi, *Velikie i bezvestnye*, 493.

62  Ibid., 495.

63  Ibid., 493.

64  Ibid.

65  Ibid., 495.

66  Ibid., 496.

67  For further detail on the history of this publication, see E. A. Takho-Godi, "A. F. Losev i sbornik *Russland* (1919): fakty i gipotezy," in *Ot Kibirova do Pushkina: Sbornik v chest' 60-letiia N. A. Bogomolova* (Moscow: Novoe literaturnoe obozrenie, 2011), 581–98.

68  A. F. Losev, *Forma. Stil'. Vyrazhenie* (Moscow: Mysl', 1995), 773–79.

69  A. F. Losev, "Die russische Philosophie," in *Russland, I Teil: Geistesleben, Kunst, Philosophie, Literatur, II Teil: Politischer Bau, Soziale Bewegungen und gesellschaftliches Leben*, ed. V. Erismann-Stepanowa, Th. Erismann, and J. Matthieu (Zürich: Druck und Verlag s Art. Institut Orell Füssli, 1919), 79–109. Reprinted in USA by Nabu Press, spring 2010.

70  Theodor Erismann was the son of the Swiss doctor Friedrich (Fedor) Erismann, the founder of social hygiene as a branch of Russian medicine, and his second wife Sophie Hass, who held a doctorate in medicine from Bern University.

71　This was the view of their daughter when asked about the collection by Magnus Ljunggren, a professor of Gothenburg University and friend of the family, in the summer of 2009 (when she was 90 years old). There are, however, reasons to doubt that this tradition is accurate.

72　See V. V. Sapov, ed., *Vekhi: pro et contra. Antologiia* (St. Petersburg: Russkii Khristianskii gumanitarnyi institut, 1998), 69, 774.

73　Losev, "Die russische Philosophie," 79–109.

74　See *O kooperativnom tovarishchestve pechatnogo i izdatel'skogo dela 'Zadruga' (Doklad obshchemu sobraniiu chlenov 'Zadrugi'): 1912-1919* (Kharkov, Moscow, Petrograd, 1919), 25.

75　Ibid., 7–13.

76　A. F. Losev, "Russkaia filosofiia," in A. F. Losev, *Strast' k dialektike* (Moscow: Sovetskii pisatel', 1990), 72.

77　Ibid., 91.

78　Ibid., 98.

79　Ibid., 77.

80　Ibid., 74.

81　Ibid., 90.

82　A. F. Losev, *Filosofiia imeni*, in A. F. Losev, *Bytie. Imia. Kosmos* (Moscow: Mysl', 1993), 773.

83　On Losev and his The Dialectics of Myth, see Philip T. Grier, "Adventures in Dialectic and Intuition: Shpet, Il'in, Losev," in *A History of Russian Philosophy 1830-1930: Faith, Reason, and the Defense of Human Dignity*, ed. G. M. Hamburg and Randall A. Poole (Cambridge: Cambridge University Press, 2010), 326–45.

84　See also S. V. Iakovlev, "Otsenka nigilizma v rabotakh S. L. Franka i A. F. Loseva," in *Sbornik "Vekhi" v kontekste russkoi kul'tury*, ed. A. A. Takho-Godi and E. A. Takho-Godi, 251–57.

85　Losev, *The Dialectics of Myth*, 96.

86　See E. Takho-Godi, "Aleksej Losev's Antiutopia," in *Aleksei Fedorovich Losev: Philosophy and the Human Sciences*, ed. Robert Bird, *Studies in East European Thought* 56: 2-3 (2004): 243–46.

87　N. Berdiaev, "Predsmertnye mysli Fausta," in *Osval'd Spengler i zakat Evropy* (Moscow: Bereg, 1922), 64.

88　Losev, "Ia soslan v XX vek...", 402.

89　Ibid., 392.

90　The title of this conversation later became the title of a book addressed to Russian youth, A. F. Losev, *Derzanie dukha* (Moscow: Plitizdat, 1989).

91　Losev, *Derzanie dukha*, 296.

92  Ibid., 294.
93  Ibid.
94  Bibikhin, *Aleksei Fedorovich Losev*, 170–71.
95  Ibid., 216.
96  Ibid., 170.
97  Ibid., 167.
98  Ibid., 170.
99  Ibid., 233–34.
100 A. F. Losev, *Vladimir Solov'ev i ego vremia* (Moscow: Molodaia gvardiia, 2009), 485–90.
101 Bibikhin, *Aleksei Fedorovich Losev*, 170. Losev misquotes Angelus Silesius here: his exact words were "without me God may make no single smallest worm."
102 Ibid., 155.
103 Ibid., 170.
104 Ibid., 30.
105 Ibid.
106 This is my decoding of the text.

# Part IV
# *Vekhi* and the RUSSIAN RELIGIOUS RENAISSANCE

# 10

## Inside Out:
## Good, Evil, and the Question of Inspiration

*Oliver Smith*

> Russian atheism is by no means a conscious rejection, the fruit of a complex, agonizing and prolonged effort of the mind, the heart and the will, the product of personal experience. No, most often it is taken on faith, and preserves the characteristics of a naive religious belief, only inside out.
> —Sergei Bulgakov

> Sir, didst not thou sow good seed in thy field? From whence then hath it tares?
> —Matthew 13:27

Perhaps the most fundamental theme running through the *Vekhi* collection is the division between inner and outer, internal and external. The "common platform" of all the authors, Mikhail Gershenzon tells the reader in his "Preface," is "the recognition of the theoretical and practical primacy of spiritual life over the external forms of community," with an emphasis on the "individual's inner life" (xxxvii).[1] This division between internal and external appears in one form or another in all of the essays. It can be observed in the critique of the Russian intelligentsia's alleged propensity for disregarding the internal work of personal development in favor of external social engineering; its inability to digest ideas or beliefs rather than simply gathering, herd-like, under the latest flag; and its dependence on external might over inner, spiritual reserve.[2] The tendency of the Russian *intelligent* to, in Gershenzon's words, live "outside himself [*vne sebia*]" (51),[3] is clearly one of the principal targets of the *Vekhi* critique. Not centered in himself and thus enjoying only minimal interaction with his inner life, the *intelligent* reads the reality around him in a similar vein. He admits of no causality but that of the material order, a causality that does not arise from a place of interiority but, so to speak, slips off the shapes of things, building its future from the mechanical flux of events. Change the flux of events—through ordering, or through the mechanical construction of society and nature, for example—and you are able to control the influx of good and evil into the world or, more precisely, radically to diminish the latter in favor of the former. "The basic philosopheme of socialism," writes Petr Struve, "its ideological axis as a world-view, is the principle that human good and evil ultimately depend on external conditions" (119).

This is all well-worn ground on which many subsequent critiques of the Soviet system, indeed of totalitarianism in general, have been founded.[4] This essay concentrates on a somewhat different aspect of this inner-outer division, namely Sergei Bulgakov's at first puzzling categorization of the unconscious religiosity of the intelligentsia—a religiosity much debated in *Vekhi*, as indeed it was before and after—as one that shares all the features of naive faith, even Christian faith, excepting the fact that it is "inside out [*naiznanku*]" (22). This phrase will be explored in the context of the tradition on which the *Vekhi* essays self-consciously draw yet rarely articulate openly, namely that of the apocalyptic strand in Russian religious thinkers such as Fedor Bukharev, Fedor Dostoevskii, and Vladimir Solov'ev. While I seek to illuminate this problematic from the perspective of *Vekhi* as a whole, I concentrate in particular on Bulgakov, whose life trajectory was inextricably bound up with the Solov'evian legacy and whose oeuvre demonstrates (with the possible exception of Nikolai Berdiaev) the strongest development of eschatological themes, the culmination of which we see in his last complete work, *Apokalipsis Ioanna* (*The Apocalypse of John*, 1948). Through the prism of Bulgakov, I therefore seek to uncover a consistent hermeneutic that weaves through the pre- and post-revolutionary periods and encapsulates both Bulgakov's own evolving conception of the workings of good and evil in Russian society and the wider framework of apocalyptic interpretation in which it was set.

## Inside Out: Good, Evil, and the Question of Inspiration

It should be stated at the outset that a religiosity "turned inside out" does not for Bulgakov equate merely to a transposition of the object of faith from God to nothing, atheism replacing theism by an inversion of its object. Conventional wisdom has of course long taught that atheism requires just as much a leap of "faith" as belief in God does, yet this is the focus of neither Bulgakov nor the *Vekhi* authors as a whole. It is fair to say that they are only tangentially interested in the ideological structures underlying Russian atheism and in the patterns of belief that fuel atheistic currents of thought, which, as the authors point out, feed on many of the same tendencies as contemporary atheism in the west.

In a recent book on Dostoevskii, Rowan Williams writes against the grain of many commentators, arguing that the novelist was not concerned in solving the so-called "cursed questions," this being especially the case as regards the question of the existence or non-existence of God. Rather, he attempted to portray what a world without God might look like, and what it might mean for human beings to inhabit such a world.[5] Atheism is not debunked as a matter of course; rather, its various, often ambiguous effects are traced through the actions of his protagonists. While the approach of the *Vekhi* authors is clearly less creative and more explicitly philosophical, they nevertheless proceed in a similar manner: their goal is not to provide an alternative worldview to the atheistic nihilism, the "heroism," or whichever term we choose to use, of the revolutionaries, but to portray the *effects* of such a worldview on the "soul" of the intelligentsia. It is only insofar as they depict the effects of atheism on human life severed from absolute values that they can be seen to propose the means for the overcoming of atheism. Yet, whereas in his novel *Besy* (*The Devils*, 1872) Dostoevskii tends to read contemporary events as ciphers for a larger reality, drawing the shapes of the future from the still-uncertain present, the *Vekhi* essays work in the opposite direction. They move from the all-too-real to the murky source of inspiration in which the real had its birth. Where Dostoevskii may be described as constitutive and prophetic, *Vekhi* is primarily diagnostic: it attempts not to lay bare the partially concealed content of the soul of the Russian intelligentsia but to interpret the development of the same from its actual history, to read the signs of the disease from its manifestly evident symptoms.

Nevertheless, *Vekhi* occupies a kind of liminal zone: its concrete time is a Russia poised between two revolutions. Its authors' reading of history, which is described by Bulgakov as "not mere chronology, relating the sequence of events," but "life experience, the experience of good and evil" (17), has therefore both a diagnostic and a prophetic aspect. On the one hand, that such experience had come to a head, and that, as a consequence, a kind of veil had dropped from the face of the Russian intelligentsia during the revolution of 1905, was axiomatic for the *Vekhi* authors. No longer was it a question of intuiting the darkness within; the darkness was there for all to see. For Bulgakov, the days of the revolution had revealed the "full-blown image of the *intelligent*" (21), while Struve speaks in almost identical terms: "the intelligentsia ... became fully manifest in the revolution of 1905–07" (118). Yet, on the other hand, the precise contours of this definitive revelation, for all its demonstrative power, appear to many readers of *Vekhi* to be particularly difficult to chart. This is in large part due to the fact that *Vekhi* is not primarily concerned, unlike its predecessor *Problemy idealizma* (*Problems of Idealism*, 1902), with the critique of philosophical and political systems; nor, unlike its successor *Iz glubiny* (*Out of the Depths*, 1918), is it focused on the study of a single historical event and its underlying causes. Read a hundred years after its publication, this series of essays "about the Russian intelligentsia" appears to its reader to be a bridge spanning its two sister volumes: it has neither the emotional detachment of the earlier nor the apocalyptic catastrophism of the later essays, yet it draws on the same wellspring that gave life to both.

While *Out of the Depths* appropriates the full force of biblical apocalypticism (its title being merely the most explicit self-representation of authors who, in the words of Struve, were all "undergoing a common torment"),[6] the apocalyptic context of *Vekhi* exists mostly in veiled form.[7] Struve, the editor of the later essays, spoke of *Vekhi* in the post-1917 landscape as "merely a *timid* diagnosis of the vices of Russia and a *weak* premonition of that moral and political catastrophe"[8] which was to befall Russia. While *Vekhi* may not have quite the tragic purpose and feeling aroused by later events, Struve surely understates the import of the 1909 volume. Indeed, if one were to pick a biblical parallel for the continuity between the two volumes, one could do worse than comparing them to pre- and post-exilic

## Inside Out: Good, Evil, and the Question of Inspiration

Jeremiah. *Vekhi*, taken as a whole, is a particular form of jeremiad, a lament that singles out not only the sins of the present but also the fruit that may be reaped through the perpetuation of such sin.[9] It is this adumbration of a still uncertain future—far from timid in its discourse—that moves through *Vekhi* as a shadow-context on which the authors both consciously and unconsciously draw.[10] In particular, the very liminality of the historical space in which it resides—the instability of the present moment—lends a portentous air to the essays' urgent appeal to turn inward. In this threshold time, the emergence and propagation of evil is predicated not on historical events or movements but on the quality of the inner life of individuals, and the personal relations between them that constitute society. Good and evil are borne not somewhere in the ether but within concrete persons, and it is the contention of *Vekhi* that the Russian intelligentsia, as a social body, has become a dangerous incubator of a virulent spiritual malaise whose maturing fruit is envisaged in apocalyptic terms.

A comment made by Semen Frank gives us the most concise expression of the *Vekhi* perspective on what had happened in their recent historical past: the "most tragic," he writes, "and, on a superficial level, surprising development [*s vneshnei storony neozhidannyi fakt*] of our recent cultural history" is that "subjectively pure, disinterested, self-sacrificing devotees of the social faith turned out to be not only the political allies but the spiritual kin of robbers, murderers, hoodlums and debauchees" (153).[11] The words "on a superficial level, surprising development" (alternatively, "unexpected fact from an external perspective"), arrest our attention here. How could it be that the conscious and unconscious religious aspects of the intelligentsia to which each author points—Berdiaev's "thirst for justice on earth that is rooted in the soul of the Russian intelligentsia" (7), Bulgakov's "eschatological dream of the City of God and the future reign of justice" (21), Frank's "spontaneous sense of vital love for people" (141), those defining characteristics that draw the Russian intelligentsia so close to authentic, religious maximalism (*podvizhnichestvo*)—could not only be corrupted but corrupted so definitively and so absolutely? In Bulgakov's words from the dialogues that were included in the collection *Out of the Depths* of 1918: "There occurred some kind of black transfiguration: the people of God became a herd of Gerasene swine."[12] Apparent good somehow mutated into manifest evil in the blink of an eye, and it is the nature, foundation, and consequences of this transformation that the *Vekhi* authors are at such pains to disclose.

For the *Vekhi* authors, the answer to the dark riddle of Russian revolutionary experience does not lie in the prevalence of certain worldviews—atheism, nihilism, materialism, and the rest. Such trends existed in the west, as Bulgakov, Struve, and others point out, often in just as emphatic a form. Nor does the answer lie in the historical fruit of these worldviews, in this case revolution. "Revolution, meaning certain political actions," writes Bulgakov, "does not in itself predetermine the specific spirit and ideals that inspire it" (38). Political uprisings, even revolutions, are not in themselves evil. The *Vekhi* contributors are very far from the political reactionaries they were sometimes painted to be. The source of evil, according to them, should rather be sought in the nature of the human possession of these ideals, the enervating spirit of the revolution, the inspiration that lurks behind the flag-waving of countless "-isms" and political maneuverings. But for Bulgakov and others, it is the character of this inspiration which is so hard to pin down. Even when they read back from its manifestations in Russian reality—criminality, violence, hatred—it is still hard to locate the point of departure from where the rot began.

This may explain one of the indicative rhetorical devices of *Vekhi*: metaphors of clothing and dress, Bulgakov's "inside out" being no exception. The effect of veiling or distorting the appearance of something is to mislead and confuse. Comparing German and Russian students, Aleksandr Izgoev writes that though the former "gets drunk, cracks stupid jokes, and behaves outrageously," he does not "array his drunken cavorting in the elegant garb of *Weltschmerz*" (79). In a similar vein, Berdiaev talks about the intelligentsia dressing in "the European garb of Marxism" (4). Struve suggests that Herzen "sometimes wore the uniform, as it were, of the Russian *intelligent*" (121), and Frank uses the same word "uniform [*mundir*]" as Struve to talk about living people who have "garbed their soul in the *intelligent*'s moral uniform" (137). These metaphors relate, in part, to the superficial absorption of western ideas by Russian intellectuals, whereby ideals and philosophical trends were "signed up to" unreflectively without any inner movement on the part of their holders—pure "fanaticism," as Berdiaev puts it (14).

## Inside Out: Good, Evil, and the Question of Inspiration

Were these sartorial metaphors no more than a commentary on the superficiality of the Russian reception of ideas, however, their role in engendering the kind of urgency the *Vekhi* contributors wished to inculcate in their readers would not be nearly so great. A good deal of that urgency, so clearly felt even from a century's distance, derives from the fact that these metaphors of veiling and unveiling, of disguise and impostorship, draw, whether self-consciously or otherwise, on the apocalyptic tradition of past Russian thought. Here the question of the quality of the political and philosophical culture of Russia is supplemented by wider questions governing the nature of good and evil, their interaction within the human heart, and their final resolution in a suprahistorical landscape. This overlaying of a larger and more comprehensive narrative atop of the *Vekhi* critique of contemporary societal ills comes into greater focus when set against the background of the apocalyptic imaginings of two particular thinkers, Bukharev and Solov'ev, whose own, peculiar interpretations of the two apocalyptic books of the Bible—Daniel and Revelation—are particularly instructive to consider in this regard.

In 1860, Bukharev published a work entitled *O pravoslavii v otnoshenii k sovremennosti* (*On Orthodoxy in Relation to the Contemporary World*), which sought to practice a kind of biblical exegesis that could be applied not only to questions of doctrine or historical context but also to the most pressing problems of modernity. In the fourth and final chapter, he offers an interpretation of the prophet Daniel's vision of the Four Beasts (Daniel 7:2–8).[13] The vision is complex, but what Bukharev plays on is the element in it that endows the beasts with human characteristics. The lion is, according to the biblical passage, "lifted up from the ground and made to stand on two feet like a human being; and a human mind is given to it," and on the small horn that emerges from the final beast there appear "eyes like human eyes." The repetition of the word "like," with an emphasis on semblance and appearance, occurs in the vision as a matter of course. The fact that the beast does not have human eyes but "eyes *like* human eyes" resonates with Gershenzon's description of the intelligentsia in *Vekhi* as "man-like monsters" (61).[14] Bukharev employs these human characteristics of the beasts to construct a new series of human and humane concerns that broadly correspond with many of the Russian intelligentsia's most cherished ideals, transferring the vision from the remote environment of Babylonian mythology to a context rich in contemporary resonance:

> Even though [a person] concern himself with the maintenance of human rights, even though he spend his time reasoning as to how to elevate human dignity, reason and the human heart, yet does not do so in the manner of Christ, the Son of God, his principle will still be the beast, even though it has "eyes like the eyes of man." [...] Even though this person, who does not value conformity to the Son of God himself, be distinguished by a multi-faceted education, even if he be in our time as a Hellene had been before a barbarian in the ancient world—alas, in his motivations we still do not see a human being but only the image of a lynx or a leopard, attractive to the eye and no more.[15]

Bukharev is indicating that the presence of the most laudable, perhaps even ethically unavoidable, ideals *without* an inner conformity to the principle of authentic humanity—Christ, the Son of God—may not only mask the hypocrisy of the actor but itself represent the sign of the beast. The principle of humanity—the carrier of the image of God in the world—does not arise from within but is conferred from without. "A human mind is *given*" to the beast, according to the Book of Daniel. This does not render the ideals that emerge evil or misguided: the criterion for their judgment lies not here but in the source of their birth, in the heart of the intelligentsia itself. However strong the moral imperative of each stated ideal from an objective perspective, therefore, they tell us nothing about the spirit of its adoption. Indeed, the Russian tradition holds that the most perfect expression of the religious ideal in word and action may mask the purest embodiment of evil. "The most profound meaning of world history," as Solov'ev said in February 1900, "is the fact that in the final historical appearance of the evil principle there shall be such a great deal of good."[16]

Solov'ev, in whom the apocalyptic strand of Russian thought found its most compelling articulation, went on, in the introductory words to his public reading of *Kratkaia povest' ob Antikhriste* (*A Short Story of the Antichrist*, 1900), to give a kind of manifesto for the future incursion of evil in the world, leaning heavily, like the *Vekhi* authors who succeeded him, on the imagery of clothing. "It is required," he said, "that the prince of this world be allowed to show himself toward the end from the best angle, to become freely adorned in every semblance of good."[17] In the context of the *Vekhi* debate regarding the religiosity of the intelligentsia, the question that emerges from Bukharev and Solov'ev's eschatology is this: does the semblance of authentic religious inspiration, the proximity of the soul of the intelligentsia to absolute good, act as a *redeeming* factor? Or is it, to the contrary, a sign of what Bulgakov terms a profound and irreconcilable "internal difference" in the face of "apparent, external, similarity" (24)? It was this point that divided the *Vekhi* authors: not the *apparent* religiosity of the intelligentsia, on which there was broad agreement, but the redemptive power of the same.

Solov'ev ended his reading of the short story that was to bewitch and puzzle many future Russian thinkers (in almost equal measure) with a short afterword, the first few sentences of which contain a summary of the intuition he wished to convey to his listeners: "Such is the impending and inevitable dénouement of world history. We shall not see it, but events of the not-too-distant future throw their prophetic shadow, and in our lifetimes more clearly and undeniably than ever do counterfeit good, fraudulent truth and fake beauty rise before our eyes. All the elements of the great deception are already before us, and our immediate descendants will see how all these things shall interweave and come together in one living and individual phenomenon, in Christ turned inside out [*Khristos naiznanku*], the Antichrist."[18] The antichrist in Solov'ev's handling is not the archetypal villain but the great pretender, the *agent provocateur* who not only infiltrates the camp of the good but champions its cause: from cessation of wars to greater cooperation between the countries of the world to human and even animal rights. This is not the antipode to Christ but his mirror image—his projection in externality, endowed with the grand mannerisms of religiosity yet, to use Struve's words, "without the content" (125). Solov'ev's Antichrist is a Christ who has slipped into his opposite without even noticing it, as if this were a perfectly natural thing to do. He has adorned himself in the inner principle of human being, the Word-Logos, but he wears it inside out: instead of the turning to God through repentance and conversion of heart, there is a turning to the material world, to the surface of things. The ideals that animate him rise not from the intimate places of the soul but are entirely self-posited: they do not penetrate the surface of things since they themselves *derive* from the surface. The interior content is spent wholly in externality, without remainder: in moralizing, in social construction, in the search for worldly over spiritual power, and in an excess of gesture and posturing.

If we concentrate on the character of Solov'ev's Antichrist alone, however, we miss the full picture. The Antichrist does not appear out of nowhere—his advent is heralded by the spread of what Solov'ev calls "counterfeit good, fraudulent truth and fake beauty." He is very much a product of his time. And what is striking about the *Vekhi* critique of the consciousness of the intelligentsia is the prevalence of the theme of perverted ideals and norms in their historical appraisal of the ills of modernity. In each human activity the authors choose to dwell on, they intuit a perversion of its ideal purpose and character. In the search for truth, instead of the use of reason to integrate and make sense of the things of the world, Gershenzon sees an empty moralizing (*rezonerstvo*), a "morbid self-analysis, a ceaseless and senseless digging in the soul" that "deforms the natural features of things, and deprives them of their essential nature." Instead of a living "legal conviction," Bogdan Kistiakovskii sees a slavish bowing to law as to a coercive force. Instead of the consciousness of the Christian ascetic (*podvizhnik*), Bulgakov sees the revolutionary hero, mangodhood rather than Godmanhood.

Faced with this mass of perverted ideals, the *Vekhi* authors look for a measure of authenticity: a conscious or unconscious trait in the Russian intelligentsia that holds out a promise of redemption. Frank finds such a trait in the "spontaneous sense of vital love for people" that at any given moment of its historical existence saves the intelligentsia from diving into the abyss, the "one thing" that "atoned" for everything else (141). Many of the *Vekhi* authors stress this commitment to self-sacrifice, the kenotic strain in the psychology of the Russian intelligentsia of active self-giving in love, which constitutes a central part of their religiosity.[19]

But what if even love itself can be corrupted? What if there is a form of self-giving that, far from affirming the other, weighs it down and deprives it of its essential nature? It is this possibility that Bulgakov explores five years after the publication of *Vekhi* in a 1914 article on Dostoevskii's *The Devils*,

## Inside Out: Good, Evil, and the Question of Inspiration

which adds the final component to his reflections on the adaptability of evil in taking on the form of the good.

Describing the love that exists between Stavrogin and Lise, he writes:

> These are not the wings with which the soul soars into the eternal blue of the heavens. These are fetters, demonic charms. This is love turned inside out [*liubov' naiznanku*], love-hate, which also possesses a certain clarity of vision, only not of good but of evil, seeing in the beloved and, at the same time, hated person not a creation of divine love but the spoils of hell.[20]

Here is a love that does not free but imprisons, a love that in its practice has dissolved in its opposite. Bulgakov's description of such satanic love enables us to complete the three potential stages of the great deceit. We have, first, the general mind-set of the intelligentsia: religiosity turned inside out, mangodhood rather than Godmanhood; second, the activity that results from this mind-set on society and the world around it: love turned inside out, love-hate; and third, the final, individual embodiment of both: Christ turned inside out, the mangod, Antichrist. In each stage, the perversion of the ideal does not present us, at least not until the final unmasking, with a transformation of good into evil, accompanied by the gradual, or even sudden, extinguishing of the former. Rather, it is the undifferentiated presence of the two poles at a single point, or in a continuum where their differentiation loses all its meaning. As Williams has written in the context of *The Devils*: "The recording of events as a single continuum without value and continuation leaves us with a mangled idea of freedom and even of truthfulness. If all we have before us is a continuum which includes equally horror and beauty, the horror is worse than it would otherwise be because there is no way of putting it into a context where it can be healed or modified. It just happens."[21] It is the reality of such a continuum that Dostoevskii portrays in the character of Stavrogin, whose very name expresses the presence of the two poles in one individual—the cross (Greek: *stavros*) and the apocalyptic horn (Russian: *rog*) of Daniel—and whose ascent to his death in a loft-attic encapsulates the fates of both Christ and Judas.[22] Stavrogin leads people to their dooms through advocating any number of ideals classifiable under various *-isms*; yet these ideals come from a place of absolute indifference: they belong not to him but to the grey matrix of this indifference. "How I wish you were hot or cold," quotes Tikhon to him from Revelation, "but as you are lukewarm, I will spit you out of my mouth."[23]

Recalling Dostoevskii's famous epigraph to *Brat'ia Karamazovy* (*The Brothers Karamazov*, 1880), "Here God battles with the devil, and the battleground is the human heart," the problem of Stavrogin takes on an additional dimension. What he represents is not the epitome of evil but the absence of any kind of battle between the warring principles, which in its own way is more terrifying. The battle that takes place within his soul continues, as it does in every living soul, but Stavrogin does not actualize it, since his will does not, cannot, give assent to the choice of either good or evil, instead resting in absolute indiscrimination. And without that battle, the human person, argues Bulgakov, itself not being evil since it is made in the image of God, becomes a channel for evil: it literally ceases to exist, or slips into non-being. Bulgakov here talks of the "absence of the living Stavrogin, his existence as mask [*lichinnost'*]."[24] The outer form persists as a hollow shell, and it is the inspiration of this mask that gives birth to the pseudo-religious transformation of the characters that surround him: to the mangodhood of Kirillov, the God-bearing nationalism of Shatov, and the murderous nihilism of Verkhovenskii. The triune arc of deification according to the Christian model—God, humanity, world, where the energies of God are channelled through humanity onto society and the world around it—is here fundamentally transformed. Humanity and God shift places: Godmanhood is replaced by mangodhood. The human form, divested of its belonging to God at its innermost core, wears its God-bearing interiority on the outside, and seeks to use its own external words, actions, and thoughts to deify its environment. Yet what is deified in the process is sheer emptiness, a form with no content, the absent humanity of Stavrogin. This absence begets not a form of Prometheanism—a rebellion against God and the ways of God—but rather the loss of religious consciousness per se, the elimination of any residual significance that the terms "good" and "evil" might once have had.

It is the fear of such an outcome that is expressed by Bulgakov in *Out of the Depths* through the mouth of the social activist: "If only our people were theomachists, mutineers against all that is sacred; this at least would constitute a negative self-testament of their religious spirit. More often than not, though, they simply behave as louts and cattle who have nothing to do with faith whatsoever. As if there were no demons in them at all, for what would demons do with them? From demonic possession one can be healed, but not from bestiality."[25] Such bestial indifference eats away at core human attributes such as belonging, loyalty, and responsibility. Here the goal becomes not internal participation in events but the provoking of certain external effects in those around you, for no other purpose than the simple possibility of so doing.

In his essay on *The Devils*, Bulgakov states that Dostoevski had "treated in artistic terms the question of political provocation, understood not only in a political sense but in a more profound, experiential-religious sense."[26] From Stavrogin, whom Bulgakov terms a "spiritual provocateur," there emerges "the provocateur-betrayer, the 'colleague' who gives away the secrets of the party for money. [He is] a degeneration of this type, its reverse side, or its elaboration and pollution, though most probably inevitable."[27] The degeneration of the more complex figure of Stavrogin into a political chameleon brings to mind a figure whose shadow is cast across the *Vekhi* essays: Evno Azef, whom Izgoev describes as the "foremost hero of the day" (83), and who indeed conforms like no other to all that Bulgakov has to say on the nature of revolutionary heroism.

A double-agent and provocateur, Azef was involved in terrorist acts for the Social Revolutionaries while at the same time informing on his colleagues in his role as spy for the *Okhrana*, the Imperial secret police. Although much doubt has recently been cast on his actual character and activities,[28] what is clear is that by the time of the writing of *Vekhi*, barely a month after his unmasking in February 1909, he had become a sort of cipher, a receptacle into whom Russian idealist philosophers poured the eschatological forebodings of the thinkers of the past century. "Is Azef-Verkhovenskii," asked Bulgakov, putting together his name with one of Stavrogin's spiritual children, "and *azefshchina* as a whole merely a chance phenomenon in the history of the Revolution, an abnormal growth that may never have been? Or can we see in it, to the contrary, its core spiritual disease?"[29] In his essay for *Vekhi*, Bulgakov highlights the moment of personal discernment in the case of Azef, when you can "no longer tell where the revolutionary ends and the police agent or provocateur begins"

(32). Azef can be seen, and was certainly so interpreted, as the historical fulfillment of the apocalyptic incarnation of evil as interpreted by Russian thinkers. A resident of two worlds, with strong links to neither yet ready to give himself in service to either one, Azef exists on the same continuum as Bukharev's beast, Solov'ev's Antichrist, and Dostoevskii's Stavrogin. He is both betrayed and betrayer, yet exists in this contradiction in absolute indifference. In the evocative words of Vasilii Rozanov, "it was decided to crush the Christ of the Revolution by the Judas of that selfsame Revolution: to open wide the garment of Christ and under it reveal Judas."[30]

Yet the question here is not only about the mark of the beast—the character of evil's appearance in the world—but about the kind of society that facilitates such an appearance. "Azef was some kind of unique monster, and the names 'satan' and 'satanic' were often pronounced alongside his name," wrote Rozanov.[31] For the latter, however, the most incredible thing was not that this monster existed, but that he could have been believed for so long. "The whole matter rests in the inability to perceive," he wrote in a response to *Vekhi*. The revolutionaries "knew his uniform but did not know his soul."[32] Great deception can only work on those who are spiritually unequipped for its possibility. The uniform fooled them precisely because they had physical eyes, but not spiritual ones.

It was to the nature of spiritual discernment in the apocalyptic context of post-revolutionary Russia that Bulgakov would dedicate much of his later writing. In 1931, he returned to the theme of betrayal and redemption in an essay on Judas Iscariot. His major concern in this piece is not to condemn the sin of the archetypal betrayer, nor is it to offer a moralistic teaching on the corruptibility of good intention. Rather, he attempts to disclose the "mystery of Christ and Judas" as a certain "hieroglyph of fate," and the reader is left in no doubt that the fate he has in mind is that of the Russian nation.[33] "The tragedy of the apostle-betrayer, his terrible fate, stands before us with imploring eyes. It has become now our own fate, not personal, but national."[34] Each one of the characteristics with which he, alongside other intellectuals of the Russian diaspora, had characterized the Russian intelligentsia are here ascribed to Judas, who is described as a "monomaniac [*odnodum*]," a person "blinded by utopia" who above all "needed a task" to which to dedicate himself.[35]

Bulgakov is no longer trying to warn of the adaptability of evil to all semblances of good, as did Solov'ev and Bukharev in the century before him, but instead to reveal the apostle in the betrayer, and the betrayer in the apostle, in such a way that neither dissolves in the other, both remaining as aspects of an antinomy that is never subsumed in identity. It is an attempt, it may be suggested, to understand the Christ-Judas mystery—the ultimate *crux theologiae* according to Bulgakov—*sacramentally*, as the very economy of the Gospel, the inner spring on which all else rests. The atheistic movement in Soviet Russia is here interpreted as neither anti-religious nor pseudo-religious at first, but as a moment in the soul of a nation which can only be fully comprehended when taken in the fullness of its linkages with historical time. One needs, wrote Bulgakov, "to understand the contradictions in the Russian soul in their connection, as the disclosure of one whole, linking the past with the present and the future."[36] For Bulgakov, only in so doing could one intuit that this "diseased love for Christ, this struggle against Christ in the name of the truth of Christ" is actually "titanic, that is, simultaneously heroic and demonic."[37] Just as God sends Judas on his path of misery "in order to lead him to redemption,"[38] "in the Christ-murdering hearts and souls of Russia there is concealed Christ's Resurrection."[39] This may be wishful thinking, born of desperation; there may even be something to Ivan Il'in's accusation that Bulgakov had spoken "in defense of Judas the Betrayer in an attempt to proclaim him the patron saint of the Russian people (for 'we too have betrayed Christ')."[40] Bulgakov, however, is not trying to force a silver lining onto the most inappropriate of rainclouds. His is not the facile mission of the theodicists against whom Vissarion Belinskii spoke so forcibly at the beginning of the Russian intelligentsia's path to self-discovery.[41] Suffering and evil are not justified through their involvement in a narrative or sophistic dialectic which will supposedly result in the triumph of the good. Nor is Bulgakov's view wholly aligned to that of his fellow *Vekhi* contributor Berdiaev, who in his 1923 work *Novoe srednevekov'e* (*The New Middle Ages*) depicted European civilization as having removed itself altogether from the battle between good and evil through a kind of inner banality, arguing that "Russia would rather give birth to the antichrist than to a humanistic democracy and neutral humanistic culture."[42] The anti-Christian values of a Soviet-style regime are not, in Bulgakov's view, by some mystical proximity in distance closer to authentic Christianity than are the values of a secular society which has lost a sense of both divine and demonic. Indeed, as we have seen, it was the absoluteness of such a loss—the lukewarmness of Stavrogin, the abolition of any distinction between good and evil—that he regarded as the essence of the Russian condition. Instead, he saw the revolution in Russia as an unprecedented call to an entire nation to turn away from outward planning toward the only place that remained: the interior space of authentic humanity. This call was not closer to its desired destination by virtue of its residence at the opposite pole. But it *was* more pressing because of the radical nature of the choice facing Russia and the Russian intelligentsia.

In his contribution to *Out of the Depths*, Sergei Askol'dov draws on the Parable of the Tares from the Gospel of Matthew (Matthew 13:24–30) to paint a picture of the contemporary state of the Russian nation:

> In all this great fortitude, in the non-acceptance of evil inside one's soul, in the practical resistance to it, alongside the crafts of evil—indeed already in some ways differentiating themselves from these—are there not maturing in the people's soul yet other holy crafts for that battle which will take place in the final days, in those days when to take part in the antichristic state will be an unforgivable sin, a definitive alignment under the banner of the enemy of Christ? So alongside the choking tares there grows good wheat, the number of the righteous is continually being renewed, and the spiritual qualities needed for the creation of the new organism of the Kingdom of God are coalescing.[43]

Askol'dov's choice of biblical allusion is not accidental, and it illuminates the particular constellation of Christian eschatology and Russian experience that lurks behind so many of the earlier arguments of the *Vekhi* authors. The word translated into English as "tares" (in modern translations, "weeds") refers to the plant commonly known as darnel (*Lolium temulentum*), whose seeds are sown amongst the good (wheat) seeds by an enemy "while everybody was asleep" (13:25). Darnel is so like wheat in appearance that in the early stages of its growth it is all but indistinguishable from the genuine article.[44] There is no external criterion fully capable of telling them apart, just as is the case for the good and ill of the Russian revolution. Through its description of the growth of the wheat alongside the darnel, the parable introduces, in the words of the contemporary theologian Robert Capon, a parallel insistence on the cosmic reach of God's kingdom and what he calls the "catholicity of evil […] the radical intermixture of goodness and badness in the world."[45] Moreover, unlike other Gospel parables of judgment, the ground is not nurtured for the production of evil, which appears as if from nowhere: "There is no openness here, none of the simplicity that characterizes the straightforward hostility of the birds or the rocky ground or the thorns. Rather, there is the full-blown paradox of the appearance of evil in a situation where there is absolutely no reason to expect it."[46] These words bring to mind once more Frank's bewilderment at the peculiar convergence of selfless revolutionary and callous murderer in the events of 1905, which were "on a superficial level [*s vneshnei storony*]" a "surprising development" (153). How could this occur? Who is to blame? According to the parable, the bad seed is sown by an enemy who works while the laborers are sleeping, and it is this sleep, not the conscious intentions or even unconscious urges of the sowers, that facilitates the incursion of evil onto the land. In the interpretation of Filaret, Metropolitan of Moscow, sleep in this context means "carelessness and a lack of vigilant attention both to oneself and one's actions."[47] It is this "sleep" from which the *Vekhi* authors wish to awaken their readers, in order to direct them once more toward the imperatives of constant self-judgment, self-questioning, and self-doubt.

*Vekhi* was a call to regain a sense of human involvement in the history of a nation, and a world, that avoided the extremes of absolute control and absolute helplessness. Its demand for a return to fostering inner life—in Bulgakov's words, for the intelligentsia to "be corrected not from without but from within" (34), should be seen not only in the context of a return to traditional values, to the prerogatives of personal spirituality over external organization, but also in the sense of a re-equipping for the spiritual struggle that continues without human intervention, yet which will not be decided without it.

## Notes

1. Quotations from *Vekhi* in English, and their page references, are taken from Marshall S. Shatz and Judith E. Zimmerman, eds. and trans., *Vekhi/Landmarks: A Collection of Articles about the Russian Intelligentsia* (Armonk, NY: M. E. Sharpe, 1994).

2. It may be suggested that Kistiakovskii is an exception to this trend. Yet, although his essay aims to counter the Slavophile view that whereas to the west belongs the way of "external truth, the truth of the state," to the Russians belongs the way of "inner truth," his ultimate view is that the Russian relationship to law is as to something *exclusively* external, as "coercive law" rather than "legal conviction" (95, 107).

3. References to the original Russian text of *Vekhi*, and quotations from *Iz glubiny* (*Out of the Depths*), are taken from V. V. Sapov, ed., *Manifesty russkogo idealizma* (Moscow: Astrel', 2009), here 509.

4. Ol'ga Sedakova, one of the most penetrating critics of contemporary Russia, echoes the premonitions of *Vekhi* from the perspective of one who has lived through the horrors of the last century. "It seems to me," she said in a recent lecture, "that if the twentieth century has taught us anything, it is that it is no longer possible to offer up any kind of universal projects.... There is but one solution: the personal turning of each individual toward their very selves, toward their inner person." See Ol'ga Sedakova, "Posredstvennost' kak sotsial'naia opasnost'," in *Posredstvennost' kak sotsial'naia opasnost': sbornik* (Moscow: Magistr, 2011). Electronic version available at http://www.intelros.org/lib/statyi/sedakova2.htm.

5. Rowan Williams, *Dostoevsky: Language, Faith and Fiction* (London: Continuum, 2008), 4–5.

6. Sapov, *Manifesty russkogo idealizma*, 635.

7. Robin Aizlewood calls *Out of the Depths* a "reprise" of *Vekhi* "in apocalyptic mode." See R. Aizlewood, "'Besy', Disorientation and the Person," *Slavonic and East European Review* 88, no. 1–2 (2010): 291.

8. Sapov, *Manifesty russkogo idealizma*, 635.

9. In 1911, Lenin spoke of the two great obstacles facing the regrouping of the proletariat around the revolutionary cause as "Stolypin's gallows and the *Vekhi* jeremiads [*vekhovskie ieremiady*]." Although the word here had the same negative connotations it had acquired in the English language, the resonance is nevertheless telling. See V. I. Lenin, "Razviazka partiinogo krizisa," *Polnoe sobranie sochinenii* (Moscow: Gos. izd. pol. lit.,1955), vol. 21, 1.

10. *Vekhi*'s discourse, as Aizlewood has pointed out, "best adumbrates the apocalyptic mood that pervades *Iz glubiny*." Aizlewood, "'Besy', Disorientation and the Person," 299.

11. For an account of the looting, mindless vandalism, and violence that followed the Revolution, see Orlando Figes, *A People's Tragedy: The Russian Revolution: 1891–1924* (London: Jonathan Cape, 1996), 520–35.

12. Sapov, *Manifesty russkogo idealizma*, 707. See also the similar statement from the third dialogue: "Where there once rose a grandiose temple, there suddenly appeared only fetid, slimy, putrid dirt." Ibid., 727.

13  Daniel 7:2–8. The vision includes a lion, a bear, a leopard and a beast so monstrous that the prophet has no name for it. For a history of the interpretation of the vision, see John Collins, *Daniel: With an Introduction to Apocalyptic Literature* (Grand Rapids, MI: Eerdmans, 1984), 74–83.

14  In an interesting passage, the Writer from Bulgakov's dialogues in *Out of the Depths* combines this vision of apocalyptic dehumanization with its concomitant militarization: "See how even the appearance of the soldier has changed. He has become somehow bestial, terrifying, particularly the sailor. I admit that these 'comrades' sometimes seem to me creatures wholly devoid of spirit and possessed only of the lower mental faculties, a particular species of Darwinian monkey—*homo socialisticus*." Sapov, *Manifesty russkogo idealizma*, 714.

15  Fedor Bukharev, *O pravoslavii v otnoshenii k sovremennosti* (St. Petersburg: Strannik, 1860), 307.

16  Cited in Nikolai Kotrelev, "Eskhatologiia u Vladimira Solov'eva (k istorii 'Trekh razgovorov')," in *Eskhatologicheskii sbornik*, ed. D. Andreev (St. Petersburg: Aleteia, 2006), 253.

17  Ibid.

18  Ibid.

19  The kenotic aspect of the Russian intelligentsia has been stressed many times in academic literature. See, for example, Marc Raeff, *The Origins of the Russian Intelligentsia: The Eighteenth-Century Nobility* (New York: Harbinger, 1966), 162–64.

20  Bulgakov, "Russkaia tragediia," in *Sochineniia*, 2 vols. (Moscow: Nauka, 1993), vol. 2, 511.

21  Williams, *Dostoevsky: Language, Faith and Fiction*, 73.

22  See Lena Silard, "Svoeobrazie motivnoi struktury Besov," *Dostoevsky Studies* 4 (1983): 159–60. Note also Hippolytus of Rome's association of the little horn that sprouts amidst the other horns of the final beast in Daniel's vision with the antichrist, and the stone that strikes the statue in Daniel 2 with Christ: "The other little horn that grows up among them meant the Antichrist in their midst; the stone that smites the earth and brings judgment upon the world was Christ." Hippolytus, "Treatise on Christ and the Antichrist," in *The Writings of Hippolytus, Bishop of Portus: Fragments of Writings of the Third Century*, 2 vols. (Edinburgh: T. & T. Clark, 1869), vol. 2, 18.

23  Revelation 3:16. See Fedor Dostoevskii, *Polnoe sobranie sochinenii* (Leningrad: Nauka, 1974), vol. 11, 11.

24  Bulgakov, "Russkaia tragediia," 502.

25  Sapov, *Manifesty russkogo idealizma*, 728.

26  Bulgakov, "Russkaia tragediia," 505.

27  Ibid., 521.

28  See, especially, A. Geifman, *Entangled in Terror: The Azef Affair and the Russian Revolution* (Wilmington, DE: Scholarly Resources, 2000).

29  Bulgakov, "Russkaia tragediia," 523.

30  Vasilii Rozanov, "Zagadki russkoi provokatsii. Ocherk," in *Sobranie sochinenii. Zagadki russkoi provokatsii*, ed. A. Nikoliukin (Moscow: Respublika, 2004), 76.

31  Vasilii Rozanov, "Mezhdu Azefom i 'Vekhami,'" in *Sobranie sochinenii. Staraia i molodaia Rossiia (Stat'i i ocherki 1909 g.)*, ed. A. Nikoliukin (Moscow: Respublika, 2004), 266.

32  Rozanov, "Zagadki russkoi provokatsii," 74.

33  Sergii Bulgakov, "Iuda Iskariot—apostol-predatel'," in *Put' parizhskogo bogosloviia* (Moscow: Izdatel'stvo khrama sviatoi muchenitsy Tat'iany, 2007), 294, 353.

34  Ibid., 353.

35  Ibid., 315–16. Compare this to Berdiaev's diagnosis of the intelligentsia's disease in *Vekhi*: "Moral pathos degenerates into monomania" (7).

36  Bugakov, "Iuda Iskariot," 354.

37  Ibid., 359.

38  Ibid., 322.

39  Ibid., 363.

40  Ivan Il'in, "Arkhimandritu Konstantinu <28.VI.1951>," *Pis'ma k arkhimandritu Konstantinu (Kirillu Zaitsevu)*, at http://kaplun.narod.ru/ilyin.htm.

41  See especially the letters to Vasilii Botkin in Vissarion Belinskii, *Izbrannye filosofskie sochineniia* (Moscow: Gos. izdat. pol. lit., 1948), 558–98.

42  Nikolai Berdiaev, *Smysl istorii. Novoe srednevekov'e* (Moscow: Kanon, 2002), 231.

43  Sapov, *Manifesty russkogo idealizma*, 669.

44  In rabbinic tradition, darnel is called "false wheat," and its emergence is connected with the generation of the Flood, when "even the earth acted lewdly; wheat was sown and it produced pseudo-wheat." See *Midrash Rabbah*, 10 vols. (London: Soncino Press, 1961), vol. 1, 28.8, 229.

45  R. F. Capon, *Kingdom, Grace, Judgment: Paradox, Outrage, and Vindication in the Parables of Jesus* (Grand Rapids, MI: Eerdmans, 2002), 94.

46  Ibid., 95.

47  Filaret, Sviatitel', Mitropolit Moskovskii, "Beseda iz pritchi o plevelakh," in *Slova i rechi*, 4 vols. (Moscow: Novospaskii monastyr', 2005), vol. 2, 239.

# 11

## D. S. Merezhkovskii Versus the *Vekhi* Authors
*Bernice Glatzer Rosenthal*

Dmitrii Sergeevich Merezhkovskii (1865–1941) was a seminal thinker. In the 1890s, he popularized Nietzsche's thought and reawakened Russians' interest in antiquity and in the classics of world literature, and his lecture "O prichinakh upadka i o novykh techeniiakh v sovremennoi russkoi literature" ("On the Causes of the Decline and on the New Trends in Russian Literature," 1892, published 1893) became the manifesto of Russian symbolism.[1] In the early twentieth century, he pioneered the study of Fedor Dostoevskii, Nikolai Gogol', and Lev Tolstoi as religious writers and co-founded the Religious-Philosophical Society of St. Petersburg (1901–03, 1906–17), which helped inspire a religious revival. The members were called "God-seekers" even though most of them were already believers, because they were seeking a new interpretation of Christianity. During and after the revolution of 1905, he advocated a religious revolution. Throughout, he opposed materialism, rationalism, utilitarianism, and positivism. He promoted his ideas in articles, book-length essays, and historical novels, and at meetings of the Religious-Philosophical Society. Newspapers reported on Merezhkovskii's attack on *Vekhi* and on his polemics with Petr Struve, a prominent Constitutional Democrat and a contributor to *Vekhi*.[2] Merezhkovskii's attack on *Vekhi* was part of a larger polemic with Struve and certain other *Vekhi* authors on such issues as the state, economic development, and rule by law.

A radical by temperament and by conviction, Merezhkovskii perpetuated the anarchistic, utopian strain of Russian cultural history, without the atheism. His apocalypticism mingled with other apocalyptic scenarios circulating in Russia since 1900.

This article will describe Merezhkovskii's attack on *Vekhi*, as well as responses to his attack, and analyze the larger polemics of which it was part. His attack merits detailed attention because it was one of the "landmark" responses to *Vekhi*, prompting in itself further responses. It also provides a particularly rich picture of the complex and contested cultural, religious, and political landscape in which *Vekhi*—and the polemics around it—were created. Moreover, Merezhkovskii's starting point and certain aspects of his intellectual genealogy share much with those of most, if not all, of the *Vekhi* contributors, to which can be added their common participation in initiatives such as the Religious-Philosophical Society. So, first, a few words on Merezhkovskii's views before 1908, the year his polemics with Struve began.

## Merezhkovskii's Views Before 1908

In the 1892 lecture mentioned above, Merezhkovskii decried the intelligentsia's emphasis on political and social issues to the exclusion of metaphysical questions, aesthetic criteria, and the "inner man" (the soul or the psyche). Here, therefore, and as noted above, he starts from a position not at all dissimilar to that of *Vekhi*. He accused the intelligentsia of curbing self-expression and stifling imagination and creativity, insisted that religious faith is a basic human need, and predicted that symbolism would lead to new religious truths and, eventually, to a new culture characterized by beauty, creativity, and freedom.

Merezkhovskii's version of symbolism was a surrogate religion, a religion of art, but it did not assuage his fear of death. So around 1896, he concluded that there are two eternal truths, paganism (enjoyment of life) and Christianity (personal immortality), that must be reconciled. In 1899, he "turned to Christ." In 1900, he declared that "historical Christianity" (the Christianity preached in the churches) was obsolete because the Second Coming was imminent. Jesus Christ Himself would grant humankind a Third Revelation (a Third Testament) that would solve all problems and reconcile all polarities, including paganism and Christianity, flesh and spirit, and East and West. From then on, Merezhkovskii cast all problems in terms of an eschatological dualism that only divine intervention could resolve. Very few intellectuals believed in a forthcoming Third Revelation, but his idea that Christianity had to be reinterpreted was widely accepted.

In November 1901, Merezhkovskii, Zinaida Gippius (his wife), and Dmitrii Filosofov (also known together as "the Merezhkovskiis"), obtained the government's permission to organize the Religious-Philosophical Meetings of St. Petersburg as a "mission to the intelligentsia." The meetings featured reports by clergymen or lay intellectuals, followed by discussion, on such issues as the Orthodox Church's excommunication of Tolstoi, Christian attitudes to sex, and whether new Christian dogma is needed and if so, who has the power to create it. The lay intellectuals were mostly symbolist poets and anti-positivist philosophers. The minutes of the meetings were published in *Novyi put'* (*The New Way*, 1903–04), a review founded by the Merezhkovskiis for that purpose.

The government closed down the Religious-Philosophical Meetings in April 1903, charging that they provided a "forum for heresy." Merezhkovskii was so outraged that he declared that autocracy is from the anti-Christ. Up to that point, he had eschewed political and social questions. The meetings resumed as the Religious-Philosophical Society after the Revolution of 1905 and continued until 1917. The Moscow Religious-Philosophical Society (1906–1917) was modeled on the St. Petersburg one. Several *Vekhi* authors were members of the Moscow Society.

In view of all this, one would expect Merezhkovskii to hail *Vekhi*, but he did not. He lambasted it, because he had come to the following conclusions: first, that the revolution of 1905 had religious significance: it was the beginning of the Apocalypse, the prelude to the establishment of the Kingdom of God on Earth; second, that the atheistic intelligentsia was the carrier of the Christian principle of freedom, it was practicing "Christianity without Christ"; third, that Jesus was a revolutionary and Christianity and revolution are two aspects of the same phenomenon, with Christianity being "revolution in the divine category" and revolution "religion in the human category"; and fourth, that autocracy, Orthodoxy, and *meshchanstvo* (philistinism) were faces of The Beast, but since autocracy was dead and Orthodoxy was dying, *meshchanstvo* was the most dangerous face.[3] Implicitly, *meshchanstvo* included such bourgeois values as moderation, compromise, practicality, material well-being, personal responsibility, and self-discipline, some of the very qualities promoted by the *Vekhi* authors.

Merezhkovskii urged Russians to turn the political revolution into a "religious revolution" that would culminate in a society in which Jesus Christ is the only ruler; love is the only law; and the "truths" of anarchism and socialism (personal freedom and community, respectively) have been reconciled. Merezhkovskii's "religious revolution" featured the destruction of the state, the death of the Orthodox Church, and its rebirth as a revolutionary body, an ally of the intelligentsia in a fight for freedom. Politically, he was closest to the anarchistic Social Revolutionaries (SRs), even meeting with some of them in October 1905. In January 1906, fearful of publishing their book *Le Tsar et la Révolution* in Russia, the Merezhkovskiis left for Paris; they returned to St. Petersburg in July 1908. By then, a "second wave" of symbolists—Aleksandr Blok, Andrei Belyi, and Viacheslav Ivanov—had emerged, but Merezhkovskii was still influential.

His "religious revolution" entailed a new set of eschatological dualisms. In the essay "Prorok russkoi revoliutsii (k iubileiu Dostoevskogo)" ("Dostoevskii, Prophet of the Russian Revolution," 1906), he counterposed earth and heaven and interpreted the revolution of 1905 as a revolt of the earth against the otherworldliness of "historical Christianity." In an essay titled "Revoliutsiia i religiia" ("Revolution and Religion," 1907), he treated the Roman papacy and the Russian tsardom (*tsarstvo*) as negative dualisms that originated in the same idea, theocracy, but proceeded along opposite paths. In the west, the Roman papacy became a state. In the East, the state absorbed the church. "In both cases there occurred the identical abolition of the Church, the kingdom of love and freedom, the kingdom of God, by the state, the kingdom of enmity and violence, the kingdom of godlessness."[4] According to Merezhkovskii, autocracy reflects, in external political form, an internal religious need, the need of the human soul for Divine oneness, monotheism: one tsar on earth, one God in heaven. That is why the overthrow of the Russian autocracy has "deep religious significance" (189).

The bulk of "Revolution and Religion" was devoted to the interplay of the two phenomena in Russia from the time of the Old Believers (the first dissidents, in his view) to Nikolai Novikov, Petr Chaadaev, Gogol', Vladimir

Solov'ev, Tolstoi, Dostoevskii, and the Russian decadents (symbolists in the 1890s); the latter were the "first self-generated mystics in Russian educated society outside any church tradition" (214). In the last section, he proclaimed that "The end of Orthodoxy is the end of Autocracy and vice versa.... There is no Orthodoxy without the Roman Caesar just as there is no Catholicism without the Roman archpriest." By the "end of Orthodoxy" he meant the triumph of the "new religious consciousness," that is, the triumph of his interpretation of Christianity: "Only the lie of Orthodoxy [Autocracy] is rejected" (218–19). When the revolutionary and religious movements fuse, Russia will emerge from the "Orthodox Church and the Autocratic Tsardom into the universal church of the One Archpriest and the universal Tsardom of the one Tsar—Christ" (221).

Clearly, Merezhkovskii and the *Vekhi* authors were on different wavelengths. Merezhkovskii favored extreme solutions, opposed politics and law per se, rejected nationalism,[5] and expected a miraculous break with the old order. As Marshall Shatz and Judith Zimmerman point out, his attack on *Vekhi* "was an attack on the contributors' recognition, in various ways, of Russia's need for a solid structured, autonomous set of political and social institutions.... Hence *Signposts* criticized the intelligentsia for its negative attitudes toward the main elements of this structure: the state, the rule of law, national consciousness, historical tradition, etc. Hence also, the book's rejection of revolution in favor of gradualism, political education, and respect for historical continuity."[6]

## MEREZHKOVSKII'S ATTACK ON *VEKHI*

Merezhkovskii titled his attack on *Vekhi*, made in April 1909, "Sem' smirennykh" ("Seven Humble Men").[7] He starts out by saying that it is difficult to tell the truth to those one is close to, and he was close to some of the *Vekhi* authors. Nevertheless, he has decided to speak out because the matter is so important. He also writes that in judging the *Vekhi* authors, he is judging his former self ("In beating them, I beat myself"), but that his *mea culpa* should not be taken as an attempt to "sugarcoat" the pill; its bitterness may be the saving medicine (71). There is thus a complex and polemical combination of self-knowledge and superior sagacity, and of turning the rhetorical weaponry of *Vekhi* back on itself, in Merezhkovskii's attack.

"Seven Humble Men" consists of a series of bullet-like summaries of the articles followed by longer attacks on those by Sergei Bulgakov, Mikhail Gershenzon, and Struve. Merezhkovskii pounced on words or phrases that struck him as particularly outrageous, in some instances magnifying them to the point of distortion and/or pushing them to an extreme conclusion. That said, he raised important questions and deployed his extensive knowledge of Russian and European history and literature in his attack.

Merezhkovskii began his onslaught with a reference to Raskol'nikov's dream (in Dostoevskii's novel *Prestuplenie i nakazanie* [*Crime and Punishment*, 1866,]) in which a little mare yoked to a huge wagon is beaten to death for not heeding the owner's commands. The wagon, Merezhkovskii explained, is Russia; the little mare is the Russian intelligentsia, and the *Vekhi* authors beat her with words. Nikolai Berdiaev accuses the intelligentsia of "populist obscurantism"; Semen Frank, of "sectarian fanaticism"; Bulgakov, of "social hysteria"; Bogdan Kistiakovskii, of "lack of legal consciousness"; and Struve, of "bottomless frivolity." Gershenzon calls the intelligentsia a "frightened herd," an "assembly of the sick." Aleksandr Izgoev indicts it for "onanism, the sexual life of a seventeen-year-old" (72).

"Suddenly the little horse kicks: the intelligentsia affirms that it has the all-purifying fire—liberation" (72), but the beating continues. Gershenzon reviles the intelligentsia as a "monster that looks like a human being." Bulgakov condemns it for "heroic sanctimoniousness" and "self-deification" and calls it a "legion of demons." Frank accuses the intelligentsia of a "Hottentot morality"[8] and "hooliganistic violence"; Izgoev charges it with "murder, plunder, thievery, of all kinds of debauchery and provocation."

"But the little mare doesn't die." With her last strength, she tries to pull the wagon. Still, the beating goes on. Gershenzon urges the intelligentsia to bless the state authorities (*vlast'*) that with bayonets and prisons still protect us from the people's wrath (72). Merezhkovskii found this (infamous) statement particularly outrageous, and repeated it (80).

"Suddenly there is a miraculous transformation." Like the little boy in Raskol'nikov's dream, Bulgakov embraces the dead mare. The Russian intelligentsia becomes the beautiful Shulamite seeking her beloved (in the *Song of Songs*). This is an allusion to Bulgakov's statement that the intelligentsia, having refused Christ, unconsciously yearns for Him. "He stands and knocks at that heart, that proud, recalcitrant intelligentsia heart.... Will His knock someday be heard?" "Seven humble men," Merezhkovskii continued sardonically, seven colors of the rainbow that merge into one whiteness, into a "common cause" (49).

Turning to Gershenzon's "Preface," Merezhkovskii noted that the words "faith" and "religious" are in quotation marks for good reason. The *Vekhi* authors have different faiths. Berdiaev and Bulgakov are Orthodox Christians. Struve, if he is a Christian at all, is not Orthodox. Gershenzon, Frank, and Izgoev are believers, but not Christians. Kistiakovskii's religion is unknown. Actually, Struve was Orthodox. Gershenzon, Frank, and Izgoev were Jewish, but Gershenzon has been called a "Jewish Slavophile" and Frank converted to Christianity in 1912.

Gershenzon also said that despite "seeming contradictions," i.e., on the "religious" nature of the intelligentsia, the contributors have a common platform, namely that the "inner life of the individual is the only creative force in human society." Merezhkovskii vehemently objected to this statement, not because he disputed the importance of the "inner life of the individual," but because, in his view, affirming that the individual is the *only* creative force in human society "means that there is no Christianity," because "Christianity affirms that the creative force of the person (*lichnost'*) is not the only one, that the religious limit of the person is union, *sobornost'*, sociality, the church as the body of Christ, a new divine-human I, only in which can the fullness of every separate human being be realized" (74). *Sobornost'*, the social ideal of the Slavophiles, Solov'ev, and many others, connotes an organic community whose members retain their individuality. The erudite Merezhkovskii knew that *sobornost'* had an explicitly Christian origin, the Church as the body of Christ.

There is no personal salvation outside the social, Merezhkovskii continued. "'Then all will be one, as You Father in me and I in You, and so they will be one in Us.' The Church is founded on this principle; annihilate it and you annihilate her. If the religious force of the person is the only one, then there is no religious force in society, no church, no Christianity, no Christ. This is not a 'seeming contradiction' or a small matter, but a bottomless abyss into which everything disappears."

Finding holes in the *Vekhi* authors' "common platform," Merezhkovskii compared them to seven doctors seeking a life-saving medicine. Berdiaev prescribes "religious philosophy"; Frank, "religious humanism"; Bulgakov, "Christian asceticism"; Struve, "a mystique of the state"; Izgoev, "love for life"; Kistiakovskii, an "authentic legal consciousness"; and Gershenzon, "making the monster into a human being." They seek the truth (*pravda*), but truth is not love and a rainbow is not a bridge (over the abyss).

Indeed, their "common platform" is only a common hatred, Merezhkovskii charged. In so doing, he turns a key aspect of the *Vekhi* critique against *Vekhi* itself and uses Bulgakov to expand on his theme. The basic idea of the symposium, the hidden axis around which everything turns, is encapsulated in Bulgakov's words: "The concept of revolution is negative; it has no independent content, but is characterized only by destructiveness. Therefore the pathos of revolution is hatred and destructiveness." Bulgakov did not say this in *Vekhi*. What he did say is that the Russian revolution developed enormous destructive energy, like a great earthquake, but that its constructive forces were much weaker. Still, Merezhkovskii had a point. It was their opposition to revolution that united the *Vekhi* authors.

Bulgakov's conclusion is implicit but obvious, Merezhkovskii contended. If revolution is destruction, hatred, and negation, then reaction, the restoration of what has been destroyed, is creation; the extinction of hatred is love and the negation of a negation is an affirmation. Finally, if revolution is anti-religion, then reaction is religion and perhaps the reverse, religion is reaction, a conclusion already reached by the enemies of religion (75–76). This is an example of Merezhkovskii's practice of taking a statement to an extreme conclusion, thereby misrepresenting the author's views. Here is another example: "Following Bulgakov's conclusion, we proceed from a 'terrible judgment' on the Russian intelligentsia, the Russian revolution, to a 'terrible judgment' on all European culture," which was forged in the crucible of revolution. Here, he exaggerates Bulgakov's anti-Europeanism. But Merezhkovskii was right when he observed that Christian ascetics esteemed by Bulgakov as the possessors of Christ's truth (*istina*) regarded all European culture as anti-Christian and that St.

Seraphim of Sarov condemned the entire Enlightenment as the work of the anti-Christ.

Merezhkovskii then posited two conceptions of world history. One affirms endlessness, perpetual development, the inviolable law of causality. For this conception, free will, the indispensable premise of religion, is a metaphysical and teleological superstition. The other conception affirms an *end*, a *break*, overcoming the external law of causality by inner freedom, by the intrusion of the transcendental order into the empirical, which seems to be a *miracle* but is really the fulfillment of another law, a higher law incommensurate with the empirical. Every development is a preparation, a maturation, the beginning of a break, the beginning of the end. The freedom of the Son is not the destruction but the fulfillment of the law of the Father. The first conception is scientific, *evolutionary*; the second is religious, *revolutionary*. In the last analysis, and only in the last analysis, they are not opposed. Every break is a limit, the end of development, a *goal* in the teleological order. Every development is a preparation, a maturation, the beginning of a break, the "beginning of the end," a cause in the determinist order. In this sense, evolution and revolution are two sides, the immanent and the transcendental, of the universal historical dynamic (76).

The apocalypse was given to us as a primarily Christian understanding of world history, Merezhkovskii continued, "catastrophic, revolutionary, bounded, and cut short." Lightning, thunder, fire, and earthquakes, are vessels of the anger of the Lord. Battles, uprisings, national defeats (presumably he had the Russo-Japanese War in mind), horses knee-deep in blood, corpses of kings devoured by birds of prey, all these signify the fall of the Great Babylon, the greatest of all revolutions, the final storm. Compared to this, all previous revolutions are pallid summer lightning. Babylon, the Kingdom of the Beast, is indeed destroyed, but the Kingdom of God is created. "The rapture [*vostorg*] of destruction is the rapture of the creator; the rage of hatred is the rage of love." But Bulgakov sees only negation, only hatred and destruction, while to Struve the apocalypse is only an anecdote (Merezhkovskii here exaggerates by trivialization Struve's opposition to the apocalyptic mind-set). Summarizing this aspect of his critique of *Vekhi*, Merezhkovskii stated: "To reject the positive religious content *not only in the empirical but in the mystical revolution* means to reject the apocalypse—the entire Christian eschatology, the entire Christian dynamic of the Coming Christ and consequently, of the Advent of Christ, because the Coming and the Advent are one" (77).

The revolutionary conception of world history was born in Christianity, Merezhkovskii contended. Only among Christian peoples do we find an endless search for the City of God, the unconscious teleology that fires the heart of the Russian people to the present day. We find it in the schismatic sectarians, in the intelligentsia, and in all Russian apostates. (Merezhkovskii's rejection of "historical Christianity" made him an apostate in his own way.) This unconscious eschatological feeling is what makes the intelligentsia national (*narodnyi*)—at least, more national than the authors of *Vekhi*, who confuse Babylon with Jerusalem. For them the liberation movement ends with the October Manifesto. So, without the name of God, the intelligentsia is—according to Merezhkovskii's polemical conclusion— closer to God than are the *Vekhi* authors. The intelligentsia "is not yet with Christ but Christ is with them." [9] Merezhkovskii never stopped trying to get the intelligentsia to accept Christ. His goal was a Christian intelligentsia.

Turning to Gershenzon's article, "Tvorcheskoe samosoznanie" ("Creative Self-Cognition"), Merezhkovskii objects to the author's negative view of Peter the Great and of the intelligentsia (Peter's spiritual descendants, according to both Gershenzon and Merezhkovskii). In "Seven Humble Men," Merezhkovskii's view of Peter was uniformly positive.[10] He praised Peter as the first *intelligent*, the first Russian apostate, and the first Russian revolutionary, and pointed out that none other than Aleksandr Pushkin called Peter the greatest revolutionary. He accused Gershenzon of wanting to crush Peter like a fly (an exaggeration) and of demonizing both Peter and the intelligentsia. "To spit on Peter means to spit in Russia's face" (79).

Unlike the Slavophiles, Merezhkovskii approved of Peter's reforms, especially his opening of a "window on the West." He believed that Peter had no choice but to subdue the obscurantist, blindly traditional church. Moreover, by the time Peter abolished the Patriarchate, the Orthodox Church was already dead, morally and spiritually. Merezhkovskii considered Peter's ability to break with the past in order to make a frenzied leap into the future the most Russian of all Russian traits. Seeing the same trait in the intelligentsia, Merezhkovskii claimed that it would complete Peter's work by liberating Russia. "It was not for nothing that the Decembrist Revolt began at the pedestal of the Bronze Horseman" (79). He ignored Gershenzon's charge that the intelligentsia stifled individuality, self-knowledge, and personal development, charges Merezhkovskii himself had made in his 1892 lecture and for years after that.

As for Struve's article, "Intelligentsiia i revoliutsiia" ("The Intelligentsia and Revolution"), Merezhkovskii lambasts Struve's depiction of the intelligentsia and his apotheosis of the state. He accuses Struve of attempting to flee to pre-Petrine Russia and the year 1612, when the Muscovites drove out the Poles in a battle with anti-state "thievery." Although Struve did not name the present-day Hermogens, Minins, and Pozharskiis, it is clear that he considered the intelligentsia the "thieves." Struve considers anti-religion and anti-state positions to be two sides of the same apostasy. In this, and only in this, according to Struve, is the key to understanding the revolution. To Merezhkovskii, the "key" is the intelligentsia's religiousness, which Struve dismissed as a "legend."

To Hermogen, Minin, and Pozharskii, the mystique of the state lay in the idea of autocracy, Merezhkovskii continued. But where is the mystique in constitutional monarchy? In imperialism? In the Third Duma or Stolypin's ministry as objects of faith? Struve is grasping at straws. Although Merezhkovskii objected to Struve's mystique of the state, he believed that the people do need a mystique. The idea of Autocracy, however, is a mystical temptation. "Perhaps the chief sin of the intelligentsia, the chief difference between the Russian intelligentsia and the people, is that the intelligentsia not only failed to overcome this tempting mystique, but did not even feel it" (80). The people still do, Merezhkovskii asserted. In fact, he himself had succumbed to it. In his study of Tolstoi and Dostoevskii (1900–01), he had called the autocrat the visual symbol of God on earth. But then he realized that every autocrat is a pretender who attempts to take God's place. Previous revolutions have resulted in the victory of yet another pretender (or despot), like Cromwell, Robespierre, and Napoleon. He wanted the Russian religious revolution to end the cycle of revolution and despotism altogether.

Merezhkovskii also addressed Bulgakov's views on autocracy. He quoted Bulgakov's statement that "in the soul of the Russian people there has always been a battle between the precepts of Fr. Sergius and those of the Zaporozhian Sech, of Razin and Pugachev." "But Bulgakov knows and we know" that Father Sergius posited an unbreakable tie between Orthodoxy and autocracy. The intelligentsia broke, or tried to break, that tie—Merezhkovskii was here referring to the religiousness he discerned in the intelligentsia, not to their views on the Orthodox Church. He objected to Bulgakov's description of the intelligentsia as a "legion of demons" and his desire to expel them from Russia. Like Fr. Sergius, "Bulgakov sees the salvation of Russia in her only national idea, in her universal historical calling of *messianism*." The "national idea," Bulgakov says, "is based first of all on *messianism*, into which national feeling naturally flows. That is how Dostoevskii, the Slavophiles, and Vladimir Solov'ev understood [it]" (81). This is yet another example of a certain shared heritage and ideas, in the context of radical ideological difference, for Merezhkovskii was a Slavophile and messianist too, in his own way. He believed that Russians were the first universal people (an idea he took from Dostoevskii), that the apocalypse would begin in Russia, and that the Russian spirit would save the world.

"Bulgakov knows and we know," Merezhkovskii continued (conflating Slavophilism and the state ideology of Nicholas I), that Slavophile messianism consisted of three links tightly soldered together: Orthodoxy, autocracy, and nationality. Bulgakov wants to exclude autocracy, but what then, he asked, will connect Orthodoxy and nationality? What will be the embodiment and dynamic of the Orthodox Church outside historical power? These are good questions, followed by a hypothetical answer. "If the soul of Russia is Orthodoxy, then the body is autocracy" (81). "There is no soul without a body and no body without a soul. There is no Roman Catholicism without the Pope, the head of the Church. There is no Eastern Christianity without Caesar, also the head of the Church, not only in historical experience but according to messianic revelation" (81). In other words, Orthodoxy is the soul of autocracy and autocracy is the body of Orthodoxy.

Merezhkovskii repeated this idea in an article titled "K soblaznu malykh sikh" ("On the Temptation of the Little Ones").[11] The subject of the article was an open letter by Berdiaev to Metropolitan Antonii, in response to the latter's open letter welcoming *Vekhi* and condemning the "new religious consciousness" as a "dangerous heresy." To Merezhkovskii's dismay, Berdiaev agreed. By the time Merezhkovskii returned to St. Petersburg, Berdiaev had returned to the Orthodox Church and was denouncing the "new religious consciousness" as a heresy. In the open letter, Berdiaev called the Orthodox Church his "spiritual mother" and accepted the state as necessary for sinful humanity (whereas at one point during the revolution of 1905 he had advocated Christian anarchism).[12] Berdiaev also said that even though "we overcame temptation" (the "new religious consciousness") he realized that "for many of our brothers, overcoming temptation is terribly difficult." Of course, Merezhkovskii did not consider the "new religious consciousness" a mere temptation. Most objectionable to him, however, was Berdiaev's distinction between the empirical, human church, which can err, and the mystical, divine Church, which preserves eternal truth (*istina*). Merezhkovskii believed that the divine and the human cannot be separated; because Jesus Christ, the Godman, was both. He accused Berdiaev of confusing Christ and anti-Christ and urged him to overcome that temptation (as Merezhkovskii himself had done): "When I began the trilogy *Christ and Antichrist*, it seemed to me that two truths existed—Christianity, the truth of heaven, and paganism, the truth of the earth—and that the absolute religious truth lay in the future union of these two truths. But as I was finishing it, I already knew that the union of Christ and Antichrist was a blasphemous lie: I knew that both truths—of heaven and earth—had already been united in Jesus Christ."[13]

Time and again, Merezhkovskii insisted that empirical objections to the idea of absolute monarchy (*edinovlastie*) have no force, because the issue is not transitory forms of a single power, but its eternal limits, not that which is, but that which may or must be. So, "just as abuse of papal power does not invalidate the idea of the papacy, the abuse of tsarist power does not invalidate the idea of the kingdom (*tsarstvo*)." Even Dostoevskii asserted that "under autocracy such freedoms were possible that republicans never even day dream about." And in Solov'ev's theocracy, the tsar is the indispensable member of the triad of tsar, prophet, and priest. Merezhkovskii objected to Dostoevskii's idealization of autocracy and to the tsar's central place in Solov'ev's theocracy. In Merezhkovskii's version of theocracy, Jesus is the only ruler.

Merezhkovskii predicted that constitutional monarchy would fail because the people did not understand the principle of shared power. They would ask, "Is the Tsar the Lord's anointed or is he not?" Seeking to regain their lost sense of cosmic unity, they would turn to a new and terrible form of Caesaropapism. He turned out to be right: Stalin became the autocrat and the new god.

"Our contemporary slavophiles are groping in the dark," Merezhkovskii concluded, but they would not find Russia's "national face." This is an allusion to an article by Struve, in which he accused the intelligentsia of an "anemic" and "colorless" cosmopolitanism.[14] Merezhkovskii objected to aspects of slavophilism but, as noted above, was himself a Slavophile, and a messianist, in his own way.

Merezhkovskii contended that *Vekhi* demonstrated the opposite of what it set out to prove. It proved instead that Russian liberation has hidden religious meaning and that "liberation will be religious and religion will be liberation" (83). He concluded his attack on *Vekhi* with a battle-cry that echoes—and outdoes—the rhetorical flourishes with which seven of the eight *Vekhi* essays end: "The Lord lives, our souls live. Long live the Russian intelligentsia and Russian freedom" (83). It is indicative of the complexity and diversity of currents around *Vekhi* that Vasilii Rozanov (1856–1919), another leading member of the St. Petersburg Religious-Philosophical Society, faulted Merezhkovskii's attack on *Vekhi* and praised the *Vekhi* authors for battling their past, i.e., the passionate Marxist and positivist convictions they had once held. For Rozanov, the symposium shows that the intelligentsia lives, and not only lives but has a great future ahead of it, a limitless road. The *Vekhi* authors did not "kill the intelligentsia" (a reference to the slain mare), they killed themselves and were resurrected; they were buried and revived. "How can a specialist in Christian affairs [like Merezhkovskii] fail to understand this?"[15]

At the beginning of this section, I noted that Merezhkovskii pounced on words and phrases he considered particularly outrageous. Reading his attack on *Vekhi* and his articles against Struve, one would not know that he agreed with them on matters of personal freedom and the importance of the inner life, and that he shared their desire to create a new religious culture and a new Russian person—a new Russian person with different qualities, of course: Merezhkovskii's ideal person would be daring, courageous, and willing to break with the past and make a frenzied leap into the future.

## A Larger Polemic I. Merezhkovskii vs. Struve

Merezhkovskii and Struve had been at loggerheads since early 1908, when Struve published an article titled "Velikaia Rossiia" ("Great Russia").[16] Their dispute centered on the question of the state, and of the state and culture. Taking his title from Stolypin's speech to the Second Duma, Struve explained that, "to us," "Great Russia" means a new Russian statehood (*gosudarstvennost'*) "that relies on the historical past of our country and its living cultural traditions, but is at the same time creative, and like all creativity, is revolutionary in the best sense of the word." He wanted the state to institute a "revolution from above" that would raise the cultural and economic level of the people, release their creative energies, respect personal freedom, emancipate the Jews, and grant autonomy to the Poles. Economic progress and patriotism would overcome ethnic differences and dampen revolutionary fervor. Apropos of foreign policy, one of Struve's goals was Russian domination (both economic and cultural) of the Black Sea basin and the Near East.

To accomplish all of this, the Russian state must be strong; its strength must be based, at least in part, on economic development, and the state must pursue a "politics of power." Power is not a rational but a religious principle. Every vital state, for example Great Britain, always has been and always will be imperialistic. The idea of an eternal peace is utopian. "Nietzsche talked about the coldness of the state.[17] On the contrary, its rays warm all aspects of national life."[18]

Struve considered the state a mystical entity, a living organism, a collective person. Citizens are comparable to the cells of a body and are motivated (partly) by will. Loyalty to the state is above reason, an expression of an innate human striving, religious in nature, to transcend the limited sphere of personal existence. The sacrifices people willingly make in war cannot be explained by reason alone. Struve praised Otto von Bismarck for solving the Prussian political crisis of the 1860s by "taking possession" of the "national idea" and unifying Germany. Presumably Struve had in mind the impasse between the tsar and the first two Dumas. Bismarck created a powerful state without degrading the people or destroying the law, by organically combining historical traditions with new and democratic state institutions. Struve also praised Oliver Cromwell, calling him the most important creator of English state power, because he instilled self-discipline in the people, labor discipline in particular—a quality, he said, that Russians lack.

Merezhkovskii denied each point.[19] "Great Russia" is a terrible artificial being, like Hobbes's Leviathan; "living Russia will stifle in its dead embrace." Struve's patriotism is another word for barbarism. Nation is a beast to nation. In war, one beast falls on another and bites off chunks of meat, he said, giving the Franco-Prussian war as an example. Bismarck is a "beast in capital letters." But man is not a beast; he tries to rise above animal existence.

Struve's "politics of power" reminded Merezhkovskii of "laughing lions," "blond beasts," and other items from the Nietzschean inventory that Merezhkovskii claimed to have jettisoned. He also claimed that Struve is a utopian. Turning reaction into a revolution from above requires as much of a miracle as turning stones into bread, or a serpent into a fish. Man must strive toward religious truth. The state is not a religious conception: it is godless, inherently unprincipled, and hostile to human personality. Though Struve advocates equal rights for Jews and autonomy for the Poles, if *raison d'état* so required he would persecute them.[20] Merezhkovskii may have been right. Struve advocated equal rights for Jews, but he also defended the Russian people's right to its "attractions and repulsions," especially since among certain sectors of the Russian people "the force of repulsion from Jewry is very great."[21] A few years later, Struve resigned from the presidency of the St. Petersburg Religious-Philosophical Society because he thought it devoted too much attention to the Beilis Case (1911–13). Mendel Beilis, a Jew, was accused of ritual murder, on charges trumped up by the government in order to divert popular anger from itself to the Jews. Merezhkovskii was one of Beilis's most vociferous defenders. Rozanov's expulsion from the Religious-

Philosophical Society because of a series of articles in which he claimed not only that Beilis was guilty, but that ritual murder is a Jewish tradition, was largely his doing.

Merezhkovskii also disputed Struve's contention that the state is a creator of culture. Culture can flourish without a powerful state, he argued, giving ancient Greece, Renaissance Italy, the disunited Germany of Goethe and Schiller, and the Jews as examples. Goethe and Schiller would be impossible in Bismarck's Germany. Macedonia and Prussia lowered the cultural level of Athens and Weimar. The Jews, "the most anarchistic of all peoples," gave the world Christianity. He did not mention the Ten Commandments, presumably because he rejected law per se. To Merezhkovskii, freedom was the absence of law.

He also pointed out that Struve ignored the combination of apocalypse and revolution in Cromwell's "prophet soldiers" as well in the American Puritans from whom the French Revolution borrowed the idea of the rights of man. Struve is a "zoological patriot" and a "maximalist" whose real religion is the state.

Struve replied that Merezhkovskii's views were "the last gasp of slavophilism" and, at the same time, "the last anchor of the Russian revolution." By making the state his enemy, Merezhkovskii has "turned the police psychology inside out" and entered into the blind alley of pure destructiveness. Macedonian culture was the universal form of Hellenism; Christianity was as much a product of Hellenism as of the Hebrews, and the greatness of Bismarck is a historical fact. Bismarck was not a miracle worker (an allusion to Merezhkovskii's belief in miracles), but with brilliant daring and power he managed to turn reaction into a revolution from above. Bismarck's Germany gave us Wagner and Nietzsche. Cromwell is greater than Stenka Razin, Carlyle is greater than Bakunin, and the dangers of chaos and anarchy are the greatest of all. Merezhkovskii should realize that religious communities like Calvin's Geneva are the greatest threats to personal freedom. Both he and Struve deployed their knowledge of European history on behalf of their arguments.

Struve also contended that apocalypticism does not solve real problems, and that Merezhkovskii's apocalypticism is a materialization of the Kingdom of God. Jesus said that "The Kingdom of God is Within You." True mystics regard religion as a purely spiritual force.[22] In a previous essay, Struve had given Tolstoi as an example of a purely spiritual Christianity. Merezhkovskii replied that Tolstoi was an anarchist and as such an opponent of "Great Russia" in any form.

Filosofov (the third of the "Merezhkovskiis") entered the fray with an article titled "Spor vokrug 'Vekh'" ("The Dispute about *Vekhi*," 1909). One of his main points is that the supra-personal Leviathan state that Struve advocated in "Great Russia" contradicted the liberal individualism he had advocated in an earlier article, "Religiia i sotsializm" ("Religion and Socialism," 1909).[23]

Merezhkovskii and Struve disagreed on other issues as well. Struve opposed dogmatism in religion and politics; Merezhkovskii sought new Christian dogma. His article "Bor'ba za dogmat" ("Struggle for Dogma," 1908)[24] was a response to Struve's essay "Intelligentsiia i narodnoe khoziaistvo" ("The Intelligentsia and the National Economy," 1908),[25] in which Struve advocated a new religious attitude to the economy in order to increase production and sanction the creation of wealth. In this context, Struve mentioned Max Weber's book on the Protestant ethic. Merezhkovskii accused Struve of a dogmatism of his own in the form of reliance on economic processes.

To Merezhkovskii, dogma was the building block of a religious-social cosmos and the point of departure of a religious society: "Without dogma, cosmos becomes chaos." The content of dogma is non-rational, outside reason. "Dogma is a crystal of revelation." "Every dogma is a revelation. Every revelation will be a dogma." Christian revelation is revolutionary. Christ rejected Jewish law and the iron yoke of Greco-Roman slavery in favor of freedom, he argued, and freedom is the testament of the first Christians.[26] Merezhkovskii should have known that Jesus did not reject Jewish law: that was Paul's doing. Jesus said, "Think not that I am come to destroy the law or the prophets: I am not come to destroy but to fulfill. For verily, I say unto you, till heaven and earth pass, one jot or one tittle shall in no wise pass from the law, till all be fulfilled" (Matthew 5:17–18). Merezhkovskii interpreted Jesus's statement to mean that there would be no law in the Kingdom of God on Earth. Dogma is dynamic, Merezhkovskii continued. It can become obsolete or turn into sterile dogmatism. For example, the living dogma of the great (French) revolution—liberty, equality, fraternity—turned into "dead dogmatism, the basis of bourgeois-capitalist slavery." Accusing the clergy of "dogmatic scholasticism," Merezhkovskii desired a new revelation of eternal truth to be resolved in dogma, and proclaimed that "in the final analysis, the issue is which dogma will save Russia." He considered adogmatism a negative conception that cannot combat nihilism. "True dogma is not a burden, but wings." "The struggle for a saving truth is a struggle for dogma." "Dogma in religious consciousness is a ray of light; in religious activity, it is a sword."[27]

Merezhkovskii and Struve called each other utopians. Merezhkovskii was indeed a utopian, but he raised important questions about the viability of a constitutional monarchy and the moral ambiguities of Struve's "politics of power." He was correct in challenging as utopian Struve's contention that reaction could be turned into a revolution from above.

## A Larger Polemic II. Economic Development and Rule by Law

Berdiaev, Frank, and Bulgakov advocated economic development, not to enhance state power but to abolish poverty by creating wealth—material and spiritual—and increasing production. In his contribution to *Vekhi*, Berdiaev wrote that "in the thought and feelings of the Russian intelligentsia, the claims of distribution and equalization always outweighed the claims of production and creation" (2). In 1906, he had advocated a "neutral socialism" (as opposed to what he called "socialism as religion"), which would guarantee everyone the necessities of life. Frank asserted in his *Vekhi* essay that it was time "we advanced from distribution and the struggle for it to cultural creation and the production of wealth." However, he maintained, in order to produce wealth, one must love it, and *"the Russian intelligentsia does not love wealth."* Indeed, it hates and fears it. "In [the intelligentsia's] soul, love of the poor turns into love of poverty" (148). And, in the same critical spirit, Frank argues that the intelligentsia "values only distribution, not production or accumulation, only equality in the enjoyment of goods and not their actual abundance" (150). Frank considered wealth a metaphysical concept that includes culture. He disapproved of the American ideal of mass prosperity, because he considered it overly materialistic. Like many educated Europeans, he regarded Americans as uncultured; he once called the United States "Genghis Khan with a telegraph."

Bulgakov viewed the struggle with poverty as a moral obligation, partly because he had experienced poverty personally and had witnessed its destructive moral effects. In March 1909, he presented a lecture, "Narodnoe khoziaistvo i religioznaia lichnost'" ("The National Economy and the Religious Person"), in which he advocated the formation of an Orthodox work ethic that emphasized personal responsibility, self-discipline, and hard work subsumed in an Orthodox metaphysics.[28] His purpose was to combat Marxist materialism, on the one hand, and the apostolic communism preached by the Christian Brotherhood of Struggle on the other. His ideal was a modern industrialized Christian society and a Christian economy based on love of neighbor and the mystical unity of all humankind, a society in which the material necessities of life were available to all.

Merezhkovskii certainly favored cultural creation, but he objected to emphasizing economic development, first because it was a secular goal, and second because the *Vekhi* authors who advocated it had been Marxists. Merezhkovskii probably viewed their desire to increase production as a residue of Marxist materialism. And since he assumed that the Apocalypse was imminent, he could also assume that there would be no poverty in the City of God on Earth.

Merezhkovskii did not respond specifically to Kistiakovskii's defense of law, even though he agreed with Kistiakovskii on personal freedom and the inviolability of the person. This was not just because Merezhkovskii opposed law per se, but also because he believed that these goals could be accomplished by love. Fond of contrasting "the eternal freedom of love" with the "eternal slavery of law," he regarded law itself as violence and as a snare of the devil, who makes law appear necessary by endowing it with the semblance of reason.[29] People obey the law not out of conviction but because they fear punishment. A vehement opponent of capital punishment, he claimed that the difference between legal force, which holds violence in reserve, and actual violence is only a matter of degree; both are sinful. Autocracy and murder are merely the most extreme forms of force. Once people realize that force is evil, the state will collapse. Deprived of the means to enforce its will, it cannot exist. "No violence, no law; no law, no state."[30] Religious revolution is not violence; it is the refusal to use violence. After the Third Revelation, love will become an active force; people will find the strength to "live in love," which they now lack. Love is Christ's commandment; it is a terrible commandment because it is so difficult, but to deny love is to deny God. The power of love, not force and violence, must prevail. Only when voluntary acceptance of Christ's law (love) replaces legal force will people be free.[31]

One would think that by refusing to accept violence, Merezhkovskii was advocating passive resistance (like Tolstoi), but he waffled on the use of terror. To him the crucial question—whether love for a higher ideal makes it "necessary to kill or impossible to kill"—was still unresolved. The solution of the religious issue of the use of force requires a miracle.[32] He said this in a review of *Kon' blednyi* (*Pale Horse*), a novel written by the SR terrorist Boris Savinkov, a personal friend. Moreover, in a final minor twist on the question of law, despite his rejection of it Merezhkovskii used the law when it suited his purpose. For example, when the government confiscated the manuscript of his play *Smert' Pavla I* (*The Death of Paul I*, 1908), Merezhkovskii sued the government under the relaxed censorship laws of 1906 and won. The manuscript was returned to him. Similarly, when the government confiscated the manuscript for his novel *Aleksandr I i Dekabristy* (*Alexander I and the Decembrists*, 1913) he sued the government and got his manuscript back.

## Conclusion

Merezhkovskii's attack on *Vekhi*, and his quarrel with Struve and certain other *Vekhi* authors, stemmed from profound religious and political disagreements. Appalled by the violence and chaos of revolution, they advocated a constitutional monarchy, rule by law, personal responsibility, and finding realistic solutions to Russia's problems. Merezhkovskii opposed the state and law per se, expected divine intervention, and was willing to accept violence and chaos as part of the apocalyptic transition to the Kingdom of God on Earth. What the *Vekhi* authors considered virtues, Merezhkovskii considered *meshchanstvo*. Put differently, Merezhkovskii was a maximalist; the *Vekhi* authors were moderates, though not all of them remained moderates. Their disagreements show that the intellectual battles of the time were not just between secularists and believers, but among believers as well.

## Notes

1. D. S. Merezhkovskii, "O prichinakh upadka i o novykh techeniiakh v sovremennoi russkoi literature," *Polnoe sobranie sochinenii* (henceforth PSS), vol. 18 (Moscow, 1914), 175–275.

2. See, for example, V. V. Rozanov, "Merezhkovskii protiv 'Vekh,'" *Novoe Vremia*, 27 April 1909, A. Liubash, "Duel' Merezhkovskogo i Struve," *Slovo*, 23 April 1909, and S. L. Frank "Merezhkovskii o 'Vekhakh,'" *Slovo*, 28 April 1909.

3. D. S. Merezhkovskii, *Griadushchii kham*, PSS, vol. 14, 5–39: 8–11.

4. D. S. Merezhkovskii, "Revoliutsiia i religiia," in *Ne mir, no mech*, PSS, vol. 13, 36–97. English translation in *A Revolution of the Spirit: Crisis of Value in Russia 1890–1924*, ed. Bernice Glatzer Rosenthal and Martha Bohachevsky-Chomiak (Bronx, NY: Fordham University Press, 1990), 189–221. Citations are from the English translation. It will henceforth be cited parenthetically.

5. On 26 October 1914, Merezhkovskii gave a lecture titled "O religioznoi lzhi natsionalizma" ("The Religious Lie of Nationalism").

6. Marshall S. Shatz and Judith E. Zimmerman, eds. and trans., *Vekhi/Landmarks: A Collection of Essays about the Russian Intelligentsia* (Armonk, NY: M. E. Sharpe, 1994), xxi. Citations from *Vekhi* are in this translation, and are henceforth cited parenthetically.

7. The speech "Sem' smirennykh" was delivered to the St. Petersburg Religious-Philosophical Society on 21 April 1909, published in *Rech'*, 26 April 1909, and included in *Bol'naia Rossiia*, PSS, vol. 15, 71–83. It will henceforth be cited parenthetically.

8. The phrase stems from a reporter's account of a Hottentot's definition of good and evil: "good" is when the Hottentot steals someone's property; "evil" is when someone steals his property.

9. Merezhkovskii, *Griadushchii kham*, 34.

10. It was not always so. In his historical novel *Khristos i Antikhrist: Petr i Aleksis* (*Christ and Anti-Christ: Peter and Alexis*, 1904) Merezhkovskii depicted Peter's flaws as well as his virtues. In "Revolution and Religion," he faulted Peter for ignoring the "free

spirit of the West," taking "its form without its content, its light without its fire, its flesh without its spirit" (193).

11  D. S. Merezhkovskii, "K soblaznu malykh sikh," in *Bol'naia Rossiia*, 84–91. Metropolitan Antonii's letter was published in *Slovo*, 10 May 1909. Berdiaev's letter was published in *Moskovskii ezhenedel'nik*, 15 August 1909.

12  Berdiaev's views on this and other subjects changed during the revolution of 1905.

13  Quoted in C. Harold Bedford, *The Seeker: D. S. Merezhkovskiy* (Lawrence, KS: The University Press of Kansas, 1975), 91.

14  See P. B. Struve, "Intelligentsiia i natsional'noe litso" (first published in *Slovo*, 10 March 1909), and the follow-up article "Polemicheskie zigzagi i nesvoevremennaia pravda" (first published on 12 March 1909), both in P. B. Struve, *Patriotika* (St. Petersburg, 1911), 370–79. An English translation of the first as "The Intelligentsia and the National Face" can be found in Rosenthal and Bohachevsky-Chomiak, *A Revolution of the Spirit*, 267–70.

15  Rozanov, "Merezhkovskii protiv 'Vekh,'" 3.

16  P. B. Struve, "Velikaia Rossiia" (first published in *Russkaia mysl'*, January 1908); see also his "Otryvki o gosudarstve" (first published in *Russkaia mysl'*, May 1908): both in Struve, *Patriotika*, 73–96 and 97–103.

17  Zarathustra called the state "the coldest of all cold monsters."

18  Struve, "Otryvki o gosudarstve," 99.

19  See D. S. Merezhkovskii, "Krasnaia shapochka" (first published in *Rech'*, 24 February 1908), and "Eshche o 'Velikoi Rossii'" (first published in *Rech'*, 16 March 1908): both in *V tikhom omute*, PSS, vol. 16, 50–56 and 57–65.

20  Struve also debated with Bogdan Kistiakovskii on the Ukrainian question. Kistiakovskii wanted cultural autonomy (but not separation) for minority nationalities and the use of the Ukrainian language in schools. Struve advocated the dominance of Russian culture and the Russian language. For details of this debate, see Susan Heuman, *Kistiakovsky: The Struggle for National and Constitutional Rights in the Last Years of Tsarism* (Cambridge, MA: Harvard University Press, 1998), 133–46. To the best of my knowledge, Merezhkovskii did not discuss the Ukrainian question.

21  Struve, "The Intelligentsia and the National Face," 267–70.

22  P. B. Struve, "Spor s Merezhkovskim," in Struve, *Patriotika*, 110–28. First published as two articles in *Rech'* on 28 February 1908 and 8 March 1908.

23  D. V. Filosofov, "Spor vokrug 'Vekh,'" *Russkoe slovo*, 17 May 1909, 8.

24  D. S. Merezhkovskii, "Bor'ba za dogmat" (first published in *Rech'*, 14 December 1908), in *Bol'naia Rossiia*, 102–09. The topic of the need, or lack of need, for new Christian dogma had been discussed at the St. Petersburg Religious-Philosophical Meetings in 1904.

25  P. B. Struve, "Intelligentsiia i narodnoe khoziaistvo" (*Slovo*, 16 November 1909; *Russkaia mysl'*, December 1908), in Struve, *Patriotika*, 362–69.

26 Merezhkovskii, "Bor'ba za dogmat," 104–05.

27 Ibid., 105–09.

28 S. N. Bulgakov, "Narodnoe khoziaistvo i religioznaia lichnost'," first published in 1909, reprinted in S. N. Bulgakov, *Dva Grada. Issledovaniia o prirode obshchestvennykh idealov* (Moscow: Tovarishchestvo tipografii A. I. Mamontova, 1911), vol. 1: 178–205. Details in Bernice Glatzer Rosenthal, "The Search for a Russian Orthodox Work Ethic," in *Between Tsar and People: Educated Society and the Quest for Public Identity in Late Imperial Russia*, ed. Edith W. Clowes, Samuel D. Kassow, and James L. West (Princeton, NJ: Princeton University Press, 1991), 57–74.

29 Merezhkovskii, *Ne mir, no mech*, 147 (see also 36–42).

30 Merezhkovskii, *Griadushchii kham*, 21–22.

31 Merezhkovskii, *Bol'naia Rossiia*, 24, 30.

32 D. S. Merezhkovskii, "Kon' blednyi," PSS, vol. 15, 15–31: 23–31.

# 12

## FEUERBACH, KANT, DOSTOEVSKII:
## The Evolution of "Heroism" and "Asceticism" in Bulgakov's Work to 1909

*Ruth Coates*

Sergei Bulgakov famously structures his essay for *Vekhi*, "Geroizm i podvizhnichestvo. (Iz razmyshlenii o religioznoi prirode russkoi intelligentsii)" ("Heroism and Asceticism [Reflections on the Religious Nature of the Russian Intelligentsia]"), around the binary opposition expressed in its title. Sections one to four develop a portrait of the Russian *intelligent* as a self-glorifying "hero" bent on saving the Russian people, while sections five to seven describe the type of the Christian ascetic who serves the world in a spirit of humility. Bulgakov argues that Russia requires the second type, for the first will lead her to destruction. The worldview expressed in his essay is the most Christianized of all those of the *Vekhi* contributors, and, more specifically, it is the only one to be colored by Russian Orthodoxy. The symposium captures Bulgakov midway on his intellectual trajectory from orthodox Marxism via Kantian idealism to the Orthodox priesthood.[1] The philosophical premises of his argument are still Kantian, but the tone is religious. Nevertheless, Bulgakov has yet to find his own Orthodox voice; instead he relies almost entirely upon that of Dostoevskii, not least for the heroism/asceticism opposition itself.

Russian Orthodox culture has always been constructed on the fundamental opposition of the sacred and the profane.[2] Since the time of the seventeenth-century schism, the forces ranged against orthodoxy have been equated with the Antichrist, and the notion of a false religion, pseudo-orthodoxy, has become established. In modern secular Russian culture no one has assimilated this ancient archetype more than Dostoevskii. In his artistic system of values, the image of Christ, the God-man (*Bogochelovek*),³ the center of the Orthodox faith and the treasure of the Russian people, is set against the image of the man-god (*chelovekobog*), the all-powerful human pseudo-savior that is the fantasy of the deracinated atheistic socialist *intelligent*. In *Brat'ia Karamazovy* (*The Brothers Karamazov*, 1881), the novel with which Bulgakov most closely engages, the opposition is embodied in Ivan/the Grand Inquisitor and the elder Zosima/Christ. The spiritual fate of Russia, for Dostoevskii, depends upon a choice between the God-man and the man-god.

Nevertheless, the manifest parallels between Dostoevskii and Bulgakov that are apparent even from this brief summary are by no means fixed. They have been arrived at by a process of evolution which can be traced through an examination of some of the essays Bulgakov wrote prior to *Vekhi*. The object of this chapter is to analyze the development of the terms "heroism" and "asceticism" in Bulgakov's early work in order to shed light not only on his dynamic relationship with Dostoevskii, but also on his developing understanding of and sympathy for his native Orthodox tradition.

## Heroism

Dostoevskii made the term *chelovekobog* his own, but it derives indirectly from the thought of two German philosophers, both Young Hegelians and proponents of atheism: Ludwig Feuerbach, best known for his *Die Wesenheit des Christentums* (*The Essence of Christianity*, 1841) and Max Stirner, author of *Der Einzige und sein Eigentum* (*The Ego and its Own*, 1844). It is known that Dostoevskii was familiar with the ideas of Feuerbach and Stirner, both from discussions with his early mentor Belinskii and from meetings of the Petrashevskii circle.⁴ Neither Feuerbach nor Stirner actually themselves use the German equivalent of *chelovekobog* (*Menschgott*) or the abstract nouns *chelovekobozhie* and *chelovekobozhestvo* (*Menschgottum*).⁵ It is likely that these derive instead from the critical reception of Feuerbach's system as anthropotheism. In fact, to designate his "new philosophy" Feuerbach briefly employs the Greek-derived term anthropotheism (*Anthropotheismus*) in his short monograph *Vorläufige Thesen zur Reform der Philosophie* (*Preliminary Theses on the Reform of Philosophy*, 1842).⁶

Walicki, and after him Frank, both cite the *petrashevets* Nikolai Speshnev as a probable mediator between the German philosophers and Dostoevskii.[7] Their claim is based on a letter, not actually addressed to Dostoevskii, in which Speshnev writes, "Anthropotheism [*Antropoteizm*] is also a religion, only a different one. It divinizes a new and different object, but there is nothing new about the fact of divinization.... Is the difference between a god-man and a man-god really so great?"[8] Did Dostoevskii take the term *chelovekobog* from Speshnev, and was Speshnev concretizing the abstract noun *chelovekobozhie* to mark the progression from a Feuerbachian to a Stirnerian worldview?

These questions are relevant because much of the interest in Bulgakov's reception of Dostoevskii lies in the tension between Feuerbach and Stirner, between *chelovekobozhie* and the *chelovekobog*. In his 1905 essay "Religiia chelovekobozhiia u L. Feierbakha" ("Ludwig Feuerbach's Religion of Man-Godhood"), Bulgakov demonstrates a thorough knowledge of the polemics between the two. His exposition of Feuerbach's work is geared around two main points. First, he discusses the fact that Feuerbach's position is not strictly speaking atheism, but anthropotheism (*antropoteizm*) (77–78):[9] his objective was "not to abolish religion, but to humanize it."[10] Humanity was to re-appropriate the divine essence it had projected onto an illusory god, to take back what was its own. In Feuerbach's words: "Man is the god of man: *homo homini deus est*" (75). Second, he emphasizes that what is divinized by Feuerbach is not the self but the human species, humanity as a whole: "His *homo homini deus est* should be translated thus: the human race is the god of the human individual, *the species is the god of the specimen* [*vid est' bog dlia individa*]" (79). The individual person is limited and flawed; only the human race as a whole is perfect. Thus the divine predicates—goodness, truth, immortality—have their locus in humanity. Stirner's answer to Feuerbach's "positive, humanistic" atheism is a more radical amoralistic, individualistic, atheism (91–2). In Bulgakov's view, Stirner correctly exposed Feuerbach's anthropotheism as just another manifestation of religion; he debunked the latter's divinization of humanity as another form of enslavement of the individual, and he mocked his sentimental attachment to moral values as having no foundation. "Mir geht nichts über Mich"—"There is nothing higher than Me," was Stirner's response to *homo homini deus est* (92). Thus, according to Bulgakov, "Stirner is the truth, the disclosed secret, of Feuerbach" (97). Feuerbach leads to Stirner.

Nevertheless, Bulgakov devotes only one chapter of his essay to the Feuerbach-Stirner polemics. The essay makes it clear that at this time Stirner, and his successor Nietzsche, are not essential to Bulgakov. Rather, his overriding objective is to counter Feuerbachian anthropotheism as an integral and central part of his polemic with Marxism. In Bulgakov's view, expressed in this essay and elsewhere, supposedly scientific theories of social progress of all complexions are the inheritors of Feuerbach, as they all accord humanity the highest value, even in those cases, such as Marxism, in which their founders disavowed Feuerbach's sentimentalism (as the late Engels did): all are atheistic humanists. "Their atheism is just as much an anthropotheism [*antropoteizm*] as Feuerbach's, and in this sense all its representatives, regardless of their shade, are in principle opposed to the more radical atheists Nietzsche and Stirner, who in the name of atheism also deny anthropotheism, and having denied the heavenly God, do not want an earthly divinity either" (99). In what follows I shall argue that Bulgakov's obsession with Feuerbach and his connection with Marxism strongly affects Bulgakov's initial reception of Dostoevskii, focusing on his reading of Ivan Karamazov in the 1901 essay "Ivan Karamazov kak filosofskii tip" ("Ivan Karamazov as a Philosophical Type"). Analysis of Bulgakov's essay for *Vekhi*, however, reveals a discernible shift away from the Feuerbachian *chelovekobozhie* and towards the Stirnerian *chelovekobog* as the prototype for the "hero"-*intelligent*. This shift brings Bulgakov into a position of greater agreement with Dostoevskii's worldview, as indeed the essay as a whole demonstrates.

"Ivan Karamazov as a Philosophical Type" is one of the essays included in the 1903 collection *Ot marksizma k idealizmu* (*From Marxism to Idealism*). An examination of the references to Dostoevskii in the collection as a whole reveals the overwhelming importance of Ivan Karamazov to Bulgakov during this transitional period: eleven out of twelve references are to Ivan, the "Legend of the Grand Inquisitor," or the philosophical issues that Bulgakov associates with these. (The twelfth reference is to Dostoevskii's "Pushkin Speech"—delivered on the occasion of the unveiling of the Pushkin monument in Moscow in 1880—in the context of a discussion of the problem of nationalism: the "Pushkin Speech" will dominate Bulgakov's thinking later, in the *Vekhi* essay.) One reason for this is that Bulgakov identifies with Ivan, whose condition in the novel, like Bulgakov's own, "is one of mistrust, of a loss of faith in the old, which has not yet been replaced by the new" (88).[11] This transitional status of Ivan is reinforced by the position accorded to the essay in the collection: fourth, immediately after the three essays included to represent Bulgakov's Marxism (dating from 1896–98), and thus the first properly transitional text.

Another reason for the prominence of Ivan and the "Legend" in the collection concerns the precise nature of Bulgakov's interest in man-Godhood at this time. After all, there are several other *loci classici* treating this theme in Dostoevskii's oeuvre—Raskol'nikov's "Napoleon" theory, Kirillov's suicide rationale, Shigalev's theory of despotism, the character of Stavrogin—with all of which Bulgakov was of course familiar. But these are all treatments of the *chelovekobog*, the strong, self-willed, unprincipled individual with charismatic power over the ordinary majority. As such they lend themselves less well as material through which to polemicize with the *chelovekobozhie* of scientific socialism.

It is of course possible to object that Ivan Karamazov has been associated just as much, if not more, with the theme of amoralistic individualism ("If God does not exist, all is permitted") as with the theme of atheistic humanism. And indeed, it is very interesting to observe how Bulgakov manipulates Dostoevskii's material to fit his own philosophical and political agenda. This manipulation can be illustrated by examination of Bulgakov's treatment of Ivan's protest against the suffering of the innocent, and through his interpretation of the "Legend of the Grand Inquisitor."

After introducing the theme of man-Godhood through a presentation of Ivan's views on the matter as quoted to him by his hallucinated devil, Bulgakov moves on to a discussion of Ivan's well-known rejection of a divine order which tolerates the unacceptable suffering of innocent children. Ivan, he argues, cannot accept the premise that present suffering can be justified by future happiness. Bulgakov presents this as a rejection of eudaemonism, the theory whereby the value of an action is determined by the degree of its capacity to produce happiness. In his polemic with Marxism he is at this time arguing that socialism built on a positivistic foundation replaces religion with belief in progress, which offers as a justification for present suffering under capitalism the happiness of the free humanity of the future order. Bulgakov rejects this as a form of eudaemonism, arguing that a valid ethics must do justice to the principle, derived originally from the Gospel but now established within contemporary consciousness, of the essential equality of persons as moral subjects. It is unjust to require that those living now, or in the past, should sacrifice their happiness for the sake of future beneficiaries.

In using Ivan to demonstrate his own argument, Bulgakov is either blind to, or deliberately overlooks, the obvious fact that Ivan is objecting not to the theory of progress and the socialist paradise, but to the Christian concept of heaven, and not to the notion that the suffering of children benefits others now or in the future and is therefore justified, but that the happiness of those same children in the next life makes up for their suffering on earth. Had he not overlooked this, Bulgakov would have had to acknowledge that his hero Ivan is diametrically opposed to Bulgakov himself on the question of theodicy. While Ivan cannot be reconciled to accepting a justification for suffering that is inaccessible to his "Euclidean" mind, Bulgakov argues at length elsewhere in *From Marxism to Idealism* that the moral meaningfulness of our lives is predicated upon the fact that we have to deal with evil as it presents itself in our experience, namely, as irrational, while accepting in faith that, in the metaphysical sphere, evil has a rationale (227–29).[12] As it is, Bulgakov recruits Ivan as an ally in the fight against scientific socialism. Thus he is here interested in reading Ivan as a character who struggles with the moral implications of his atheism rather than as a character who struggles with the apparent injustice of the Christian world conception.

In his polemics with scientific socialism Bulgakov also argues that the belief in progress and the future new human being depends of necessity on an act of faith—that it is a pseudo-religious belief, which is therefore also subject to doubt. In his presentation of the "Legend of the Grand Inquisitor" Bulgakov shifts the dominant of his interpretation of Ivan from the character who struggles with the moral implications of his atheism to the character who harbors doubts about the *capacity* of humanity to achieve man-Godhood (as opposed to the desirability of it doing so) (99). Humans are too weak to take up the challenge of freedom, thinks the Grand Inquisitor/Ivan (100). Against the grain of the usual interpretation, Bulgakov reads this idea not as a riposte to Christianity (though he does not suppress the object of the Grand Inquisitor's polemic in his summary of the story) but as a riposte to scientific socialism's dream of a transformed humanity: "to the question as to whether humanity is capable of leaving its present, debased condition and making room in itself for the onset of a new, free, autonomous moral life, of carrying out the task allotted to it in the future, the Grand Inquisitor answers with a spiteful and passionate 'no'" (102). This ambiguous and curious wording (the reference to a "present, debased, condition" and "future" onset of a free life) reveals again what is Bulgakov's primary motive for using Dostoevskii at this stage in his career, namely to refute the theory of progress. In order to foreground the concept of man-Godhood in the first sense of a transformed collective humanity, he does not exploit the obvious potential for exposing the Inquisitor as a man-God in the second, Stirnerian sense.

When Bulgakov does eventually address the problem of the despotic ruler, it is once again to use Dostoevskii's material as a vehicle to air another of the arguments central to his conflict with Marxism, namely that as a positivistic worldview it cannot philosophically justify its core value of equality, and that its theory of progress is predicated on a disregard for the equal value of all. He argues that the Grand Inquisitor is anti-Christian (anti-Christ) in the sense that he rejects the Christian precept of the moral equality of all humans before God (which Bulgakov sees re-stated in the Kantian dictum that the person must be viewed not as a means but an end in itself) and replaces it with the pagan (pre-Christian) differentiation between the ethics of the master and the ethics of the slave. Not unexpectedly, Bulgakov draws a comparison to Nietzsche's neo-pagan, anti-Christian ethics, also pointing out that the latter regarded the emergence of a master-race as the goal of history (104–05). Bulgakov states that Dostoevskii wanted to show how an atheistic ethics is always in danger of reverting to pagan norms: "People are equal in God, but they are not equal in nature, and this natural inequality defeats the ethical ideal of their equality wherever this ideal is voided of its religious sanction" (104).

The connection with paganism and the point about people being unequal in nature are surely not Dostoevskii's, but Bulgakov's own. Still, what is most striking is that Bulgakov resists making the usual and apparently obvious point that the "Legend" illustrates how, for Dostoevskii, socialism must always end in tyranny. This entrenched view of Dostoevskii's, founded on the premise that socialism is intrinsically atheistic, is precisely the one that Bulgakov is fighting to overcome, so it is not surprising that he does not want to draw attention to it here. Though Bulgakov agrees that *Marxism* is intrinsically atheistic, the new ideological position that he is forming at this time is that social democracy as such is not only compatible with philosophical idealism and with Christianity, but that its values of justice and equality have no foundation without them. Thus Bulgakov's conclusion about Dostoevskii and socialism is a blatant imposition of his own view upon Dostoevskii: the latter "regarded the socialist worldview … as something of the order of a moral illness, but an illness of growth, as a transitional worldview that preceded a higher synthesis which, I might add, would consist in the merging of the economic demands of socialism with the principles of philosophical idealism, and the justification of the former by means of the latter" (109).

Though "Heroism and Asceticism" is not "about" Dostoevskii, its argument and vision are much closer to him than the essay discussed above that *is* "about" him. We can speculate that the change in emphasis has to do with "events." Between 1900 and 1905, Bulgakov's polemic with Marxism and other forms of positivistic socialism was conducted on the plane of theory. "Heroism and Asceticism," on the other hand, is an analysis of the Russian intelligentsia based on Bulgakov's experience both of the revolution of 1905 (which inspired the *Vekhi* symposium) and of the second State Duma of 1907, of which Bulgakov was a member. In confronting the political reality facing Russia at this time, the apparent inability of the radical left to engage with the political process and effect concrete reforms, Bulgakov willy-nilly psychologizes his objections to *chelovekobozhie* in the form of a critique of the leaders of the revolution seen as so many *chelovekobogi*.

In this connection, it is interesting to note that Bulgakov is the only *Vekhi* contributor to develop the theme of "the heroism of self-worship," the savior mentality, in his critique of the intelligentsia. On the other hand, both Nikolai Berdiaev and especially Semen Frank highlight the theme of anthropotheism.[13] Defending absolute values, Berdiaev sees the intelligentsia's "worship of man and worship of the people" as idolatrously replacing love of God and the truth (6), and concurs with the earlier Bulgakov in regarding scientific positivism as a "special religion" (8). For Frank, faith in the future happiness of the people "takes the place of authentic religion in the consciousness of the atheistic intelligentsia" (142), and he actually rehearses Stirner's challenge to Feuerbach that only amorality can derive from the rejection of absolute values (135).[14] However, in his analysis of the contradiction in terms that is the intelligentsia's ideology of "nihilistic moralism" (seen as embodying the tension between Feuerbach and Stirner), Frank nevertheless contends that, in the classic Russian *intelligent*, moralism displaces nihilism (149). Bulgakov's new emphasis on the self-worship of the *intelligent*, rather than the latter's worship of the people, reflects his greater immersion in Dostoevskii relative to the other contributors: he makes ten references to the novelist in his essay, while Berdiaev mentions him only once, and Frank not at all.[15]

If Bulgakov has previously focused on scientific socialism as a pseudo-religion, as anthropotheism, in "Heroism and Asceticism" the focus is on the intelligentsia as a pseudo-religious sect. Dostoevskii is explicitly credited by Bulgakov with being the first person to point out the intelligentsia's religious traits (20).[16] In his turn, Bulgakov draws our attention to its spirit of martyrdom, its utopianism, its Puritanism, and its dogmatic fundamentalism on the question of atheism, which he wittily describes as the faith into which all members of the intelligentsia are uncritically baptized (22). And if previously Bulgakov has analyzed as a philosophical consequence of Feuerbach's thesis the tendency to deify the common people, in "Heroism and Asceticism" he notes that the intelligentsia's intense feeling of guilt before the Russian people is the atheist's reassignment of the Christian's sense of her or his guilt before God (21).

Further, as indicated above, if Bulgakov has been previously preoccupied almost exclusively with Feuerbach's and Marxism's "religion of man-Godhood," within a few paragraphs of the third chapter of

"Heroism and Asceticism" this theme transmutes into the theme of *self-worship*. Thus he begins the chapter by stating, "The intelligentsia rejects Christianity and its standards and appears to accept atheism. In fact, instead of atheism, it adopts the dogmas of the religion of man-Godhood, in one or another of the variants produced by the Western European Enlightenment, and then turns this religion into idolatry." However, he goes on to argue that "the basic tenet" of man-Godhood—the "belief in the natural perfection of man and in infinite progress ... effected by human forces"—leads to "man [putting] himself in place of Providence and [seeing] himself as his own savior" (26). He concludes that the essence of man-Godhood is self-worship. In Russia, the intelligentsia sees itself as the savior of the Russian people, as Russia's hero: "*Heroism*—for me, this word expresses the fundamental essence of the intelligentsia's world-view and ideal, and it is the heroism of self-worship" (26–27). Later on in the essay he will state unequivocally that "the hero ... is the man-God" (39).

As we saw, in the Feuerbach essay of 1905 Bulgakov regarded Feuerbach and Stirner as ideological opposites, despite their shared atheism. The former had a substitute religion, that of *chelovekobozhie*; the latter had no religion except the elevation of the self. In "Heroism and Asceticism" Bulgakov admits a synthesis of the two, despite being aware of the ideological tension between them, as is apparent in the following statement:

> Our intelligentsia is almost unanimous in striving for collectivism, for the closest possible communality of human life, but its own temperament renders the intelligentsia itself an anti-communal, anti-collective force, since it bears within itself the divisive principle of heroic self-affirmation. The hero is to some extent a superman, confronting his neighbors in the proud and defiant pose of a savior. (29)

This insight had been reached by Dostoevskii long before. Unlike Stirner's *Einziger*, his *chelovekobogi* (Raskol'nikov, the Grand Inquisitor) are interested in the social sphere, and see themselves as the saviors of mankind. They combine egoism, or at least desire to rule, with altruism. In Russia, illogically, "Stirner" did not supersede "Feuerbach." Rather, egoistic amoralism, the logical outcome of materialistic atheism, existed side by side with faith in humanity and devotion to its cause. In "Heroism and Asceticism" Bulgakov understands this, which brings him into line with Dostoevskii's own treatment of the man-Godhood theme.

## Asceticism

We should view Bulgakov's engagement with asceticism in the context of the widespread preoccupation with the relationship between the "spirit" and the "flesh" in the culture of late imperial Russia. Since about 1900, in pursuit of a "new religious consciousness" and under the influence of Nietzsche, the literary avant-garde, led by Viacheslav Ivanov, Dmitrii Merezhkovskii, and Vasilii Rozanov, had set its face against the institutional Church, among other reasons because of its perceived denigration of the material world and bodily life. This perception was connected with the resurgent dominance of monasticism in Russia and the fact that the Church leadership was appointed from the (celibate) monastic clergy. A second reason asceticism was viewed with great hostility was because it was considered selfish to pursue one's own salvation in isolation from society at a time of unprecedented social and political upheaval. In this respect, Dostoevskii's passionate advocacy in *The Brothers Karamazov* of the Russian monastery and the institution of holy elders as the source of Russia's salvation fell on stony ground, despite the popularity that he otherwise enjoyed in the first quarter of the twentieth century.[17] Thus Bulgakov's Dostoevskian defense of the Christian ascetic in "Heroism and Asceticism" constituted a bold, counter-cultural move. It also marked a significant shift in his own, originally rather negative, appraisal of asceticism.

Bulgakov's most extensive treatment of asceticism prior to "Heroism and Asceticism" is found in a 1903 essay entitled "Ob ekonomicheskom ideale" ("On the Economic Ideal").[18] The terms used in his article are exclusively *asketizm* and its derivatives, where *asketizm* is opposed to hedonism, so it is true to say that Bulgakov moved between 1903 and 1909 from *gedonizm i asketizm* to *geroizm i podvizhnichestvo*. I will comment on the shift in terminology in due course. In 1903 Bulgakov had abandoned the philosophical materialism of Marxism and was working toward a justification of the Marxian beliefs in social justice and equality on the basis of Kantian idealism. His essay employs a rigorous Kantian methodology to scrutinize the value of wealth as one of the foundational values of political economics (the other is justice), and specifically to solve the economic problem of luxury. The question Bulgakov poses is: how justified is the relative ideal of wealth when examined in the light of the absolute ideal of the good?

Bulgakov sets up an opposition between two inadequate materialistic attitudes to wealth, which he will go on to resolve idealistically. These inadequate attitudes are at one extreme Epicureanism, the validation of the sensual world as the only existing one through the embrace of hedonistic consumption: this is the attitude of both materialist varieties of socialism, including Marxism, and contemporary capitalism.[19] At the other extreme is asceticism, which is deemed to be a materialism of a negative type, recognizing the world as exclusively sensual and rejecting it out of hand. Asceticism regards the body and its life as an absolute evil, and strives to liberate the spirit from the material sphere (271). Asceticism is intrinsically anti-cultural: it denies economics, whose premise is the validity and desirability of the growth of needs, and it denies history as a record of common human endeavor, admitting only of a moral individualism based on the need to save one's own soul (272–73). Thus the definition of *asketizm* that Bulgakov is working with is: "denial of the world."

I would contend that Bulgakov's attitude to asceticism as defined above is primarily derived from Vladimir Solov'ev, in terms of both the content of his view and the methodology that he uses to establish the "correct" attitude to the problem of wealth. From an essay, published in the same year, "Chto daet sovremennomu soznaniiu filosofiia Vl. Solov'eva?" ("What Does the Philosophy of V. Solov'ev Give to Contemporary Consciousness?"), we know that Bulgakov was familiar with Solov'ev's work in 1903, and what his essential evaluation was of it at this stage.[20] Like Solov'ev in *Chteniia o bogochelovechestve* (*Lectures on Godmanhood*, 1878), he identifies as the "pessimistic philosophy of asceticism" first neo-Platonism, then Buddhism. (Schopenhauer and Tolstoi are adduced as contemporary examples.) His basic approach to cultural history is also the same as Solov'ev's: hedonism and asceticism are seen as "abstract principles," one-sided responses to the problem of the body and its needs that ought to be supplanted by a higher, that is, a historically more recent, integral approach (and this methodology perhaps constrains Bulgakov into a very narrow interpretation of asceticism) (280).

What is interesting, though, in the light of the *Vekhi* essay, is that Bulgakov perceives asceticism in Christianity to be the same "denial of the world." The ascetic worldview "was adopted by an ascetic understanding of Christianity that is closer to Buddha than to Christ. Based on a one-sided and therefore untrue interpretation of the Gospels' teaching on wealth, this worldview often transforms God's world into the exclusive kingdom of Satan, into which not a single ray of divine light penetrates." To which aspect of Christian culture is Bulgakov referring? Surely to the extreme ascetic practices of the heroes of the Christian East, judging by a list of these heroes cited in a footnote to illustrate his point that the motto of the ascetic is: "mortify your flesh, curtail your needs, reject wealth as a temptation and the greatest of evils" (272). This suggests that in 1903 Bulgakov was not yet familiar with the hesychastic tradition that had so recently undergone a revival in his own country, that he had not yet read the ascetic writings collected in the *Philokalia*, that he was unaware of its teaching about the spiritual rewards of the ascetic life, and particularly that he had not learned of the teaching about the participation of the body in those rewards. It is certainly clear that he had not yet met his future friend, the defender of asceticism Pavel Florenskii.[21] On the evidence of the sources that he cites, Bulgakov's knowledge is drawn from scholarly works like M. Korelin's *Vazhneishie momenty v istorii srednevekovogo papstva* (*Important Moments in the History of the Medieval Papacy*, 1901) and those of Protestant theologians like Adolf von Harnack (*Das Wesen des Christentums*, 1900) and Francis Peabody (*Jesus Christ and the Social Question*, 1903).

It is also highly probable that Bulgakov's view of Christian asceticism is colored by his reading of Solov'ev, whose hostility toward monasticism was expressed many times in his career, most memorably in the essays "Ob upadke srednevekovogo mirosozertsaniia" ("On the Collapse of the Medieval World-Conception," 1891) and "Zhiznennaia drama Platona" ("The Life Drama of Plato," 1898). It is well known that Solov'ev perceived monks to have turned their backs on a needy world in order to pursue their own private salvation, whereas according to him their duty was to Christianize the world. The moral task of Christianity was seen by Solov'ev to be social, not individual. As a Christian socialist, Bulgakov naturally sympathized with Solov'ev's moral vision. Indeed, displaying typical Solov'evian historicism, he states in his essay that the ascetic worldview, with its rejection of history and social morality, is alien to contemporary Europeans, part of an outworn phase in human development that cannot be revisited (272).

Asceticism as "denial of the world," we can see, is unacceptable to Bulgakov. In "On the Economic Ideal" he is defending the "world," the material-bodily principle, *as an economist*. The basic premise is Kantian: the ideal of wealth should not be rejected, but rather subordinated to the higher ideal of the good. Bulgakov's defense for this is that material wealth is a prerequisite for spiritual growth.[22] The meaning of human existence is to serve the highest principle, the absolute good, by means of spiritual labor (272). This act of service is a free choice, made in the light of conscience and of the consciousness of one's duty (Kant's categorical imperative). The process is also the objective: through the service of a higher ideal a person grows spiritually and becomes more and more free—that is, morally developed. Perfection, however, is an unattainable ideal lying beyond the bounds of history and the individual life. But in order to begin this process of spiritual service and spiritual growth, one must first have attained a certain level of material wealth, or must experience freedom from poverty. Below a certain level of prosperity, humans are the slaves of nature and cannot fully exercise free moral choice. A negative asceticism is of no use to the poor (and is therefore inappropriate in Russia). Culture is the record of the spiritual labor of human beings, but without material well-being, there can be no culture (275–79).

This argument anticipates an important point made against asceticism in the *Vekhi* symposium, where it is taken by the other contributors, as it was in 1903 by Bulgakov, to mean "denial of the world." This argument is made in connection with the theme of culture-building in the widest possible sense, from the production of wealth through the creation of a legal state to the writing of philosophy, and is a product of the same Kantian framework that Bulgakov is using in 1903. At its greatest extreme, denial of the world incorporates denial of life itself. The *Vekhi* contributors are unanimous in regarding the Russian intelligentsia as ascetics in this sense, and thus as psychologically unfit for the urgent task of reforming Russia. For example, Berdiaev observes an "ascetic view of philosophy" that militates against the development of independent and original national thought (2). Aleksandr Izgoev is pessimistic about the intelligentsia's potential for creating culture given its cult of martyrdom: it "has formed a peculiar monastic order of people who have condemned themselves to death, and, moreover, to the most rapid death possible" (85). Frank points out a fundamental contradiction between the exclusively material ideal that the intelligentsia holds out for the people and the psychological fact that "the Russian intelligentsia does not love wealth," of either the spiritual or the material kind (148). To a greater extent than any of the other contributors, Frank repeats Bulgakov's earlier argument that Russia is too poor to afford asceticism: her priority must be to produce wealth.

But for Bulgakov in "On the Economic Ideal," once a certain level of material wealth has been achieved, the ascetic *method*, if not the philosophy of asceticism, acquires a positive value and comes into play as an essential moral practice for maintaining a person's spiritual growth. It does this by ensuring that our natural hedonism—a love of the good things of life—does not become a negative hedonism—enslavement to materialistic values and material goods. People in wealthy societies are always going to be tempted by negative hedonism, and will only be able to overcome this temptation through conscious moral effort, or *askesis* (*uprazhnenie*). Failure to do so will lead in due course to cultural collapse.[23] Luxury, then, cannot be defined objectively. Luxury is the victory of sensuality over the spirit, whether in an individual or a society. Thus Bulgakov wants to see the philosophy of asceticism as having been surpassed, although its method is presented as a timeless feature of our moral being. His main concern seems to be to Christianize Kantian ethics, to replace its apparently effortless exercise of duty with a vision of moral choice as a difficult and unending struggle for self-mastery. At the same time, Bulgakov wants to bring ascesis out of the monastery and into society: "Our time knows ascetics whose lives are a constant feat of the spirit [*podvig dukha*], constant sacrifice and self-negation, although nowadays one encounters these ascetics more frequently in the world than in the monastery or the desert" (282).

"Heroism and Asceticism" represents a development of this argument, and of course an application of it to the Russian intelligentsia. Now thinking about asceticism in a different way, as "self-overcoming," Bulgakov has gone beyond his fellow contributors, who are still applying a notion of asceticism as "rejection" or "denial," whether of the world, as we have seen, or of the self. For them asceticism is seen negatively from the point of view of a Kantian emphasis on culture-building and individual responsibility. Since 1903 Bulgakov, on the other hand, has moved deeper into the psychology and culture of Orthodoxy, and his understanding of the moral life, though still wholly compatible with Kantian ethics, has become further Christianized.

Both the changes and the original Kantian position are reflected in Bulgakov's choice of vocabulary. The most significant new terms are of course the Slavonic *podvizhnichestvo* (asceticism) and *podvizhnik* (ascetic) (deriving from the noun *podvig*—"exploit," "feat," "heroic deed"), but also *smirenie* (humility), *grekh* (sin), and *poslushanie* ("penance" or "obedience"). The morphology of *podvizhnichestvo* conveys the element of struggle in moral choice more effectively than the Greek *askesis* (exercise), which connotes a sense of discipline that seems to fit better with the Kantian notion of duty. The terms *smirenie* and particularly *grekh* personalize the Kantian imperative to aspire to the Good. One is humbled more in the presence of a superior being than that of a principle, and one sins not against an ideal but against a Person. *Grekh* also reinforces powerfully the notion of struggle in the exercise of our "free" will. The choice between right and wrong is not merely a rational act (as Kant implies), but an effort of the will that must first overcome an innate tendency to do the wrong thing. Thus Bulgakov writes of "the power of sin, its agonizing weight, its ubiquitous and profound influence on all human life" (36). Nevertheless, some truly Kantian/Protestant vocabulary and concepts remain, including: *dolg* (duty)—which is frequently mentioned, *obiazannosti* (obligations), *samokontrol'* (self-control), *samodistsiplina* (self-discipline), and the like.

Nevertheless, asceticism is being used differently in the *Vekhi* essay, as part of a polemic against the Russian intelligentsia. The binary opposition *geroizm/podvizhnichestvo* is not, as was the opposition *gedonizm/asketizm*, a false opposition of two equally flawed attitudes to be reconciled in a higher synthesis, but an irreconcilable opposition of an attitude presented as essentially false to one presented as essentially correct. This is of course the opposition of man-Godhood and Godmanhood, of divinized humanity (the intelligentsia "hero") and Christ the God-man, or the ascetic-imitator of Christ: "Is the standard for examining oneself the image of the perfect, Divine personality [*Bozhestvennoi lichnosti*], incarnate in Christ? Or is it self-deified man in one of its earthly, limited guises (humanity, the people, the proletariat, or the superman)—a projection, in the last analysis, of one's own ego in a heroic pose?" asks Bulgakov (36). In fact, it is misleading to use the abstract noun *bogochelovechestvo*, with its Solov'evian ring, because in the essay Bulgakov actually only uses the proper noun *Bogochelovek*, and that only once, as he prefers to refer directly to *Khristos*—Christ. This is because this essay is written primarily and indeed overwhelmingly under the influence not of Solov'ev but Dostoevskii, who at this point clearly colors Bulgakov's interpretation of asceticism. Dostoevskii explored the struggle between atheistic socialism and Christianity through the medium of fiction, and thus preferred embodiments of the man-god and the saintly Christian to their philosophical abstractions. This suits Bulgakov's purpose as he opposes the Russian *intelligent* intent on saving the world to an image of the Christian citizen doing penance within it (39).

It will be said that Dostoevskii was more interested in saintly elders and the "God-bearing" Russian people than in doctors, engineers, and lawyers. One response to this is that Bulgakov's citizen-ascetics are his vision of the humbled intelligentsia "proud men" that Dostoevskii called for in his "Pushkin Speech," which Bulgakov mentions with approval in his essay. Dostoevskii wished to reunite a deracinated intelligentsia with the people, and this is the theme with which Bulgakov ends his essay. In his previous work he had condemned Dostoevskii's religious nationalism for its politically conservative and romantic attitude to the question of the rule of law,[24] but in "Heroism and Asceticism" the national idea is defended against the intelligentsia's cosmopolitanism, which overlooks the importance for the people of the Orthodox faith. The people's "ideal is Christ and his teaching, and their standard is Christian asceticism," claims Bulgakov after Dostoevskii (44–45), and he even follows Dostoevskii in identifying the people's ascetic ideal with the Orthodox monasteries and elders in their midst: "Like the icon-lamps glimmering in the monastery cloisters, whither the people thronged through the centuries in search of moral support and instruction, these ideals, this light of Christ, illumined Rus'" (45). Thus, under the influence of Dostoevskii and the logic of his man-god/God-man opposition, Bulgakov sympathetically reconnects the ideal of the citizen-ascetic with its monastic source.

As Bulgakov emerges from Marxism, he begins to place greater emphasis on the psychology of atheism than on its philosophy. As he emerges from Kantianism he begins to invest more in the concrete human personality than in the theoretical individual. By the time he wrote "Heroism and Asceticism," he saw the human being as a genuine agent whose efficacy rests on a choice between pride and humility, self-elevation and self-effacement. Humility is not seen as inactivity or as the mark of a weak character, but as a constant battle for perfection on the model of Christian asceticism. Meanwhile, perfection is no longer a philosophical ideal but a personal God: "The Christian saint is the person who, by means of continuous and unremitting effort [*podvigom*], has most completely transformed his personal will and his empirical personality until they are permeated to the fullest possible measure with the will of God. The model of total permeation is the God-man, arriving 'not to do his own will, but the will of His Father that sent him'" (39–40). Bulgakov is indebted to Dostoevskii for his vision of Russia as the battleground on which Christianity fights the atheistic forces of modernity for control of the country's future.

## Notes

1. For a detailed account of Bulgakov's intellectual development until 1922, see Catherine Evtuhov, *The Cross and the Sickle: Sergei Bulgakov and the Fate of Russian Religious Philosophy* (Ithaca, NY: Cornell University Press, 1997). Bulgakov entered the priesthood in January 1918. See also Rowan Williams, ed., *Sergii Bulgakov: Towards a Russian Political Theology* (Edinburgh: T & T Clark, 1999).

2. See Ju. M. Lotman and B. A. Uspenskii, "The Role of Dual Models in the Dynamics of Russian Culture," in *The Semiotics of Russian Culture*, ed. Ann Shukman (Ann Arbor: Michigan Slavic Contributions, 1984), 3–35.

3. The term *Bogochelovek* is the Slavonic rendering of the Greek *theanthropos*, which was widely used by the Greek Fathers to convey the hypostatic union of the two natures—divine and human—in Christ. Origen was the first to use the term, in *de principiis*. *Theandros* was used as a variant. See G. W. H. Lampe, *A Patristic Greek Lexicon* (Oxford: Clarendon Press, 1961), 615–16.

4. See Andrzej Walicki, *The Slavophile Controversy: History of a Conservative Utopia in Nineteenth-Century Russian Thought* (Oxford: Clarendon Press, 1975), 538, and Joseph Frank, *Dostoevskii: The Seeds of Revolt, 1821–1849* (London: Robson Books, 1977), 182–98.

5. Established by means of an electronic search of the texts via Zeno.org. Accessed on 25 January 2011. It is worth noting that Bulgakov uses *chelovekobozhie* (alongside *antropoteizm*) in his essays before *Vekhi*, but switches to *chelovekobozhestvo* in the *Vekhi* essay itself. I do not think there is an obvious explanation for the switch.

6. The passage reads as follows: "Der Theismus beruht auf dem *Zwiespalt* von *Kopf und Herz*; der Pantheismus ist die Aufhebung dieses Zwiespaltes im *Zwiespalt*—denn er macht das göttliche Wesen nur *als transzendentes* immanent—; der Anthropotheismus *ohne Zwiespalt*. Der Anthropotheismus ist das zu *Verstand* gebrachte Herz; er spricht im Kopf nur auf Verstandesweise aus, was das Herz in seiner Weise sagt. Die Religion ist nur Affekt, Gefühl, Herz, Liebe, d.h. die Negation, *Auflösung Gottes* im Menschen. Die neue Philosophie ist daher, als die *Negation der Theologie*, welche die Wahrheit des religiösen Affektes leugnet, die *Position der Religion*. Der Anthropotheismus ist die *selbstbewußte Religion* – die Religion, *die sich selbst versteht*." Vorläufige Thesen zur Reform der Philosophie, in Ludwig Feuerbach, *Kleine philosophische Schriften (1842–1845)*, ed. Max Gustav Lange (Leipzig: Felix Meiner, 1950) (Philosophische Bibliothek, Bd. 227), 55.

7. There is evidence that Speshnev became a prototype for the character Stavrogin in *Besy* (*The Devils*, 1871–72). See Frank, *Seeds of Revolt*, 258. Stavrogin is the ultimate Dostoevskian amoralist of the Stirnerian type.

8. V. E. Evgrafova, *Sotsial'no-politicheskie i filosofskie vzgliady petrashevtsev* (Moscow: Gosudarstvennoe izdatel'stvo politicheskoi literatury, 1953), 496; Frank, *Seeds of Revolt*, 262; Walicki, *The Slavophile Controversy*, 538–39. The addressee is K. E. Khoetskii. Speshnev's wording does seem to echo Feuerbach's understanding of anthropotheism

as a form of religion ("self-conscious religion, religion that understands itself"). If, as seems likely, he coined the term "man-god" for the first time, it is reasonable to suppose that he did so against the background of the prevalence of the use of "God-man" to denote Christ in Orthodox religious discourse.

9   S. N. Bulgakov, "Religiia chelovekobozhiia u L. Feierbakha," in *Dva grada. Issledovaniia o prirode obshchestvennykh idealov*, ed. V. V. Sapov (Moscow: Astrel', 2008), 67–119. *Dva grada* was originally published in 1911. Page references to essays in *Dva grada* refer to the Sapov edition and are included in parentheses in the text.

10  Translations of text from Bulgakov's essays prior to *Vekhi* are my own. For text from the *Vekhi* symposium itself, I have used Marshall S. Shatz and Judith E. Zimmerman, eds. and trans., *Vekhi/Landmarks: A Collection of Articles about the Russian Intelligentsia* (Armonk, NY: M. E. Sharpe, 1994). Page references to essays in *Vekhi* refer to this translation and are included in parentheses in the text.

11  Sergei Bulgakov, *Ot marksizma k idealizmu. Sbornik statei (1896–1903)* (Frankfurt am Main: Posev, 1968). Facsimile of the original publication in St. Petersburg, 1903. Page references to essays in *Ot marksizma k idealizmu* are included in parentheses in the text.

12  See "Chto daet sovremennomu soznaniiu filosofiia Vl. Solov'eva?," in Bulgakov, *Ot marksizma k idealizmu*, 195–262.

13  The opposition true religion/false religion is present at least implicitly in all of the essays, except those of Izgoev and Kistiakovskii, but remains undeveloped by Gershenzon and Struve. It is of course not a coincidence that it is the religious philosophers who are most interested in this theme.

14  Stirner is mentioned three times by Frank, Feuerbach once.

15  Izgoev and Kistiakovskii make no reference to Dostoevskii. Struve does so in a generic way twice. Interestingly, Gershenzon, the "Tolstoian," makes five mentions of Dostoevskii.

16  Struve gives Solov'ev this honor (119).

17  For an overview of religious attitudes in late imperial Russia, see my "Religious Renaissance in the Silver Age," in *A History of Russian Thought*, ed. William Leatherbarrow and Derek Offord (Cambridge: CUP, 2010), 169–94.

18  "Ob ekonomicheskom ideale," in Bulgakov, *Ot marksizma k idealizmu*, 263–87. Translated by Williams, *Sergii Bulgakov*, 27–53.

19  Bulgakov illustrates extensively from the German social scientist Werner Sombart's *Der moderne Kapitalismus* (1902).

20  See note 12, above.

21  The first published correspondence between Bulgakov and Florenskii is postmarked March 1906. See *Perepiska sviashchennika Pavla Aleksandrovicha Florenskogo so sviashchennikom Sergiem Nikolaevichem Bulgakovym*, ed. Igumen Andronik (Tomsk: Vodolei, 2001), 16.

22   In fact, this is one of two discrete defenses. Bulgakov also argues that matter is the medium through which a higher, non-material end is served. This argument is of great interest for his subsequent work, particularly *Filosofiia khoziaistva* (*The Philosophy of Economy*, 1912). However, since it has no bearing on the *Vekhi* essay, I shall not analyze it here. See Sergei Bulgakov, *Philosophy of Economy: The World as Household*, trans. and ed. Catherine Evtuhov (New Haven, CT: Yale University Press, 2000).

23   One might well reflect on the recent banking crisis in the light of this perception.

24   See the 1906 article "Venets ternovyi. Pamiati F. M. Dostoevskogo," in Bulgakov, *Dva grada*, 478–93.

# List of Contributors

**Robin Aizlewood** holds an honorary position at UCL, having been director of the UCL School of Slavonic and East European Studies, and also of the inter-university Centre for East European Language-Based Area Studies. He is the author of two books on Maiakovskii's verse (*Verse Form and Meaning in the Poetry of Vladimir Maiakovskii*, 1989, and *Two Essays on Maiakovskii's Verse*, 2000) and a wide range of studies of nineteenth- and early twentieth-century Russian philosophy and literature, both prose and poetry.

**Ruth Coates** is senior lecturer in Russian studies at the University of Bristol, UK. She is the author of *Christianity in Bakhtin: God and the Exiled Author*, 1998, and numerous articles on the Russian intellectual tradition. She is currently researching the reception of the doctrine of deification in Russian culture, with an emphasis on the late imperial period.

**Stuart Finkel** is associate professor of history at the University of Florida in Gainesville. He is the author of *On the Ideological Front: The Russian Intelligentsia and the Making of the Soviet Public Sphere*, 2007, as well as articles on both Russian intellectuals and the formation of the Soviet security apparatus. His current research involves the so-called "Political Red Cross," which lobbied on behalf of political prisoners in the Soviet Union from 1918–38, and he is also examining the remarkable life of this organization's longtime leader, Ekaterina Peshkova.

**G. M. Hamburg** is the Otho M. Behr Professor of History at Claremont McKenna College, California. He is co-editor (with Randall Poole) of *A History of Russian Philosophy, 1830–1930: Faith, Reason, and the Defense of Human Dignity*, 2010. With Semion Lyandres, he edits *The Journal of Modern Russian History and Historiography*.

**Frances Nethercott** is reader in Russian history at the University of St Andrews, UK. She is the author of *Une rencontre philosophique: Bergson en Russie, 1907–1917*, 1995, *Russia's Plato: Plato and the Platonic Tradition in Russian Education, Science and Ideology, 1840–1930*, 2000, and *Russian Legal Culture Before and After Communism: Criminal Justice, Politics and the Public Sphere*, 2007. She is currently working on developments in Russian historiography during the late imperial and early Soviet eras.

## List of Contributors

**Randall A. Poole** is associate professor of history at the College of St. Scholastica in Duluth, Minnesota. He is the translator and editor of *Problems of Idealism: Essays in Russian Social Philosophy*, 2003, co-editor (with G. M. Hamburg) of *A History of Russian Philosophy, 1830–1930: Faith, Reason, and the Defense of Human Dignity*, 2010, and author of numerous essays on Russian intellectual history and philosophy. In 2012 he was a visiting professor of Russian intellectual history at the University of Toronto.

**Vanessa Rampton** has recently completed a PhD on conceptions of freedom and selfhood in pre-revolutionary Russia at King's College, University of Cambridge. She is co-editor of a special edition of *Studies in East European Thought* on contemporary Russian culture and has published articles on Russian nationalism and on Dostoevskii and works as a translator for the English version of the President of Russia's official website, eng.kremlin.ru.

**Christopher Read** is professor of modern European history at the University of Warwick. His research focuses on the intellectual, political, and social history of the Russian Revolution. His books include *Religion, Revolution and the Russian Intelligentsia: The Vekhi Debate and its Intellectual Background*, 1979, *Culture and Power in Revolutionary Russia*, 1992, *From Tsar to Soviets*, 1996, *Lenin: A Revolutionary Life*, 2005, and *The Russian Revolution 1914–22*, 2012. He is currently an editor for a major international research and publishing project to commemorate the approaching centenaries of the First World War, the Russian Revolution, and the Russian Civil War, and is writing a biography of Stalin.

**Bernice Glatzer Rosenthal** is professor of history at Fordham University. She has published extensively on the early twentieth-century religious revival and on Nietzsche's influence on Russian and Soviet culture. Her recent publications include *New Myth, New World: From Nietzsche to Stalinism*, 2002, "Religious Humanism in the Russian Silver Age," in *A History of Russian Philosophy*, 2010, and "Occultism as a Response to Spiritual Crisis," in *The New Age of Russia: Occult and Esoteric Dimensions*, 2011, which she co-edited with Birgit Menzel and Michael Hagemeister. Her first book, *D. S. Merezhkovsky and the Silver Age: The Development of a Revolutionary Mentality*, 1975, is being translated into Chinese.

List of Contributors

**Oliver Smith** was until his untimely death in April 2013 lecturer in Russian at the University of St Andrews, UK. He is the author of *Vladimir Soloviev and the Spiritualization of Matter*, 2011, and numerous articles on the Russian theological and philosophical traditions. His last projects involved biblical reception and the prophetic tradition in Russian cultural history.

**Elena A. Takho-Godi** is professor of Russian literature at Moscow State University and a corresponding member of the Russian Academy of Natural Sciences. She is the author of more than 250 publications on Russian literature and thought. Her recent monographs include *Khudozhestvennyi mir prozy A. F. Loseva*, 2007, and *Velikie i bezvestnye. Ocherki po russkoi literature i kul'ture XIX–XX vv.*, 2008. She is the editor of the series "Losevskie chteniia," whose most recent publications are *Sbornik "Vekhi" v kontekste russkoi kul'tury*, 2007, *Antichnost' i kul'tura Serebrianogo veka*, 2010, and *F. M. Dostoevskii i kul'tura Serebrianogo veka: traditsii, traktovki, transformatsii*, 2012.

**Evert van der Zweerde** is professor of political philosophy at Radboud University, Nijmegen, Netherlands. He is author of *Soviet Historiography of Philosophy; Istoriko-Filosofskaia Nauka*, 1997, and co-editor of *Vladimir Solov'ev: Reconciler and Polemicist*, 2000, *Civil Society, Religion, and the Nation*, 2004, and *Orthodox Christianity and Human Rights*, 2012. He has published numerous articles on Russian philosophy and civil society. The current focus of his research is democratic theory.

# Index

Aeschylus  215
Aizlewood, Robin  7-46, 171-187, 260n7, 260n10
Akhmatova, Anna  226
Aksakov, Ivan S.  40, 71
Alekseev, P. V.  45n33
Alexander I  283
Alexander II  16, 156
Alexander III  156
Aliaev, G.  43n8
Alloi, V.  43n5, 43n11, 84n24, 188n6
Althusser, Louis  127n55
Alyoshin, A.  190n24
Anarchism; anarchist; anarchistic  27, 91, 226, 263, 266, 275, 279-280
Andreev, D.  261n16
Andreev, Leonid  89
Antisemitic; antisemitism  88-89, 96
Antonii (Metropolitan)  274, 285n11
Antonovich, Volodymyr  140n6
Aristotle  115, 124n15, 215, 222
Artsybashev, M.  102n19
Ascetic; asceticism  36, 39-40, 51, 65n11, 65n14, 85n40, 127n61, 154, 161-163, 215, 230, 252, 270, 287-288, 294-304
Ashley, J. Matthew  166n3, 166n11, 167n15
Askol'dov, Sergei  258
Atheism; atheist  28, 32-33, 35-36, 39, 51, 56, 59-60, 82, 92, 158, 161-162, 181, 184, 199, 228, 231, 243, 245, 248, 257, 263, 265, 288-296, 303-304
Augustine of Hippo  146, 165
Authority, religious  62
Autocracy; autocratic  15, 18, 20, 59, 74, 88, 90, 92, 95, 97, 99, 115, 122, 154-156, 160, 162, 265-267, 273-276, 282
Autonomy, individual  28, 52, 133-134, 136-137, 150, 155, 158, 190n24, 203
Autonomy, political  112, 277-278, 285n20
Averintsev, A. A.  191n28, 237n22
Avksent'ev, Nikolai  97-98
Azef, Evno  255-256, 261n28, 262n31

Bakhtin, Mikhail  191n24
Bakunin, Mikhail  28, 59, 199, 279
Barber, Benjamin  124n12
Barna, Luba  168n30
Barta, Peter I.  190n21
Barth, Karl  165
Bauman, Zygmunt  57, 67n42
Bazarov, Vladimir (Rudnev)  94
Bedford, C. Harold  285n13
Beilis, Mendel  89, 278-279
Belinskii, Vissarion  35, 59, 92, 100, 262n41, 275, 288
Belokonskii, Ivan  228
Belyi, Andrei  216, 226, 236n5, 266
Benson, Peter  102n8, 143n36
Berdiaev, Nikolai  10, 13, 20-38, 41, 45n34, 45n36, 51-52, 56-58, 62-63, 65n5, 67n29, 71-74, 78-79, 90, 93, 96-98, 105-106, 109-111, 116, 125n25, 127n63, 130-133, 137, 142n23, 144n45,48, 154, 169n42, 45, 175-181, 185-186, 189n13, 190n16, 192-193, 199, 202, 205, 207, 209, 216, 220-226, 229-236, 244, 247-248, 257, 262n35, 268-271, 274-276, 281, 285n11, 295, 301

# Index

Berdiaeva, Lidiia  224
Besançon, Alain  124n8
Bibikhin, V. V.  237n22, 237n24-28, 238n33, 35, 43, 239n51, 54, 241n94-99
Bird, Robert  236n3, 240n86
Bloch, Ernst  151
Blok, Aleksandr  226, 266
Boborykin, P. D.  61, 64n2
Bogdanov, Aleksandr  25, 94, 144n45
Bohachevsky-Chomiak, Martha  66n22, 168n32, 284n4, 285n14
Botkin, Vasilii  262n41
Brensted, M. M.  224
Briand, Aristide  96
Brooks, Thom  124n14
Brun-Zejmis, Julia  189n12
Buddha  299
Bukharev, Fedor  65n8, 168n36, 244, 249-251, 256-257
Bulgakov, Mikhail  236n7
Bulgakov, Sergei  10, 13, 20-21, 24, 28-29, 32-41, 45n34, 52-54, 58, 65n6, 65n13-14, 66n27, 79, 81, 90, 92, 98, 105-107, 109, 111, 115, 117, 130-131, 133, 144n49, 147-154, 156-159, 161-164, 166n6, 167n21, 169n44-45, 175, 177-182, 184-186, 188n11, 192-193, 199, 202, 205, 207, 209, 220-222, 225-230, 234, 243-248, 251-257, 259, 261n14, 268-274, 281-282, 287-307
Bunyan, John  38
Burbank, Jane  62, 85n41
Burchard, Kristiane  47n58
Burke, Edmund  84n27
Burleigh, Michael  168n34

Calvin, John  279
Calvinism  38
Capon, Robert  259
Carlyle, Thomas  38, 193, 279
Cauderay, Laurent  142n28
Cavanagh, Clare  191n28

Cavanaugh, William T.  166n1, 166n11, 167n26
Chaadaev, Petr  23, 26, 28, 51, 59, 171-191, 266
Chamberlain, Lesley  45n35
*Change of Signposts* (*Smena vekh*) 79-81
Chekhov, Anton  52-54, 59, 65n10
Chelpanov, Georgii  215
Cherniavsky, Michael  155-156
Chernov, Viktor  94-98, 129
Chernyshevskii, Nikolai  12, 25, 59, 65n15, 92, 100-111, 186
Chicherin, Boris  26, 112, 155
Christ; Christian  34-38, 51, 53, 56, 65n14, 82, 89, 97-98, 111-113, 116-117, 119, 123, 137, 139, 144n49, 149-151, 155, 158, 161, 163, 176, 183, 193, 197-198, 202-205, 219, 227, 230, 236, 244, 250-254, 256-258, 263-276, 279-280, 282-283, 287-288, 292-297, 299-304
Christianity; Christian  34-38, 51, 53, 56, 65n14, 89, 111-113, 116-117, 119, 123, 137, 139, 144n49, 149-151, 155, 158, 161, 163, 176, 183, 193, 198, 202-205, 219, 230, 244, 252, 254, 257-258, 263-276, 279-282, 287-300, 303-304
Chulkov, Georgii  226
Church, Russian Orthodox  18, 32, 36-37, 117, 194, 199, 265-267, 272, 274-275, 287
Cicero  108, 124n11, 124n16
Clemenceau, Georges  96
Clowes, Edith W.  31, 46n49, 64n2, 237n15, 286n28
Coates, Ruth  10-47, 287-304
Cohen, Hermann  143n41
Coleman, Heather J.  47n56
Collini, Stefan  61-62, 67n31, 68n45
Collins, John  261n13
Communism; communist  43n4, 100, 119, 154, 165, 189n12, 230-232, 234, 282

Community  12-13, 32, 37, 108, 112, 114, 128, 135, 143, 172, 266, 269, 279
Confino, Michael  63, 68n45
Conservative  16, 37, 47n53, 74, 83n16, 90, 122, 153, 209, 303
Constitution; constitutional  15, 17-19, 69, 87, 93, 105, 114, 122, 135, 137, 145n53, 156, 163, 263, 273, 276, 281, 283
Constitutional Democrats (Kadet)  18, 61, 69, 81, 87, 90-91, 93-95, 99, 105, 118, 129, 135, 263
Copleston, Frederick C.  190n16
Craig, E.  142n19
Creative; creativity  12-13, 29-30, 37, 39, 50-53, 60, 76-77, 92, 97, 101, 110, 122, 128, 133, 138, 148, 150, 154, 161, 163-164, 173, 185, 203, 209, 214-215, 220, 223, 229-230, 234-235, 245, 264, 269, 272, 277
Cromwell, Oliver  273, 278-279
Culture, religious  10, 14, 32, 47n56, 277

Dahrendorf, Ellen  140n2
Daniel', Iulii  235
Davydov, Iu. N.  141n8
de Madariaga, Isabel  169n40
de Vries, Hent  166n1
DeBlasio, Alyssa  45n36
Democracy; democratic; democratization  16-20, 42, 70, 87-88, 91, 94-95, 99, 105-114, 116, 118, 121-123, 135, 228, 257, 278, 294
Dennes, M.  236n3
Derrida, Jacques  109, 125n18, 125n23
Descartes, René  182
Dogma, dogmatic  35-36, 38, 66n27, 70, 73, 146, 202-203, 209, 233, 265, 280-281, 295-296
Dolinin, A. S.  190n20
Dostoevskii, Fedor  26, 28, 30-31, 38, 45n36, 51-54, 56, 59-50, 80, 93, 116, 152, 174-175, 177, 179-182, 186, 190n21, 208, 218, 221, 226, 244-245, 252-254, 256, 263, 266-268, 273-275, 287-297, 303-304
Downey, John K.  166n2, 167n17
Drahomanov, Mykhailo  140n6
Duddington, Nathalie A.  125n31, 166n13, 216, 237n9
Duma  15, 40, 89, 106, 115, 118, 273, 277-278, 294
Duncan, Peter J. S.  190n21
Durylin, S. N.  220, 226
Dynnik, M. A.  126n52
Dzhimbinov, Stanislav Bemovich  42n4, 189n12

Egorov, Dmitrii Fedorovich  217
Ehlen, Peter  45n34
Eikhenbaum, Boris  192-195, 210n1
Emel'ianov, B.V.  124n6
Emerson, Caryl  42n2, 46n41, 191n24
Engelstein, Laura  143n38
Enlightenment  25, 35, 38, 40, 57-58, 60, 163, 203, 271, 296
Erismann, Friedrich (Fedor)  239n70
Erismann, Theodor  228, 239n70
Erismann-Stepanova, Vera  228
Ermichev, A. A.  191n25
Ermishin, O. T.  238n29
Ern, Vladimir  221
Erofeev, Viktor  238n31
Eschatologicial; eschatology  148-149, 151-153, 156, 158, 161-162, 244, 247, 251, 255, 258, 264, 266, 272
Ethics  37-38, 41, 129-131, 133-136, 159, 164, 214, 231, 292-293, 301-302
Evgrafova, V. E.  305n8
Evtuhov, Catherine  66n22, 127n56, 144n49, 166n7-8, 305n1, 307n22
External  12-13, 28, 32, 37, 57, 73-74, 76, 79, 93, 97, 128, 135, 138-139, 146, 153-154, 157-158, 161-165, 172, 179, 184-186, 189n13, 201,

205-206, 208, 210, 243-244, 247, 251-252, 254-255, 258-260, 266, 271

Fedorov, Nikolai 22, 29, 40
Fedotov, Georgii 62-63
Fet, Afanasii 51-53
Feuerbach, Ludwig 168n30, 287-306
Fichte, Johann G. 26, 179
Figes, Orlando 19, 44n13, 44n21, 45n23, 45n25-26, 45n28-29, 260n11
Filaret (Metropolitan) 199, 259, 262n47
Filosofov, Dmitrii 265, 280
Finkel, Stuart 14, 19, 21, 69-82, 85n32, 127n59
Fischer, George 93
Florenskii, Pavel 31, 217, 220-221, 224, 299, 306n21
Forster, E. M. 232
Foucault, Michel 143n38
Frank, Joseph 305n4, 305n7-8
Frank, Semen 10-11, 13, 20-22, 24, 28-30, 32-35, 38-39, 41, 43n11, 45n34, 50-52, 54-56, 64n3, 78-79, 90, 93, 95, 97, 105-107, 109, 111, 113, 120, 127n71, 130-131, 160, 163-164, 175, 177-179, 181, 185, 194, 202, 214, 216, 220-225, 227, 229, 231-234, 247-248, 252, 259, 268-269, 281, 289, 295, 301, 306n14
Freedom 21, 28, 38, 51, 72, 91, 93-94, 109-115, 122, 128-140, 148, 151, 154-156, 158-159, 172, 203, 234-235, 253, 264-266, 271, 275-277, 279-283, 293, 300
French, R. M. 46n39, 168n33
Freud, Sigmund 232
Freund, Julien 124n8
Friche, Vladimir 94
*From Under the Rubble* (*Iz-pod glyb*) 67n29, 117, 126n45

Gacheva, A. G. 46n44
Galai, Shmuel 143n31
Gaponenkov, A. A. 238n44
Gardenin, Iu. See Chernov
Garshin, Vsevolod 52
Gaut, Greg 168n37
Geifman, A. 261n28
Genghis Khan 282
Gershenzon, Mikhail 10, 12-13, 18, 20, 28-30, 32, 34, 36-39, 43n5, 43n11, 51-53, 58, 65n7, 84n24, 90, 92-93, 97-99, 105-106, 111, 113, 117, 122, 128, 137, 144n47, 171-175, 177-181, 184-186, 189n13, 193, 202, 209, 214, 227, 234, 243, 249, 252, 268-273, 306n13
Gertsen, A. I. see Herzen
Ginzburg, Aleksandr 235
Ginzburg, Lidiia 191n24
Gippius, Zinaida 265
Glatzer Rosenthal, Bernice 14, 27, 66n22, 168n32, 263-286
Glen-Doepel, William 166n14
Glinka-Volzhskii, A. S. 226
God 20, 31, 36, 51, 80, 146-147, 149-151, 154-155, 158, 161, 165, 173, 195-196, 198, 200-202, 204-207, 217, 221, 227, 233, 235, 245, 247, 250-259, 263, 265-266, 271-276, 278, 280, 282-283, 288-293, 295-299, 303-304
Goethe, Johann Wolfgang 279
Gogol', Nikolai 56, 59, 226, 263, 266
Gol'denveizer, Aleksandr 197-199, 201-204
Gor'kii, Maksim 216
Green, Robert H. 47n56
Grier, Philip T. 240n83
Griftsov, B. A. 222
Groys, Boris 24, 45n37
Gurian, Waldemar 153, 167n27
Gusev, Nikolai 193, 204-205, 211n3-4
Gustafson, Richard F. 168n35
Guyer, Paul 143n36

# Index

Haardt, Alexander  112, 236n3
Habermas, Jürgen  40
Haimson, L.  102n9
Halfin, Igal  168n34
Hamburg, Gary M.  14, 26, 43n7, 44n12, 64n2, 66n24, 83n17, 144n45, 144n50, 167n14, 168n35, 190n19, 190n24, 192-210
Hardeman, Hilde  85n33
Harnack, Adolf von  299
Hass, Sophie  239n70
Hauerwas, Stanley  166n6
Havel, Václav  40
Hedda, Jennifer  47n56
Hegel, G. W. F.  26, 28, 110, 175, 224, 227, 288
Hermogen (Patriarch)  36, 273
Herzen, Aleksandr  28, 59-60, 67n32, 92, 100, 116, 173, 182, 188n11, 190n24, 199, 248
Heuman, Susan  143n33, 285n20
Hippolytus of Rome  261n22
Hobbes, Thomas  278
Hollerich, Michael  167n26
Humanism; humanistic  29, 50, 111, 113, 139, 147-148, 150-154, 158, 160-165, 257, 270, 289-291
Huntington, Samuel P.  17, 44n18
Husserl, Edmund  224
Huxley, Aldous  232

Iakovlev, A. A.  42n3, 46n45, 65n7, 67n30, 84n20, 188n6, 190n14-15, 191n26, 236n2
Iakovlev, S. V.  240n84
Iazykov, Nikolai  187
Idealism  10-11, 19, 23-24, 26, 28, 31, 38-42, 53, 129-131, 133, 155-164, 182, 230, 246, 287, 290-294, 298
Il'in, Ivan A.  220-221, 227, 240n83, 257, 262n40
Il'in, V. see Lenin
Il'in, V. N.  222
Inner  12-13, 17, 38-39, 51, 56, 59, 76, 91, 93, 97, 99-100, 110, 128, 136-138, 148, 154-155, 158, 163, 173, 182, 184-187, 192, 198, 201, 206, 208, 214, 230, 243-244, 247-248, 251, 257, 259, 264, 269, 277
Isupov, K. G.  191n25
Iur'ev, B. see Chernov
Iurkevich, P.  27, 119
Ivanov, Viacheslav  27, 177, 215, 220-221, 225-227, 237n23, 266, 297
Ivanov-Razumnik, R. V.  61, 67n33-34, 81
Izgoev, Aleksandr (Lande)  10, 13, 25, 27, 33-34, 36-37, 43n11, 51, 54, 65n12, 69-85, 90, 105-106, 111, 115, 119, 175, 181, 185, 248, 255, 268-270, 301, 306n13

Jakim, Boris  125n31, 166n13, 168n29
Jubara, A.  236n3
Judas Iscariot  253, 256-257
Justice  20, 58, 89, 109-110, 113-117, 122, 130-134, 137-140, 149, 177, 233, 247, 292, 294, 297-298

Kamenskii, Z. A.  187n1, 188n4
Kant, Immanuel  26, 38, 112, 130-137, 141n15, 143n36-37, 150, 155-156, 158-159, 161, 165, 179, 202, 227, 287-304
Kantorowicz, Ernst  156
Karamzin, N. M.  40
Karsavin, L. P.  31
Kasso, Lev  89
Kassow, Samuel D.  286n28
Kazakova, N.  124n7, 126n53
Keck, Timothy  143n41
Keep, John  19, 44n14, 44n16, 44n21-22, 45n24, 45n32
Kelly, Aileen M.  42n3, 101n2, 109-110, 116, 124n7, 129, 140n2, 169n45
Kenworthy, Scott M.  47n56
Kesler, Charles R.  124n16
Khoetskii, K. E.  305n8

Khomiakov, Aleksei  23, 26, 28, 45n36, 229
Kireevskii, Ivan  37, 77
Kistiakovskii, Bogdan  10, 13, 20-21, 27-28, 33-34, 37, 43n11, 51, 64n4, 67n32, 90, 92-93, 105-106, 111, 113, 115, 118-119, 122, 128-145, 178, 181, 185, 252, 260n2, 268-270, 282, 285n20, 306n13
Kivelson, Valerie A.  47n56
Kizevetter, Aleksandr  92-93, 98-100
Kline, George L.  46n40, 190n18
Kochan, Lionel  19, 44n14, 44n16, 44n21-22, 45n24, 45n32
Kofmel, Erich  124n14
Kolerov, M. A.  43n5, 43n11, 188n6-7
Kolesnikov, Ivan Vasil'evich  192-193
Korelin, M.  299
Kornblatt, Judith Deutsch  168n35
Kosakovskii, V.  235, 239n56
Kotkin, Stephen  168n34
Kotliarevskii, S. A.  76
Kotrelev, Nikolai  261n16-18
Kozlov A. A.  27
Kremnev, G. B.  46n46
Kretzschmar, Dirk  44n20
Kudrin, N.  82n4
Kuße, Holger  104, 236n3, 237n21
Kutuzov, Mikhail  53
Kuznetsov, P. V.  191n25


Lacoue-Labarthe, Philippe  45n27
Lampe, G. W. H.  305n3
Lang, Virgil R.  168n30
Lange, Max Gustav  305n6
Lavrov, P. L.  25, 132
Law  13, 18, 20-21, 27, 41, 52, 70, 91, 93, 112, 114-115, 128-140, 153, 156-161, 185, 194-195, 200-201, 206, 218, 252, 263, 266-267, 271, 278-283, 303
Leatherbarrow, William  43n7, 46n48, 64n2, 189n12, 306n17
Lefort, Claude  20, 45n27
Lenin, Vladimir  45n36, 85n31, 86, 88, 90, 94-95, 98-99, 116, 119, 121, 127n64, 165, 260n9
Leont'ev, Konstantin  13, 29, 45n36, 46n46, 221
Lepekhin, M. I.  188n4
Lermontov, Mikhail  59
Liberal; liberalism  10, 16, 18, 20, 24, 28, 39, 50, 63-64, 87, 90-99, 105, 110, 112-114, 119, 122, 129, 134-140, 150, 153, 155-156, 159-160, 165, 172, 182, 202-203, 209, 214, 228, 280
*Life* (*Zhizn'*)  226
Lilla, Mark  165, 169n51
Literary; literature  14, 22, 24, 28, 30-31, 33, 41, 50, 52-53, 55-56, 60-64, 74, 79-80, 94, 104, 122, 177, 192-194, 209, 214, 218, 221, 226, 229, 232, 263, 268, 297
Liubash, A.  284n2
Ljunggren, Magnus  240n71
Locke, John  182-183, 186
Lopatin, L. M.  27, 221-222
Lopatin Philosophical Society  221-222
Losev, Aleksei  31, 214-241
Loseva, V. M.  237n10
Losskii, N. O.  27
Losskii, Vladimir  46n52
Lotman, Ju. M.  305n2
Löwith, Karl  153, 167n27
Lozinskii, Evgenii  73, 83n15
Luhmann, Niklas  17
Lunacharskii, Anatolii  25, 144n45
Lur'e, Semen  92-93, 99-100
Luzin, Nikolai  217


Mach, Ernst  177
Machajski, Jan Wacław (Makhaev)  73, 83n14-15, 94, 102n14
Madison, James  108
Maklakov, Vasilii  89
Makovitskii, Dushan  194-199, 201-202, 204, 211n14, 212-213
Mamardashvili, Merab  30

# Index

Manchester, Laurie 47n56
Mandel'shtam, Osip 187, 191n28, 226
Manemann, Jürgen 166n2, 167n17, 167n22
Manin, Bernard 104, 108, 124n16
Mannheim, Karl 62
Manning, R. 102n9
Marchenkov, V. 236n6
Markovich, V. V. 224
Marx, Karl 65n14, 72, 154, 157
Marxism; Marxist 25, 49, 61-62, 71-72, 90, 105-106, 111, 115, 119, 130-131, 133, 148, 150-151, 154, 165, 175, 179, 225, 227, 230-231, 248, 276, 282, 287, 290-295, 297-298, 304
Materialism; materialist 10, 33, 70, 72, 87, 119, 131, 137, 148, 158, 227, 230, 233, 248, 263, 281-282, 296-298, 301
Matthieu, Jean 228, 239n69
Mel'gunov, Sergei 228-229
Merezhkovskii, Dmitrii 27, 88, 104, 118, 120, 144n45, 177, 263-286, 297
Messianism 169n45, 274
Metaphor, metaphorical 32-37, 50, 56, 64, 117-118, 165, 248-249
Metaphysics, metaphysical 26, 30, 37, 52, 56-57, 118, 129-134, 137-139, 152, 157-158, 160, 164, 217, 227, 233, 264, 271, 281-282, 292
Metz, Johann Baptist 147-148, 150-153, 156, 159, 167n21
Michelson, Patrick Lally 47n54, 142n28
Mikhailovskii, N. K. 25, 59, 71, 81, 92, 100-111, 132
Mil'china, V. A. 188n3
Milbank, John 166n6
Miliukov, Pavel 21, 61, 67n33, 67n38, 91-92, 98, 100, 129, 140n4, 156
Mill, John Stuart 135, 143n35
Minin, Kuz'ma 273
Mints, I. I. 87
Modern; modernity; modernist 18, 20, 22, 27, 49, 96, 100, 110, 118, 146, 150, 153-154, 160, 202, 205, 207, 209-210, 215, 222-223, 249, 252, 258, 282, 287, 304
Monastic; monk 33-34, 39, 52, 297, 299, 301, 304
Moralism; morality; moralistic 51, 74, 112, 128, 131, 134, 138, 153, 155-157, 163-165, 178, 209, 233, 256, 268, 295, 300
Morozova, Margarita Kirillovna 220
Morson, Gary Saul 46n47, 73, 84n19
Mouffe, Chantal 109, 125n19
Murav'ev, V. N. 69, 77-78
Mysticism 27, 97, 100, 177-178, 227, 229-230

Nahirny, Vladimir C. 64n1, 66n15, 67n35, 68n46
Napoleon 273, 291
Nekrasov, Nikolai 52
Neo-idealism; neo-idealist 10-11, 13, 23-24, 129-130, 132-135, 150, 154, 156, 159-160
Neo-Kantian; neo-Kantianism 26, 130-131, 179
Nerler, P. M. 191n28
Nesmelov, V. I. 27
Nethercott, Frances 14, 21, 49-67, 144n50
Nicholas I 274
Nicholas II 15, 88, 156, 204
Nicholas of Cusa 217, 222, 237n8, 237n11
Nietzsche, Friedrich 29, 57, 111, 179, 263, 277-279, 290, 293, 297
Nihilism; nihilist; nihilistic 28, 34, 40, 51-52, 55-56, 93, 107, 112, 128, 148, 163-164, 178, 181, 184, 214, 231, 245, 248, 254, 281, 295
Nikolaev, S. 195
Nollan, Valeria Z. 47n57
Novgorodtsev, Pavel 77, 84n27, 133, 138, 142n29, 144n44, 154-155, 157, 159-160, 164, 227

# Index

Novikov, Nikolai  59, 266

Oakeshott, Michael  124n8
Oberlander, G.  101n2
October manifesto  15, 75, 106n20, 155, 272
Octobrists  90, 97
Offord, Derek  43n7, 46n48, 64n2, 189n12, 306n17
Ogarev, Nikolai  199
Ollig, Hans-Ludwig  142n19
Ospovat, A. L.  188n3
Ostovich, Steven T.  166n2, 167n17, 167n26
*Out of the Depths* (*Iz glubiny*)  10, 24, 29, 31, 39, 41, 56, 69-71, 74-82, 86, 107, 164, 226, 246-247, 254-258
Ovsianiko-Kulikovskii, D. N.  61, 67n33
Ozhegov, S. I.  46n50

Paert, Irina  36, 47n55
Palamas, Gregory  217
People, the  35, 37, 51, 61, 70-71, 76, 78, 80-82, 91, 93-94, 100, 108, 113-118, 162-163, 177, 198, 200-201, 205, 216, 247, 258, 268, 273, 276-278, 295, 301, 303-304
Person; personhood; personality  12-13, 18, 28, 37, 44n12, 56-57, 72, 97, 112, 130-139, 147-148, 150-151, 155-164, 174, 177, 180-187, 189n13, 201-203, 205-207, 230, 233-235, 247, 250, 253-254, 256, 269, 277-278, 282, 289, 292, 293, 295, 300-304
Peterson, Erik  152
Pethybridge, Roger  85n31
Peter I (Peter the Great)  37, 77, 156, 272, 284n10
Petrashevskii, Mikhail  288
Petrazhitskii, I. I.  142n23
Petrunkevich, Ivan  92

Philosophy, European  219
Philosophy, political  19, 39, 104-123
Philosophy, religious  25, 36, 41, 104, 162, 178, 214, 270
Philosophy, Russian  11, 13-14, 22-27, 30-31, 41, 177, 180, 182, 189n12, 214, 216, 219, 226-231
Philosophy, western  24
Pipes, Richard  19, 21, 25n25, 49, 63, 86-87, 161
Pisarev, Dmitrii  25, 54-56, 59, 66n16-18
Plato  108, 124n11, 124n14, 215-217, 221-222, 224, 299
Plotinus  215, 217, 222, 224
Plotnikov, N. S.  43n5, 43n11, 44n12, 104, 125n30, 182, 188n6-7, 190n19
Pobedonostsev, Konstantin  95, 160
Polenov, Vasilii  197-198
Polovinkin, S. M.  238n36
Poltoratzky, Nikolai P.  83n17, 101n2, 210n1
Polybius  108
Pontius Pilate  236n7
Poole, Randall A.  14, 19, 24, 32, 42n2, 43n6, 44n12, 46n38, 141n16, 142n20, 142n28-29, 144n45, 48, 50, 145n54, 146-170, 190n19, 22, 24, 240n83
Popov, P. S.  222, 229
Populism; populist  25, 51, 61, 82n4, 87, 90, 95, 98-100, 177, 228, 268
Positivism; positivist  10, 25, 112, 130, 133, 149, 153-154, 156-164, 172, 179, 231, 233, 263, 265, 276, 292-295
Pozharskii, Dmitrii  273
Preobrazhenskii, E.  85n38
*Problems of Idealism* (*Problemy idealizma*)  10-11, 19, 24, 26, 39, 41, 132-33, 155-156, 159-160, 162, 164, 182, 246
Proclus  217, 224
Proskurina, V. Iu.  43n5, 43n11, 84n24, 188n3, 188n6

Protestant; Protestantism  38-39, 202, 280, 299, 302
Pugachev, Emel'ian  274
Pushkin, Aleksandr  54, 56, 59, 80, 116, 180-181, 187, 191n25, 220, 227, 272, 290-291, 303

Quenet, Charles  191n27
*Questions of Philosophy and Psychology* (*Voprosy filosofii i psikhologii*)  172, 193

Rachinskii, G. A.  220-222
Radishchev, Aleksandr  28, 40, 59
Raeff, Marc  64n1, 261n19
Rampton, Vanessa  14, 20, 27, 26n36, 128-140
Rationalism, rationalist  10, 24, 26, 38, 186, 209, 231, 263
Rawls, John  109-110, 113
Razin, Stepan  274, 279
Reactionary  15-16, 29, 53, 73, 95-96, 122, 129, 248
Read, Christopher  14, 19, 21, 43n8, 65n15, 67n35, 83n16, 86-102
Reagan, Ronald  87
Reform, reformist  15-16, 19, 37-38, 73-75, 94, 115, 120, 122, 134, 137, 172, 288, 294, 301
Religion  14, 18-19, 32-39, 41, 52, 56, 72, 91, 97-98, 100, 105, 112-113, 122, 133-134, 146, 151-157, 161-162, 164, 175, 178, 198-199, 202-204, 206, 227-228, 264-266, 269-271, 276, 279-281, 287-289, 292, 295-296
Religious-Philosophical Society  215, 220-221, 226, 263, 265, 276, 278, 284n7
Revolution  16, 20, 25, 62, 69, 75, 77, 80, 82, 86, 89, 91-92, 96-98, 101, 115, 120, 122, 137, 155-156, 160, 173, 194-195, 199, 205-206, 208, 214, 225-226, 232-233, 235, 246, 248, 255-256, 258, 265-267, 270-273, 277-279, 281, 283
Revolution (1905, 1917)  10-11, 15, 25, 42, 50, 56, 58, 70, 75, 77, 79, 82, 99-101, 105, 107, 114, 122, 137, 153, 160, 164, 184, 225, 246, 263, 265-266, 275, 294
Rhetoric; rhetorical strategies, devices  14, 24, 27, 32, 50, 56, 58, 189n13, 248, 268, 276
Rimskii-Korsakov, Nikolai  215
Robespierre, Maximilien  273
Rosenthal  see Glatzer Rosenthal
Rossiter, Clinton  124n16
Rousseau, Jean Jacques  113, 121
Rozanov, Vasilii  27, 30-31, 46n46, 177, 256, 262n30-32, 276, 278, 284n2, 297
Rumiantsev, Nikolai  228
Ruppert, Hans Jürgen  166n9
*Russian Thought* (*Russkaia mysl'*)  74, 79, 92, 203, 206, 221

Sabashnikov, M.  225
Safranski, Rüdiger  107, 122, 124n9
Saltykov-Shchedrin, Mikhail  60
Sapov, V. V.  42n3, 82n2, 101n4, 123n1-2, 4, 141n8, 187n2, 188n5, 188n11, 260n3, 6, 8, 12, 261n14, 261n25, 262n43, 306n9
Savinkov, Boris  283
Scanlan, James  31, 43n4, 46n49, 168n28, 189n12, 191n24
Schapiro, Leonard  86, 129, 137, 140n2, 144n46
Schelling, Friedrich W. J.  38
Scherrer, Jutta  47n58, 126n54
Schiller, Friedrich  65n13, 279
Schlögel, Karl  107, 116, 123, 124n7
Schlüchter, Anita  140n3
Schmitt, Carl  109, 121, 125n19, 146, 152-153, 165, 167n24-26
Schopenhauer, Arthur  199, 298
Schrooyen, Pauline W.  126n34
Schwab, George  167n24-25

# Index

Scott, Peter  166n1, 166n11, 167n26
Sedakova, Ol'ga  260n4
Semenova, S. G.  46n44
Seraphim of Sarov  271
Serfdom  16, 92
Sextus Empiricus  217
Shakhovskoi, D. I.  126n43
Shatsillo, Kornelii  143n31
Shatz, Marshall S.  8, 42n1, 43n10, 64n3, 83n15, 84n20-22, 24-25, 85n40, 122, 123n3, 124n7, 10, 13, 125n27, 126n38, 46, 48, 51, 127n56, 61, 140n1, 143n37, 144n47-48, 168n30, 169n48, 188n7, 260n1, 267, 284n6, 306n10
Shaumyan, Sebastian  218, 237n18
Shelgunov, Nikolai  56
Shelokhaev, V.  122, 124n7, 126n37, 126n39, 127n62, 66, 69
Shestov, Lev  24, 31, 186
Shevtsov, Vera  47n56
Shishko, Leonid  98, 100
Shpet, Gustav  31, 240n83
Shukman, Ann  305n2
Silard, Lena  261n22
Silesius, Angelus  235, 241n101
Silver Age  11, 22, 31, 56, 106, 155, 187, 209, 219
Simmel, Georg  130
Siniavskii, Andrei  235
Sivkov, Konstantin  228
Slavophile; Slavophilism  13, 26, 28, 32, 37-38, 51, 71, 77, 92, 119, 136, 174, 179, 181-182, 227, 229, 260n2, 269, 272, 274, 276, 279
Smith, Oliver  14, 32, 35, 243-260
Sobornost'  13, 21, 37, 77, 269
Social Democrats (SD)  87, 90, 94-94, 99
Socialism; socialist  20, 33-34, 39, 59, 75, 87, 90, 94-97, 100, 129, 134-140, 148-150, 153-154, 158, 162, 164, 203, 216, 232, 244, 266, 280-281, 288, 291-295, 298, 300, 303

Socialist Revolutionaries (SR)  87, 90-91, 94-96, 129, 266, 283
Sociology; sociological  13, 21, 27, 49, 60-62, 71, 81, 83n9, 94, 119, 132, 231
Sokolov, Boris  228
Sokolov, K. B.  65n10, 66n24, 67n34, 67n37-38
Sokolova, V. M.  220
Solov'ev, Vladimir  13, 19, 22-23, 26-29, 31, 34, 39-41, 60, 65n8, 97, 106, 111-113, 116, 119, 125n28, 144n43, 153-155, 161, 166n13, 169n44, 172, 177, 180, 182, 186, 188n7, 190n24, 193, 202, 207, 211n8, 215, 218-220, 226, 229-230, 233-234, 244, 249-252, 257, 261n16-18, 267, 269, 274-276, 298-300, 303
Solzhenitsyn, Aleksandr  67n29, 87, 117, 126n45
Sombart, Werner  306n19
Spengler, Oswald  79, 216, 240n87
Speshnev, Nikolai  289, 305n7-8
Spiro, Sergei  193
Spivak, M. L.  236n5
Stadzhi, F.  215
Stakhovich, Aleksandr  195-196
Stakhovich, Sofiia  198
Stalin, Iosif  119, 217, 232, 276
Stammler, Rudolf  166n8
State  17-18, 36, 38, 58, 60, 70, 75-77, 80-81, 88-89, 91, 93, 112, 115, 117, 119, 135-136, 138-139, 146, 152-156, 160, 175, 181, 195, 228, 258, 263, 266-268, 270, 273-283
Staten, Henry  125n23
Steinberg, Mark D.  47n56
Stepun, Fedor  237n21, 239n54
Stirner, Max  288-290, 293, 295-296, 305n7, 306n14
Stolypin, Petr  16, 102n20, 204, 260n9, 273, 277
Strakhov, Nikolai  55, 66n19
Strauss, Leo  17, 44n19, 124n14
Stringfellow, William  166n6

# Index

Strong, Tracy B.   167n24, 169n53
Struve, Petr   10, 13, 21, 28, 33-34, 36, 38, 43n11, 47n53, 58-60, 65n6, 67n32, 74, 79, 82, 86-87, 89-91, 93-94, 96-98, 105-106, 109, 111, 116-118, 127n63, 130-131, 133-134, 137-138, 142n26, 143n31, 144n51, 155, 160-164, 175, 181, 184-185, 188n7, 192-215, 226, 244, 246, 248, 251, 263-264, 268-271, 273, 276-281, 283, 285n20, 306n13-16
Sudov, A. D.   45n33
Sukhodub, T.   43n8
Sullivan, Lawrence E.   166n1

Takho-Godi, A. A.   43n8, 125n28, 140n3, 236n3, 237n19-20, 238n32, 238n37-38, 239n53, 239n60, 340n84
Takho-Godi, E. A.   14, 31, 43n8, 125n28, 140n3, 214-241
Tarasov, Boris   191n27
Theocracy   36, 154, 168n34, 266, 275-276
Theology   47n54, 202
Theology, political   19, 146-165, 305n1
Tihanov, Galin   30, 46n48, 189n12
Tilly, Charles   125n17
Tiutchev, Fedor   51, 53
Tocqueville, Alexis de   18, 44n15
Tolstaia, Aleksandra   198
Tolstaia, Sofiia Andreevna   197-198
Tolstoi, Lev   23, 26-28, 30, 51-53, 60, 73-74, 80, 83, 89, 105, 112, 119, 161, 172, 177, 188n7, 191n24, 192-213, 226, 263, 265, 267, 273, 280, 283, 298
Tolstoi, Sergei   197
Tompkins, S. R.   101n2
Treadgold, Donald W.   168n30
Troitskii, V. P.   236n7, 238n32, 238n37-38
Trotskii, Leon   94

Trubetskoi, Evgenii   116, 126n41, 220, 225-226
Trubetskoi, Sergei   23, 26-27, 46n42, 57, 65n8, 66n24
Truth   13, 20, 53, 73, 78, 87, 93, 105, 109-110, 114, 137, 172, 175-181, 185, 192, 197, 199, 203, 227, 230, 233, 251-252, 257, 260n2, 264, 266-267, 270, 275, 278, 281, 289-290, 295
Tsarism; tsarist   18, 59, 62, 88-89, 128, 134, 154-155, 160, 162, 275
Turgenev, A. I.   188n3
Turgenev, I. S.   55, 59, 64n2, 80

Union for the Revival of Russia   228
Uspenskii, B. A.   305n2
Uspenskii, Gleb   52
Utilitarianism   73, 101, 263
Utopian; utopianism   29, 53, 149, 159, 263, 277-278, 281, 295

Valentinov, Nikolai (Vol'skii)   94
Valliere, Paul   167n14, 168n36
Value, absolute   93, 137, 147, 156, 160-161, 163, 175-177, 245, 295
Value, relative   137, 163
Values, religious   13, 32, 35, 60, 178
Van der Linden, Harry   144n41
Van der Zweerde, Evert   14, 19, 37, 104-126
Vechev, Ia. See Chernov
*"Vekhi" as a Sign of the Times ("Vekhi" kak znamen'e vremeni)*   87, 95
Velikanov, Petr   204-205
Verdi, Giuseppe   215
Viazemskii, Petr   171, 188n3
Virtue   17, 20, 108, 195, 283
Viviani, René   96
Voegelin, Eric   153
Von Bismarck, Otto   277-279
Voronskii, A.   85n38
Vysheslavtsev, B. P.   222

Wacker, Bernd 166n2, 167n22
Wagner, Richard 279
Waldron, Jeremy 140, 145n55
Walicki, Andrzej 125n29, 129, 140n2, 144n43, 145n54, 168n28, 168n31, 289, 305n4, 305n8
Weber, Max 38-39, 65n14, 83n9, 280
Wells, Herbert G. 232
West, James L. 286n28
Willey, Thomas 143n41
Williams, Rowan 147-149, 168n30, 245, 253, 260n5, 305n1
Windelband, Wilhelm 130, 141n19
Witte, S. Iu. 16, 18
Woehrlin, William F. 66n23, 82n1, 83n18, 84n26, 85n28, 169n50
Wortman, Richard S. 156, 169n41
Wrangel, Petr 105

Zaitsev, Kirill (Archimandrite Konstantin) 262n40
Zander, Lev 167n14
Zen'kovskii, V. V. (Zenkovsky) 25, 46n40, 180, 190n18
Zhukov, V. N. 211n18-19
Zimmerman, Judith E. 8, 42n1, 43n10, 64n3, 83n15, 84n20-22, 24-25, 85n40, 122, 123n3, 124n7, 10, 13, 125n27, 126n38, 46, 48, 51, 127n56, 61, 140n1, 143n37, 144n47-48, 168n30, 169n48, 188n7, 260n1, 267, 284n6, 306n10
Zlatopol'skaia, A. A. 191n25

www.ingramcontent.com/pod-product-compliance
Lightning Source LLC
Chambersburg PA
CBHW071401300426
44114CB00016B/2144